BREAD CRUMB

A GREEK'S ODYSSEY

Tony Christ

Copies of this book may be obtained by contacting:
BookMasters Distribution Center
1-800-247-6553
http://www.atlasbooks.com

Written by Tony Christ
Edited by William Collins

Published by Kristos, L. L. C., © 2003
Tony Christ 703-538-3077

ISBN: 0-9725288-7-3

Published in the United States of America

Dedicated to my wife, Lee Ann,
and to my children,
Brian, Katelyn and Ashley

Table of Contents

Acknowledgments

My ongoing gratitude goes to Dino and Despina Bayz for their tireless translations of over 100 letters from Greek and Turkish to English that got the ball rolling. Much thanks to Father George Papademetriou, Professor of Theology at the Hellenic College in Brookline, Massachusetts, for copies of published material on the Christian Holocaust; and to Father Steve Zorzos of Saint Sophia Cathedral in Washington, D. C., for reviewing the religious sections. I am indebted to Mr. Tom Vasil, Mr. Anthony Vondes, Mrs. Christina Regas, Mr. Vince Allen and Mr. Lincoln Vance for the wealth of information they provided, as well as for their direct contribution to the story.

I would like to thank my three aunts whose contributions were invaluable: Aunt Sultana for tolerating all my requests and patiently answering all my questions; Aunt Afrodite, whose unflappable memory and numerous sessions of classic conversations were priceless; and thirdly, Aunt Katina, whose beautifully written letters over four decades were key in framing the book. Of course, I am indebted to my mother, Helen (Elenitsa), and my brother, Jon, for their contributions and corrections, largely in Part II.

I handwrote the book in long hand through at least five iterations over six years. I am grateful to two talented ladies who typed and edited, and at times rewrote my scribble. Without the talent and patience of Lynn Hurst and Deborah Truscott, I am certain this book would look a lot differently. I am equally indebted to my editor, Mr. William Collins, the grammarian, whose meticulous attention to detail was invaluable in getting the book ready for publication.

My thanks go to two old friends, Mr. Frank Doe and Mr. Dennis Crawford, for reading the book and for their numerous positive suggestions.

I could never repay the priceless contributions made to this story by His Eminence, Archbishop Iakovos, who gave the title to the book and relayed stories about Bread Crumb's youth. I would also like to thank Paulette, Archbishop's assistant, for putting up with my persistent calls over six years. Much thanks to Ted Flynn for coaxing Bread Crumb out of an unending edit and into a cover, and for a lot of other advice.

Finally, I must acknowledge Lee Ann for her tolerance, dedication and support, without which I would have never completed this project, and Brian, Katelyn and Ashley, who have tolerated my sitting in the family room for six years covered with papers while obsessively crafting Dad's story. Well here it is!

Preface

It is with pride, pleasure, a feeling of responsibility, as well as a surge of emotion from my past—a different era—that I have agreed to write this preface on the life and times of Chrysostomos Chrysostomidis, the man whom, in our younger years, I affectionately dubbed "Bread Crumb" because of his small size, blue eyes, fair hair and infectious smile. It is my hope that the generations of today will be mindful of the crisis period from which we emerged, for this is the best protection against future crisis: to closely hold our traditions and remember our past.

The story of Bread Crumb from Imbroz is in many respects the story of an extraordinary man who prided himself in living an ordinary life.

It was a tumultuous time on our tiny island of Imbroz, an island off the coast of Greece that had changed little since the dawning of Christianity—simple people with a simple faith in God, family and country.   Indeed, through centuries of invasions, occupations, repressions, oppressions, massacres and persecutions at the hands of the Ottomans, the ways of these Greek Orthodox Christians never wavered, never changed. Their faith remained steadfast.

Although I have not spoken publicly during my life as Archbishop of the Americas of the atrocities that surrounded us as children, I now feel it is important they be brought to the fore—not for retribution but as a clarion call for present generations to be vigilant and take care. When Chris and I were children, our world was in turmoil…crisis after crisis. Our little island was lost to the Mohammedans and our culture and people destroyed. And those of us who survived…well, we wished to look forward. We wished to focus on the future, on hope and optimism. No need to dwell on our own past hardships—we would use our knowledge of suffering, of oppression and inhumanity to serve as a reminder of what to hold precious, of what to strive for to bring out the best of mankind. We would serve as silent guardians…silently pointing a new direction through our positive actions. On this, the eve of the passage of our generation, it is imperative that future generations not forget these tumultuous errors long past, lest they be repeated.

The childhood experiences Chris and I shared on Imbroz began quite peacefully, although the threat of the Mohammedan aggression surrounded us. Soon the religious persecution and suffering spread to our island. Such persecution was not new in the eyes of history. The Turks had executed and persecuted the Christians countless times as far back as King Alp Arslan in the 11th century. Then came the Ottomans in the 13th century, under King Osman, who declared a warrior or Gazi state. Bound to Jihad, the holy war, against the Orthodox Christians, they instituted some of the harshest and cruelest methods ever seen in the world. Male children of enslaved Christian families were taken and raised to become fanatical killers of their own Christian people. Over time, the Ottomans systematically slaughtered millions of Asia Minor's Christian inhabitants, including Armenians, Kurds, Serbs, Albanians, and Greeks. They promised that those who died in battle against a nonbeliever were guaranteed passage to heaven. This ensured for the Christians a greater hell on earth.

After the turn of this century, the Young Turks under Atatürk began this pattern of persecution again in earnest. A renewed purging of the Christian culture was put in motion by new Mohammedan zealots. The world seemed to turn a blind eye. A "democratic constitution" had been enacted by the Turks in 1908. By 1912 the Young Turks, supported by the Christian minorities, had taken control of the military. What followed over the next decade was an unrelenting genocide of millions of Orthodox Christians, many of whom had supported the Young Turks to power. Our families were uprooted and properties were stolen or destroyed. We were forbidden to speak Greek and forced to attend Turkish schools. Businesses collapsed from extortion and outright theft, and our economic status was often reduced to starvation. On our way to school we saw our countrymen hanging from trees, crudely lettered signs on their bodies announcing crimes they had allegedly committed, but for which they were never tried. Surely, the world would notice...but in 1923, the world was distracted by its so-called peace at Lausanne and ignored the violations which ensued.

The culmination of this holocaust occurred in Smyrna in 1922, where, in the span of only three days, three hundred thousand innocent Christians were ruthlessly slaughtered. The venerable Archbishop of Smyrna, refusing to leave his people, was beheaded, dismembered and dragged through the streets while the world didn't see. By this time, the number of Christians remaining in Asia Minor had been reduced from 4.5 million to less than half a million. On my own tiny island, the number of Greeks dwindled from 12,000 to 1,000 and finally to 200. We believed now the world would see, but soon the depression came, then World War II. The civilized world was immersed in crisis, and we became a tragic footnote of history.

After World War II, things began to improve. Never again, vowed the world, would such atrocities and inhumanity occur. The heroes, the survivors, who became strong, who learned firsthand the price of peace and the responsibility of privilege, made their brave vows of a better tomorrow. They believed it was possible to guard precious freedom and protect our children from such unconscionable atrocity. We would be vigilant, we would not become distracted. Never again.

And for a time we were vigilant. A generation has gone by…we have beloved peace. We have glorious prosperity. We have marvelous technological gain, medical progress. We have televisions. We have high-speed travel. Another generation begins. We have satellites, we have cable, walkmans, video games, VCR's, the internet…and we have declining academic scores and apathy, the seed of crisis. We have decaying family values; we have political debates based on a lack of morals rather than a prospect of ideals. We have intellectualized away our moral and spiritual underpinnings…but we have 168 channels by satellite dish! What we have is distraction…yet God's will and the cycle of life undauntedly advance.

Have we lost our focus? Have we lost the spirit exemplified by the life of my friend, Chris Chrisostomidis, and other men like him? Ask yourself this as you read about his life's journey and a spirit that moved him with grace through times of tribulation and turmoil, times of triumph, pride, love, sacrifice, peril, and inhumanity, never wavering, never losing sight of all that is precious and all that kept him strong. His was a journey that led him to America and freedom, while never forgetting his humble roots, nor the people who shared his love and spirit along the way. His were simple beliefs that seem all too lacking today.

Today the story of Bread Crumb, a true hero, is a story for all ages, for all times, and one whose traditions must not be forgotten during our current period of social unraveling. As a man who has devoted his life to God and mankind, who has weathered the seasons of time, I admonish you, both parents and children, to learn from this man. Parents: prepare your children to be the future heroes that God and circumstance may demand they become. Nurture them. Instill in them the spirit that will keep them strong in times of hardship and will keep then humble in times of blessing. Children: learn your lessons well. Stay together and remember that if the clouds of time grow dark, you must keep your faith and remain strong, for eventually those clouds will give way to the sun again.

Please remember you are all guardians of your beliefs and your human rights. God bless you all and God bless America. Go in peace with God forever.

†Archbishop of the Americas, Iakovos
December 1, 2000

Introduction

The cathartic events that began to unfold on September 11, 2001, and threaten our nation's stability compel me to write this brief introduction. The psychotic violence that came to America was a reality check. The response was a war on terrorism wherein modern western governments battled 12th century Afghanistan, with undermining pervasive interests lurking in the shadows. These acts of terror on America parallel the repeated violence commonplace during Bread Crumb's early years. Many rightly feel that the tapestry of human life is checkered with the periodic peril of hideous global crisis. Were the tragic events of September harbingers of future protracted crises? Are the present perils we face new and different, or are they eerily similar to the violence of Bread Crumb's era? Could our generation of American Christians be lulled into yet another global crisis? What will the first decade of the new millennium hold? Can Bread Crumb's story shed light on our contemporary travail?

Recently the United States' war on terrorism transfigured into a war against Iraq and Saddam Hussein, a tin dictator of a despotic regime, ushering in a perilous new standard of pre-emption, supposedly for sovereign safety, a standard for which we will be accountable. Was Saddam's reign a cause of evil or merely a symptom? Will proactive interference become our duty-laden distraction? Can we afford the cost?

To extend our economic freedom we must not ignore our faith. America's spirituality has supported its system of free choice. Our unparalleled belief in individual sovereignty has sharply advanced social welfare. Freedom and free will are basic democratic precepts fostered by Christianity and are not readily found in other countries or faiths. Many states' governments and religious philosophies are infected with some form of social determinism that denies individual free will and supports central controls and globalization in its stead. Our ability to temper nationalism and materialism with spiritualism will strengthen our resolve and extend our unique social freedoms.

Individual freedom, once surrendered, becomes sullied with central government whose promises of welfare and security are often not delivered. Slowly, social determinism supplants the individual's freedom to choose, dealing an unwelcome loss to welfare and an unhealthy dependence on government. Once surrendered, freedom is not easily regained. Faith and humility before God become unimportant and are subordinated to nationalism. Nationalistic faith requires an additional and unannounced loss of personal freedom and yields a greater corresponding reduction in social welfare. Our new-found surge of nationalism risks the emergence of a false sense of moral purpose and security, while deflecting our attention from what is important. Social determinism and nationalism are preconditions of a crisis period. It is important to remember that our material superiority is transient and doesn't condone arrogance or insure success.

The story of Bread Crumb will renew the power of the human spirit. Who amongst us can say they are over-inspired? Bread Crumb's story is a testament to free will and faith. His journey will give us courage to exorcize the demons in our life, both external and internal, while illuminating a timeless wisdom for all. Bread Crumb's Odyssey should inspire us to defend our unique freedom of choice, most especially against those who would destroy it if they could.

Tony Christ
April 3, 2003

Part I
The Old World

1
Visions

I look for aged pots
Of prehistoric days,
And then I measure them in lots
And lots of different ways.
And then (like you) I start to write.
My words are twice as long
As yours, and far more erudite.
They prove my colleagues wrong!

—Agatha Christie
Come Tell Me How You Live, 1944

The late winter of 1994 had been unseasonably harsh for metropolitan Washington, D. C. Sheets of ice had covered roads and toppled power lines for weeks. The thaw finally came by mid-March, and now, on this particular Sunday, just days later, the appearance of my little friends had banished winter's drear and the pageantry of spring was begun.

As a general surveying his troops, I walked with hands crossed behind my back, though my face reflected the pleasure and simple pride of beholding one of God's most captivating sights: my azaleas beginning to bloom. Bright colors—corals, pinks, reds and violets—adorned the backyard of my half-acre of paradise. Over the years, I had planted azaleas everywhere until azaleas spilled over on top of azaleas. Late March often proudly sees their showy blooms, joined a little later by like-colored blossoms of the towering rhododendrons.

It was my habit to awaken as early as five in the morning so I could walk outside among the blossoms. As no other time of day, the morning's soft dawn light made my little backyard a fairyland full of God's wonder. *Nothing more beautiful in nature have I seen than my azaleas in full bloom*, I thought as I paced in sight of them, wanting to touch and greet each and every one of the tiny buds still sparkling with dew. So began my Sunday. Soon I would be sipping coffee with Elenitsa, my wife of forty-six years, when she would join me for breakfast. From there, the day's pace would accelerate to a peaceful bustle as we would dress for church, allowing enough time to pick up Christina Regas, our friend of many years.

It was the usual church service, and afterwards I enjoyed the short social hour with friends and neighbors whom I had only recently had time to know in my retirement years. Today's big news was the tragic death of two Greek Orthodox priests killed by a drunk driver in New York. Being kinsmen, their death struck the congregation here deeply, though many had never met them.

Brunch at the Marriott was a special treat which we enjoyed only a handful of times throughout the year. Certainly the arrival of my azaleas as harbingers of spring warranted such a treat! Yes, it might have been a typical Sunday morning in routine and people and faces, but the difference was a new presence—a cool spring breeze, a final farewell to a lengthy winter's chill. The change had infected everyone.

As soon as we had returned from church and brunch, I resumed my vigilant backyard review. Lifting my voice to penetrate the cracked back door, I called out to Elenitsa, "Honey, you see the azaleas?" I began picking up fallen branches and straightening up around the bushes, not even bothering to change out of my Sunday clothes. I felt unusually tired, again, yet I pored over my azaleas intently, my eyes refusing to leave the first buds of spring.

In a distant echo I heard Elenitsa respond from the house. "Yes, dear," she replied dutifully. She didn't share the excitement over my garden.

"Remember, we have to go to the children's house to help them move," she said, walking toward the door.

As I entered the kitchen, I saw Elenitsa putting away dishes. "I'm going to the other room to rest a bit," I told her. "Wake me a little before three."

"Okay, Chris," she smiled, and continued her work in the kitchen.

Walking through our family room to a small side room, I opened the blinds and sat in the corner of the sofa, directly exposed to shafts of warm sunlight. I loved the sun, though recent years had labeled sunlight a danger, and Elenitsa often worried about my overexposure. I ignored the risk. Old men often ignore new risks in pursuit of the comfort of old habits. Such were my naps in the sun. Burrowing through my closed eyelids, the muted light was restful.

My life over three quarters of a century has been blessed. I, along with my family on Imbroz, had survived the Christian Holocaust and the Young Turks' conquest of that little Greek island in 1923, though losing everything to the occupation that followed. My youth was impoverished under the harsh rule of the Mohammedan Turks, the devastating economic conditions they imposed leaving deep scars on many of our people—those who survived. To my continual amazement, in spite of this desperate backdrop, I had somehow managed to follow Papa's dream for me—to land in America, America the free! Here, I met Elenitsa, was blessed with three children and now four grandchildren…and counting.

To some, my life of hard work may not seem blessed, but in America, I own my own home and small business. I have social and economic freedom and peace. My family has stayed together, well fed and well loved—not torn apart by the ravages of a tyrannical occupation. What more could a man ask for, praise God!

Yawning, I placed my hands behind my neck with fingers interlaced, as was also my habit. I felt the friendly warmth of the sunlight on my shoulders and arms, my neck and my head, lulling me to doze. So tired, I seemed to have no energy. I had experienced unusual fatigue like this several times over the last couple of months, but had said nothing to Elenitsa or the children. This time the sensation was very heavy. My body succumbed to it while my mind remained restless and wakeful, my thoughts wandering across my life.

I arrived in America in April of 1945 along with the returning G. I.'s. I worked long hours every day, year in and year out, with an occasional half-day off on Sunday to go to church. I am

5

enormously proud to be an American and to be able to provide for my family. The ability to do such simple things that so many people take for granted—things impossible under the Turks' tyranny—is a source of unending joy for me. You see, I am the fortunate one, for I know joy every day of my life. Most Americans don't know how good they have it—if people only knew the value of things around them. I am an ordinary man, it's true, but I thank God for the privileges I enjoy every waking day of my life.

This afternoon was no different. Out of habit, my hand went to the collar of my tee shirt and found the relic coin fastened there by a safety pin, as it always was, and I thanked God for my blessings yet again. If a holy coin and my indomitable faith had allowed me to survive the Christian Holocaust, then could anyone fault me a little appreciation for His favor?

My fatigue deepened in my sunny spot on the sofa. My life had always been meticulously organized, methodical and focused, but now my thoughts resembled a series of unconnected images passing on a screen. Images of my wife Elenitsa appeared. She was saying, "Chris, you must have regular checkups and eat the right foods…."

"Yes, dear," I said.

My children appeared before my eyes, one by one. The images were so stark and lifelike I almost thought they were real. The first child I saw was Anthony, my eldest son.

"Hi, Dad," he said, his voice deep with affection.

Then Jon, my second son, and my daughter Ianthe appeared. "Hi, Dad," they called cheerfully.

Now the grandchildren appeared, Brian and Katelyn. "Granddad, hi!"

Finally little Ashley appeared, but she was crying. "Granddaddy, don't go!"

"What's all this?" I asked. "I'm not going anywhere," and I reached out to ruffle her hair, but she couldn't seem to hear me.

Suddenly I saw myself at the health club on the treadmill. I had gone yesterday for the first time in a number of months, the bleak winter and my nagging fatigue having kept me away. I was going faster and faster on the treadmill and the images seemed to be coming faster and faster in my mind; confusion was blurring my thinking. I felt as though I were moving in slow motion, the parade of people and memories of my life increasing in speed at an alarming rate. They were moving in a different world, at a different time and speed, and I could not pass through to theirs except in brief snatches that were whisked away to be quickly replaced by the next.

Darkness came over me for a brief moment, then a voice: "Chrysostomos?" It was very distant and muted at first, then much louder. "Chrysostomos?"

"Mama?"

"Chrysostomos." Her voice seemed to fade again.

"Mama, so long has it been...Is it really you?" Then I saw her with Papa, but they couldn't hear me. I was back in time to the old country, and suddenly there I was, a boy leaving home to find his way in the world—only I was an observer, not a participant.

"Papa and I don't have money to give you," Mama was saying, "but here, take this," and she handed me a package. I could see Papa's store, its windows boarded. It was in disrepair, in need of paint and maintenance. Losing myself in memory, I felt the presence of the Turks, that sharpening of the senses, that unceasing alertness that caused any Greek Christian on Imbroz to constantly check over his shoulder, or drop his voice to a barely audible whisper whenever Greek, the outlawed tongue, was spoken outside the relative safety of the home. It was second nature. It was how we lived.

"Mama, don't worry," I could hear my young image saying. "I'll work and send you money. Don't worry, I'll take care of you." Big words for such a little man—I was hoping the words sounded more confident than I felt.

Mama was crying, though trying her best not to.

"Mama, Papa, I love you," I said, embracing my parents. Mama kissed me through her tears, their salty moisture calling forth an involuntary response in my own eyes against which I struggled valiantly. Papa patted me on the back trying to offer the assurance we both knew he did not feel. It was an ordeal no parent should have to bear, yet they were making the bravest face possible and I loved them dearly for it.

"Take care of yourself," Papa forced a smile, such love in his voice.

The images were so vivid. My lips moved again, "Mama, Papa, I love you!" but I was whispering to an empty room. I was no longer a boy but an old man in the twilight of his life sitting in the sunshine in my house in America. These things I had not thought of for a long time, and the memories now caused me to swallow hard. An ache came from deep within me.

When I left Imbroz that day, such a long time ago, it was to find work and my way through a world in crisis. Life was so hard in the Old World. Little did I know that for the next seventeen years I would not see my parents except for a few brief visits; after that, I was never to see them again.

I moved restlessly on the sofa, aching to see Mama and Papa again, but instead I heard a choir singing. I saw myself with Elenitsa in church this morning at Saint Sophia, the cathedral in Washington.

"Alleluia, alleluia, alleluia! Wisdom! Attend! Let us hear the Holy Gospel. Peace unto all," Father John intoned.

"Glory to Thee, Oh Lord! Glory to Thee…Amen," the choir responded according to the unchanging Divine Liturgy passed down from St. John Chrysostom in the fifth century.

"Alleluia, alleluia, alleluia!" the choir and the priest sang out, the full, deep tones resonating through the shafts of colored light streaming through stained glass windows at St. Sophia, a truly Byzantine cathedral. Even as a child, I had found the Liturgy exhilarating and inspirational, but I had been very tired this morning in church. I did something I had never done: I remained seated while the others stood. We always stand at certain parts of the service to show respect to God, but today I felt so weak and tired.

The image of the church slipped and faded as I grew more tired…but all at once other images came vividly into view.

There was Charlie Howard, my bookkeeper of 40 years and good friend. "Chris, how are the fish biting?"

"Oh, pretty good, Charlie!" I answered, at once animated by my favorite topic. For the last twenty years I had fished every chance I got. But Charlie was already fading before I could really talk on the subject, and the next thing I saw was the ocean. Even better, I was on my small boat, one of my favorite places to be, only it seemed, this time, something was wrong. The fog was thick and the water choppy. The boat was stilled.

"Captain Christ, what should we do?" came a plea from the stern of the boat, a note of desperation in the thin, dry voice of my friend, Paul Yeonas.

"Just fish, Paul, just fish…someone will come along," I could hear myself saying.

Suddenly I was high above the scene and saw Elenitsa crying. My sons, Jon and Anthony, were talking anxiously. "The Coast Guard has been looking for two days," said Jon.

The images came faster: back to Constantinople, the crossroads of my life, when I was a busboy at the Park Hotel, the job I had waited so long and had worked so hard to get at a time when there simply was no work, let alone for a teenage boy—such hard times!

It was there I learned to speak French in addition to my Greek and Turkish. It was there that I would meet my ticket to America…

Now James Hatzi, my brother-in-law, appeared. "Chris, let's go down to the docks and eat fresh oysters!" he was calling to me. I was in Brooklyn with Jim and my sister Sultana, and going to the docks to eat oysters was always fun. Jim was a good, hard-working man and I still miss him. He died of cancer only a year ago—yet, now, I felt he was nearby, as if he was in the room with me. There he was on the screen in my mind saying, "Here, Chrysostomos, have an oyster. Here, take it!"

"Okay, Taki," I said, calling him by his Greek name, but as I reached for the oyster, Taki faded and darkness replaced him.

Now I was back on the health club treadmill running faster and faster. My mind sped backward in time with total disregard for place or circumstance, continuing its snapshot review of my life.

An image formed of early morning in the summer of 1958 at my Tastee Freeze carryout restaurant. It was my pride, my American dream. Eighteen hundred square feet of restaurant at the beach, and it was all mine. God bless America! I was in the parking lot, hosing down the pavement. On the street a colored man was rapidly pedaling his bicycle toward me. Getting closer, I saw he was Bernard. Bernard was in his early twenties. He did not drive a car, but he had a very special bike with a headlight in front, two saddle bags on each side, a pair of big rear view mirrors, a multitude of reflectors and horns—and a fox tail hanging off the back! I've never seen a bike decorated like Bernard's. When he pulled up, the headlight was still on although it had been light for about 40 minutes. "Sorry I's late, Mr. Christ. I left when it was dark but it took this long to get here! I's sorry, Mr. Christ. I's sorry."

Gradually, the image of Bernard faded into darkness with the hose pushing debris, sand and dirt in a crescent around me. I sighed and turned on the sofa. Memories kept flooding me and it seemed useless to try to sleep. The next image that appeared was of me lying in a hospital bed with a tube in my side—my gall bladder operation. Dr. Mandes was in the doorway talking with my wife, my sons, my daughter and daughter-in-law.

"His gout medication has caused a reaction with his gall bladder medicine," Dr. Mandes said.

Well, if that doesn't top it all! I thought. My philosophy has always been to stay away from doctors and, up until that incident, I had been pretty successful for over seventy years. Elenitsa goes to doctors once a week, but if I can go without seeing a doctor at all, that is fine with me! Don't get me wrong—I know many doctors and I believe we have a mutual respect for each other. I just don't think my health is their business.

"How is he doing, Doctor?" Ianthe was asking.

"He's been here for eight days!" Anthony exclaimed.

"Well, he had a drug reaction and a fever," Dr. Mandes explained patiently. "The next couple of days will tell. If he beats the infection and breaks the fever, he should do well..."

"Jon," I called suddenly, "wait a minute, please..."

My unease faded as the memory melted into darkness and I stirred against the cushions of the sofa, my body twinging as my mind careened through caverns of distant memories. Was I forgetting something? My house mortgage was paid off, my bills were all paid, all my important papers were in order on my desk. Organization and order, things must be in order.... Suddenly, I was on the treadmill back at the health club. Not again! I only have a little more time before Elenitsa and I have to be at Anthony's to help them move. I felt so weak...I must get some rest! But my meandering mind ignored my body's request.

Ed Hammond, my attorney, appeared before me while running on the treadmill. "Chris," he said, shaking his head. "If they haven't paid the rent in two months, I guess I'll have to write them a notice letter." He was referring to the tenants of a store I rented out.

"Okay, Ed," I told him reluctantly. "Do what you have to do."

"How's the fishing, Chris?" he asked, changing the subject.

"Well, pretty good, Ed. The croakers are biting, and if you go to the twelve-mile buoy you can catch trout. I caught ten yesterday. Would you like a couple?" I often offered fish to my friends.

"No thanks, Chris," Ed smiled. "I'm not a fish-eater, but thank you anyway...." His image began to fade and his voice echoed into silence. Maybe now I could get a few minutes rest.

Instead I saw my oldest sister, Katina, large as life and standing right in front of me. "Chrysostomos, I remember you as a boy fishing with your friends on the island. Now, after so many years you have come to America and made a success for yourself and your family..."

"Katina, don't go," I tried to say, but the image left me as the others had, another taking its place. At first I couldn't make it out, but a moment later I saw that it was the silk dress jacket Mama had woven for me when I was a teen leaving to find work in Constantinople. Once again I was standing with Mama and Papa in front of our small house. "Chrysostomos," Mama said, "take care of yourself...be careful...your father and I love you very much...." Then Mama gave me my silk jacket wrapped in a bundle with some other clothes, along with another, smaller package. "Here is some cheese and bread I prepared for your trip," she said. Good-bye, Chrysostomos. Have a safe trip. God be with you!"

That silk jacket still hangs in my closet today, some sixty years later. Mama, Papa, I miss you so.

As the image of Papa, Mama and my sunny island home disappeared, I found myself in the midst of a severe blizzard. The wind was howling and the snow was blowing almost horizontally.

My eyelashes had ice on them and it hurt just to blink. Although it was long past sun up, the storm was so intense the day seemed dark as night. A figure, barely discernible through the swirling white powder, was standing by a gate. To the right was a pup tent. The figure was a soldier standing at attention with an unloaded rifle on his shoulder. He was wearing a heavy, drab coat, and strips of cloth were wrapped around his hands, neck, face and feet for protection from the frigid wind.

The year was 1941, and I was that figure standing guard near the Russian border in northern Turkey. Many young Christian conscripts froze to death in northern Turkey during the Second World War. Like me, they had all been forcibly conscripted into the Turkish military—the infamous work battalions. It was unclear then which was worse: the elements or the Turks. Although we were issued a jacket and a pair of pants, only some of us were lucky enough to get boots, and none was prepared for the frigid weather and deplorable conditions near the Russian border.

The truth was that neither the Turkish gendarmes—Turkish military officers dispatched to keep "order" in the towns and villages—nor the military proper cared how many Greek boys froze to death as long as there was a good supply to take their places. The battalions were designed to kill us off. Wind chills of forty degrees below zero were commonplace and temperatures of twenty below zero were normal. I was lucky to have survived my time in the work battalions. Many young Christians did not.

When I was still a very young child in the years before the Turks came to my home, we were a happy and stable people. Imbroz, that small sunny island I remembered from my childhood, is the rhythm of my heart. I carried it with me to America, and I will carry it with me to my grave. Neither the Turks nor death itself will separate me from my roots and my traditions. Imbroz is my way of life. I know no other.

My thoughts continued to page through my life, spontaneously and unapologetically. Fog seemed to swirl around me, and I experienced a sense of vertigo. Then slowly, in my mind's eye, other images began to take form. As if peering from the bow of a fast-approaching boat, I saw it from a distance—Imbroz, my tiny island, just as it was three-quarters of a century ago. So beautiful my island looked, so steeped in tradition! Groves of olive trees graced the landscape and sheep grazed on the rocky hillsides as they had for untold centuries.

Suddenly, I found myself on the outskirts of town, my impassioned heart quickening its beat. There was our stone home, only one room with a loft above, and next to it was Papa's store. They were in perfect order, just the way Papa kept them. Both were freshly painted in white with Greek blue doors and windowsills. Where were Mama and Papa? It was nighttime. I was on the little road in front of our house heading to the center of the town. Where were all the people? Now I heard faint voices singing in the distance. As I moved closer, the voices grew louder and more resonant—a church choir, my church on lmbroz.

Puzzled, I stood in the darkness, listening to the sound of the choir. Much like any Christian Orthodox church throughout Byzantium, our choir's melodious sound resonated heavenward. But this wasn't Sunday service, it couldn't be—this was well after dark!

Holy, holy, holy, the choir sang, *Lord of Sabbath, heaven and earth are full of Thy glory. Hosanna in the highest: blessed is He that cometh in the name of the Lord. Hosanna in the highest.*

The church was filled with people dressed in their very best. In the lantern light, I made out eggs dyed red on a table in the back of the church. It was Lambri! the Feast of Light, the Saturday night before the Orthodox Easter.

Here I sat with Papa at the end of the second pew, a five-year old boy with sandy hair and blue eyes, wearing my finest Easter clothes. Papa looked at me out of the corner of his eye and smiled warmly, a smile I returned in kind. Starting a family late, he was over forty when I was born. Not a tall man, he was a little stout around the middle…like me now, I guess. His large handlebar mustache stretched nearly from ear to ear, offset by unusual piercing blue eyes. I had his light hair and eyes. In contrast, Mama had long brown hair and soft brown eyes.

Feeling the exuberance and excitement of a five-year-old child at the service of lights, I was breathless with anticipation, and there was the priest, Father George, chanting in ancient Greek:

"It is meet and wise to praise Thee, to glorify Thee, to bless Thee, to give thanks to Thee, to worship Thee, in all places of Thy dominion, for Thou art God ineffable, incomprehensible, invisible, inconceivable, existing always as Thou dost exist, Thou and Thine only begotten son and Thy Holy Spirit. Thou has brought us from nothingness into being, and when we fell away didst raise us up again...."

No holiday shines as brightly, filling Heaven, earth and all in between with an essential light. Not even Christmas was deemed greater than the Easter celebration of Christ's resurrection. The celebration began on Holy Saturday evening and culminated on Easter Day, all following Holy Week and forty days of Lent.

It was near midnight, for all the oil lanterns were being extinguished, and within moments the bishop came out with a candle chanting, "*Christos anasti* [Christ has risen]." The candlelight spread as each member of the congregation lit his candle, one after the other. Suddenly caps went off in an explosion of sound and the parishioners responded exultantly, "He truly has risen, Christ is risen!" over and over. The Easter celebration had begun.

Everyone began filing outside the church, and I saw the *phenos,* or bright lantern. In this case it was a bonfire readied in a pit days before. The flames from the *phenos* cast shadows along the church wall and men on horseback fired guns into the air. People circled the bonfire excitedly and a horse reared up at the sight of the leaping flames its dark shadow dancing on the church wall. The Easter celebration of the Resurrection of Christ had begun in earnest. Although soon we would sleep, we would awaken on Easter Day to dress again in our fine clothes and celebrate with the traditional Easter feast of paschal lamb surrounded by all the simple joys that our bucolic life couched in faith offered.

This is the way it had always been, and this is the way I believed it would always be. These were truly the happy times of my early childhood—before the Turks arrived when I was not yet six years old. As we left the church that night, a cool Mediterranean breeze was blowing. Hundreds of oil lanterns were relit and devout parishioners, in their best dress, moved in festive celebration toward their homes.

Ah, to recapture the fleeting memories of youth—what a life I've lived. The recounting light now shone brightly in the forgotten crags of my mind illuminating places and times so long left behind.

2
My Early Childhood

Women scantily clad, carrying babies in their arms or on their backs, marched side by side with old men hobbling along with canes...about 1,200,000...started on this journey.... "Pray for us...we shall not see you in the world again"...they prodded pregnant women with bayonets.... All perished.

—Henry Morgenthau
Ambassador Morgenthau's Story, 1919

"Papa," I asked as we stood outside of the little stone church, "are Yiayia and Papouli Dracoulas coming with us?" Yiayia and Papouli were my maternal grandparents.

"Yes, son, they are," Papa said. Although my grandparents spent time with us, they lived mostly with Uncle Russo and Aunt Cleo on Samothráki Island. They had traveled that evening to attend the service with us, but due to the crowd we had yet to find them and the darkness was making it more difficult.

"There is Yiayia!" I cried suddenly. Taking my father's hand, I started pulling him through the church crowd.

"Ioanni..." someone called.

"Mr. Chrysostomidis," another friend cried out. "Christ has risen!"

Starting at midnight on Easter, neighbors greeted each other with "Christ has risen," to which the reply was "He has truly risen." This happened everywhere we went. Everyone knew Papa. He was on the town council, kept the village records, and saw practically everyone at his small store. He also served as the town dentist when someone needed a tooth removed. More importantly, he was wise and always had words of wisdom for all who crossed his path, and particularly for me. Whether I was at home or far away I never tired of Papa's words.

"Hi, Yiayia!" I greeted my grandmother. Yiayia Sultana was a small woman who always had hugs and kisses for me.

"Hello, my precious! Come here, let me see you." As my grandmother embraced me I smelled her familiar fragrance. Although she seemed old to me, I was told that her mother, Great Yiayia Theopisti, was almost one hundred years old. Since she lived on Samothráki with Uncle Russo and Aunt Cleo, I had never met her.

"Yiayia," I asked, "what do you have in the sack?"

"I have some Easter bread, cheese and Easter eggs."

I saw my mother approach us. "Hello, Mama," my mother greeted Yiayia. "How was your trip?"

"Not bad," Yiayia responded. "We brought the donkey. Your father had something he wanted to bring for Ioanni."

"Did you bring the *tsoreki* (Greek sweetbread), Mama?" my mother asked.

"Yes, and cheese, Easter eggs, a spinach pie and maybe some other things."

Papa had brought our donkey, too. Costa and Sultana rode on the donkey because they were too small to keep up. Although Yiayia and Papouli Dracoulas were getting old, they were able to walk all the way from Castro where the boat docked. Papouli and Yiayia Chrysostomidis, Papa's parents, were older and lived in a village on the other side of the island. They would not be coming for Easter dinner tomorrow.

Our house was a fifteen-minute walk from the church and the center of town. As we headed home I saw my aunt and uncle, Thea Kirata and Theo Demetrius. Theo Demetrius was my father's brother and my favorite uncle. He and Thea Kirata would attend Easter dinner, too.

"Hello, Blue Eyes," Theo Demetrius said, making me laugh. "How are you today?"

Although I had not seen my uncle in church, I had seen Jimmy Coucouzes, who was now walking up to join us.

"Hello, Mr. Chrysostomidis," Jimmy greeted my father. "Hello, Mrs. Chrysostomidis. Christ has risen!"

"He has truly risen," we responded.

Jimmy Coucouzes and his family lived in another city, Igios Theodora, but Jimmy's aunt was Maria Karezou who lived next door to us. He was six years older than I was and very tall and thin. Even as adults many years later, he would tower over me.

"Hi, Christo," he said falling into step with me. "I liked the service tonight, didn't you?"

"Yes, I did," I agreed, tilting my head to look up at him.

"When are you going to grow taller, my little friend?" Jimmy asked, and when I laughed, he laughed with me.

"Did you take communion today?" he went on.

"No." Eyes cast down, I shook my head.

"I did," Jimmy told me matter-of-factly. "Do you know you should take communion at least six times a year as well as all major holidays, or you might be damned for all eternity?" Jimmy was very interested in the church.

"No," I replied, wide-eyed. I would be sure to tell Mama and Papa what Jimmy said.

"Hey, maybe we can play ball tomorrow," he suggested. "Want to?"

"Sure, Jimmy!" I nodded happily.

Jimmy Coucouzes always liked me and I liked him. Our paths would cross half a dozen times during the course of our different, yet parallel, lives, and through trials and tribulations we would remain friends.

As we journeyed home, the pleasing aroma of freshly cooked and seasoned lamb filled the night air, only sharpening the hunger I was feeling despite the late hour's fatigue blunting my senses. When we reached our house Mama and Papa continued their preparations for Easter dinner. Yiayia and Thea Kirata helped Mama tend to various dishes on the stove, a heavy steel cylinder with a firebox that burned either wood or coal, and which was our only source of heat on cold nights. It had a flat top for cooking and its shaft, or chimney, vented through the roof. Papa shooed the women away so he could stoke the stove and lay additional logs on the fire. The lamb, seasoned with salt, pepper and garlic cloves, was stuffed into a pan, covered completely, ready for the oven the next morning. Many people had already placed their lambs in large outdoor baking ovens earlier on Saturday, but Papa believed that it would be tastier if cooked early Easter Day. He also made a traditional chicken and rice soup with whipped lemon and egg, which, famished from the deprivation of Lent, we drank before going to bed. In less than a moment, I fell into a deep sleep.

Before he married Mama, Papa had purchased our land and built our house on a small lot along the road to Panayia. He had worked years to do this. Our home was no more than 800 square feet and faced the mountains. It was adjoined by another house on the left, and our small store was detached to the right. Other houses were strewn along the road. Papouli Chrysostomidis once had had a small store and he helped Papa to build ours. Our fields were across the road from our house except for one, which was almost a mile away. Behind our house and over a hill lay the Aegean Sea.

On Easter Day there would be no work. Papa's store would be closed, unless someone really needed something. Christ had risen and it was a time for celebration! It was a day to be spent in the company of family and close friends, a time for showing reverence and joy over Christ's resurrection, and a time to thank God for our blessings. It was a time for dressing up in our finest clothes, cracking painted eggs, and baking *tsoreki* and other assorted treats.

The next morning, I awoke to the wonderful aroma of roasting lamb. Mama was making rice pilaf, and on the stove Yiayia's spinach pie was heating up. Katina and I excitedly helped Mama while Yiayia and Thea Kirata cleaned and chopped vegetables for the salad. Papa, Theo Demetri and Papou were turning and seasoning the lamb. Yiayia and Papouli Chrysostomidis arrived during our preparation. When dinner was finally ready, the adults ate at our kitchen table. For the children, who were usually fed first, Papa brought a second table over from the store along with four chairs. Even little Costa had his own chair. Lamb, rice, bread and spinach pie were my favorite foods. Olives picked from our trees and Greek cheese adorned the salad, and Papa served the adults red wine made from our grapes. Katina, Sultana, Costa and I drank goat's milk.

Before we began to eat, Papa said a prayer. We all bowed our heads and closed our eyes—but just as we began to pray, our door opened and there was Bishop Iakovos, wearing the traditional black headdress and carrying a staff. Although not very tall, he was still a little taller than Papa. He was also a few years younger than Papa, but already he had white hair in his beard. Bishop Iakovos was a very intelligent man and spoke a number of languages. Though Papa was not formally educated, he was self-taught and well read. Papa was Bishop Iakovos' friend and mentor.

When he appeared everyone quickly stood up. Mama and Papa went to his side to greet him. As was the tradition, Mama kissed his hand and said, "Hello, Your Grace."

Papa said, "Welcome, we are very glad that you came, Your Grace...please, sit down."

When Bishop Iakovos sat down, he was drawn into conversation with my uncle, my Thea and my mother.

"How would you like your lamb?" Papa asked, gesturing to the roast.

"From the top, please," the Bishop responded.

"Rice pilaf? Salad? Easter bread? Cheese? Spinach pie? Olives? And some wine?"

Iakovos acknowledged each with a small though eager nod. He had eaten with us before and he loved everything my parents made. My father and mother were excellent cooks, and the Bishop always ate a very full meal when he had dinner at our home.

After they had eaten, the adults sat and talked, and Katina and I were allowed to go outside and play. Jimmy Coucouzes came over as promised from his aunt's house next door, and we began a game of kick ball. It was a beautiful Easter Sunday. Jimmy and I ran around the yard fast and hard for a long time. Even though Jimmy was older and taller, I was quicker and could almost hold my own. Katina was pretty good, too.

When Mama finally called us in, Papa was talking with the Bishop, Papouli and Theo Demetrius about the Turks. Eventually they began to discuss the massacre at Smyrna, which had occurred about six months earlier, in September of 1922. There was not a gathering of Greek men on our island that did not discuss the massacre of the Christian population of Smyrna with a mixture of disbelief, frustration, fear and uneasiness. Smyrna was an old and beautiful Greek city that had been founded in 3000 B. C. It had stood as an important and prosperous economic center for 30 centuries—but in only three days' time, an undetermined number, believed to be two to three hundred thousand Christians, were slaughtered, including our revered Archbishop Chrysostom. The city burned nearly to the ground—except for the Turkish section.

"Archbishop Chrysostom went to the French consulate," Bishop Iakovos told Papa. "At the risk of his own safety, he went to plead for the inhabitants of Smyrna. The consulate there urged him to stay and take refuge, but he refused, saying it was his duty to stay with his flock. That was the last time," Iakovos went on sadly, "this venerable and eloquent man was seen alive." Mama sent us children outside to play again. The Christian massacres on the mainland were not really proper subjects for the ears of small children, but I hid by the crack in the front door where no one could see me and listened for a while longer.

"Shortly thereafter the Turkish military took him to Nureddin Pasha, the Turkish commander-in-chief, who turned him over to a mob in front of the military headquarters of the Kemalist forces. They spat upon him, tore his beard out by the roots...he was beaten, stabbed and dragged about the streets before finally being beheaded and dismembered.

"With his disciplined army, Mustapha Kemal could have easily prevented this brutality if he chose," our Bishop continued, choking with emotion. "Mustapha Kemal was determined to make a complete and irretrievable ruin of Christianity in Asia Minor by turning a blind eye to his generals! Meanwhile, his militia, aided by the general citizenry, slaughtered the Christian population."

"So many people killed, Your Grace," Uncle Demetrius commented sadly. "So many people killed."

"The plan was to give the city up for a few days to lust and carnage," Iakovos continued, "to make it appear as if it was mob related, but it wasn't."

"Yes, this massacre is such a terrible thing," Papa interjected, "that surely the allies must respond. Certainly the civilized world is horrified by this latest slaughter!"

Iakovos shook his head doubtfully. "In the year A. D. 156, Polycarp, the patron saint of Smyrna, was beheaded, dismembered and burned in the now ancient stadium, the contours of which are still plainly visible," he reminded the men. "Now, nearly 1,800 years later, Christians are still being slaughtered."

"But the world won't tolerate this!" Papou exclaimed, echoing Papa's sentiments.

"There are outcries from all Europe and the United States," Iakovos replied, "but nothing has been done. Instead, there is talk of a 'peace agreement' with the Turks that would uproot Greek Christians from Asia Minor. There is even some discussion that our island will be ceded to Turkey!"

"Imbroz! Will Mother Greece or the allies allow it? Why?" Papa exclaimed, trying to make sense of it all.

"I don't know. I'm afraid it seems to many to be a small price to pay for peace," Iakovos said. "But in the meantime, the slaughters of countless innocent Christians continue."

Papa was aghast. "You mean giving up a Greek island with a population that dates itself back to antiquity is a *small* price?"

"I'm afraid so, Ioanni. Since Greek independence in 1821, the Mohammedan Turks have craved the Greek border islands and have consistently sought means to conquer them. They will do anything to get them."

"In a sense," Papou mused, "the islands serve as an imaginary demarcation line between Christianity to the west and the Mohammedans, who have overrun Byzantium and the Roman Empire, to the east."

"And strategically," Papa added as sober realization sank in, "since they sit at the mouth of the Dardenelles Straight, they are coveted by the Ottomans all the more."

"That is true, Ioanni," Iakovos nodded.

"Unbelievable to think that the world would sacrifice us to appease the Turks!" Papa exclaimed.

"Stop that talk," Mama broke in quietly. "The children might hear."

On that note I backed away from the door a little, but I was still close enough to hear Papa say, "The Turks have been persecuting the Greek Christians on the mainland for hundreds of years. Christian Byzantine civilization has again and again developed in Asia Minor only to be crushed later by Asiatic invasion. This tragic drama has repeated for centuries, yet there is a difference this time."

"Yes," Theo Demetri said, "since 1914 the campaign to eliminate the Greeks and Christians has intensified and grown particularly vicious. The Byzantine age is gone."

"And the Mohammedans," our Bishop added, "through influence and forceful conquest, have confiscated all the ancient artifacts and religious relics of that era. The exterminations carried out by the Committee for Union and Progress and the Young Turks, who have used the Mohammedans as a means to their ends, have indeed put an irreversible end to our cultural heritage."

"Yes," Papa acknowledged, "I know it has been very bad on the mainland since the end of the Balkan Wars in 1912—over ten years now! Turkish independence is certainly a contradiction of terms. Let's thank God that our small island has been spared from the likes of Mustapha Kemal Atatürk and his Young Turks."

"Yes," Theo Demetri repeated, "thank God we have been spared."

"At least for now," mused the skeptical bishop, and a sober hush fell on the group.

"Ioanni," the bishop went on quietly, "one day soon I would like you to come to Nicholas Vasil's house. I think you should hear something he has to say."

The air was heavy with meaning. "Of course, Father," Papa responded after a brief pause.

[The agenda of these new Ottomans—known as the "Young Turks"—has been a well-kept secret documented by a few historians of the period. Many Greek and Armenian Christians of Asia Minor were tortured, beaten, violated, robbed of their lawful property, and murdered for their Christian beliefs. The magnitude, breadth and viciousness of the atrocities were in many instances greater than Hitler's persecution of the Jews, but this slaughter of Christians never gained the social attention of the massacres in Germany.]

I left the porch and decided to play. Other than the adults' political discussions, these were the happiest days of my young life. With Jimmy and my siblings, I kicked and chased my ball, which was leather and about twice the size of a softball. We had fun playing a game of keep away until early evening when Jimmy's parents called from his aunt's house for him to leave.

"Bye, Jimmy," I said with a smile.

"When do you think you might grow taller?" he teased. I shook my head and laughed.

Suddenly a thought struck him that made him grin. "Your grandfather bakes bread," he told me. "Your father runs a store and he bakes bread, too. Certainly you are no more than a crumb of bread. I will call you Bread Crumb!"

The name stuck. Among the things I remember best from my childhood are Greek Easter with the Bishop, family gatherings, kicking my ball with Katina and Jimmy—and of course, my nickname, "Bread Crumb."

* * * * *

After the holiday, life returned to normal. The one small schoolhouse, the Central School, contained all twelve grades, and was about an hour's walk from home. I went with Katina, who was almost seven. Class began early in the morning and the teacher, Mrs. Tiganis, was very strict. She was a large, broad woman with big hands. We sat stiff and straight, our hands at our sides, in wooden chairs pushed against two long tables. Our eyes had to be focused forward and we weren't allowed to talk. If we had to go to the bathroom, there was one break at midday in which to do it.

One day a sixteen-year-old student named George turned his head to talk to the girls behind him. Mrs. Tiganis saw him and she grabbed her switch in one hand and George's ear lobe in the other. She took him outside and switched him so hard we could hear him yell. For the rest of the day, George had to stand facing the corner. You can imagine the effect this had on the rest of us. To see our biggest schoolmate disciplined like that was very sobering and underscored the importance of manners and respect, while ensuring attentive silence in our small school community.

Although stern, Mrs. Tiganis had a very inquisitive, educational side. She was always making us think about something and she was adept at keeping our interest. I was in her school only a year and a half before the Turks came, but in that brief time I learned how to read, write and do arithmetic. Although some children were brighter and others slower, we had no significant discipline problems that I was aware of. The rule was simple: Children did what their parents, teacher, priest and other adults told them, without question or debate. As a child, you literally spoke only when spoken to. When I see children today and the liberal manner in which they are brought up, I often think back to my childhood and wonder if our permissive ways with today's young are well advised.

Even though school began so early in the morning, we still had chores to do before we went. From the time I was five, I fed the goats and donkey and brought in water from the well, while Katina fed the chickens before we went to school. We also had to pull the cover up on the bed we shared with Sultana, my younger sister—a big mattress with a warm blanket in the loft of our little house. Costa, the baby, stayed with Mama and Papa downstairs. Then we washed up and ate a breakfast of bread and cheese along with water or milk and sometimes fruit. Cheese, olives and bread composed our lunch, many times with an occasional bit of leftover dinner such as a piece of spinach pie. Mama would wrap up our lunch and give it to Katina to take to school for us.

There were many other chores apart from our morning tasks. I brought in wood for our stove on a regular basis, and performed many other tasks that did not need to be done every day. Children in America have no idea of the demands placed on youngsters of my generation and the generations before in the old country. I have always believed that the chores I did in childhood were positive to my development, giving me a sense of accomplishment and pride at a very early age. We developed discipline and control. Above all, my early years gave me a respect for the little things in life, a sense of value and preparation for adulthood.

Papa usually had opened our store by the time we left to go to school. The store was our livelihood, and he worked long hours there. We would always wave and call out to him as we walked by. Most of the time he would run out and give us a hug and kiss, but even if he didn't, he always acknowledged us from the doorway as we passed the store on our way to school.

Life was hard, but it was full and rewarding. Our wants and desires were contained within the walls of our cottage homes, the boundaries of our churches, the limits of our towns and the shores of our island. For a time we were safe from the holocaust occurring throughout the Balkans and Anatolia. Our full and contented lives within our Christian culture would soon be irreversibly violated by the encroaching pan-Turkic menace.

3

The Turkish Occupation

*War should be undertaken only if it is absolutely
necessary and vital. If the life of the nation is
not exposed to danger, then war is murder.*

—Mustapha Kemal Atatürk, 1924

For a few fleeting months following the Easter celebration of
1923, our lives moved through time in the same ageless, familiar
manner that was the ancient rhythm of our island. However, the
unsettled borders in the aftermath of the Balkan Wars of 1912–
1913, followed by World War I, had economically devastated
Mother Greece, leaving the Christians of Asia Minor easy prey for
the barbaric Young Turks. Exposed and vulnerable, our island
stood without an ally or an advocate. We became a bargaining chip
of appeasement for Atatürk and the Young Turks.

In January 1923, after eleven years of uprooting and
unspeakable violence, the Exchange of Populations Agreement was
signed by Greece and Turkey. Although the agreement was fairly
structured, Turkey imposed its own terms. Thus, 1,290,000 Greek
Christians were exchanged for 480,000 Mohammedans. This, then,
was the fate of the Greek civilization in Asia Minor that had
survived for thirty centuries; although the people had suffered
many conquerors, hardships and martyrdom, they had never been
uprooted. What manner of man spawned the annihilation of the
Christians?

The seeds of a holocaust were sown at the dawn of the
twentieth century in Salonika when a group of sinister and brutal
nihilists gained control of Turkey and conducted what became one
of the bloodiest deliberate campaigns of religious persecution and
ethnic cleansing in history, the first unconscionable annihilation of

a marked population in the twentieth century, the Christian Holocaust or genocide.

Formed in the late nineteenth century, the group of radical and ruthless military officers known as the "Young Turks" attempted several coups against the Sultan of the Ottoman Empire, none bringing lasting success. The guiding core of this group was called the Committee of Union and Progress, or C. U. P. Among the leaders of the Committee were Talaat Pasha, Ahmed Amal Pasha, Enver Pasha, and Ahmet Jamal. Ahmet Jamal would ascend to command the Turkish fleet by 1917. Ismail Enver Pasha would be minister of war, and during World War I he became commander-in-chief. It was said that he was a militarist and an egotist with no grasp of politics. Mustapha Kemal Atatürk would finally depose the Sultan and ban the sultanate in 1922. It was he who would be responsible for the slaughter of Greeks in Smyrna and much of the Pontus that same year. With Kemal Rya and Jamal Pasha, these were some of the Young Turks who, along with others, were the controlling members of the C. U. P. A prominent member of this band of parasitic predators was Dr. Selanikli Najim, their chief ideologist. Over time these bloodthirsty intruders implemented a systematic program of dislocation and annihilation against the Christian population in the remnants of the Ottoman Empire still under their control.

These men finally gained support through the 1908 constitution, which initially toppled the Sultan's reign (though the Sultan briefly took back control in 1909, only to be ousted again and finally replaced by his brother, who would serve as a figurehead Sultan dominated by the C. U. P.) and purported freedom from religious persecution and equal rights for the Christian minorities. Their actual agenda began to reveal itself in 1909, when they conducted an experiment that succeeded in exterminating 30,000 Christians in Adana, a town broadly composed of those who had supported, to their demise, the C. U. P. The folly of the Christians' early monetary support of the Young Turks would become increasingly apparent as the genocide continued to spread.

The Young Turks' program began with the systematic disarmament of minorities. They postulated that with the new constitution, there was no longer a need for the population to bear arms. They were free under a government that would protect their rights. Gun control laws were passed, followed by an amnesty that allowed people to turn in their guns without being in violation of the new arms laws. Christians serving in the military were reassigned to duties that did not require firearms. Once disarmed, they became easy prey for the Mohammedans of modern Turkey.

These twentieth-century Ottomans succeeded where five hundred years of Ottomans had failed in the extermination of the Christian population of Asia Minor. In 1915 and 1916, the "Butcher Battalions," formed by Talaat and Enver, exterminated seventy-five percent of the two million Armenian Christians in the region. Typically they would enter a village and order all males from ages ten through 50 to assemble, then march them out of town for a number of miles so the shots of their executions could not be heard by the women, children and elderly who were left behind, thus easy prey for the next round. Sometimes, the women and children were not shot, but driven to the desert and ultimate death by starvation.

Although the Armenians bore the brunt of the early holocaust, all Christians in Anatolia felt the pressure: Serbs, Hertugonians, Italians and, of course, the Greeks. By 1916, under the veil of political reform, the ensuing massacres of the Christian populations throughout the Ottoman Empire resulted in a blatant transfer of wealth to the now-controlling C. U. P. The genocide sealed the extinguishment of Byzantine Christian culture.

The Armenian massacres escaped international attention, overshadowed, as they were, by the First World War. The purging of Greek, Serb, Italian and Russian Christians began in earnest at the end of the First World War, and did not significantly relent until the Black Sea Christians were uprooted and slaughtered following the Lausanne Agreement in 1923.

Between 1920 and 1922, Mustapha Kemal Pasha, or Atatürk ("the Father of Turkey"), would gain control of Turkey and pass a law prohibiting any Christians from living in Anatolia east of Rankia Bostangi. Thus, Christians were driven west toward the Aegean and the Mediterranean, into Smyrna and other coastal cities. Smyrna had been given to Greece after World War I under protection of a mandate by the Allies, who subsequently refused to support Greece in her defense of the city.

History has largely ignored these events, placing whatever blame it was willing to acknowledge upon the triad of Enver, Talaat and Jamal, proclaiming Mustapha Kemal a great man and leaving the other members of the C. U. P. unscathed. Although time may weaken the testimony, selective truth and concealment of truth equal falsehood.

Our families, our villages, and our clergy knew these events. They are events I know only too well. The thin veil of political reformation cloaked the most heinous persecution of Christian populations in the twentieth century while the rest of the world turned a blind eye. Political reformation became a means of conducting ethnic and religious purification. The prize was immense for the Young Turks, for the Christian population in Asia Minor was wealthy, educated and productive.

It wearies me now to ponder the long spiral of the human condition...the oppressed become the oppressors; the leaders, the followers; the downtrodden, the conquerors; the young, the old; its never-ending coils continue twisting and turning through time.

* * * * *

"Christo," Papa said one evening shortly after Easter in 1923, "tonight we are going to Papou's house." I was excited about the excursion, but had a sense that this was not an ordinary social visit. Bishop Iakovos soon arrived and would apparently be accompanying us this evening.

At Papou's house, the greetings were short and mechanical, and Papou and Yiayia did not make a fuss over me as they usually did. I spotted a thin man, a woman, and three young boys sitting quietly at the end of the room. I was too young to understand its meaning, but they all had the same detached despondent look about them, which made an impression on me.

The bishop introduced Papa, "Ioanni, this is Nicholas and Anastasia Vasil, and their sons Athanasis, Nicholas and Philipos. They are the ones from Smyrna I told you about. I think you should hear what they have to say."

30

"It is a pleasure to meet you," Papa said seriously.

"Mr. Chrysostomidis," he started his tale, "I understand you are a good man... We escaped from Smyrna on a Greek ship flying the American flag. Six months ago, it dropped us 70 miles northwest of here on the island of Lesbos, where we stayed in a one-story house outside the island's capital of Mitilini. So many refugees are there that the conditions are deplorable, so we came here for a brief stay with Anastasia's second cousin before leaving for Greece. We are blessed to have made it this far."

"I see," Papa said gently. "Can you tell me what happened?"

"It started in earnest two weeks before the city was burned. The Turkish military uprooted countless Christian families from inland as well as from surrounding provinces and drove them into Smyrna. During this period, advance elements of the Turkish army were drifting into the city. We heard regular reports of theft, rape and murder during those few days of increasing occupation. Realizing the mounting severity of our plight, many of us stayed indoors and prayed." He spoke in a dry monotone without emotion. "On the eve of the slaughters, the population of the city had swelled from 200,000 to more than 400,000."

"First the Turkish military incited the Mohammedan population against the Christians, the Mohammedans forming mobs, looting, and starting fires throughout the Christian sector. Then the gendarmes entered the city and..." Here he faltered for a moment before continuing, "a horrific, incomprehensible bloodbath began." He stopped, and Papa waited quietly for him to continue.

"I had a stone and concrete factory. All was lost. My wife sewed a few gold coins into the clothes of my three sons. Luckily, I had sons and not daughters. That night, the Turks broke into my home." He lifted his hand and stared briefly as a memory caused a look of mild surprise. "They tried to cut off my finger to get a gold ring," he said, showing his hand to Papa, "but I was able to remove it in time to save my finger." Again he paused and quickly passed his tongue across his tight, dry lips.

"Poor Leonides, my friend and neighbor. He suffered a terrible death. He had a young daughter of sixteen—"

At this point, Papa turned to me, "Christo, go out and play with Mr. Vasil's sons, please."

I wanted to stay and hear the story, but I knew better than to argue. "Yes, Papa." I looked shyly at them. The three others went outside, but I lingered at the door.

"I'm sorry, go on," Papa said.

He shook his head and began again, still devoid of emotion. "He was forced to watch while three Turkish soldiers repeatedly raped her. When he tried to defend her, he was stabbed with a saber in his intestines and stomach. Three times this happened. He sat on the floor, trying to hold his entrails in while he slowly bled to death, unable to defend his daughter who lay on the ground before him. God rest their souls."

"Yes, God rest their souls," Papa repeated as Bishop Iakovos crossed himself while mumbling a prayer.

Vasil continued recounting the horrors. "We were powerless, defenseless. We fled our home. We roamed the streets with thousands of others while our homes burned. Many people were stabbed to death or shot randomly in the streets. Countless young girls were raped in plain view. Somehow, we survived, my family and me," shaking his head with wonder. "We hid for two days in the yard of an old factory near the docks while the city burned. The sky glowed red from the city's blaze for more than a week, smoke from the smoldering ruins and the stench from the dead and dying filling the air. We had no food or water and finally had to leave our lair, which we did at first light on the third morning. With the help of an American naval officer, we boarded the Greek ship, one of a few that the Americans had agreed to allow to be transferred under their flag, God be praised."

Papa was agitated. "Smyrna is an international port—"

"No," he said in anticipation of the question. "From the factory I could see crowds of people forced to the sea by the fires. Yes, ships were docked bearing French, British, and German registry. Many of the poor souls were trying to board by climbing up the sides of the big ships, only to be repelled. To my knowledge, only a few were accepting refugees."

"In the midst of this chaos, the regular Turkish Army arrived. They were purportedly there to bring order out of the mayhem that they themselves had created. They proceeded to do this by firing round after round at point-blank range into the throng, now defenseless and trapped, the water at their backs and the burning city before them. No mercy was shown. Countless women, children and the elderly were slain next to the men." He drew a breath and sighed.

"May God let their poor souls rest in peace," Bishop Iakovos reverently interjected, momentarily capturing the group's attention.

"The kind bishop has found this place for us to stay," Nicholas continued. "Shortly, we will be going to Greece. But I warn you, you are not safe here. Be careful. You must all leave before you succumb to the same fate. No Christian is safe in these parts of the world any longer." Mr. Vasil began to tremble, and his voice became rough and contorted.

Bishop Iakovos broke in, "You will be safe here. You must get some rest." Turning to Papa, he said, "I fear he is right. Our island home is at great risk."

"Yes...what a tragedy these poor people have endured and witnessed."

They talked for a while on lighter subjects, but Papa knew they were tired, and he had to open the store early the next morning. Rising to take his leave, Papa shook Nicholas Vasil's frail hand and said, "Christ be with you." Then Papa kissed the bishop's hand, the children were gathered, and we left.

The brief meeting with Nicholas Vasil and his family was an ominous sign of the imminent loss of our beloved island home to the barbarians of the Smyrna genocide. When the Treaty of Lausanne was signed that same year of 1923, the world would read that it annexed Imbroz to the Turks and decreed three things: The island would be governed by an organization composed of Greeks, a local administrator would recruit a local police force, and the customs and institutions of the local Greek population would be protected. The world was satisfied.

Papa believed that these bloodthirsty Turks had no intention of abiding by the treaty—and he was right. Instead, harsh occupation laws were imposed. Immediately, Greek schools were closed and Greek children were forced to attend Turkish schools. It became illegal to fly the Greek flag or to speak Greek—all in direct violation of the publicized treaty. The Greek way of life existed no more on Imbroz, except in the hearts and minds of the conquered people.

In his capacity as a city council member of Panayia, Papa had been responsible for maintaining all the records in city hall. He foresaw that the Turks would inevitably confiscate the city's records, so he carefully kept our family records separately at home. His children, and his children's children, would know their proper births and identity, as well as their heritage, relatives and traditions. He would not abdicate these intangibles in the face of overbearing intimidation, coercion and repression. To be sure, we kept our records in our heads.

I live in Panayia, the capital city of Imbroz Island, I recited to myself. *I was born on December 15, 1917. I am named Chrysostomos Ioanni Chrysostomidis for my grandfather and father, as is our custom. I am the second of four children. I have two sisters, Katina and Sultana, and a little brother Costa. My father's name is Ioanni Chrysostomidis. His parents are Katherine and Chrysostomos, and his sisters and brothers are Zafira, Kiraha and Demetrius. My mother's name is Theopiste Dracoulas Chrysostomidis. Mama's parents are Dracos Dracoulas and Sultana Dracoulas, and her sisters and brother are Ioanni, Keratsa, Yramatiki, Constantinos, Basilic and Thea Cleo....* These were the things I memorized from our family records.

Papa was a stubborn man. Unlike many Greeks who fled the island, Papa refused to leave his home and the property he had worked for so long and so hard. He believed doing so would play right into the Turks' unspoken agenda to drive the entire Christian Greek population from their homes. He was not about to give the Turks what they wanted so easily! Somehow, in the face of Turkish oppression, Papa remained an optimist. No matter how dire the circumstances were, he held out hope that things would change. They never did.

When the Turks first arrived, our family stubbornly tried to proceed with its normal activities, but change was everywhere. Every day more Greek families left the island and the economy grew increasingly poor. Like the other children of the island, my sisters and brother and I now attended Turkish school. Although Mama and Papa still spoke Greek at home, we were forbidden by law to do so in public or at school. Turkish teachers took the place of Greek teachers—and of course, Turkish was the language of the classroom.

Just a few months earlier, in a past that now seemed like a dream, Papa had worked happily in his store, often with Mama's help. I also helped in the store, and I enjoyed it so much that I once told Papa I would like to quit school and work with him, but he wouldn't let me. Everyone came by to see him and the store was well stocked with sugar, flour, bread, Greek cheese, milk, olives, wine, coffee, tea, Greek cookies, fabrics, thread and much more. Our small store was not only Papa's joy, it was also the way we made our living. Now, in the face of a population in exodus and a suffering economy, Papa struggled hard to keep the store open and the inventory grew more and more sparse. Sometimes, even the essentials were hard to come by for weeks.

One winter day in 1924, as I stood next to Papa at the counter, two Turkish gendarmes came to the store. They were both armed with rifles and sabers, and they towered over Papa. The bigger of the two laid his saber on the counter and looked at Papa. "Fine store you have here," he said in Turkish.

"May I help you?" Papa inquired politely.

"Yes," the gendarme told him. "What is your name?"

"Ioanni," Papa said.

"Well, Ioanni," the gendarme said, "we need supplies for the Turkish military police."

Papa didn't say a word, and a moment later the gendarme lifted a bag of flour on his shoulders and carried it out to his donkey-drawn cart. Next, the gendarmes took a bag of sugar and another of rice, until the cart was full of staples.

"Excuse me," Papa said. "You owe me 1,500 drachmas."

"Of course," the first gendarme said sarcastically. "Ismet, pay Mr. Ioanni his 1,500 drachmas."

The Turk ripped off a corner of Papa's wrapping paper from the roll he kept on the counter top and scribbled something on it. "Here," he said, pushing the paper at Papa, "an I-owe-you."

"But there is no name on this," Papa protested. "No amount, either."

"You do not need names or amounts," the first gendarme said as he buckled his saber back on. "This is by order of Kemal Atatürk for the Turkish police. We will remember and pay you later." In an eruption of laughter the gendarmes left the store, and the Turkish military police never repaid us.

Turkish interlopers were murdering, stealing, and violating our rights. Christian worship was barely tolerated. The priests were trying to hold our population together in the face of unbelievable persecution and exodus.

One morning on my way to school, as I walked along the road idly humming a tune to fill the time, I rounded the usual bend to face a small pasture and slowed to let a small band of chickens scatter before me. Their squawking interrupted my absentminded humming, as a strange awareness that something was wrong overcame me. Then I saw it. My heart stopped beating altogether as I froze, rooted among the chickens. I saw his feet first as they swayed slightly in the air. One shoe was missing. To my horror, my eyes traveled up as I fought to resist, fearing what I might see, but on they went, up into the branches of the tree to the rope from which the body hung. It was a Greek man. On him was a sign: *This man caught stealing chickens.* I didn't know the man, but I knew it was a lie. Even if true, the punishment hardly fit the crime.

Similar events were growing more and more common all over the island. People were fleeing daily for unknown destinations, leaving behind generations of possessions for the Turks to seize. As the population dwindled the Turks became more brazen and less accountable in their persecutions, and there was greater pressure on those Greeks left behind. Papa and the other city council members had been discharged, and the Turkish authorities who replaced them were indifferent to complaints. The tedious passage of Turkish time was torturous.

* * * * *

The year was 1927. Panayia was a much different place. Though the multitude of Greek monuments from the Classical, Hellenistic and Byzantine eras still remained, in the five years since the massacre at Smyrna and the martyrdom of Archbishop

36

Chrysodom, Imbroz had changed enormously. The collapse of Smyrna closed the Hellenic and Byzantine influence in Asia Minor on a note of utter destruction for the Christian minorities.

"Christo, we must be hopeful," Papa told me. "Without hope, life would be empty." He had read about the United States and its freedom and justice, and believed that America would come to our aid. "They will not allow this to go on," he said. "The United States is just and good and they will protect our rights." Even though the Americans never came, Papa always spoke kindly and had a deep respect for the United States, a respect he nurtured in me from an early age. Had it not been for his encouragement I would not have found my way here. From that time on Imbroz, coming to America was my dream.

I nodded solemnly. Such high-minded concepts did little to allay my ten-year-old fears, and yet, there was a comfort in them, too.

"You will be a success if you go to America, my son."

"Yes, Papa," I said. "I promise I will go to America and be free. I will never forget."

It had been a year now since Papa was forced to close the store. He simply had no more goods to sell. By now our diet had been reduced to bread, olives and Greek cheese, supplemented by an occasional plate of fish when we were able to catch it. Two-thirds of our sheep had died or were stolen. Miraculously, though, Papa had been able to put red meat on our table for Christmas and Easter. There was increasingly less food to eat, however, and my siblings and I came home from school with hunger cramps in our empty stomachs. The Turks spread an abundance of hunger and sadness across our island. People were slowly wasting away.

That year, for the first time, Papa could no longer provide the basic necessities for his children, and soon my sister Katina went to stay with Thea Cleo and Theo Russo on Samothráki Island. Cleo and Russo had no children and welcomed her. There she would help them with their store and attend a Greek school.

About a year later, my turn would come. The day Mama called to me, I knew immediately things were more dire than ever before. "Chrysostomos, come here!" The tears that threatened in her proud eyes were the only hint of the despair she must have felt at that moment, though she would die rather than admit it. "Papa and I have decided to send you to Samothráki Island for a while to stay with Theo Russo, Thea Cleo and your sister. You will see your sister, Katina." My parents were proud and would never admit defeat, but I knew then how financially strapped we were. "They have plenty of food," Mama said, "and you can attend Greek school."

Even so, I felt all the fear and uncertainty of a ten-year-old boy leaving home to find his way in the world. Papa knew this, and he tried to reassure me. Papa was full of other advice, telling me how I should behave if a Turk confronted me. "Chrysostomos, when a Turk comes before you and speaks to you, look him in the eye and smile, then bow at the waist...see?" Papa placed his hand lightly at his waist and bowed to demonstrate. "Now, you try it."

"Yes, Papa." We tried bowing for about five minutes.

"It shows respect, my son," Papa told me. "Always look into their eyes. That way, they won't bother you."

"I'll remember."

The night before I left Imbroz was a cool Saturday evening. Papa pulled my arm to sit down next to him on the porch. I felt the cool evening breeze from the east off the Aegean. Papa took my hand and held it for a few minutes as he talked. Even if we were far apart, Papa told me that night, we would always be together in our thoughts and love. Although at the time I was too young to understand much of what was happening, I fully realized that the events of recent years had irreversibly changed our lives. The carefree happy days of my early childhood were distant memories.

"Christo, wherever you go, remember to remain humble and reverent and God will take care of you." Then Papa told me stories about the ancient Greek philosophers, how they lived and what they believed. Papa often quoted the ancients. Listening to him tell stories, I felt my tensions and anxieties dissipate. Even though I would see him for brief moments later in my life, this is how I will always remember my father: telling me stories about the ancients the night before I left home.

We talked of America, and how the ideas of the ancients had sown the seeds that that country had cultivated and allowed to flourish. On the eve of my departure from the only home I had ever known, thousands of miles across vast oceans from that awesome land of opportunity with barely a cent in my pocket, the possibility of ever seeing America seemed as real as having afternoon tea with Plato or Socrates. But Papa was convinced that this was what I must do, so I had to believe that it was possible.

Soon a figure was approaching from Panayia, a man with a white beard and staff dressed in the black robe and headdress of a holy man. It was Bishop Iakovos. After greeting Papa, he turned to me.

"Chrysostomos, I understand you will be going to live with your Thea and Theo?"

"Yes, Your Grace, I am going tomorrow after church."

"I see."

"I will be helping Theo Russo in his store."

"My, my," he smiled. "A big job for such a young boy." Then he added, "Christo, you have been noticed by many on our island. You are special. You must never forget that. Wherever you go, whatever you do, you must not forget your home on Imbroz, or your Mama and Papa and brother and sisters."

I was honored and humbled, "I won't forget," I told him gratefully. "I will never forget."

"Come here, my son."

The Bishop bowed his head and said a prayer for me. I bowed my head, too, and prayed that God would watch over and protect us.

"Amen," Bishop Iakovos said, and I kissed his hand and bowed. He was more than our religious leader, he was a friend of Papa's and a familiar face at our house. I felt he always liked me and showed me special attention, and I liked him very much. I knew he had made this special visit for me.

"God be with you my son," he said.

It was dusk now and Mama started to usher me to bed along with my brother and sister, but I could hear Papa and the Bishop talking downstairs. Although I did not understand everything, I listened intently.

"Is there any news from the mainland?" Papa asked. "Will the Greek government intervene? Or the Americans? Or the Europeans? What about the violations of Article 14?"

"The world does not care," Iakovos said.

"But one day someone will correct the injustices we are facing," Papa insisted. "The civilized world will not close the door forever. Sometimes, justice—like God—acts in strange ways."

"Yanni," the Bishop said, using Papa's nickname. "The Turks have been forcing many to sell their land at gunpoint. In the night and for no reason, they have taken men from their homes and they are never seen again. They have assaulted women, and when charges are brought to the magistrate, they are dismissed or simply not pursued. What will you do when things do not get better, but worse?"

"I will not run from tyranny," Papa insisted. "I will not give up everything I have lawfully worked for all my life! That is what the Turks plan on, uprooting us. Of what value is freedom if you must lose everything to pursue it? I was born on Imbroz. It is my home and one day I will die here."

"At least you will preserve your life," Iakovos told Papa. "Remember Archbishop Chrysodom refused refuge, saying, 'I am a shepherd and must stay with my flock.' He was decapitated, his head paraded up and down the streets of Smyrna!..." The Bishop was agitated and his voice trailed off. "Chrysodom was offered safety but he chose to stay with his people," he went on a moment later, repeating a story we all knew. "He tried to save his people from the Turkish slaughter and became a martyr for our faith!"

At once, Papa grinned. "Oh, my friend...even though they have yet to find a cure for the common birthday, I do not intend to be a martyr. However, there is no life for my children here. One day, they must all leave."

"Yanni, you can't fight the Turkish gendarmes!"

"No, I can't," my Papa said, "but as long as I am here living my life the way we have for generations, our island will be alive."

Papa, don't worry, I thought to myself. *I will go to America one day. I will find a way.*

The conversation drifted from subject to subject. The men discussed the bullet holes in the double eagle that ornamented our Metropolitan Church and the establishment of monopolies in the wine and tobacco trade that eventually extinguished production. They talked about the surprise tax raids on our homes and property, which were, at the least, an invasion of our right to privacy and often resulted in theft of land and property. They talked of the closure of our schools and the forcible renaming of our cities and towns as well as our island itself. Our Greek homeland with centuries of Christian character buried in its soil could never be forgotten.

I don't know when the Bishop left. I was starting to doze, and when I finally went to sleep that night my thoughts were on Turkish Gendarmes and Greek philosophers. Even at age ten, although uncertain about leaving home, my strong resolve was to help Mama and Papa, my brother and my sisters. The Turks had brought many unwelcome changes to my small island home over the past four years and Mama and Papa tried to deal with them as best they could. Now it would be my turn to help.

4
Separation

As I pass through my incarnations
In every age and race,
Make my proper prostrations
To the Gods of the Market Place.
Peering through reverent fingers
I watch them flourish and fall...
And the hearts of the meanest were humbled
And began to believe it was true
That all is not Gold that Glitters,
And Two and Two make Four—
And the Gods of the Copybook Headings
Limped up to explain it once more.

—Rudyard Kipling
"The Gods of the Copybook Headings," 1919

When morning came I was up and dressed even before Mama called us to get ready for church. I had finished my chores and was ready for breakfast when Mama and Papa walked up to me.

"Chrysostomos, I want you to wear this," Papa said.

"What is it?" I asked curiously.

"It is a very ancient relic coin that is rumored to have pieces of the Cross in it," Papa told me. "It has been in my family for generations and now it is yours. Wear it all the time, next to your heart. It is a holy relic. Through this ancient coin, God will protect and watch over you every day of your life."

My eyes were glued to the worn, tarnished coin. It appeared to have a faded, primitive rendering of Christ with a halo engraved on its face. "I will, Papa, I promise," I said, nodding earnestly. "I will wear it every day." Papa carefully handed the relic coin to Mama, who pinned it to the collar of my tee shirt over my heart. Then she

42

and Papa embraced me for a long moment. "Come on, now, let's eat breakfast," Mama said finally, interrupting her stoic silence.

That morning we had bread and a thin piece of Greek cheese. Papa and Mama drank coffee and we children shared a little goat's milk. I was very hungry. Since the Turks came—and especially since Papa closed his store—we never seemed to have enough food.

After breakfast, Mama prepared a small sack of cheese, olives, and bread for my trip to Samothráki Island.

"Mama, you don't have to," I said. "Keep the food, I can wait to eat until I get to Thea Cleo's."

"Chrysostomos," Mama remonstrated, "it will be almost a full day...and besides, it is only a couple of pieces of cheese, a few olives and a piece of bread. I also made you a treat—some baklava. Now remember, your Great-Yiayia Theopisti will be there, too. When you talk to her, talk loudly. She is a little deaf. She is very, very old."

As we left that morning, I glanced back at the only home I had known. I paused for a minute, swallowing hard at the thought that I would not see my home for a while. A ten-year-old's pain of separation is hard to conceal. Although I was trying very hard to be brave, it was difficult to leave my home and family. The occupation of Imbroz that had uprooted so many had finally uprooted me.

"Mama," I asked suddenly, "did you remember to pack my ball?"

"Don't worry," she smiled. "Your ball is in your case with your other things."

The ball Jimmy and I once played with was wrapped with yarn and encased in leather and was not perfectly round. Still, we had a lot of fun with it. I remembered a time when this ball had gotten me in trouble. We were playing and had lost track of the time. Mama and Papa didn't know where we were and they were upset and worried. Papa took a switch to me, the one and only time he ever did, which made it all the more memorable. The ball was my one childhood toy.

The walk to church my last morning home was solemn and uneventful. The church was only a half-mile from our house. We brought my possessions along with us in Mama's small worn suitcase and a terry cloth bag for the trip to the port at Castro, which was an hour-and-twenty-minute walk from Panayia. I wore my church clothes, Papa wore his white shirt and his church jacket, and Mama wore her good Sunday dress.

The people at church had a worn and haggard appearance. The number of parishioners had substantially declined since the coming of the Turks. Outside the church doors, two Turkish policemen were a daunting reminder of the occupation. Church was the only thing from our past that was allowed—or tolerated—by Atatürk, the Turks showing little curiosity about any of our traditions.

The choir had started and the priest had already begun the liturgy. Papa and Mama were sticklers for being at church on time. "On time" meant five minutes after the service started, which by Greek standards is pretty early. The Turkish presence outside made the congregation, the choir and the priest sing and chant louder. 'Not even the Turks could stop Christianity' was the message!

Bishop Iakovos delivered a sermon on the inner strength of Christianity and admonished the congregation to keep their Christian beliefs and stay strong. "These are difficult times we live in," he began. "Many in our villages have left or are leaving for Greece and other destinations, abandoning everything they own. We will remember them in our prayers and ask God to bless them wherever they are." During four years of occupation, the island's population of twelve thousand had been more than halved, and the economy had collapsed. Some people had disappeared mysteriously at night, never to be heard from again by family or friends. Others had been shot. There had been a few instances of public hangings for trivial violations of nonsensical Turkish whim or law, like the "chicken stealer" I saw. Most fathers kept their daughters very close during this time, and with good reason.

Sometimes, Turks offered to buy homes and property for the price of a chicken. More often people simply abandoned their houses, leaving land, possessions and even their loved ones behind to flee Turkish persecution. It was mostly the young, who had had their futures so irreversibly violated, who left their island home.

Following their flight, belongings and property converted to Turkish ownership.

We were luckier than most because we had grain field, an olive grove and a vineyard, as well as a few remaining sheep and chickens. These possessions and some small savings in the form of gold coins left us better off than most. It was due to our meager belongings and Papa's strength of will that we survived those difficult years. Papa never let us know the true depth of our economic difficulties, and he sheltered us as much as possible from the Turks.

In the end, the Church was the only part of our cultural tradition that was allowed by the Turkish rulers, because forcibly closing the churches would have provoked open revolt on the island. Even so, the Turks showed no respect for the Christian population and very little respect for life in general. This was what my island home had become. These were the events unfolding before me—the destruction of my youth, my life.

Suddenly, it was as if the Bishop were expressing Papa's thoughts. "These are your homes. This is your island," he told us emotionally. "Do not leave them easily. You have done nothing wrong. In the name of the Father, the Son, and the Holy Spirit. Amen." I was pleased to see that Jimmy Coucouzes was at church with his parents that morning. He usually went to the church in Ayii Theodori, but occasionally he attended in Panayia to hear the Bishop and visit his aunt. As the thinning congregation filed out the church doors, Jimmy sought me out.

"Hey, Bread Crumb!" he called out. "When are you going to get bigger?"

I smiled, wondering the same thing. I was ten now, and Jimmy was sixteen. If anything, Jimmy towered over me more than he had three years ago.

"What are you doing?"

"I'm going to theological school," he told me. "Bishop Iakovos helped arrange it."

"Good, Jimmy!" I said, genuinely pleased. "May God be with you."

"Thanks," he smiled.

"I'm leaving today for Samothráki Island to work at my uncle's store," I told him, proud that I had news of my own to share. In those days, circumstances often forced young boys into older roles.

"But Bread Crumb," he protested. "You are too small to work."

"I've worked for Papa the last three years. Anyway, this is what I want to do—it beats going to a Turkish school."

"God be with you, my little friend." A silence fell between us. "Do you have your ball?" Jimmy asked suddenly.

I grinned and walked over to Mama's bag where my ball was packed. "Go and play with your friend," Mama told me. "But just for a minute, or you will miss your boat."

"But Sultana," Papa said, "we have to go now."

"Don't deny them a moment of children's play," Mama urged. "Jimmy Coucouzes is going to seminary and Christo is going to Samothráki. Who knows when they will see each other again?"

There was a small yard on the side of the church where Jimmy and I kicked the ball, frolicking back and forth. For a few brief moments we were untroubled children playing an uncomplicated game in a complex and often hostile world. At the time I had no idea that these few minutes playing ball with Jimmy Coucouzes marked the early end of my childhood and the beginning of my circuitous and often bewildering journey to America.

"Chrysostomos! We have to go now!" Papa finally called.

"Good luck, my little friend," Jimmy said affectionately, placing a hand on my shoulder as I bent to pick up my ball.

"Good bye, Jimmy!" I tucked the ball under my arm and waved, then ran to catch up with my family. We parted on different paths with no idea if and when we might meet again.

The walk to Castro seemed quick. Costa and Sultana, only five and seven years old, rode the donkey. The rest of us were afoot, and for a while I tried to walk stride for stride with Papa and Mama. As we left the town behind us, it dawned on me that I would not be sleeping in my house, nor returning to church the next week. I would be leaving Panayia and Imbroz for the first time in my life. A gust of warm wind rolled across the lush green grass that bordered the road on the outskirts of town, and for a brief moment the agony of conquest was quelled and the scent of fond memories returned, as I silently bid good-bye to my home.

When we reached the dock, Papa called out to a man whom I did not recognize. "Hello, Captain Koutris! I have your young passenger here for you!"

Captain Koutris was the most experienced captain in Castro and a friend of Papa's.

"Hello, Mr. Chrysostomidis! Is that the little fellow?"

"Yes," Papa nodded, "Christo, say hello to Captain Koutris."

"Hello," I said. Papa gave Captain Koutris a few coins and told him that Aunt Cleo and Uncle Russo would pick me up at the Samothráki dock at first light. Mama gave me the small case with my belongings, as well as the bread, cheese and olives wrapped up in cloth for my trip. A single tear ran down the contour of her face in silent recognition that the time for my departure had come.

Captain Koutris had a chiseled, lean and worn look about him. He was taller than Papa and wore a knit fisherman's cap on his head. His mustache was white and brown and formed an inverted vee to the edges of his lips. His ears and nose seemed disproportionately large, but his sizeable eyes were engaging and friendly. My best guess was that he was at least as old as Papa.

"I have a bottle of water for you," Captain Koutris said, "but if you have to go to the bathroom, better run to those bushes now." I looked first at him and then at the bushes and decided it was a good idea. When I returned, Mama grasped me around the shoulders and gave me a final tearful sigh and gripping hug.

"Chrysostomos, I will miss you very much," she said, her voice thick with emotion. Suddenly my little brother and sister ran up to hug me. After a long minute of mutual embrace, I began to disengage. Then Papa stretched his hand out to me.

"Papa," I said, trying to reassure him, "don't worry, I will be fine." The appearance of Papa's warm, gentle smile set me at ease.

A short distance away, Captain Koutris stepped into his boat. "Mr. Chrysostomidis," he called out, interrupting us. "Hurry! We must hurry to catch the tide."

"Chrysostomos, my son," Papa said, "remember what I have told you."

"I will, Papa," I promised, my voice sounding very adult. As I stepped back, I looked Papa in the eye and bowed. Papa returned my bow with a big smile, and then we both laughed. Although caring for the family put a lot of pressure on Papa, he never complained and always showed us compassion, humor and wit. Since the arrival of the Turks almost four years earlier, we had been rendered powerless to provide for our material needs or to control our destinies. This would be my chance to be on my own and to help my father and my family. I welcomed the responsibility.

Everyone followed me onto the dock as I got on the boat, calling out farewells. As I turned and stepped down into the small craft, I hardly realized the significance of this childhood separation.

Captain Koutris looked at me with concern. "Are you ready, Chrysostomos?"

"Yes," I nodded, not trusting myself to speak. Captain Koutris understood and turned away busying himself with some task. Mama and Papa stood waving as my boat pulled out to sea, their figures growing smaller and smaller. "Good-bye Mama, good-bye Papa," I said silently.

I had seen the sea many times, played and fished in it too, but I had never gone out to sea in a boat before. Yet, it was not the voyage that preyed on me. As the figures of my family grew smaller in the distance, it was the fear of separation and the uncertainty of my future that made me uneasy, not the tossing waves and open sea before us. Soon Mama, Papa, Sultana and Costa were no more than silhouettes on an ever-shrinking shoreline, yet my eyes and my thoughts were with them. Long after they disappeared from view I felt an emptiness deep inside. I clenched the medallion coin pinned to my shirt and prayed for God to protect my family from the Turks. Fate and necessity often expose life's fragility, yet our will confirms life's strengths.

As the day wore on, I began to take stock of the little boat we were in. "How fast are we going?" I asked Captain Koutris.

"Oh, we're moving at about three knots," he said. It suddenly felt good to talk, and my mind was soon occupied with more questions about the sea. "When will we arrive?"

"We should reach Samothráki Island, God willing, in about eight to nine hours." He paused, then added, "We will wait offshore until dawn so that we don't run up on any rocks." After he answered, he resumed rowing.

I didn't want to think about breaking up on rocks in the night, and instead my thoughts returned to my family. After a while I focused on the dinner Mama had packed me. The Captain offered me some water, but declined my offer of olives, bread and cheese, and continued his rhythmic rowing. I ate quietly and without much appetite. Even the dessert, baklava, did not offset the solemn sadness of separation. Small swells rippled past the little boat, trailing off into faint ribbons around the wake. Eventually his small sail picked up a seaward breeze, yet Captain Koutris continued to row.

We idly chatted most of the remaining afternoon. The sun was setting and my little island was no more than a speck on the horizon. A silence had fallen between us now, each of us within our own thoughts.

"Young man," the Captain said, breaking into my reverie, "I can see that you are tired. It will be a long night on the water. You should go to sleep. There is a blanket behind you in the stern."

Although I didn't want to admit it, Captain Koutris was right. I was tired, and it had been an emotional day of long good-byes. I found the blanket and pulled it around me. For a long time I lay awake, watching quietly as Captain Koutris rowed on in the growing darkness. The repetitive, rhythmic swells were medicine for my anxious concern and hollow grief. *One day, I will be a captain and have my own small boat on which I will go out to sea,* I thought dreamily...finally falling to sleep.

Later that night Captain Koutris startled me out of a fitful doze. "Samothráki Island!" he exclaimed, as if surprised he had actually found it. "There it is...now I will rest, my little friend, until first dawn." In the moonlight I saw him sit and drink a considerable amount of liquid from a jug he kept by his feet, which I suspected was not water. Then he ate some food he had stored below his seat. I was awed by the man's stamina. He had been rowing all of this time and barely seemed fazed. "In a short while you will see your aunt and uncle," he told me, catching my gaze. I nodded silently and a few minutes later I fell back to sleep. For the remainder of the night I dozed uneasily, rocked by the gentle Aegean swells, chilled by the early morning air, and anxious at the prospect of my first day away from home.

"Child, wake up," Captain Koutris shook me. "Wake up, we will be there soon!" With the aid of daylight, the small vessel had closed the distance to Samothráki Island. The morning air was still very cool and I clutched the tattered blanket around me.

"We will be at the dock in less than an hour!" the Captain told me with a rare smile. "Your aunt, uncle and sister should be there to greet you. Look for them!" In the distance I could make out the piers of the harbor, but I couldn't see anyone waiting there. Even as we neared the dock, I saw no signs of my sister, aunt or uncle, and apprehension fluttered uneasily in the pit of my stomach. We docked the boat in silence and I stepped onto an empty pier. Suddenly, I saw a small group of people walking toward the dock—it was Aunt Cleo, Uncle Russo and my sister, Katina. I smiled in the early morning air at the sight of familiar faces. Suddenly, with family around me, it felt good to be on Samothráki.

"Good-bye, son," Captain Koutris said as he watched my family crowd happily and noisily around me. "God be with you, Chrysostomos."

"Wait!" I cried, breaking free of Aunt Cleo's embrace. "Uncle Russo, Aunt Cleo, I want you to meet Captain Koutris from Imbroz."

He was a little uncomfortable being the center of attention; his was a solitary existence that seemed to suit him just fine, but I felt very close to the man with whom I had shared the first twelve hours of my new life.

"Good-bye, Captain Koutris!" I said as he handed me the last of my gear. "Please tell Mama and Papa that I made it all right."

"I will, son," the Captain promised, as his sail caught the morning breeze.

I turned back to my aunt, who caught me up in another embrace. Aunt Cleo was my mother's sister and, although younger, she looked and acted a lot like Mama. "Oh, my child!" she crooned. "You must be hungry and cold! Look, I brought you some food," she said, offering me some neatly wrapped spinach pie.

Over my aunt's shoulder I studied Katina. She had grown more than I had during the ten months she had been away, and now she was at least a head taller than I was. She had put on weight as well. Wasn't I ever going to grow?

Katina caught my eye. "Come here, Chrysostomos!" she cried, and I wiggled out of Cleo's hug and into hers. Next to us, Uncle Russo stood passively. He was a quiet, expressionless man without Papa's mental depth or humor. Nonetheless, he was my uncle and I respected him. Like my father, Uncle Russo had a large handlebar mustache, but Papa's mustache was brown and blond while Uncle Russo's, like his full head of hair, was black. I remembered the old saying among Greeks on the islands that dark-complexioned Greeks betrayed their Turkish blood. Uncle Russo's graven features, brown eyes and dark skin could easily have been confused as Turkish. It was wise not to mention that to him, however! I was a little intimidated by his looks at first.

Also at the docks to greet me was Yiayia Sultana, Mama's and Aunt Cleo's mother, whom I had not seen since Easter several years earlier. After the death of Papouli Dracoulas, she had remained on Samothráki Island, not venturing across the water to visit us on Imbroz. She was about my height and smoked Turkish cigarettes that she rolled herself. Slender yet strong, she could carry two jugs of water on her shoulders simultaneously in spite of her age.

"Oh, my pretty child," she exclaimed, hugging me to her and rocking me from side to side. "How good it is to have you with me!"

A minute later I turned in my grandmother's arms and smiled at my uncle. "Uncle Russo," I said formally, pulling out of my grandmother's embrace, "I will do my best to help you at the store." I followed this little speech with a modest bow, and Uncle Russo smiled faintly in response. Then he turned to begin the forty-minute walk home.

Katina came up alongside me. "Chrysostomos, it's not too hard working in the store. I will show you what I know. Don't worry," she added reassuringly, not realizing that working in the store was all I really wanted to do. "You will catch on quickly…and oh, you will also attend school with me—a Greek school!"

This news didn't excite me the way Katina thought it would. "I think I would rather work than go to school," I offered.

The truth was, I wasn't at all interested in school. I had to get on with my life. Beside beginning under the Greeks and continuing under the Turks, I had spent four years in school and that seemed quite adequate. As we trudged down the road, Aunt Cleo gave me some grapes, olives, cheese and bread to eat for breakfast, and hurried us along. Even though it was still early morning, we had to get back quickly so that Uncle Russo could open his store. Samothráki Island was as Imbroz used to be—bustling with economic activity. A man with two donkeys loaded with goods passed us. There were people beginning their day in the fields, and as we neared the village the activity increased. I saw at once that the pulsing, upbeat life of this Greek Christian island stood in sharp contrast to the depressed economy and despondent mood of Turkish-occupied Imbroz.

The familiar culture and customs of Samothráki set me quickly at ease, yet the plight of my family and homeland was never far from my thoughts. As we made our way to my aunt's and uncle's house, I bit off a piece of bread and smiled at Katina. We had always been close, and I had missed her. She was older than I was by a year, but since I was the oldest son, the responsibility for her fell on me. It was up to me now to show my maturity and that I could contribute and help. For the rest of my life I gladly accepted this responsibility. To me, it was always a privilege and an honor to be helpful to my family. It was a lesson I learned at an early age, a lesson that my maturity and tireless energy facilitated. Circumstance and necessity required my effort to result in success.

5
Samothráki Island

Yes, as through this world I ramble,
I see lots of funny men
Some will rob you with a b-gun
And some will rob you with a pen.
But as through your life you'll travel,
Wherever you may roam,
You won't never see an outlaw
Drive a family from their home.

—Woody Guthrie
"The Ballad of Pretty Boy Floyd," 1939

Uncle Russo's house was about two hundred meters off the main road outside the island's capital city of Protevosa. It was twice the size of our house on Imbroz, with two separate rooms downstairs adjoined by a kitchen—but it lacked the freshly painted white walls and cheerful Greek blue doors and shutters of our house, and the outhouse was built of wood rather than stone.

It was, in fact, the largest house I had ever been in, yet for all its impressive size it was empty, for Aunt Cleo could not have children.

Uncle Russo said nothing during the walk, but when we reached the house he turned to me. "Welcome, Chrysostomos," he said. "You rest and eat today, and after school tomorrow you may come to the store and work." Uncle Russo was a man of few words and an expressionless delivery.

"Yes, Uncle Russo," I nodded obediently.

"Now you'll greet your great-grandmother, Yiayia Theopisti," Aunt Cleo interrupted, and presented me to the oldest lady I had ever seen. She sat in a chair with a cane across her knees, and I could see that she was very wrinkled. "Yiayia," Thea Cleo said, "this is Chrysostomos, Theopisti and Ioanni's son, your great-grandson."

Great-Yiayia Theopisti's eyes sparkled as she surveyed me, then she took my hand and welcomed me with a hug. "What a beautiful, precious child," she declared. Instantly, I felt a bond with her that oddly seems to occur between a very old and a very young relative. The stories about her were true, I was convinced: She was every bit of a hundred years old. After my obligatory kiss, she continued rolling a cigarette in her lap. For a few minutes I could not take my eyes off of her—she was ancient.

"Cleo," Uncle Russo said, turning to my aunt. "Fix the children something to eat. I will be back this evening."

Uncle Russo with his dark mustache and hair was a sculptured site of a man. Because Aunt Cleo resembled my mother, she had many similar habits and mannerisms, even down to her meal preparation. Therefore, I felt comfortable with her right away.

Inside the house Aunt Cleo started to make a stew with real lamb meat. To a boy who had not had meat for some time, the smell of the stew was a torment. I could barely contain my excitement. While we waited for the stew to complete cooking, Katina was full of questions about family and friends on Imbroz. I did my best to keep my thoughts off my hunger to answer her questions.

"Christo," she asked anxiously. "Tell me how Mama and Papa really are. We hear such rumors!"

"Everybody is fine. Mama said to tell you she and Papa miss you very much."

"But, what about the Turks?"

I hesitated. The vision of a dead man swinging from a tree leapt into my mind, but "The Turks don't bother us much" was all I said. Why should I worry her further? "We mind our business and they mind theirs most of the time."

"Do Papa and Mama have enough food?"

"Yes," I said, without elaborating on the sparseness of our diet. She looked at me doubtfully, but changed the subject.

"So, Christo, what have you been doing at home?"

"I have been going to a Turkish school, and I don't like it," I said honestly. "I *wanted* to come and work for Uncle Russo,

Katina. It will be much better than wasting time in Turkish schools, better and more helpful to the family. I can earn some money to send back to Mama and Papa."

"Who will take it to them?" she asked, puzzled.

"Captain Koutris," I told her.

Katina nodded thoughtfully. "And your friends," she asked. "Demetrius Terzes and Yanni Apistola. How are they?"

"They are fine," I said patiently.

"Are Maria and Ismini well?" she went on. "Harralombous, Sofia and George?"

"They are all well and ask for you."

She was getting nowhere. "Does Sultana still pick her nose?"

Suddenly we erupted into laughter. Boy, I had missed her!

"I am learning to sew," Katina told me a little later, "and going to school. One day I'll help Mama and Papa sew garments to sell to the Turks. That will help us earn some money."

"I'm through with school," I announced, although I knew my Mama and Papa would not agree. "I'm ready to work. I'll show Uncle Russo what a good worker I am, and then he'll agree to let me quit school." Even though I was only ten, I knew I was mature and able to pick up things more quickly then most kids. Katina, however, wasn't as sure about my plan as I was.

"Remember," she said, "you are a boy and not yet grown."

"I have helped Papa at our store since I was eight years old!" I said defensively, but before Katina could respond, Aunt Cleo called us to the kitchen.

"Children, the food is ready!" she announced. "I will give you a little now to eat and the rest we will have this evening when your Uncle Russo returns from the store."

"Yes, Thea," we said, and launched ourselves toward the stew.

"Not yet!" a voice rang out loudly. It was my great-grandmother Theopi, smoking her cigarette and hoisting a large jug of water. "Christo, into that room," she ordered, nodding in the direction of a small bedroom, "and get ready to take a bath."

"But Great-Yiayia, I had a bath before I left Imbroz!" I protested.

"Cleanliness," she intoned firmly, "is next to godliness." The sinewy, wizened woman stood in the doorway, a trail of smoke hanging in the air from the tip of the cigarette that dangled from the corner of her wrinkled mouth. As she steered me toward the tub, I discovered that her hands were disproportionately large and her grip was surprisingly firm.

Half an hour later, scrubbed within an inch of my life and smelling of strong soap, I was finally allowed to eat. Good thing, too, because I was near collapse! The lunch was satisfying and filling, and I thought about Mama and Papa who had so little to eat. I promised myself I would never go hungry again, and neither would my family. Tomorrow I would start work for Uncle Russo, and he would quickly see how good a worker I was.

After lunch Aunt Cleo wanted to read with us in Greek, partly because Katina had missed school on account of my arrival.

"Christo," she asked, "do you know how to read in Greek?"

I nodded.

Aunt Cleo handed me a reader, and Katina helped me once or twice. My Greek was not as sharp as Katina's, even though Papa had made sure we read at home, but I wasn't far behind her.

Before we finished our Greek lesson, my eyes began to grow heavy. The long trip had fatigued me, and the bath and food had made me sleepy. Aunt Cleo cut the lesson short and led me to bed for a nap. Within seconds I was fast asleep.

When I awakened later that afternoon, Aunt Cleo gave permission for Katina to take me outside and show me around, providing that we tended the chickens, goat and donkey. I was very familiar with tending animals since it was part of my daily chores on Imbroz.

* * * * *

About two hundred feet from Aunt Cleo's house was a small shanty—I dare not call it a barn—which housed the dozen-and-a-half chickens that belonged to Aunt Cleo and Uncle Russo. Behind it a goat was tied to a pole, and behind the goat a donkey was tied to the tree. Katina showed me every nook and cranny of our uncle's and aunt's property, including the outhouse which was located, most inconveniently, I thought, about ten meters further from the house than was ours at home. We walked a little way toward town and got a good view of the city including Uncle Russo's store, which was bigger than Papa's. Uncle Russo sold all the things we used to sell in our store before it closed. As we approached, Uncle Russo, who was waiting on a customer, saw us and nodded. Watching him, I grew excited about my first day of work, eager to prove myself.

It was late afternoon when Katina I returned to the house. A little later Uncle Russo closed the store and arrived home for dinner. After dinner we sat for a while in the room that served as a dining and living area, the largest room in the house. While Aunt Cleo was sewing in a chair and Uncle Russo was snoring away in another, I surveyed the room carefully. On the wall directly across from me were an icon of the Virgin Mary and a picture of Jesus. Below these was a small table containing the Bible, a cross on a chain, two candles and what appeared to be a bottle of holy water. All God-fearing, reverent Greek Orthodox Christians of the time, including my parents, erected home altars in either the bedroom or living room for the purpose of worship and to remind the family that God was always present.

Near the altar was the door to the kitchen, and I could see the stove, used for heating as well as cooking, standing against the wall. At home, our stove was in the middle of the room because Papa believed that the heat would be distributed more evenly, but Uncle Russo's stove was much larger and could hold more fuel, in the form of wood and coal, in its chamber. This meant the stove burned hotter and had to be stoked less frequently than ours on Imbroz.

In fact, my aunt's and uncle's kitchen had another notable convenience. Although meats still had to be seasoned, wrapped and buried to keep from spoiling for several days, Uncle Russo did have a basin in the kitchen with a pipe and faucet above it. The pipe ran inside from the well about twenty-five meters in front of the house. Over time, I became quite used to this improvement, which reduced the need for hauling water into the house. In the mornings we simply worked the handle up and down to pump water from the spigot for washing up, as well as for Uncle Russo's tea or coffee, but for bathing and cooking, we still had to carry in the water. The creature comforts of Uncle Russo's house were remarkable to me.

Life in the first three decades of the twentieth century was not what it is today. The broad distribution of many twentieth century miracles, including plumbing, autos, electricity, radio—and later, television—was nonexistent in my world when I was growing up. I marvel at the prevalence of these things in America today, but with no knowledge of them in my childhood we did not miss them at all.

Looking back on my early years, I sometimes wonder privately if children today will have the strength to face adversity, even as I hope that their world will remain at peace. I lavished my children and grandchildren with material things that I was deprived of growing up, and in my old age I wonder if that was wise. I wanted them to live the material childhood that I was denied.

"Time to go to sleep, children!" Aunt Cleo's voice interrupted Uncle Russo's snoring as well as my study of the living room and kitchen.

"Huh?" Uncle Russo snorted from his chair.

"I'm having the kids go to bed, that's all," Aunt Cleo said.

"Oh." Uncle Russo closed his eyes and returned to his nap.

"Good night, Uncle Russo," Katina said.

"Good night, Katina, good night, Chrysostomos," Uncle Russo muttered, eyes closed.

At home, Katina and I had shared a feather mattress on the floor of the loft above the single downstairs room. In my aunt's and uncle's house, two small rooms in front adjoined the large kitchen-living room in the rear. Katina and I slept in the small room to the right, which contained a feather mattress upon a wood-frame bed. Although narrow, my sister and I did not take up much room and could fit easily on the bed. A year or so later, Uncle Russo would get me my own bed and place it next to Katina's.

Both Katina and I wore nightgowns that were not unlike long tee shirts. I slept on the inside against the wall and Katina slept on the outside. That way, she told me, she would be certain I wouldn't fall. Although she was only a year older than I, even at that age she towered above me and liked to mother me at times, but I didn't mind too much.

When I got under the covers that first night, my body was tired but my mind was wide awake. I thought of our island, of Uncle Demetrius, of Papa, of Father George and Bishop Iakovos. I thought of Jimmy Coucouzes calling me "Bread Crumb" and asking, "When will you get taller?" My young thoughts wandered to Smyrna and the slaughter of the Greek population I barely understood. In a nightmarish succession of visions, I saw poor Archbishop Chrysodom beheaded and innocent children and women run through by the bayonets of the Turkish gendarmes. Young girls were torn from their families, and their fathers were stabbed, shot, or bludgeoned to death. The nightmarish visions were so vivid and real that my heart raced. The visions were realistic and unrelenting, however, there was no sound. I had to remind myself that I was in Greece, safe in my uncle's house. I saw a calming vision of the gentle Bishop Iakovos before I finally drifted into sleep.

The nightmares returned later in the night. I dreamed that I was in Papa's store the day the two Turks came in and robbed us. The smaller Turk stood with his back to me, and Papa was reasoning with the bigger one. Suddenly, the big Turk laughed and pushed Papa on the ground, then picked up his rifle that had been leaning on the counter. He was still laughing at Papa as he pulled out his long bayonet from a sash on his side and mounted it on his rifle.

"No, no!" I screamed. "Don't hurt my Papa!"

Just as the big Turkish gendarme was to run Papa through, the smaller Turk abruptly turned around. It was Uncle Russo in the uniform of a Turk.

"Now it is your turn," he said to me, mounting his bayonet on his rifle. An instant later I awoke, breathless and sweating. I remembered Papa's words, "Be brave my son, God is with you," and I drifted back to sleep, mumbling, "I am in Greece...I am in Greece..."

I knew what had influenced my dream. Although he hated the Turks more than anyone I knew, Uncle Russo simply looked very Turkish. I don't know if he really had any Turkish blood in his past, but I remember Mama once telling Aunt Cleo that she was sure he did and that he would ruin our Greek heritage. I flopped back against the mattress. Uncle Russo was not a Turk, I told myself, no matter how Turkish he happened to look.

The next morning I was up at daybreak, waking Katina as I climbed over her to get out of bed.

"Chrysostomos, what are you doing up so early?"

"Aunt Cleo is up," I said, although I wasn't really sure if she was. I could see the first glimmers of daybreak and to me that meant it was time to get up. I dressed and went outside to get some seed to feed the chickens, as was my habit at home. I also watered the donkey and goat. When I returned to the house I found Aunt Cleo had awakened and had placed a pot of water on the stove.

"My, my, Chrysostomos, you are up so bright and early!" she said while stoking the fire.

"Yes, Thea, and I have fed the chickens and watered the goat and donkey," I told her virtuously.

"Without anyone even telling you?" Clearly, Aunt Cleo was impressed.

"Yes, Thea. I do the same chores at home. I know how they must be done."

"I see you do!" she smiled. "Aren't your Uncle Russo and I so lucky to have such a talented little boy with us?"

I smiled back, enormously pleased with myself.

Aunt Cleo had made some hot porridge for breakfast, and after we all ate, Katina and I were off to school. Although strict, the Greek school was much more relaxed than the Turkish school on Imbroz, and in addition to reading and writing, there was discussion of the ancient philosophies. All the while, my thoughts kept drifting impatiently to the store. Would the day never end? After school I hurried to Uncle Russo's store, where I was told to simply watch for a day or two. It wasn't long, though, before I saw a number of things that I could do. Uncle Russo had more supplies than Papa had ever had, but his store was not as neat and organized, and it seemed as though he could not remember exactly where things were. I decided to help by separating the bags of flour from the bags of sugar.

"Christo, what are you doing?" Uncle Russo asked.

"I am separating the flour and the sugar, Uncle Russo.

"Yes, a very good idea," he said a little absently. Then he repeated, "Why don't you separate the flour from the sugar?" as though his repetition enabled ownership of the idea.

So that is how my first workday began. During the four years that I worked in Uncle Russo's store, I learned everything there was to know about the business, including baking bread, ordering supplies, measuring quantities, storing food, and keeping the store clean, which was my specialty. The days were not difficult, but long and challenging for a pre-teen boy. By the time I was thirteen, Uncle Russo would often leave me unattended in the store for hours on end.

After completing my fourth year of Greek school, I finally quit school altogether and worked full time for Uncle Russo. I knew I could handle it. I was very organized and always knew exactly what we had in inventory. As a result, there was no overstocking, which was important to maintaining a healthy business. I made many changes at the store and business kept increasing.

By my third year of work, Uncle Russo relied on me regarding all matters of the store. Oh yes, and that year I had finally started to grow. About the same time, Aunt Cleo wrote a letter to Mama.

Dear Theopisti, Aunt Cleo penned. *The children are fine and we are fine, and I hope you, Ioanni, Costa and Sultana are also doing well. Chrysostomos is doing such a fine job managing the store that he has quit school and is working full time. My beloved sister, since Russo and I do not have any children and you have four, could we keep Katina and Chrysostomos since they are doing so well here? Katina is finishing tailoring school, and her teacher at Greek school thinks she is bright enough to go to Gymnasium. Chrysostomos is such a big help to Russo at the store that I don't know what we would do without him—and besides, we are able to provide for them...*

My mother didn't take too kindly to her sister's request to keep two of her children, no matter how appreciative she was of her sister's generosity or how great the need. Her response was swift and immutable:

My dear beloved sister Cleo, she wrote. *Yanni and I are quite appreciative of your attention and loving care of our children during our time of need. We are also happy to know that*

Chrysostomos has been such a help to Russo. However, my little sister, you cannot have my children ready-made, and if you want children, I suggest you bear them yourself. Enclosed is a Turkish note for your trouble, and would you please send Katina home right away? We need her to help us sew clothes for the Turks. You may keep Christo awhile longer since he has proven so valuable to Russo. However, in about a year we will send for him, too.

Within a couple of days plans were made to send Katina home. On Katina's last evening on Samothráki Island, she and I talked for a while. Although no longer towering above me, she was still slightly taller, though I had reached the respectable height of 5' 4". "Katina," I said, "you must let me know how everyone is back home."

"I will write you, Christo, but you must promise me that whenever we are separated you will write me also."

"I will."

Thus began a 35-year correspondence between my sister and me that was interrupted only during my forced conscription in the Turkish work battalions. We never broke our word to one another. Over the years it would be through Katina's letters that I kept in touch with my beloved parents, siblings, relatives and friends—in short, with my roots. I had no idea at the time Katina and I first promised to write each other how brief and infrequent my trips home to Imbroz would be, nor of the few fleeting moments we would spend together as a family.

"Katina," I asked her that night, "will you be all right back home?"

"Are you kidding, Christo?" she teased. "I will have every Turk who wants a new garment muttering my name."

"You must promise to tell me the truth, Katina. You know Papa—he would never admit to needing anything, especially not to one of his children."

"Christo, what can you do? You are still so young!"

I brushed the objection aside. "Katina, I can do a lot, you will see, but you must promise to tell me what is really going on at home."

I was afraid for her, for all of them, but I had never fully told her what it was like back home. I had to hope things had improved, because I couldn't tell her now.

"I promise. Oh, Christo, I am going to miss you so!" She smiled mischievously. "Do you think you will grow any taller?"

"I hope so," I sighed. Katina was almost fifteen, and she had matured physically into an attractive young woman.

Because we were brother and sister, because we had a lot in common, because the times were tough, Katina and I had grown very close during our two-and-a-half years together on Samothráki. Although circumstance had forced us to grow up quickly, we were in many ways still children. During that time with Cleo and Russo we drew strength from each other, and after Katina left she kept her word and wrote me. She wrote mostly about the family, of course, but she also mentioned a lot of other things, and her letters were my lifeline back to my beloved Imbroz.

Costa is nine years old now, she wrote in one of her letters, *and he is talking about coming to work with you on Samothráki Island. Mama and Papa and I work very hard sewing clothes for the Turks. They don't pay much, but it is a living, and we are developing a reputation in Panayia and across Imbroz. Even the Turkish counselor comes to us to have his clothes done! 'If you want clothes made,' people say, 'you come to Chrysostomidis.'*

Another time, she wrote, *Christo, so many people have left our island. Sometimes Turks come from the mainland and take their homes, but still, many houses remain deserted and in disrepair. The Turks have not tried to close the churches, but from time to time vandals have destroyed or damaged their relics and icons. I guess we can put up with those things. What choice do we have? I think three-quarters of the people have left Imbroz, Chrysostomos, and more are leaving every day.... But I almost forgot! Jimmy Coucouzes came by to talk to me when he went to visit his aunt— just like old times! He has grown a beard, and he asked about you and sends his regards. When he finishes with his studies in Theotoko, he plans to continue his schooling as a priest. I think he wants to become a bishop and remain celibate, like old Bishop Iakovos. Isn't that something? I for one would never choose that life.*

She went on to tell me how the Turks had destroyed the town archives, *but Papa had already managed to salvage some records and some of the history of our family, including property records. He has been approached by Turkish police and asked if he wants to sell his pastures or his house. His answer, as you may expect, is always no. But there are many instances in which the gendarmes have bought houses and land for a pittance and a pound of coercion while the seller has looked down the barrel of a Turkish rifle, or been assessed a tax they could not afford—and some people flee simply because they can no longer make a living. I think we are safe from such a fate—for now, anyway. The Turks need us to make their clothes….*

When I was almost fifteen, Uncle Russo told me he would open a store for me if I stayed with him, but I missed my family and I knew I needed to go home. Oddly enough, it was my great-grandmother, Yiayia Theopisti, who was the first to realize and accept the fact that it was time for me to leave Samothráki. By this time she was nearly deaf and spent much of her day in her chair reading the Bible through a magnifying glass Uncle Russo had given her. Yet this wrinkled and frail old lady favored me. For all her one hundred-plus years, she was still somewhat mobile and remarkably insightful, and during my years on Samothráki we had grown quite close.

"Christo," she called to me one day. "Come here my precious, and let me see you."

"Yes, Great Yiayia," I said, settling myself on the floor by her chair.

"God willing, you will be a wise and successful man some day," she told me. "You will have a family of your own and you will be respected by everyone you meet. I wonder," she smiled, "will you remember your old Yiayia then?"

"Of course, Great Yiayia," I protested. "How could I forget you?"

"There is a big world beyond this island, Christo." Though she had never seen it, she spoke with the voice of great knowledge. "There is so much to see and do. You won't be truly happy if you stay here." I found her unusual words surprising and recalled Papa

64

urging me to go to America. Still, that seemed as impossible to me as a voyage to the moon.

"Yes, Great Yiayia. You are right."

"Of course I am," she said, bringing her wizened face close to mine and looking into my youthful eyes. Her eyes, still sharp and quick, were warm and thoughtful, and they had nurtured a light of confident hope within me. "And another thing...remember to bathe every morning."

"Yes, Great Yiayia," I smiled. "I will remember." For a while we both sat in silence as though we each had felt the breath of change stirring in the air around us.

6

A Brief Homecoming

The West and East came face to face at the
second class coastal town of Mudanya on a
crooked road covered with dust on the hot
Marmara coast. Despite the English flagship
Iron Duke's *ash-colored deathly turrets that*
transported the Allied generals for negotiations
with Ismet Pasha, the Westerners had come here
to beg for peace, not to ask for peace or to
dictate the conditions... These negotiations
demonstrate the end of Europe's dominance
over Asia, because as everyone knows,
Mustapha Kemal got rid of all the Greeks.

—Ernest Hemingway
Toronto Daily Star, 1922

Neither of my grandmothers was able to accompany me to the
harbor, and, after tearful hugs, I left the house with my aunt and
uncle. Aunt Cleo wept quietly the entire distance, and Uncle Russo
was silent and preoccupied. Papa had written that he would send
Captain Koutris to fetch me at first light on November tenth, and
when we arrived at the harbor that morning, Uncle Russo gave the
Captain a tip and generously gave me a hundred drachmas.
Although he had periodically sent some money to my parents as
recompense for my labor, I felt I could now earn much more on my
own. The work I had done for my uncle would normally have been
worth considerably more, but it was also my training, good training
for things to come, and I was most grateful. Besides, Thea Cleo
had sent many material things to Mama and Papa over the years. I
was leaving Samothráki with two bags full of shoes and clothes for
my sisters and brother, plus the few things I brought with me,
excepting my beloved ball, which had worn out long ago.

The sight of Captain Koutris stirred memories. His graying hair and haggard appearance spoke of the chronic poverty and blight that had become a way of life at home. I lifted my bags and gave them to the Captain to stow in the little boat. When I turned back to my aunt and uncle for a last good-bye, Uncle Russo—who never had shown much emotion—grabbed me in a heartfelt embrace.

"Take care of yourself, child," he said with misty eyes. "We will miss you very much."

By now Thea Cleo was weeping openly. "Chrysostomos, Chrysostomos, my child, what will we do without you? It is so hard to say good-bye."

I kissed my aunt and thanked them both one last time. With a final bow, I turned to board Captain Koutris' small boat. As we pulled away from the island, Uncle Russo and Aunt Cleo stood on the dock waving to me for as long as they could see me. I waved back, watching them recede in the distance, unaware that this would be the last time in my life that I would ever see them. Images of Uncle Russo with his black hair and mustache, Great Yiayia Theopisti rolling her own cigarettes, and my busy, energetic Yiayia Sultana have stayed with me through my life.

The man I was becoming had matured beyond his years, yet the thought of my return home brought forth in me the child I was. For that moment I was filled with youthful excitement and impatience. As the small boat left Samothráki Island in its wake, Papa's words were as clear to me as they had been four years before. Papa had said to love God, family and country in that order. God was inseparable from our existence. He was the source of the faith and hope we needed to survive the Young Turks and their agenda to promote Christian erosion. Family was our extension of self. To debase, defile or disrespect our family was the equivalent of doing the same to ourselves. Virtue, honesty and morality formed the adhesive that bound our family together while our material circumstances grew increasingly difficult and our environment became pervasively hostile. It was a tumultuous period of religious persecution for the remaining Christians of Asia Minor.

Finally, we drew strength from our beloved country. Greece was severely weakened by the First World War and the subsequent war with Turkey, as well as the ensuing economic depression and her own impotence to halt the abuses the barbarians had wrought on the Greeks along the Byzantine coast of Asia Minor. Papa, always patriotic, said that when your country calls you must run to her defense. In a bid for peace through appeasement, Greece and its French and English allies had abandoned us, ceding our small island and the relics of Christian Byzantium to the Young Turks. Not once over the decade, however, had Papa spoken ill of his country. Papa never lost his faith in his Greek Christian heritage, nor his hope that one day the island would be freed from unjust Turkish rule. During his thirty-five years on Turkish-occupied Imbroz, sadly that day never came. Poor Papa.

As the little boat made its way across the water, I snuggled up in the back to get some rest, much as I had done more than four years earlier. This time, I was going to familiar surroundings. I would see my family and rest in my old bed. Not even the thought of the Turks could ruin my longing to return to my little house and family I had left so long ago. Yet, my imminent reunion with Papa, Mama and Imbroz was stained by the occupation. Eventually, lulled by the roll of the seas, I dozed into a dreamless, timeless stupor, only to be awakened later, as four years earlier, by Captain Koutris.

"Christo!" he called out. "Look, we're home! There is Imbroz!"

Startled, I was instantly awake and rubbing my eyes. Then, in the clear cool autumn morning, I caught sight of my island home, still a few kilometers off.

When I glanced back at the Captain, I saw that he was looking at me with a rueful smile. "I remember when you left Imbroz…you were hardly waist high. Now you're returning a fine young man," he said.

I smiled at his praise. "How are things on the island, Captain?" I asked, trying to elicit more dialogue on conditions at home.

"There are fewer merchant ships to unload, for one thing," the Captain said. "They used to come once a week, now they come once a month. But life goes on, even with the Turks. Your Mama and Papa are okay…older, but okay."

I nodded. "Do you see them often?"

He shrugged. "I see them when we go to church in Panayia, or when your Papa comes to Castro to pick up cloth and supplies. Your Papa is a good man." He said the last with an emphatic nod.

I turned my gaze back to Imbroz. I could make out the port in the distance, and after a while I could see people standing on the docks. Although I could not make them out, I knew it was my family waiting for my arrival, a joyful sigh of recognition escaping as I impatiently awaited the boat's final kilometer. Finally, I could see faces. Sultana and Costa were waving. Approaching in the dim light of dawn, I could see that Papa looked a little pale and somewhat older than I remembered, but his broad smile covered his worn appearance. As soon as we docked, I grabbed my bags and scrambled ashore. Costa and Sultana reached me first and clung to me like little monkeys.

"Chrysostomos!" I heard my mother's voice. She was crying and making the sign of the cross; an instant later I was in her embrace. I realized that both Mama and Papa had shrunk, as well as Katina. In another month I would be fifteen, and at five feet, six inches, I was finally a little taller than Mama and Katina, and almost as tall as Papa was. My adolescent growth spurt, although unimpressive to some, had finally arrived. Greeks are not noted for their height, anyway.

While I greeted my family on the dock, Captain Koutris brought up my second bag, the package from Aunt Cleo to Mama. I had also brought two small, carved wooden characters for Costa and Sultana, a scarf Aunt Cleo had made for Katina, and an American newspaper for Papa. He loved to read American newspapers, but so rarely had an opportunity. As we left the dock to begin our walk home, everybody was chattering at once, peppering me with questions about Samothráki Island. I was telling Sultana and Costa about the size of Uncle Russo's house when my mother put her finger to her lips.

"Quiet!" she hissed in a low voice. Startled, I followed her gaze. A couple of Turkish gendarmes were walking toward us about a hundred feet away, a stark reminder of the Mohammedan social inequality toward Christians.

Although it was illegal to speak Greek on the island, the Greek population continued to do so among themselves. The consequence of being caught depended on the capricious mood of the Turk. In the excitement of homecoming I had forgotten briefly about the Turks, but the sight of the gendarmes quickly snapped me back to reality. With the occupation now ten years on, the segregation and persecution were well entrenched. As they passed, the policemen eyed me coldly. I said hello in my best Turkish, nodded courteously, and the moment passed uneventfully—but we waited cautiously until the Turks were out of sight before we resumed our conversation.

On the way home, I noticed how differently things looked. Neglect and overgrowth were irregularly apparent. Before I left, the wounds to the land and people were fresh. Now, I saw the sad, decaying remains of epidemic neglect and abuse. A broken wagon rusted on the side of the road. A fence was in disrepair, its posts leaning at angles. As we approached Panayia, things got even worse. All the houses along the road were vacant, their windows knocked out, their walls falling in upon themselves. Vegetation overgrew abandoned properties. I had never seen Imbroz with such a look of desolation. The dreary face it turned to me that day would haunt me the rest of my life.

Suddenly, I spied our little house. Mama and Papa had kept it just as it was when I had left, with its Greek blue shutters and door and the exterior walls freshly painted white! Our store next door had long since closed down, but Papa had kept it painted, too. There was nothing that made my heart feel warmer than the sight of my family and our tiny home. The loss of our island to the Turks, the migration of many of our friends, the closure of Papa's store and our subsequent impoverishment and dislocation lay in sharp contrast to our rich heritage, our home, our love, and our faith.

I had worked and lived away from home for over four years. Out of necessity I had, perhaps, grown up quicker than most. For that moment, though, I felt like a little boy again, seeing my house with my family after such a long time. The familiarity of home and family gave me a sense of warm security I had not experienced in years, and I wished the moment would never pass. Mama and Papa rarely had meat to eat, and their chickens and sheep were all but gone, yet they had prepared a feast to celebrate my arrival. We stayed up very late that evening, eating a meal of olives, cheese, bread and fresh fruit, talking and laughing—a family reunited. Feasting on light fare and each other's company, making the most of our fleeting moments together, we relished my homecoming as a warm, loving time in this starkly treacherous and troubled Turkish world.

The next morning I slept in to the unheard-of hour of nine. It was a deep, sound sleep I had not felt in years. Shortly thereafter Demetrius Terzes came by to see me. He was a childhood friend who lived in our neighborhood. He was a little taller than I, but we were the same age. Despite the passage of years, his bushy brown hair and dark eyes were unchanged and formed a contrast to my fair features. Neither of us was sure what we were going to do with our lives. Jobs were impossible to find. No work and no food made for an unsustainable combination.

Almost as soon as I had arrived, I realized that I would have to leave Imbroz again to find work, not just for my own welfare, but also for the welfare of my family. So within two weeks Demetrius and Yanni Apistola, another childhood friend, and I made a plan to go to Constantinople—Istanbul, as it was now known—to seek our fortunes. Yanni was three years older and three inches taller than either of us. We would leave by the next boat on Monday when a freighter would dock offshore at Castro. We could not afford to wait another month for the next ship.

Katina had planned a small farewell party for us. A few family members and friends would come to our house after church the night before we left, but the preceding Saturday evening was a solemn one. The realization that economic necessities brought on by the Turkish occupation would once again influence the course of my life imparted a fatalistic feeling of powerlessness. I felt alone and uncertain of the future. Even Costa, who was a repeated source of questions for me, was now quiet. From the darkness, Papa called me out on the porch.

"Chrysostomos, you remember the talk we had before you went to Samothráki?"

"Yes, Papa. You told me to go to America." I didn't ask him how he thought I might get there, but said instead, "I haven't forgotten. I'll find work, Papa, and send you and Mama money—and one day, I will go to America."

"Of course you will," Papa told me. "I don't want you to worry about your Mama and me, but I would like you, if you are able, to help your brother and sisters. Try to stay together, Chrysostomos, whatever happens to Mama and me. You are older now, but in Constantinople there are many things you have not experienced and are not aware of. There are still some Greeks, but there are many more Mohammedan Turks who mistreat Christians. Even though the fighting has ended, the Mohammedans still are very abusive toward Christians." Then he smiled a little. "Aristotle would tell you to try to understand the cause of the things you observe and take a scientific view," he went on. "Also, always remember that if you work for a Turk you must do everything better just to be found acceptable. And don't forget to show respect and humility by—"

"Bowing," I finished for him. "I know, Papa," I said, smiling as I bowed to demonstrate. Suddenly, I realized that in many ways I was much like Papa.

"What type of work do you want to do?" he asked.

"Whatever is available," I told him. To be honest, it had never even occurred to me to think about what I wanted. "I don't know, but I'll find something."

"Yes," he nodded. "You will. And Chrysostomos," he went on, "wherever you go, always be humble, honest and fair. Don't take advantage because of your position. No matter how high you go, respect your fellow man."

"Yes, Papa." I smiled at the implied confidence.

"This is just the beginning of your life," my father went on. "God willing, you will find your way to America when the time comes. Don't be discouraged by current circumstances, and never give up your dreams. Look toward the future. You can do whatever you wish to do. Follow this path and God will be with you, wherever you go."

"Thank you, Papa," thinking he was finished. "I will find a job and help you, Mama, Katina, Sultana and Costa. I won't be that far away. I will write with my address—"

But Papa had a point to make. "My son," he said, interrupting me impatiently, "the brief years of your life have been hard. I can't recall a time so difficult in all my life. And remember, wherever you are, whatever you are doing, as long as we live your Mama and I will always be with you in our thoughts and prayers. Always remain positive and keep your faith. Use your God-given intelligence and energy for the betterment of yourself and those around you. Never forget God, your family, or your home and they will be with you always." He was speaking with such intensity, with such conviction, that it was making me uncomfortable. Things always seem so much more important to adults than they do to young people who take each day for granted. The meaning of my father's impassioned words spread over me like a warm blanket. Our eyes locked in the sober sadness of final separation between father and son. Papa in his heart realized his boy was leaving for good. Should I ever return, the nurturing of childhood was now, nevertheless, at an end—and so painfully early in life.

"I will, Papa. Don't worry, I promise. And I will write—"

"One more thing," my father cut me off with a smile. "Walk like a king, with dignity and humility, and one day you will be as a king."

I never forgot Papa's words to me that evening. Although I was only going a hundred and fifty kilometers east to Constantinople, this journey would be far different from the one I had made to Samothráki where my aunt and uncle, grandmother and great-grandmother lived. This time there would be no family to greet me. This time I was truly on my own.

Then Mama came out on the porch to join us. "My, such serious talk, Yanni, for such a young man. Chrysostomos," she said, turning to me, "I have sewn you a silk jacket to take with you." Smiling, she held out a beautiful jacket of pure silk along with a pair of trousers. "Here, try it on."

I turned and slid my arms into it one at a time. It was a little big, allowing for my growth, but it felt luxurious and I was enormously proud of it. The trousers were also silk, and off-white in color. I knew she must have worked for months to make these things for me.

"Mama," I said, moved deeply by her kindness. "Thank you so much."

"Wear it in good health," she told me. "You will need a proper jacket in Constantinople. Now you have one."

Gratefully, I reached out to embrace my mother. I have kept the jacket and pants she made me all my life, just as I have worn my father's relic coin over my heart every single day. These were the sparse, material keepsakes of my youth that helped nurture my spirit. To this day they are reminders of a family that I saw less and less as the years went by.

"Come now," my mother said, briskly pulling herself from my arms. "Let's go to sleep. Tomorrow we have a big day...church in the morning and friends and relatives to see you in the afternoon. Katina has been so busy planning this farewell party for you and Yanni and Demetri! Monday morning you will depart from us again. Come now, let's go to sleep," she urged, kissing my cheek. "Good night, Chrysostomos."

"Good night, Mama. The jacket is beautiful."

"I'm glad you like it."

"Thank you, Mama. Thank you, Papa." I went upstairs where everybody was asleep except Katina. As I undressed in the dark, we talked.

"You know, Chrysostomos, some Greeks have named their dogs Pasha and call them in plain view of the Turks."

"That's funny," I said.

"You must promise me you will write me with all your news, and I will write you back," Katina said. "You are going to Constantinople, Chrysostomos! How exciting!"

"We have always written each other, Katina," I told her, "and we always will do so. Remember, you must promise to tell me in your letters how Mama and Papa are doing. The truth," I said sternly for good measure.

"Of course I will," she promised. "Chrysostomos, will you come back? Will you send for Sultana, Costa and me?"

"I will be back," I said as I fell into bed, "but you must take care of Mama and Papa while I am away. They are getting older, and you must stay with them as long as they need you. I will find work and send you money. Don't worry," I assured her again. "I will be back, I promise."

I slept with my little brother, Costa, on my old stuffed feather mattress. Katina and Sultana slept on the other. All four of us slept upstairs in the loft, the same room we had known since our births, while Papa and Mama slept downstairs on a bed which, when pushed back, doubled as a sofa during the day. That night as I lay on my bed in the loft, my stomach growled even though we had finished dinner—a sharp reminder that I was back on Imbroz. I thought about the feast we would cook after church the next day for our relatives and friends. I had gone hunting and had shot a rabbit and Papa had purchased a leg of lamb, for which I knew he must have paid dearly. Over the years I have often thought that one of the reasons I went into food service was to ensure that I had enough to eat.

That was not the only reason I was restless. The prospect of going to Constantinople excited me. I was confident I would find work and, God willing, fulfill my promises to my family and seek a new and brighter future.

The next morning I was up at dawn, as usual. When I had dressed, I went out to feed our few remaining hens and help Mama by bringing in some water. Within an hour everyone had risen, even though it was only seven and still too early for church. There was a sense that we would not be together much longer and that our few remaining moments together were best spent awake.

"Costa, you should put on your shoes and get ready for church," I said.

"Will you take me to Constantinople with you?" Costa asked.

"I can't take you now, Costa. You need to stay at home and help Papa and Mama. Maybe I will call for you later."

"You promise, Chrysostomos?" Costa asked in a serious tone. "You won't forget?"

"I won't forget," I assured him.

"What about me?" asked Sultana. "Will you call for me, too?"

"Yes, Sultana, one day I will call for you, too."

Mama had made some porridge for breakfast, along with tea and *tsoreki*, which was normally saved for New Year's or Easter. Afterwards, we readied for church and gathered at the front door. Mama called out for Maria Karazou, Jimmy Coucouzes' aunt, as we walked across our yard.

"My goodness," Maria said, glancing at me. "You have become such a big boy, and I know your parents are very proud of you." She turned to Mama: "Jimmy is studying for the priesthood at the School of Theology at Chaulkus, the Halki Seminary." Then to me: "You will see him again one day, I'm sure."

"Yes, I will," I assured her, not having the faintest inkling of how that might happen.

"God bless him," Mama said. "He will devote his life to God." While Mama and Maria carried on with small talk during the walk to church, Sultana held Katina's hand and Costa held mine. The walk passed pleasantly and uneventfully, and for a few minutes I forgot how brief my time at home with my family really was. After a while the church, the center of our lives, came into view, and I noticed how few people were gathered outside. In fact, the town square and surrounding shops appeared drab and desolate, in sharp contrast to the busy mingling of people I remembered from our pleasant and thriving pre-Turkish past.

"Papa, how are Bishop Iakovos and Father George?" I asked suddenly.

"You will see for yourself," he said.

When we arrived at church, the service had already started. Papa walked to our usual seat three rows back on the left side. The church was only about a third full and those in the congregation looked worn and gaunt, a people who had seen hard times. Since many of the younger parishioners had fled the island, most of the people at church were older, yet they were familiar to me. When they lifted their voices into song, I noticed that our once vibrant and plentiful choir had been reduced to no more than a half a dozen voices.

Bishop Iakovos was conducting the service with Father George assisting. Although I couldn't see him, I knew the Bishop was there because I could hear his voice chanting from behind the altar. When he eventually appeared to take the lead in the service, I noticed he looked the same as he had before I left—except his beard and hair had turned completely white, giving him a rather saintly aura. Much later, and for many years, our Bishop's white hair and beard would remind me of Saint Nicholas. Father George, on the other hand, had aged considerably and looked worn.

Bishop Iakovos stepped forward, blessing the chalice of wine and bread for Communion. "Take ye, eat," he recited the familiar words. "This is my body, which for you is broken unto remission of sins."

"Amen," the choir chanted.

"Drink of it, ye all: This is my blood, of the New Testament, which for you and for many is shed, unto remission of sins."

"Amen," the choir chanted again.

"Thy Gifts, of what is Thine, do we offer to Thee in all we do and for all Thy blessings." Elevating the precious gifts, Bishop Iakovos invoked God while the congregation knelt. The Divine Liturgy of Saint John Chrysostom was the center part of every Christian Orthodox service. It was read, chanted and sung in hymns in its entirety most every Sunday.

The choir's melodious tones filled the church, and then we prayed. Papa made the sign of the cross and bowed his head. I did likewise. He looked at me out of the corner of his eye and smiled warmly, a smile I returned in kind, and then we recited the Creed:

"I believe in one God, Father Almighty, Maker of Heaven and Earth and of everything visible and invisible. And in one Lord Jesus Christ, the only-begotten Son of God, begotten of the Father before all ages. Light of light, true God of true God, begotten not made, co-substantial with the Father, through whom all things were made from Heaven...crucified for our salvation under Pontius Pilate, He suffered and was buried. And was resurrected on the third day according to the Scriptures. And ascended into Heaven and sits at the right hand of the Father; and He will return in glory to judge the living and the dead; whose kingdom will have no end.

"And I believe in the Holy Spirit, the Lord, the Giver of Life, Who proceeds from the Father, Who, together with the Father and the Son, is worshiped and glorified, Who spoke through the Prophets.

"I believe in One, Holy, Catholic, and Apostolic church. I acknowledge one baptism for the remission of sins. I await for the resurrection of the dead. And the life of the age to come."

"Amen," the choir and congregation chanted in unison.

This was our life, a good Christian life, under God. We respected all life and had many quiet enjoyments. We believed that the human experience should be cherished, and that all human beings were special, unlike the Mohammedans. A momentary silent stillness gripped me while I realized the sharp contrast between hope and despair. Away from my home, I would have the chance to bring hope to my family stranded here where the future had been stolen by the Turks.

After the liturgy, it was Bishop Iakovos' habit to say a special prayer for the Christians in Asia Minor who were martyred by the Turks. This Sunday he gave a special prayer for our late Archbishop Chrysodom. Although the tragedy at Smyrna was a decade old, the harsh scars of the Holocaust and the consequences of the occupation had not healed, nor had the persecutions of Christians diminished.

"O mighty God, who acts in mysterious ways and tests our faith, we pray for the souls of our martyred brethren. God bless the poor souls of those who gave their lives as good Christians in the small towns and cities of Asia Minor. God bless our lost brothers in Phocea, the forefathers of whom founded Marseilles. God bless our dead brethren in Aleppo, Harport, Trebizonde, Bitlis, Diarbekis, Mardin, Smyrna and Constantinople, as well as many unnamed towns and cities along the coast of Asia Minor and their people who were so tragically slain.

"God, we offer a special prayer in memory of the total destruction of Smyrna and the hundreds of thousands of people who were slaughtered by the forces of Mustapha Kemal and his Mohammedan barbarians; Smyrna, home of the Odyssey, written thousands of years ago; Smyrna, which kept the lamp of learning alight through all the Dark Ages; Ionia, the land of St. John, the Divine. Six of the candles were extinguished long ago, and the seventh, Smyrna, burned brightly until its destruction that fateful day in the second week of September 1922, by the Turks of Mustapha Kemal. We pray to God that He cherish the soul of our beloved Archbishop Chrysodom, who was martyred for his faith by the Turkish military, a kind, intellectual man who spent his life doing God's work, who refused safety in the embassies to care for his people whom he loved so dearly."

Stirred by the Bishop's sermon of remembrance, women were crying and crossing themselves in respectful prayer for the victims and the dead. The sermon broke through the tedious drone of occupation.

"God give us strength to face the Turks. Please hear our prayers. Amen," a voice in the crowd said, reminding us that these were not regular times and that our island home was now part of Turkey.

After the formal church service, the Bishop gave a brief sermon. I had not heard the venerable Bishop speak for more than four years. This time, his words were memorable to me.

"Parishioners, my children," he said. "These are difficult times we live in, not only for Imbroz but for the world. The economic depression in Europe and America reaches throughout the globe. Our misery has been compounded by the loss of our small island to the Turkish intruders. This rule against law and God has endured for ten years, and because it was blessed by the Allies at Lausanne, there appears to be no end in sight for us." He paused, gazing hard into the eyes of his congregation, and when he continued his voice was steely.

"Our oppressors have outlawed our language, closed our schools, replaced our officials and our police and committed countless crimes against persons and property. The Turks have brought down upon us an unrelenting religious persecution. Many of the citizens of our small island have been violated, murdered, or made to disappear. Our properties have been taken or forcibly purchased under threat of death for the price of a few coins. Our businesses have been robbed until we could no longer keep them open. Many of our Christian brothers and sisters have fled this tyranny..."

At his words, the parishioners had snapped to full attention. All eyes were on him, for they had never heard Bishop Iakovos give such an incensed and uncensored sermon. Some of the older Greek men began casting watchful eyes on the back door to make sure no Turkish gendarmes were listening in.

"I can remember days when this church was filled with worshipers," the Bishop went on, "and the handful of you who remain is truly chosen by God. You have endured so much. Our gathering here on this day is evidence to God, Our Lord Jesus Christ, that although the Turks can and have taken our lives, our businesses, our properties, our schools and our language, they cannot take our faith or crush our indomitable will. We will face this test by the Almighty together. Nor can they smother the flame of our culture, which has existed on this island for three thousand years and will continue to exist wherever we may go.

"Although we are few in number, our resolve is immutable and indestructible. As long as there is one Greek Christian alive on Imbroz, the traditions of our Greek culture will survive. Even a flicker can become a flame. Our humility, our hope and our honesty will sustain us in the face of this cruel conquest that has uprooted so many of our brothers and sisters." His voice thundered above the congregation and people were anxiously stirring, even as their faces were flushed with excitement and a unity of spirit. This was dangerous talk.

"In God's name we pray for strength to carry on with our lives and to continue to serve Jesus Christ. In the name of the Father, the Son and the Holy Spirit, Amen."

"Amen!" the congregation said loudly and in unison.

Papa also liked the sermon, and it became the topic of conversation on the way home and at dinner. It was not hard to get a unanimous opinion on the Turks.

These thoughts, as well as the Bishop's sermon, were on my mind as I held Costa's hand on the walk back from church, when suddenly Theo Demetrius, my favorite uncle, joined us for the walk home and for my farewell dinner.

"Hello, blue eyes," Theo Demetrius said. He was still hale and hearty in his early seventies.

"Hello, Theo Demetri," I said happily.

He reached for me and we embraced. I was almost as tall as he, I realized—only two or three inches shorter.

"I have not seen you for years, and now look at you! You are a grown young man. My, my, it is so hard to believe how quickly time passes. It seems like yesterday that I was holding you on my knee." He chuckled. "Your Papa has told me that you have been managing Russo's entire store, and that when he found out you were leaving he had to hire two employees to replace you as well as work harder himself," he said, clapping my shoulder.

Actually, the only replacement Uncle Russo had hired was Pablo, but Theo Demetri's merry laugh made me smile. It was so good to see him again, and for a moment I allowed myself to forget that I would be leaving in the morning. In my mind, Papa, Mama, and Theo Demetri had not changed, yet I saw they had aged. Although the evidence of our impoverishment and irreversible decline was all around us in the form of abandoned houses and overgrown fields, our reunion brought back warm memories of my happy, thriving childhood. However, we all knew there was no future here.

Demetri had fallen into conversation with Papa, and we had all begun walking again. Costa had taken my hand once more, and Mama and our neighbor Maria were walking in front of us. Suddenly, Maria broke off her conversation with Mama and turned to me. "Chrysostomos," she said, "you will begin an adventure tomorrow that will take you to Constantinople! Are you excited?"

"Yes," I said, smiling broadly. It *was* exciting, the idea of seeing new places, of working, of being grown up, on my own, and useful to my family. It was an adventure, just as Maria said, and it would all begin tomorrow morning.

When we reached home everybody continued the preparation for a Sunday dinner, which had all the makings of a special holiday. Usually, the men helped with the meat, but cooking on Imbroz was primarily a woman's chore, and Mama had made all my favorite foods. There was *spanakopita*—spinach pie—as well as garden salad with oil and vinegar and an entire shelf of desserts she had made the night before—including my favorite, *yalatoboriko,* which is a creamy custard in a thin, filo dough covered with honey. Papa and Theo Demetri began to cook the leg of lamb, which had been trimmed and spiced liberally with fresh garlic, onion, salt and pepper. Potatoes, rice pilaf, Greek feta cheese, olives and fresh baked bread also appeared—a miraculous display of food, considering our circumstances, a festive and fitting celebration for sending off the firstborn son.

While our parents were busy cooking, Katina and I walked outside. "Chrysostomos, do you think I will ever leave this island? We make a living—all of us, even Costa sometimes—sewing clothing for the Turks. Apart from that, there's nothing here anymore."

We had had this conversation the night before, but I answered her again. "Of course, Katina, you will leave here someday. We will all leave eventually."

She looked at me with wide and fearful eyes. Suddenly I realized she was a grown woman now. She trusted what I said and I knew I had better do my best to make it a reality for her. Mobility is such a common and easy thing today. We think nothing of picking up and traveling a hundred miles or much more, but on my island, transportation was by donkey, boat or foot. Lack of money and time prevented even small excursions of 25 kilometers to the mainland or neighboring islands. In the 1930's the double-edged sword of poverty and scarcity made travel consuming, costly and most difficult. Unless my parents left, it would be very difficult for either of my sisters to leave the island by themselves, since in those days young women didn't travel by themselves. Although I had no idea how, I had promised Katina I would send for her, and I determined to keep my word. That would come later, but for now, Katina would take care of Mama and Papa.

The afternoon and evening sped by. Our little party had been warm and merry, and no one seemed to want to focus on the sadness of parting, preferring instead the prospects of the future and the contagious excitement of adventure, though unknown. Demetrius and Yanni were full of youthful exuberance. Neither of them had even been off of Imbroz, and their excitement was evident as they vied for the attention of Katina—and, indeed, anyone who would listen—by expounding the feats they would accomplish in Constantinople, each trying to outdo the other, until their predictions of fame and fortune became so outlandish that even they were laughing. Tired and happy, I slipped into my bed for the last time before my departure.

With an uncertain journey looming, sleep did not come quickly, and I was awake before the sun. I waited until I heard Mama and Papa before I rose and dressed. Soon we were all up, and Mama was calling us for breakfast.

We had hot tea and porridge along with yesterday's leftover bread, which Mama warmed up on the stove; then began the walk to Castro where Captain Koutris would ferry my two friends and me three miles offshore to the steamboat that would take us to

Constantinople, a trip that would take us two days. Mama had packed my things, including my carefully folded silk suit, into my bag and the same small worn suitcase. I said good-bye once again to my family. I still had half the money Theo Russo had given me—the rest I had given to Mama—and Papa gave me boat fare. Costa took my hand and Sultana cried. A similar scene played out with Demetri Terzes and Yanni Apistola and their families. A few moments later, we all boarded the boat and headed out to sea, three young compatriots leaving their homes to pursue their fortunes.

My friends' demeanor, I noticed, was much different than that of the previous evening. We were all somber, and I recalled with a twinge the very first time I had left the familiarity of my home and family to face the unknown. As we moved away from shore, and Mama's and Papa's images began to fade from sight, I took my medallion coin from my shirt and gazed at the ancient, worn figure of Christ, adorned with a faint halo. I clutched the coin, my family's heirloom, before returning it to my shirt. I stared at the tiny figures of my family on the shore until they faded into the horizon. Captain Koutris rowed us toward the steamboat as his eyes transferred wishes, hopes and dreams. His words I did not recall.

The steamboat journey was to take us through the Dardanelles and the Sea of Marmara to the mouth of the Bosphorus and Constantinople. After we had been at sea for about four hours we sighted the mainland. The wind had been at our backs and we had made good time. From that point on we kept land in our sight, seeing only a few towns.

It was late autumn, and the closer we traveled to Constantinople the cooler the weather got. I had a sweater on, but there were few heavy clothes in my bag. None of us knew a soul in Constantinople, and none of us had any idea of what to expect or what we would do. We were three Greek boys from an island looking for work in the city, little aware of the difficulties that lay before us. The sun was setting as we approached Constantinople, and we could see the lights of the city in the distance.

The fourteen hours since leaving Imbroz seemed much longer as our vessel cut through small swells at more than ten knots. Then, there it was, the historic city founded by Constantine, a

Roman Christian. This was the city that had served as the seat of Christianity under Constantine centuries ago. Now, in the space of a decade's genocide and uprooting, it had been purged of eighty percent of its Christian population.

In my soul I could sense the enormity of the change impending on my life. On the approaching shore my future awaited, a shore once Greek but now Turkish, like my beloved home of Imbroz. It was here, in the rightful home of Greeks, that I would try to rise above the oppression of the Turks. Although in five years I had spent barely two weeks at home, my life's odyssey, in true Greek tradition, was only now beginning in earnest.

7
The City Lights

*Gold and silver we will tell them that they have
from God; the diviner metal is within them, and
they have therefore no need of the dross which is
current among men, and ought not to pollute the
divine by any such earthly admixture for that
commoner metal has been the source of many
unholy deeds.... And this will be their salvation
and they may be the saviors of the State.*

—Plato
Republic

When we arrived in Constantinople, the last remnant of day
was fading into the city's flickering lights. Like a glowing
tapestry, the shoreline had no visible end. Even the Bosphorus
itself bore a faint reflected glow. As the last rays of sunlight
disappeared, the intensity of the electric lights magnified.
Lanterns, oil and electric, were mounted on the boats we passed in
the harbor as we entered the docking area. It was the first time any
of us had seen an electric light—let alone a whole city illuminated
by them—and the glittering sight enchanted us.

I gathered up my things and began to disembark with my
friends. Before setting foot onto the soil of Constantinople, I
instinctively said a prayer and pressed my hand against my coin.
As we disembarked, we paused uncertainly, bags in hand. Except
for my stay on Samothráki, none of us had ever been off our island,
and none of us had ever seen anything like Constantinople before.
It was overwhelming.

"Look at this," Yanni breathed, his arms sweeping wide to
embrace the scene. For a long moment we stood speechless, three
island boys gaping wide-eyed in awe. Finally, Yanni turned to me.
"Where are we going to go, Christo?"

85

"Well, first we should find a place to stay, I guess." My eyes traveled along the dock to a wooden shanty on the left. At the corner of the structure I saw the image of a large man standing in the dim light.

"We had better find a place soon," Demetrius said. "It's already dark."

Yanni's eyes followed mine and rested on the man by the shanty. "Sir!" he called out in his best Turkish. "Excuse me, sir, can you please tell us where we might find a boarding house?"

Demetri and I looked at each other, not at all sure that it was wise to talk to this Turkish stranger. As the man surveyed us a slight grin crossed his face. "Go down to the end of this road," he said, his eyes glancing in the direction we were heading. "Then turn right and walk up the hill toward Pera. That's the Christian part of the city. Or, if you wish, make a left at the road's end and you will go to Galata and Eminoun, the heart of the Muslim section." He paused. "You boys are Greek, aren't you?"

"Yes," I responded in Turkish, "we're from Imbroz Island."

"Such a long way from home, island boys."

"Yes it has been a long journey, and we are very tired. A boarding house would be most appreciated, sir," I reminded him.

"A boarding house. Oh, yes. Well, in that case continue walking up the hill into Pera for about ten or twelve blocks and you'll see boarding houses. At the top of the hill, you can see the Bosphorus on one side and the Sea of Marmara on the other. Looking down from there you'll see a large hotel, its lights reflected on the water. That's the Park Hotel on the Asiatic side of the city. You might just want to stay there and dine with the Pasha," he said, using the Turkish word for an army general. Amused at his joke, he went on, "Or in Pera," he said, gesturing to the right, "up on a hill in the European side of town, you will see the Pera Palace where diplomats and kings stay. Perhaps," he laughed, "you might find a room there!"

We ignored the teasing and I thanked the man in my best Turkish. At the road's end, we turned to the right toward the Christian side of Constantinople. This was Pera, the wealthier half of the city. Ironically, despite the religious massacres and deportation of over a million Christians throughout 1922 and 1923, most of the civil service jobs in Constantinople at that time were held by Greek Christians, and most of the commerce was handled by the Christian and Jewish minorities rather than the Turks. Even the gendarmes, who had slaughtered over three million Christians, couldn't run the city without the "infidels."

As we crossed the bridge that separated the Mohammedan from the Christian section, I couldn't help but notice high on the facing hill the beauty of the Pera Palace Hotel. What appeared to be a grand dining room was visible to our right overlooking the intersection of the Golden Horn and the Patriarchate as we crossed into Pera. Through the illuminated windows, I could make out elegant ladies and formally dressed gentlemen dining inside. I knew the older man back at the dock was kidding when he suggested we stay at either the Park or the Pera Palace, but I couldn't take my eyes off the hotel—it was so beautiful. I knew from the moment I set eyes on it that I would work there some day.

After a ten- or fifteen-minute walk, the road became paved and we reached a more populated part of the city. Although the air was chilly and the temperature dropping, our brisk walk and excitement made it hardly noticeable. Besides, we were so distracted by the great city's bustling that we paid no attention to the cool temperatures of the night.

Papa had told me about the sights of the city: the historic walls of Constantinople, the churches of Saints Sophia, Constantine and Helen, and the patriarchal church of St. George at Fanari. Saint Constantine was the emperor who had made Christianity the official religion of the Roman Empire. His mother, Saint Helen, or Elenitsa, had found the True Cross of Jesus Christ in Jerusalem on her journeys. There was also the Patriarchal Academy, called the Great School, which for centuries had graduated Orthodox Christian Priests. Near the Great School was the Patriarchate, which housed the Ecumenical Patriarch, the religious leader of the Orthodox Christian faith. As the religious hub of the Byzantine period, Constantinople was full of shrines, historic relics and Byzantine temples for worship—many of which had been sacked, looted and destroyed over time by Mohammedan Turks. The great Cathedral of Saint Sophia was now mimicked across its courtyard by the Blue Mosque with its six minarets, one of the largest mosques in the world, its size illustrating the stifling Mohammedan presence in this once great Christian city. The Turkish presence was everywhere, from teahouses to Topkapi Palace—the residence of the Ottoman sultans.

It was a city steeped in fifteen centuries of history. On one side of the Bosphorus is Europe; on the other is Asia. Trains arrived every day from Paris—the Orient Express—bringing the well to do to this melting pot of East and West, where the mingling masses of humanity seemed to cover every inch. Through here pass those trekking to all points of Asia, Europe, even the wilds of Africa.

This great city, meant to reflect the glories of Christianity, like my home of Imbroz in its humble way, was now in the hands of the Turks. Walking its streets, I wasn't sure how it all fit together, but I was sure that the Turks were responsible for my present condition. Constantinople might now be called Istanbul, but in the mind of a Greek will always be the name Constantinople.

The streets of the city were crowded with a kaleidoscope of people, some dressed in finery, others ragged and hungry. Beggars mingled with European aristocrats and greeted us at every corner. "Do you have a quarter lira, please?" a voice rasped from the shadows. A thin man in dirty rags appeared, his sharp hungry eyes fixed on us like a wolf's on a rabbit. We moved past him quickly. We were beginning to sense that, for as much splendor and glitter as the city held on the one hand, it had an equally dark and dismal side full of danger and misery.

Eventually we came to a boarding house with a sign that said "Room with a Tub." I suggested we look some more, but Yanni was tired and had already started to walk to the door. It was ten o'clock at night and we had had a long day. Once inside we learned that the room indeed had a tub, but only one mattress. Yanni and Demetrius haggled the landlord down from three Turkish pounds a month to two. We paid the two pounds and took the room, thinking we could change the next month if we found something more suitable.

To those accustomed to running water, it may have been irritating, or even amusing, to discover that, though our room had a tub, there was no running water. However, in the hall outside our door there was an electric light bulb—an unimagined luxury. With light from the hallway illuminating the room, we pondered the single mattress, knowing that the three of us could never fit on it together. Then we glanced at the tub. I could sense Yanni and Demetrius looking at me, visually measuring me, and I knew that of the three of us, I was the one—at five feet six and a hundred and thirty pounds—who could most easily fit into the tub.

Reluctantly, I dragged my bags across the little room, changed into my long johns, and climbed into my "bed." I rolled up some of my belongings, put them under my head, and covered myself with the small blanket Mama had packed, reminding myself that one day soon I would find better accommodations. With that final thought, I was soon sound asleep. If anyone wishes to learn humility, he should try sleeping in a bathtub in a Constantinople rooming house.

At dawn the next morning I was up and out of my "bed." Letting the others sleep, I went down the hall to find a bathroom. There was a steel sink with an oversized basin and next to it a commode. The commode was made of wood and, with a pipe attached that dropped straight down to the sewer, it smelled horribly. Still, it seemed quite an improvement over the outhouses back on Imbroz. After relieving myself, I threw some water on my face and hands and dried off with a hand towel my mother had packed for me. I returned to the room, grabbed my jacket and decided to go out and have a look before my friends awoke. I had some bread, cheese and olives wrapped up in a small towel, but breakfast would wait until Yanni and Demetri were up.

Now I would search for a job. I walked down the three flights of stairs and out through the front door without seeing anyone. The street was empty except for the smell of coffee coming from an all-night coffeehouse a few doors down. I followed the scent inside, the aroma of coffee overlaid by the odor of cigarette smoke forming clouds above each occupied table. Most of the patrons appeared to have been there all night. A large man with an apron came up and asked in Turkish if he could help me.

"No thanks," I said, backing out the door. I was hungry, but I didn't have extra money for food.

Returning to the rooming house, I found a cup in the bathroom and filled it with water. Back in our room I divided up the bread, cheese and olives into three separate piles, then roused my roommates. Nobility and wealth populated Pera; however, there was a much larger population of beggars and have-nots. Willing to work, I vowed I would not remain a have-not.

Our food ran out in the first week, and we had little money more than the month's rent we had paid. Every day from morning to night we had looked for jobs, but no luck. Work, it seemed, was impossible to come by, and the streets appeared filled with the unemployed, some looking for jobs and others for handouts. During the second week, I found a possible job in a grocery store about twenty-five minutes from the rooming house. The store was owned and operated by an Armenian Christian named Raki. "I am looking for a part-time delivery boy as well as someone to straighten the store, stock shelves and clean," he told me. "How old are you?"

"Eighteen, sir," I lied, standing rigidly to convey maturity.

"You're Greek?"

"Yes, sir, from Imbroz."

"I don't need you today, but come tomorrow at six in the morning," he said. "The person you're replacing fell sick, and I only need you until he returns," he went on, dictating the terms of the job. "Do you understand?"

"Yes, sir. Thank you, sir!" certain that my elation was at least partially evident on my face.

Work was so hard to come by that even a part-time, temporary job was a prize. Jobs in Constantinople during the 1930's and '40's typically required a seven-day workweek, with shifts running twelve to sixteen hours a day. The idea of beginning work at six in the morning didn't faze me. Although there were legions of beggars and dregs that formed the economic underbelly, there was an equal number of individuals looking for an honest day's work.

"Yes sir," I nodded to the Armenian, and offered a small bow as my father had taught me. "I will be here in the morning—at six!"

My new job at the grocery store included delivering orders all over the city—usually in Pera, but sometimes I was sent to the center of the Mohammedan side which was about an hour-and-a-half walk one way. I was paid seven piasters (Turkish pennies) a day, plus tips and food, which would pay the two-pound rent with a little left over. It was my first job in Constantinople and I was determined to make the best of it. I was told I was lucky to find work so quickly, and the more I saw, the more I realized that to be true. It was often said, and not in jest, that to get a job in Constantinople you usually had to wait until someone died. In my case, the sick man I replaced never returned.

"Chris, take this list of groceries to Mrs. Duma in the Turkish sector," Raki told me on my second day, "and be sure to collect."

Raki gave me directions and a grocery list. I went to the back of the store, found a box, collected the groceries and the bill, and was on my way. I might collect a tip at my destination, usually a penny or two, but many times I would get nothing. As I found out, it was very difficult to carry a box of groceries down the beggar-filled streets of Constantinople to the Mohammedan side of the city.

"Hey, boy, come here!" A shriveled hand in a tattered garment beckoned within three feet of me. "Come here, can't you hear me? Come here!"

"Sorry, I'm on delivery," I said, quickly veering from the beggar's path, but passing close enough to smell his stench.

"Some bread, please! I am starving!" An unending stream of beggars littered the street, a sad element of society that had given up hope. They served as a loathsome, frightful reminder of life on the street that lurked around the fringes of the workplace. It was a life from which so many of us were only a heartbeat away; I felt sorry for the beggars, but I had no money to help them, either.

"Please, some food! I've not eaten in a week! Please!"

Not all beggars in the Turkish section were old and feeble. Some were relatively young and as healthy as I was.

"Hey, boy, what do you have there? Come here, let us see," a shabbily dressed heavyset man called to me in Turkish while his two friends smirked over my obvious unease. "Did you hear me, boy? I said come here!" A second later he began striding in my direction.

Sensing trouble, I dashed quickly down the street, breaking into a jog. I was responsible for getting the groceries to their destination, and there was no way I was going to give them up to a street thug. I heard the laughter of the men behind me as I darted away. The beggars of Constantinople were generally shameless vagabonds, yet the sight of them instilled a fear of failure in me at a very young age, reinforcing my motivation to successfully deal with obstacles.

In Pera, the streets were cobblestone, but in the poorer Turkish sector they were mostly dirt. Finally I found Mrs. Duma's row house. She answered my knock but ignored my greeting. When I put the groceries down and gave her the bill, she silently handed me the money.

"Would you like me to help you put the groceries away?" I asked.

Wordlessly, Mrs. Duma shook her head. Despite the distance I had come, she never offered me a tip or a word of thanks.

Work with Raki was hard and demanding. I would try to arrive at first dawn, which meant I had to get up in the dark. In the morning I touched my toes to stretch twenty-five times, then cleaned my face, hands and upper body by throwing water on myself in the bathroom since there was no shower. Finally I pinned my father's relic coin on my tee shirt over my heart, buttoned up my shirt and left my room. When I arrived at work, Raki would have me do a series of chores to open the store, many of which were familiar from Papa's store and Uncle Russo's. Afterwards, he would give me some bread and tea, and occasionally a piece of kasari cheese. This was a dry, light yellow cheese which, along with feta, was one of the common cheeses of the area. I performed my duties at the store quickly and eventually took over many of Raki's responsibilities. He always had me make the larger deliveries, and although he had another helper, over time I became something of a manager.

Dear Katina, I wrote my sister a few weeks after my arrival. *I have a job in a grocery store working for an Armenian Christian. Enclosed please find half a Turkish pound for Mama and Papa. Please give my love to everyone. Say hello to anyone you may see. I miss you all. Love, Christo.*

The first month I had to bear the rent by myself, but soon Yanni got a job working on a fishing boat in the Sea of Marmara, and by the third month, Demetri had a job at a butcher's. Yanni and Demetri were not lazy, it was just very hard for three young boys from Imbroz to find work in Constantinople in 1932.

In order to stretch my monthly wage, I ate almost exclusively at the grocery store for the entire first year. A pack of cigarettes cost about a penny. A dinner at an average restaurant cost about ten cents. A suit of men's clothes cost about two pounds, which was the exchange rate for an ounce of gold. History would note that the Turkish pound began a 50-year decline at that point, eventually reaching the exchange rate of 120,000:1, underscoring the pathetic Turkish oversight of affairs. Although the rate was influenced by a number of factors, the chaos of the Turks' administration was an ongoing contributing factor in the decline.

That year I sent about seven pounds to Mama and Papa and paid about ten pounds for rent, my roommates paying the rest. The few purchases I made were for a pair of shoes, pants, two shirts, underwear and some other essentials, all of which cost me four pounds. I managed to save three pounds.

During that first year I got exactly three days off from work: the day before Easter, Easter Day, and a personal day to buy clothes. Although Raki wouldn't open the store to customers after church on Sunday, he always expected me to be there.

In my first year, I also bought a ledger book made in the United States and started to collect menus. Whenever I had a rare few minutes, I worked on my menu book and slowly taught myself French. In Constantinople the best restaurants were exclusively French, and all the waiters spoke French fluently. It was a requisite, I realized, for upward mobility in Constantinople. My first menus were from the two most luxurious hotel restaurants in the Pera section of the city. I studied the French on the menus using them like textbooks for the language, as well as for food presentation, and made notes on the sides. In this way my menu collection became something of a diary or a journal, and I would keep this journal updated for several years.

Meticulously, I pasted daily specials on the pages of my notebook, then carefully wrote out recipes in French. I had a good memory. If I saw or heard something once and focused on it, I would remember it. Collecting the menus of great restaurants and teaching myself French was more than a hobby. It was a way to improve myself, and was another step toward my goal of working at the Pera Palace.

By the next summer I was homesick. Late that autumn Raki gave me a week off, the only time during the year that business was slow and he could afford my absence. A ship left Constantinople once a week and arrived on Gallipoli by noon, then on to drop anchor about a half-mile off of Imbroz. I wrote Mama and Papa to ask them if they could arrange for Captain Koutris to row out and pick me up the morning the ship was scheduled to anchor offshore. The round trip from Constantinople to Imbroz cost almost one Turkish pound. By this time I had saved nearly seven Turkish pounds and sent home more than twice that much.

During the trip home I had time to reflect on my future, and I realized that it was time to look for another job. Raki had been a great help to me, but there was no future with him and the pay was awful. I decided to try waiting tables at one of the nightclubs in Pera. A friend had told me of a club that might hire me, where some of the waiters were making as much as a Turkish pound a week—over four pounds a month! With that kind of money I could be more help to my family and move to a larger apartment. Although dirt poor I never felt the weight of poverty. I moved through my demanding schedule with energy and enthusiasm.

When the Captain's boat picked me up that autumn afternoon in 1934, I realized just how homesick I really was. As we neared the shore, I saw that everyone was waiting for me—Mama, Papa, Katina, Sultana and Costa. Even though winter was not many weeks past, I felt the warmth of springtime wash over me at the sight of my family. Over two years had passed since I had last set foot on Imbroz.

From where she stood at the end of the dock I could hear Mama's excited voice, "Christo, Christo!" As soon as Captain Koutris brought the boat alongside the dock, everyone was running to greet me. My family and I embraced warmly, I collected my bags, and soon we began the trek home. The abandoned houses and overgrown farms were more in evidence as we walked along the road, many structures having totally succumbed to the elements. In its twelfth year, the occupation of Imbroz was now institutionalized, but our happiness at being together momentarily blotted out the decay and deterioration around us.

Throughout the following week, my parents made sure all our friends on the island saw me. It felt good to know how proud they were of their son who had gone to the city and found a job. Uncle Demetrius, Father George, Bishop Iakovos, our neighbor Maria, Katina's friends all came by to see me. With no future for them there, most of the boys had already left the island. I was dressed in a short sleeved white shirt, new tan khaki slacks and white shoes. Beneath my fresh white shirt, firmly pinned to my undershirt, in its proper place, was the coin that Papa had given me so long ago. A morning had not passed by when I hadn't fastened it to my tee shirt.

"My brother is making such a success of himself in Turkey!" Katina proclaimed to some listeners one afternoon during my visit home.

"Some success," I snorted. "In Constantinople I work all day, week in and week out, and return to my room at night to sleep in a bathtub!"

"Yes, and you are so proud of yourself for doing it!" she laughed. I acknowledged her with a broad smile. Yes, I was proud. Katina knew me too well, but I knew she also was proud of me for what I was able to do. We were downtrodden, uprooted, therefore aspirations were small. Our victories measured by the inch, and to my family I was the returning hero. Any success was worthwhile compared to the stagnancy of Imbroz. During my infrequent visits home over the ensuing decade, although my work was simple service, I would be held in the same lofty position of bearing the hopes and dreams and future of my family.

"Christo, have you met a young princess in Pera?" Katina teased.

"Oh, yes! Hundreds of princesses come into Raki's grocery every day," I teased back. Making her smile made me realize how much I had missed her during my three years in Constantinople. I had missed everyone.

In some ways, little had changed over the two-and-a-half years I had been in Constantinople. Papa gave me advice and spoke as always of the Greek philosophers, my sisters and brother peppered me with questions, and my mother cooked all my favorite things, but there was a subtle difference. It was in the way they looked at me, spoke to me, and regarded me with their eyes. It was in the way I carried myself, not as the child who had left them years ago. Now, at age sixteen, I was an independent adult, forced to grow up quickly, however, their acceptance of my independence didn't change their need or our bond.

Although things were quiet on the island, the Turks, in their underhanded way, were slowly taking ownership of the vacated properties—homesteading the abandoned homes and farms and businesses. The Turkish population had grown while the Greek Christian population was still in decline. Opportunities to make a living under the Turks were almost negligible; nonetheless, Papa still would not leave his home. Countless Greek Christians may have fled in the face of Kemal Mustapha and his relentless "cultural revolution," but not my steadfast father.

The situation on Imbroz was a smaller, quieter version of what had happened throughout Byzantium, of despondent despair. In many areas the Christian population had been virtually wiped out. Those who remained went about their lives unfettered in spirit yet mournful of the losses that surrounded them. Yet the intangibles, their customs, their beliefs, their traditional Christian religion, remained intact. The massacre which ushered in the twentieth century with the violent extermination of at least two out of three Anatolian Christians, and forcibly uprooting eighty percent of those who remained, had been reduced to a footnote in the academic history books of Western intellectuals—out of sight, out of mind. Yet the model for the great religious and political massacres that came later in the twentieth century had been spawned by Kemal Mustapha and his Young Turks; their brutal ethnic purging of Christians and Byzantine culture from Asia Minor and its old capital, Constantinople, occasioned no accountability and little, if any, outrage. For over three quarters of a century this massacre of more than three million Christians remains not only unatoned for, but almost unacknowledged. Yet it will never be forgotten by the few remaining survivors or their families.

While I was away, Papa and Mama began farming our fields themselves rather than leasing them out to other farmers. This provided them with many of the basics: wheat for flour, tomatoes and vegetables for salad, olives for oil, goat's milk for cheese and drinking, and, sometimes, chickens for eggs. A return to farming allowed my parents to provide minimally for themselves. Farming was supplemented by sewing suits and dresses for the Turkish gendarmes and officials, and by what I sent home.

I knew Papa was concerned about my brother's future. Costa was almost thirteen and Papa suggested that perhaps he could go to trade school in Constantinople the following year and learn to be a tailor. I told Papa that within a year I would have a bigger room and would send for him.

"One day, Papa," I went on confidently, "I will have my own place in America and I will bring you, Mama, Katina, Sultana and Costa to live with me."

Papa shook his head. "Christo, Mama and I are old. We will not leave Imbroz; but try to help your brother and sisters. I would like them to start a new life. You are young, Christo. Remain humble and honest and your enthusiasm for life will never leave you." Papa was smiling, but as his kind blue eyes remained on me, I saw that he looked tired. He was about sixty years old and had lived a hard life. Even if his anecdotes and philosophical observations were at times, now, a bit repetitious, he remained a source of inspiration for me every day of my life.

As of old, we all went to church as a family that Sunday, the day before my departure. Only perhaps two dozen people were in church, and I thought back on my early childhood when hundreds of people would fill the pews. On this particular Sunday, Bishop Iakovos was not present, so Father George conducted the service. Although Father George was younger than Papa, I saw that the years had taken a toll on him. He chanted the service in an unemotional, toneless manner, his face pale and expressionless. The change saddened me. He seemed almost the embodiment of the blighted life our proud island had resigned itself to for a dozen years.

After church, as we were finishing Sunday dinner, a young man came to the door. He had the full beard and black dress and collar of a priest. I saw at once that it was Jimmy Coucouzes.

"Hello, Mr. Chrysostomidis," he said, turning his head to the rest of us. "I hope I am not disturbing your dinner."

"Not at all," Papa said, greeting Jimmy with a smile. "Come in, come in, and let Mama get you something to eat." Papa seated Jimmy at the table and an instant later Mama placed a bowl before him.

"God bless you, Jimmy," she said.

Jimmy Coucouzes, my boyhood friend—soon to be a priest! He looked very dignified and proper and I knew he would be a credit to the priesthood. Imbroz always had a tradition of producing priests, especially after the Turks took control. There was not much for a young Greek man to do under Turkish rule. He could go into hard labor as I had, or he could turn to the ministry and seek a life serving God.

"I hear you are in Constantinople now, Christo," Jimmy said in a politely inquiring manner.

"Yes, I...er..." I hesitated, wondering how I should address my old friend, and then plunged on: "I have been working in a grocery store in Pera."

"Is it close to the Patriarchate?" he asked.

"Not very far at all," I replied. "About a mile."

"One day I will be there," my old friend said quietly as our eyes made contact. It was the same Jimmy. Then he reached across the table and patted me on the arm. "Well, Bread Crumb! I see you have finally grown up!"

I smiled. No one had called me that since we were children. "You are still a head taller than I am!" I blurted out.

"Then we are both taller!" Jimmy smiled, and we both laughed. Yes, we had physically changed, but we could feel that the bond of our friendship had held fast. Suddenly, I forgot Jimmy was a dignified young deacon, soon a priest, and we began chatting easily. We talked about Imbroz, Constantinople, the Turks—and, of course, our futures.

"One day I plan to go to America. There is freedom in America," I said.

"America has its problems too," he told me, "but you're right. There are over one million Greeks in America. Did you know that?"

"That is something!" I said, amazed, envisioning a place where being Christian was perfectly all right. "There is nothing for us in this part of the world," I went on. "Only in the United States will we have freedom and equal opportunity, Jimmy."

In what seemed like only a moment Jimmy stood to leave, and everyone gathered at the door to see the young deacon off.

"Jimmy, take care of yourself," I said. "It is so good to see you. Until we meet again," I added with a broad smile, our eyes affably capturing the moment.

"May God be with you," Jimmy responded. "And Christo, maybe I'll meet you in America one day."

"We will. One day we will," I told him with conviction. We watched from the door until Jimmy was out of sight—it was the custom on our island to ensure that family and friends had safely left the premises. Mama and Papa would always stand in the open doorway to see our guests off until they were out of sight, and this was a habit I took with me to America and practiced all my life.

My week on Imbroz had come and gone. The next morning I would wake up early and walk to the docks where Captain Koutris would row me out to sea to catch the boat to Constantinople. That night I slept soundly in my childhood bed and was up at first light. Although I tried to convince Mama and Papa that they didn't have to walk me to the dock, they insisted that they did. Just as we had watched Jimmy Coucouzes safely out of sight, everyone walked me to the dock to see me off. It was an unusually quiet walk.

"Christo, you must write me with your news for Mama and Papa," Katina said as she hugged me on the dock.

Katina always made the same request, that I would write her while I was gone, and once again I made the same reply. "I will," I promised her, "and let me know if you need anything. I will be moving and changing jobs," I went on, "and when I do I will write you and send my new address. Mama, Papa," I said, turning to them. "I will try to come home next summer—and Costa, you help Mama and Papa, and maybe in a year or two I will bring you to Constantinople to study tailoring."

"You promise?" my little brother asked with bright eyes.

"Well, we will see," I responded smiling.

"Sultana," I said, turning to her last. "You have grown so much! I won't recognize you next time I come home." It was a reminder of how much I would miss them during my absence and how very long that absence might be.

Good-byes were hard but important to all of us. As Captain Koutris began to paddle out to sea, my thoughts turned toward Constantinople. I imagined waiting tables in a trendy club in Pera, and calculated how much better the pay would be. At last I would be able to move out of the rooming house I had lived in for more than two years—and out of the tub that had shrunk.

It is hard for people today to understand the obstacles to advancement that existed in my part of the world so many years ago. The level of communication and transportation made the smallest distances major hurdles requiring great time and money to overcome. Work was a seven-day-a-week, morning-'til-night proposition with only an occasional day off, and the eight-hour workday was unheard of. Jobs in clubs and grocery stores and restaurants were rare and highly sought, no matter how menial they may seem to us today. The excess supply of labor ensured the work would remain grueling and extremely lengthy. From my years laboring in Turkey I developed a lifelong respect for the working man.

When we pulled alongside the ship that was to take me to Constantinople, I paid Captain Koutris and once again said good-bye.

"Will you return next year, Christo?" the Captain asked as we shook hands.

"I'm not sure."

"Well, take care and let your father know when you will return and, God willing, I will pick you up."

The steam-powered boat was larger than the one that had brought me home the previous week. It weighed anchor at 8:30 that morning and steamed off on the daylong voyage. We moved through the Dardanelles Straight past Gallipoli, into the Sea of Marmara and the mouth of the Bosphorus and the harbor at Constantinople. Although there was food that passengers could purchase aboard ship, Mama had packed me cheese, bread and olives—a meal like the ones she had packed on my other journeys, and one to which I had grown accustomed.

Arriving in Constantinople late that evening, I went to the club in Pera, which my friend had recommended, and was immediately hired as a waiter. Although I didn't particularly like the hours or the clientele, my schedule would give me days off to spend time at the Pera Palace to study its operations. Besides, the club was a popular spot and I would be able to make more than twice the salary I was making at the grocery store. The next morning I went to Raki and gave him two weeks' notice. It would be my policy to leave every job on good terms so that, if need be, I could return. My simple jobs were the assets of my life. There has never been an employer, all the way back to Uncle Russo, that I couldn't return to or who did not want me to stay. They knew I was a productive, hard worker, and that I was proud of what I did.

During the first week of my notice, Raki tried to talk me out of leaving, but my time with him—long days carting heavy deliveries for miles—was over. I immediately made arrangements to move into a small apartment with my friend at the club. The apartment had a sink with running water, electricity, a hot plate to cook on, two beds and a private bathroom. The bathroom itself only had a commode, the sink being located in the room, but for me this was an unimagined luxury! I gave Yanni and Demetri notice. They were both working and could easily afford the two pounds a month without me.

Before I left the room I shared with them, I took one last look at the tub I had slept in. Since I had arrived more than two and a half years earlier I had grown about four inches, which made my nights in the tub increasingly uncomfortable. I slept with knees drawn up first on one side, and then the other—but usually I was so tired from my days at the grocery store that it didn't matter. It was hard to believe that in my new apartment I would have a real bed!

I was sure I would continue to see Yanni and Demetri after I moved, but my busy work schedule meant I saw less and less of them as time went by. Eventually I would lose contact with them altogether. I left my old apartment and began my new life in high spirits reflecting back on my first arrival in Constantinople. No longer was I awed by the city of crossroads, by the mixing crowds of humanity, colors, and lights, for I had become a Constantinopolitan, a city boy.

Dear Katina, I wrote happily a couple of weeks later. *Remember the dinner club I mentioned to you on my visit home? Well, I have a job there now as a waiter, and I have also moved to a new apartment. My new address is at the top of this letter. Enclosed you will find a three-pound note to give to Papa. Regards to everyone. Love, Chrysostomos.*

The energy I released was renewed daily, stimulated by the odyssey I lived and by my deep desire to succeed. Although not yet seventeen years old, I was confident my life was moving in a positive direction.

8

A Waiter at Last

Out of the mud two strangers came
And caught me splitting wood in the yard.
And one of them put me off my aim
By hailing cheerfully, "Hit them hard!"
I knew pretty well why he dropped behind
And let the other go on a way.
I knew pretty well what he had in mind:
He wanted to take my job for pay.

—Robert Frost
"Two Tramps at Mud Time"

The nightlife of Constantinople in late 1935 was profitable, fast and furious. I was making good money at the club, but I was already restless. It would be better to work daytime hours, I decided, rather than late at night. The drinking and carousing at the club was not something I enjoyed, anyway. I had never forgotten my goal to work at the Pera Palace, which was about a twenty-five-minute walk from my new apartment. I was spending nearly all my extra time there. For some unknown reason, I associated it with my future success. I left early each morning for the club, passing the Pera Palace on my way. I would often stop and watch a small army of waiters and busboys setting up the dining rooms for lunch, all ordered to the smallest detail. Chairs upholstered in velvet were drawn up to tables covered with white linen and laid with polished silver on freshly pressed satin napkins abutting gleaming china. Mirrored walls reflected marble columns and dazzling crystal chandeliers. Most impressive of all, however, was the legendary cuisine.

I would sometimes leave for work extra early just to watch them readying the room for breakfast. I often wore the silk suit that Mama had made for me, so that I might look my best, and

103

eventually I got to know a few of the waiters by sight. In the tradition of a fine French restaurant, the Pera Palace featured a captain who supervised the waiters and staff, and a maitre d' who greeted the guests. One day the captain noticed me standing in the service entrance.

"What can I do for you?" he asked in French.

By now I was fairly fluent in basic French and replied as best I could.

"Nothing sir. I'm just watching, with your permission," and offered him a polite bow. The captain was a big man, dark complected with a handlebar mustache, jet black hair and a broad face. Although he spoke French, his name was Memet Kahele, and he was unmistakably Turkish.

Where are you from?" he asked in Turkish. Evidently, my "menu" French had not been that persuasive. Nonetheless, with my blue eyes and sandy colored hair it was not readily apparent that I was Greek.

"I am Greek, from Imbroz." Then I corrected myself, "Chalaka Island," using the name the Turks had given my home.

"Oh, an island boy from Chalaka! Are you looking for a job at Pera Palace? Well, I don't need anyone," he said, without waiting for an answer. "It is not easy, you know, to work at Pera Palace. We only have mature, experienced men, not boys."

"I have a job at a club nearby," I told him. "I was just stopping by to watch," I repeated.

"You can watch," the captain told me curtly, "but stay out of the way of the waiters and busboys. Stand to the inside of the door—over there." He gestured with his hand to the wall directly inside the service entrance door while his keen eyes surveyed me.

"How old are you, anyway?" he asked abruptly.

"Nineteen," I said, with an expressionless stare, although I would not turn eighteen until mid-December.

"Well, we don't need anyone," he said, turning to walk away, "but you may keep checking with us. Maybe you will be lucky." Pausing, he appeared to lose interest, turned and left.

"Yes sir!" I gasped, and bowed respectfully. His back was already turned, but I knew that he heard the eagerness in my response and instantly I wished I had been more reserved. Jobs were no easier to come by in 1935 than they had been three years earlier, and many of the busboys were older men who had worked at the Pera Palace for twenty years or more. I quelled the excitement rising inside me.

I knew I could do a good job at the Pera Palace if only given the chance. I had taught myself French, I had watched the staff as they worked, and I had gained experience as a club waiter. It was impossible for me to hide enthusiasm from Memet that day. I felt he had accepted me—or at least, and probably more accurately, tolerated my presence.

The next day was my day off at the club. I arrived earlier than usual at the Pera Palace. I stood in my suit for an hour and watched the end of the breakfast service and the setup for lunch. I know Memet saw me, but he said nothing. I came again half a dozen times over the next two weeks, usually wearing my homemade suit. Even though a busboy's wage at the Pera Palace, including tips, was a little less than I was currently making, I was drawn to it because I felt it was my future. I would not be a busboy forever, I decided, and waiters at the Pera Palace did very well.

One day as Memet passed, I bowed politely. "Nothing today," he said briefly. This continued over the next two weeks and, although proud that my presence was being tolerated, I began wondering if I would ever be hired. I patiently and diligently returned, though, whenever my time allowed, two weeks stretching out to two months, then three.

The staff at the Pera Palace was multi-cultural, composed mostly of Turks, Greeks, Armenians, French, Russians, an African and an Italian. However, all were manicured to fit seamlessly into the tapestry. Just at the time when I had resigned myself to the belief that someone would have to drop dead for me to get a job, the unthinkable happened. From my post at the right of the service door, I saw Memet come out of the kitchen with a mop and start mopping in the dining room. By now, I knew everyone's job and in the past an older gentleman had always done the mopping. A quick glance around confirmed his absence. On impulse, I strode over to Memet, bowed, and in one smooth movement took the mop from his hands. Without speaking, he submitted and released the mop to me. Finally, I had a chance to be of some help and show my worth.

I mopped the white marble floor of the Agatha Christie Ballroom in long straight lines as quickly and efficiently as possible, being careful to follow the wet mop with a dry mop so that customers would not slip and fall. I had spent so much time watching the old man who normally did this job, I knew exactly what to do without being told. When I finished, I immediately took the mop and the bucket into the kitchen, a large bustling room with shiny stainless steel sinks and counters and a white porcelain floor. An assistant to the cook tipped his head toward a small closet where I put the mop and bucket. Later, I would rinse the mop, clean and dry it, but right now there was no time. Customers were beginning to come for lunch and the setups had not been completed. I moved quickly, placing silver setups and napkins at the tables. I had watched this procedure so many times, I felt I could do it blindfolded.

After finishing the lunch setups I went back into the dining room. People were being seated by the maitre d' while the waiters, in their black jackets and ties, stood patiently by their stations, some with hands folded behind their backs in an 'at-ease' position, others with crisp, white linen towels folded carefully across their bent forearms. This was the customary, formal manner of Pera Palace waiters. The customers, meanwhile, had not noticed our anxious and hurried preparation, which is how it should be in good restaurants. Although unsolicited, I gleefully moved in an orderly manner to other tasks. After my long wait I was committed to a flawless performance.

Since no one had stopped me, I proceeded to fill water glasses with ice and water and placed them on a tray. Then I lifted the tray with the palm of my hand underneath and my other hand on the rim for balance. I served a party, standing to the left of each guest as I carefully placed a water glass by each plate. Then I cleaned the tables of departing guests and reset them exactly as I had seen it done, with a dinner fork, a salad fork, a knife and two spoons. I smiled and bowed politely at each guest who looked at me. The tasks I performed that day were easy and fluid and required little if any assistance by the regular staff. Busboys normally wore white jackets, but my plain white shirt and light-colored pants seemed to blend in enough as not to arouse comment.

I knew Memet was eyeing me and though I was only helping out, I knew I was also on trial. Since the time he had allowed me to stand by the door and observe, I had felt certain he would afford me a chance one day. A mistake might mean an end to my potential employment, so working as much from instinct and common sense as from experience, I spared no effort to do every task quickly and correctly.

After lunch Memet approached me. "Are you hungry?" he asked. "You may go to the kitchen and eat now if you are." The question was rhetorical in those days, since everyone was hungry, but the offer of food was clearly evidence of his approval.

Regretfully, I shook my head. "No, thank you," I said politely. "I am late and they will be expecting me at the club."

Memet looked at me carefully. "You are very diligent," he said, his face betraying nothing. "Why don't you come by tomorrow at the same time?"

"Yes sir," I said. It took me a minute to understand that Memet had offered me a job…at least for another day. It was too good to be true! To be hired at age seventeen as a busboy in the Agatha Christie Ballroom of the Pera Palace was a tremendous milestone in my young, hard life, a goal obtained that satisfied me to no end. I could barely believe it, and the joy in my heart was indescribable.

I gave the club a week's notice and then began my career at the Palace.

I learned later that the old man who had not shown up for work that day was named Albert Lamare. He had worked at the Pera Palace for 28 years and had died the night before. The saying had proven true—it literally had taken someone to drop dead before I got a job there.

Agatha Christi had written *Murder on the Orient Express* in one of the upstairs rooms, the haunts of the aristocracy of Europe where heads of state held numerous clandestine rendezvous that affected countless many, where vestiges of the White Russian Army intermingled with wealthy Bulgarian and Armenian traders. It was an important and very cosmopolitan hotel at the height of its celebrity. If Constantinople was rightly coined the crossroads where East meets West, then Pera Palace was as equally known for romance and intrigue. Often spies and assassins would exchange information or plot the overthrow of a European leader, independent of the guests' diverse agendas. The service was always first-class. All who frequented the posh ballroom were there to be pampered and fed. In the evenings, the finest ladies and gentlemen would attire in glittering finery, such a sharp contrast to the vast majority of the population, like those just outside the damask walls barely holding on to their fragile survival.

On my first full day there, Memet followed me into the kitchen where the breakfast cook was changing pans on the cooking line to prepare for lunch. The chef was to the side taking freshly baked bread out of the oven and placing it in a warmer to serve for lunch. He had been preparing sauces, condiments, and soups from scratch for the luncheon menu. In those days, all chefs worth their salt prepared everything from scratch.

"Victor," Memet called out to the chef, "show Christo how to wash the dishes, silver, cups and glasses. He will help you clean up and prepare for lunch. Oh, and give him a white jacket before he returns to the floor." From the outset, I was to be somewhat of a handyman for Memet. His habit of putting me in service where I was needed complemented my quick mind and allowed me, over time, to master most of the restaurant's tasks, including food preparation.

Victor nodded and beckoned me over to a linen closet where he held up a smart-looking white jacket to size me. The jacket had gold buttons down the front and completely covered the plain white shirt I was wearing. After cleaning up the breakfast dishes, I returned to the dining room—this time properly attired in my jacket—and began to clean and set up for lunch. The area used for breakfast extended into two other rooms for lunch and dinner. Filled to capacity, the Pera Palace seated over three hundred in the Agatha Christie Ballroom and its bar. Everything about the Palace, from the marble reservation podium at its entrance to its hilltop view overlooking the Golden Horn and Patriarchate on one side and the city on the other, bespoke of an opulent, first-class hotel restaurant, things I had never dreamed or imagined.

Lunch that first day was very busy. Besides my regular busing duties, Memet sent me on errands to fetch things from the laundry room and kitchen. After lunch I was given a dinner menu. It was required that a waiter memorize for recital the luncheon and evening specials and, though not required for busboys, it was a practice I embraced. I understood most of it and learned it by heart.

No member of the staff ate or drank during a meal service, but after the lunch service, Memet took me to the kitchen and said something to the chef in French that I did not quite understand, something about leftovers. I soon was pleased to discover that leftovers did not mean food left on customers' plates, but were soups or specials du jour that did not sell during a meal, all quite good but perishable. The restaurant was careful and efficient in this regard.

Gourmet meals were a perquisite the entire staff enjoyed, even down to kitchen helpers and dishwashers. For many employees the food was an annuity that supplemented their wage and bound them to the mystique of the grand hotel. It also had the benefit of allowing us to become familiar with the restaurant's cuisine, thereby making the waiters more authoritative when giving recommendations or descriptions to the customers.

I am convinced that my success at Pera Palace was owed in large part to my enthusiastic embrace of menial tasks such as cleaning, which many more experienced than I would shun. I am equally confident that this approach invites success in many vocations.

As with all the jobs I had had, I worked a long day at the Pera Palace, busing breakfast, lunch and dinner, and cleaning up afterwards. Memet's rules were simple: *I will give you a job, and I will feed you; you must arrive promptly every day and you cannot leave until I tell you.* His rules were fine with me. Our customers were the finest ladies and gentlemen in Europe, and my adrenaline would speed up my metabolism such that my often-fatigued condition would be barely noticeable; I was up to the task.

"Christo," Memet told me finally, "you may go home now, but be back at six-thirty in the morning."

"Yes, sir!" I responded crisply.

It was almost eleven-thirty. Without a word I bowed respectfully and left. I didn't even know what my pay would be. It was two weeks before I learned it would be five Turkish pounds a month, although some months I could make an equal amount from tips. It was customary for the waiters to share a nominal amount of the tips with the busboys. My workweek was eighty to one hundred hours or more, and I didn't get a day off during my first year, but I had no complaints. In mid-December I would turn eighteen, yet I was led to believe by others that my maturity and poise far surpassed my years. I had been working for almost eight years, and now I was working at the finest restaurant in Constantinople.

I didn't get to sleep that first night until well after midnight, but I was up at first light, very hungry and a little stiff from my long first day of work. Having no shower facilities, I washed my face, teeth and underarms. The light fuzz on my face did not yet require shaving. I touched my toes to stretch, dressed, pinned on my relic coin and said a prayer of thanks to God and asked Him to watch over me. I left for work before six o'clock, hoping that I would be offered breakfast at the restaurant. When I arrived at the Pera Palace it was barely six-thirty and no one was there except the chef and his assistant.

"Good morning, sir," I said, bowing respectfully to the chef.

"You're here early," he commented.

"I'll start setting up for breakfast," I offered, donning a white busboy's jacket, then I hurried into the dining room. My stomach was demanding breakfast, but never mind, I would eat later. The large crystal chandeliers had not been turned on in the dining room, but there was adequate light from the windows to do my breakfast setup. Whatever your vocation, become immersed in it and your day will be self-gratifying and your work will receive positive attention. Within minutes a waiter arrived, a forty-year-old Greek named Aristis Plaka.

For several moments Aristis watched me setting up with an experienced eye. "What are you doing?" he asked me finally in Greek.

"Setting up for breakfast, sir," I responded.

"Make sure you crease the napkins like this," he said, making a fold and then applying pressure with his palm as if to iron the fabric.

I bowed my thanks and continued working.

A few minutes later Memet arrived. As soon as he saw me he called me over. "Christo, Good morning."

"Good morning sir," I responded, a little nervous.

"Today is Saturday and we are having our buffet. I want you to come with me so that I can show you how we set it up." He took me to a room off the dining room in the front of the house where there were long folded tables. "These tables will be set up in a line like this," he said, gesturing with his hands along the back wall of the room. "Allow room so customers may pass on both sides, Christo," he added, gesturing to another busboy, "Pedro will help you. Aristis, you supervise," Memet said with a side glance. Aristis, unexpecting, acknowledged with a head bowed over his morning coffee.

"Yes sir," I responded automatically. The tables were long and a little difficult to handle, and we had to be careful not to bump them into anything. After setting them up and covering them with spotless, white tablecloths, the chef's helper and I brought out large chafing dishes from the kitchen, filled them with hot water, lit paraffin beneath to keep them warm, then placed food trays on top. Like many of the serving pieces at the Pera Palace, the chaffing dishes were silver and very ornate. By the time we had finished arranging the buffet, the chandeliers had been turned on, more than half the waiters had arrived, and guests were being seated. Another long workday had begun.

* * * * *

My eighteenth birthday came and went, the Pera Palace consuming my long days. During Christmas and New Year's we were very busy with parties and special functions. Within a month, I had mastered all my assigned tasks and a few others as well. Many times my days stretched into sixteen hours or more. At first I was sore and tired from the rigors of my job, but after a while I grew used to my grueling schedule and even became proud of it. I was working seven days a week, week in and week out. Although I planned to ask for a day off, I wanted to make sure that I was secure in my job first. I wanted to become irreplaceable. I focused all my energy on my job.

I became friends with the chef, who was also there sixteen hours a day. He was a Frenchman, Victor François, and he spoke fluent German, English, Turkish and even some Greek. Although the two of us normally conversed in Turkish, he often helped me with my French. He was a very skilled chef and prepared everything daily from scratch, including breads, desserts, condiments, vinaigrettes, dressings, soups and sauces—unheard of production these days. Chefs were real chefs in those days. Nothing was pre-packaged or canned. Some nights, when I did not have time to eat properly, Victor gave me kitchen leftovers to take home. My diet was certainly much improved when I joined the staff at the Pera Palace. The restaurant business has often attracted poor rural boys with sparse diets.

After I became established, I wrote Katina. *I have changed jobs and am working at the Pera Palace Restaurant where all the aristocrats of Europe dine! I am presently a busboy but hope to be a waiter soon. Enclosed you will find three Turkish pounds. Did you receive the money I sent last month? Hope everyone is well. Love and regards to Papa, Mama, Sultana, Costa and anyone who might ask for me.*

Sometime later I received a response to my letter. "Dearest Christo, "Katina wrote. "We were so excited to receive your letter. You are in our thoughts every day. Papa is so proud that you found such good work. Please write again with all your news. Regards to Janni and Demetri…do you still see them? Love from your sister, Katina."

It was good to get news from home. It was a relief to be able to sent money home regularly.

As time passed, I continued to collect daily menus, studying them as an opportunity to improve my French and to expand my knowledge of food. Sometimes, when needed, I would help the chef prepare food. My ease in learning and eagerness in the kitchen made me an instant success. My menu scrapbook served as a chronicle of my interest in the restaurant industry—a fascination born of necessity, which started with Papa and continued as a young man busing tables in Constantinople.

As time went on, I continued to be the one Memet called upon whenever he needed anything. "Christo, where is the small cocktail table?" he'd ask. "Please find it right away," or, "Christo, we have a party of twelve in the small dinning room! Please do the setup..."

Even the waiters joined in. "Christo, will you please bring my lemonade from the kitchen," or "Christo, check with the kitchen for my fruit bowl for that table in the corner." One thing I learned from a young age is that there was never enough time to finish; there was always something to do and never time to complete life's work. I stayed busy.

"Christo, you see how this is done with egg whites," the chef, Victor, told me gravely in French, explaining a recipe to me. "The gravy must start with the correct roux. You see, fresh churned butter." (Roux is the base of sauce, usually flour and butter, that gives it body.) Victor's soups, sauces, and soufflés were what filled our dining rooms with customers. Never take shortcuts with food, he insisted. Always use the best ingredients and you will have an excellent result. Increasingly, the chef or one of his helpers would ask for a hand. "Christo, can you please help me prepare these Lyonnaise potatoes," or "Christo, I have a roast for the large party under the chandelier, would you please baste it for me?" and on and on. My knowledge of food grew considerably with Chef Victor in the kitchen, as did my respect for proper preparation. Frankly, not to boast, I had a knack for food preparation. The long hours and hard work of my first three and a half months at the Pera Palace were paying off. I was an insatiable sponge improving my French as well as the skills I needed to be a waiter, while learning to prepare French dishes. My energy and interest were inexhaustible.

It was now 1936, and Memet had promised me a day off after the New Year. The parties had tapered off, but the hotel remained full and always something seemed to come up to prevent me from taking a day. Not until early spring did I finally get my holiday.

That day there were many things I had to do. I posted a letter to Katina and enclosed two Turkish liras to Mama and Papa. I went shopping for a new pair of shoes, two pairs of black waiter's slacks, two new white shirts, a bow tie and a black waiter's jacket. My money was spent on necessities that supported my trade as well as my family. It cost me almost two months' pay, and over half my savings, but I viewed it as an investment in my future. On my way back from the shop I stopped by the Patriarchate, which housed the Patriarch and a Byzantine Orthodox church. It was beautiful, with marble, gold, stained glass windows and walls adorned with brightly painted icons. The Patriarchate had withstood the ravages of time, dating back to the fifth century, a Christian oasis from antiquity in the desert of Mohammedanism. I offered a prayer thanking God for my good fortune and one for my family's health and welfare.

Later that day I made a rendezvous with Demetri and Janni. It seemed ages since I had seen them. We were all working in the same city, but with such torturous workdays, we seldom saw one another. We had planned for some time to go to the Cathedral of the Whirling Dervishes, a Mohammedan sect who, as part of their religious ceremony, spun endlessly round and round. It was a good excuse for three teens to have a reunion. Upon our arrival we found both men and women dressed in Turkish hats and colorful full-length gowns that streamed and swirled around them as they spun, feet moving in small staccato bursts. The smell of incense and strange food frying in the distance added an exotic air to an already exotic city. My friends and I watched, mesmerized, for more than twenty minutes, wide-eyed and captivated by this timeless and dizzying ceremony. Upon leaving we spun in laughter until we all had fallen dizzy on the ground.

Afterward, we walked to the Church of Christ Pantokrato where a particularly fascinating relic, the mummified hand of Saint John the Baptist, was displayed in a gold case. Though perhaps gruesome to some, such relics remain a tangible sign of God's presence in the world. While the Christian population dwindled, its rich traditions and relics still shone deeply in Constantinople.

Being teenage boys, the grisly and dizzying sights did not crimp our appetites. We went to a sidewalk cafe and treated ourselves to a hot meal—liver and onions, potatoes, salad, bread, cheese and cold beer. We had much to celebrate together.

Through tenacious, methodic labor, we had significantly improved our plight since our arrival as three inexperienced boys from Imbroz some three years earlier. We feasted and reveled, reminisced and swapped stories, then fell with the setting sun into a silent and reflective camaraderie. It was good to sit peacefully with my old friends. No one spoke of homesickness, nor, strangely, even of Imbroz, but we felt it. It was our bond. As the night's darkness deepened we gradually shook the spell, regretting a single day's brevity, and sadly said our farewells. Demetri and Janni headed back to their room and I went home to wash clothes and get ready for work the next morning.

Rejuvenated and refreshed from my day off, I arrived at the restaurant early the next morning. I wore my new white shirt, black slacks and shoes, and I set up the whole dining room for breakfast by myself. When Memet arrived, I gathered my nerve, looked him directly in the eyes and addressed him in my best French.

"I would like to become a waiter."

"In time you will wait tables, Christo," he promised. That night, by chance, two waiters did not show for dinner. Often necessity invites promotion in the restaurant business. Assisted by Aristis I waited on my first party. They were an older couple, distinguished in appearance and expensively dressed. The man had white hair and a white beard and wore a white dinner jacket. His wife, her white hair piled luxuriously high, wore a beautiful ruby-studded pearl necklace. They appeared to be German, but their French was perfect.

I bowed and asked for their order as if I had been a waiter all my life. The man turned to his wife, "What will you have, my dear?"

"What would the young man recommend?" she replied.

"Tonight we have Potage crème d'Orge," I said smoothly, "as well as Langousta en belle vue sauce remoulade, Sigara börek, Perdreaux rotis pommes frites salade verte, Kadin gŏbagi au kaymak, Corbeilles de fruits, and Café."

"That sounds perfect," she approvingly responded. "Then I'll have the same," her husband said.

This was my cue to bow. "Right away," I said sharply, and retired to the kitchen.

It was the waiter's task to be inconspicuous and make the meal delightfully uneventful. The dinner I served the German couple went well and afterwards I collected my first tip, five piasters.

My second party that night consisted of two elderly couples whom I recognized as frequent patrons of the restaurant. One of the men had been a general in the White Russian Army before the Bolsheviks. I stood at the right shoulder of one of the gentlemen and bowed. "Monsieur, may I take your order please?" I asked politely.

The man facing me across the table apparently recognized me as one of the busboys. "Well, you are a waiter now!" he commented pleasantly in French. "What is your name?"

"Chrysostomos, sir," I replied, surprised that he had noticed me in the past.

"And you are Greek Orthodox, is that right? Yet your French is so good."

I felt myself flush with pleasure. "Thank you, sir!" I bowed politely, beaming over his compliment.

That night my station included four tables for three sittings. Busing and cleaning up after dinner, as well, I made upward of half a Turkish pound.

That night I thanked God for his guidance and the strength he had given me. After nearly four years in Constantinople, I had learned a valuable lesson: If you set your mind to something and focus all your energies on it, you can accomplish your objective. I was a Greek island boy struggling in Turkey to make a living during those hard years between World Wars, and I had accomplished the near impossible—I had become a waiter at the posh Pera Palace, a fashionable spot for the upper crust to mingle. Diplomats, merchants, kings and dukes, a melting pot of espionage and intrigue, all came to dine at the Pera Palace. In Turkey, where the have-nots were the distinct majority, I learned something that would prove true throughout the world: There will always be a demand for fine food and those who prepare and serve it properly. For a Greek boy from the islands with little education, advancement in the food industry was indeed a blessing. I had mastered a transportable trade.

All that winter, spring and summer I continued to wait tables, gaining experience and confidence. I had saved some money and had moved to my own one-bedroom apartment with a sink and a shower. From that day on, every morning at the crack of dawn I would take a shower. The apartment was only three-quarters of a mile from the Pera Palace and featured a hanging electric light with a string to turn it on and off. Voilà!

* * * * *

It had become Memet's habit in the three years I was at Pera Palace to call my name, and one night it occurred in a most unexpected circumstance. In late November of 1937, there was a group of Turkish dignitaries, a couple of whom were chatting with a young woman about twenty feet beyond us.

"Christo!" Memet called in a low voice.

"Yes, sir?" I bowed.

"I want you to take his Excellency's party." It took me a moment to fully grasp whom he meant. Then I saw him, Mustapha Kemal Atatürk, the "Father of Turkey." My view was a little obscured by the figure of the young woman he was talking with, but there was no mistaking him, a slight man of about my height, dark complected.

"Yes, sir. Right away!" I said with a sharp bow, and Memet turned to take me to the party. "Your Excellency, Christo will have the pleasure of serving you this evening. Lemel is not here tonight."

"This way your Excellency," I said crisply, barely making eye contact. I bowed and gestured toward two tables in the far corner of the ballroom Memet reserved for special guests. Atatürk was a nationalist and a member of the Committee of Union and Progress that twenty-five years earlier had orchestrated the Christian Holocaust. It was quite unusual for a Christian to have this assignment.

Atatürk barely acknowledged me with a glance, never pausing in his conversation with the young woman. I did not recognize all of the men in the party, except for one from newspaper photos, Fayik Okte, the previous Tax Director of Constantinople. Another older man bore a striking resemblance to a man I saw in my father's news clippings as a child, the notorious Doctor Selanikli Nazim, the chief ideologist of the Young Turk movement which, through the C. U. P., laid down and executed the policies against the minorities. My pulse quickened with thoughts of the genocides, yet not a hair of my manicured presence betrayed a whisper as I seated the "Father of Turkey."

Before the rest of the party was seated, a large man among them issued an order. "Raki and hors d'oeuvres for the Father of Turkey!"

"Right away, Pasha," I responded with a bow. Raki was a popular licorice liquor in Turkey. A few moments later, while I was pouring it, the same man said, "Leave the bottle." I bowed and withdrew to bring the hors d'oeuvres and assorted condiments to tide the group over until dinner was served. Again, the same man, "Bring another bottle."

"Right away, sir."

While I served his drink, Atatürk suddenly acknowledged my presence with a bold stare. "You're Turkish, are you?" He queried with a penetrating stare.

"No, sir, I am not." In that moment, while gazing into his dark foreboding eyes, my life as well as the lives of my family and kinsmen flashed across my mind: Athanasis, the boy from the slaughters in Smyrna, the conquest of my island home, the expulsion of the Christian officials, the Turkish schools, the laws and taxes passed to cripple us, and interwoven throughout, the unspeakable violence which permeated every aspect of my life under the Turks. Images of the harsh, stifling violence of this ruthless man who had bullied, brutalized and methodically butchered the Christian minorities for decades flashed in that one moment that our eyes locked. I had every reason to hate him, and yet, surprisingly, I felt no hatred. I felt the drone of my impoverished island existence that he reflected, the blunted hollow feeling I had toiled so long to forget. I felt a soul-wrenching sadness as I looked at him, a slight, aging man feeling the effects of the liquor and the flowery fragrance of the young woman who, at that moment, was the object of his attention. From Salonika, his appearance revealed his mother's Jewish background. This was the man at the center of so much power, which he wielded so prejudicially and so cruelly. The moment passed, and I went on with my duties, going through automated motions of European manner and décor in service to the anti-Christian of my age.

Over the next hour or so, the Father of Turkey and much of his party fell increasingly under the influence of drink. They did not linger after dinner, and as Mustapha Kemal staggered toward the exit numbed by alcohol, he clutched the perfumed young woman for support. Atatürk, the man credited with the creation of so-called Modern Turkey, staggering out of a ballroom, clutching a young woman for support, was a telling image. Yet the memory of the cold dark stare in the moment when our eyes met was one that would fix permanently in my mind. A year later, he died at the age of 57.

* * * * *

There wouldn't be time to go home that year, but I felt adequately established financially to make good on my promise to bring my little brother Costa to Constantinople for schooling. I was filled with pride and pleasure when I wrote to Katina.

A few weeks back I was made a waiter at the Pera Palace restaurant I mentioned to you, where I serve in the Agatha Christie Ballroom. I have my own apartment now. I have also made arrangements for Costa to study at a haberdashery not far from the apartment. I will pay the fee. It will take him about a year to finish the apprenticeship and become a tailor, and he will stay with me. Tell Papa the school has a good reputation, and I am sure it will be of value to Costa. Write to me and tell me when I might expect him.

Tell Mama not to worry, Costa will be with me. I miss you all and our home very much. How are Papa and Mama?

Love, Chrysostomos

By the end of October I had a reply: Costa would arrive on the evening of November fifteenth. On the fifteenth, Memet gave me the dinner shift off so that I could meet him. When the boat docked, I saw Costa walking down the plank. My heart ached as I watched him carry a small, worn suitcase that I recognized as Mama's and Papa's, and a somewhat larger duffel bag with pull strings slung over his shoulder. He had grown considerably in the two and a half years since I had last seen him, and he was almost as tall as I was, but Costa didn't look like me at all. Where I resembled Papa, with his light complexion and blue eyes, Costa had Mama's brown hair and brown eyes. My brother and I had not spent much time together and I was looking forward to his stay.

"Costa!" I waved to get his attention.

"Hello, Christo!" and his tired figure broke into an immediate run. "I haven't seen you in such a long time!"

We shook hands, then embraced, our faces wreathed in broad smiles. He was wearing his best clothes: his only white shirt and a jacket Mama had made for him. Nothing was held back in our reunion.

Reaching for his duffel bag, I said, still grinning, "Come, I'll take you to my apartment. I have the evening off so we have time to get you situated. Then we will go out for dinner."

Costa was fifteen years old and thrilled to be in Constantinople with me. "I can't believe I'm here!" he exclaimed over and over, his voice laced with excitement. "You know, Christo, this is the first time I have ever left our home!"

"Is that so?" I asked him in mock surprise. "Well, you look so much a man of the world, I would never have known that!"

Costa laughed good-naturedly at my teasing. His face was full of wonder as he took in all the sights on the walk back to my apartment. A waiter's wage at the Pera Palace was a significant raise in pay for me. Besides the luxury of a sink and bathroom with a shower, the apartment had a closet and chest for Costa's clothes and I had bought him his own bed, placing it against the wall at a right angle to mine. In the middle of the room was a small table with one chair. I sat in the chair and signaled Costa to sit on the bed. "My own bed!" he exclaimed.

"Tell me," I began, eager for news of home, "how are Mama and Papa and everyone?"

"They are fine," Costa said. After the updates on family, he hesitated. "You know, big brother, there are not many Greeks left on Imbroz anymore. More Turks are coming over from Turkey and homesteading abandoned properties that Greeks have left behind. The Turks are the police and the government. They control every aspect of our lives. Slowly they will take all the property, Papa says. But," he added brightly, "a few of Papa's friends have been talking with the Turks and there is some discussion of reopening a Greek school on the island."

"And the churches?" I asked.

"Some of the churches have closed. They have been looted and the graveyards desecrated, Christo. But ours is still open."

"And Bishop Iakovos...is he well? Does he still visit Papa?"

"Yes, Christo, and he and Papa still talk late into the evening about the ancient philosophers, the Church, the Turks—about everything, you know, just as they used to." I smiled. It was reassuring somehow to know that some things don't change.

"How are Uncle Demetri, Uncle Russo and Aunt Cleo?" I asked.

"They are fine. Your letters bring smiles to Mama's and Papa's faces, Christo. You are a celebrity, did you know that?" Costa spoke proudly, in a tone that was half-serious, half-joking. "I have thought about you for years, anxiously awaiting the day you would call for me, and now here I am! There aren't many who have left the island and become a success!"

I blushed a little at my brother's praise. "Is the money I'm sending home enough?" I asked next.

"We have enough to get by," he told me. "Papa and Mama make a little sewing clothes for the Turks and Papa still has a few gold coins, so we have managed." Costa looked at me gravely. "But last winter was hard. Most of Papa's sheep were stolen. We would not have made it without your help, and now here I am," he excitedly said.

"Did you ever doubt that I would send for you?"

"Of course not!" We both chuckled with joy.

"Let's go get something to eat," I said with a smile. "Aren't you hungry?" I asked, knowing the answer from a boy from Imbroz. "We've talked for over an hour and it's almost nine o'clock. We will have a treat, little brother. I will take you out to eat at a posh restaurant."

In all my years in Constantinople, I had only eaten out a couple of times, and never at a fine restaurant. Tonight I would treat both of us to dinner. We left the little apartment and explored the streets, with me pointing out everything of interest I could find.

"Look, Costa!" I exclaimed. "On the hill there you can see the Pera Palace and to the right, on the Golden Horn, is the Patriarchate.

"That's where you work?"

"Yes," I replied. "There are some beautiful Byzantine churches, too—the holy church of the Theological School of Chalki and the Cathedral of Saint Sophia. Some day I will show you. There, on the hill," I pointed, "can you see the tower? It's part of the old walls of Constantinople, built by Constantine. And just up the road is the Patriarchal Church of St. George, and on the hill by the Patriarchate is the Patriarchal Academy of Constantinople. It is amazing, Costa," I went on enthusiastically, "how historic this city is—for both Christianity as well as the Hellenic tradition. Even with so many of the ancient relics lost and destroyed, the city is still steeped in Christian tradition. There will be time to explore during the day."

Costa's eyes were as wide as saucers as he took in the sights around him. "Would you like to have dinner at the Park?" I asked my brother suddenly. "The Park is on the Asiatic side of the city overlooking the Bosphorus and Sea of Marmara, and it's the equal of the Pera Palace, where I work."

Costa hesitated. "I've never eaten at a restaurant," he said.

"Don't worry, little brother, you are with me and you will enjoy it!" I was enjoying playing the host, and perhaps the earlier praise made me want to live up to—to surpass—expectations. Although the Park Hotel shared the culinary limelight in Constantinople with the Pera Palace, in terms of lavish opulence of marble and crystal, nothing could quite rival the Pera Palace. Nevertheless, waiters often moved back and forth between jobs at these two fine restaurants, and I had heard the food at the Park was also excellent. What better time to sample it than with my little brother on my night off?

"I'll order for you, Costa. The menu is in French."

"In French!" Costa exclaimed. "I didn't know you spoke French!"

Again a rush of pleasure filled me. I had worked hard and was proud of my accomplishments. "You have to speak French to be a waiter at a place like the Pera Palace or the Park Hotel," I explained. "The food is French, you see, and—" I broke off abruptly and pointed to the right. "Look, there are the docks where you came in today. On the other side is the Asiatic section of the city. That means we're not far from the Park—over there, see it? It overlooks the water." Within a few minutes we were walking up to the entrance.

Taking in the glitter and ornate dress of diners around him, suddenly Costa hung back. "Big brother," he said uncertainly, "maybe I'm not dressed up enough to go here."

"Of course you are, Costa," I encouraged him. "You look fine, truly."

The maitre d' greeted us with a smile. "Good evening, gentlemen."

"Good evening," I responded giving him a respectful bow. In a flash of recognition, I realized that I knew him from the Pera Palace. He had worked as a waiter when I was a busboy. Evidently, he came to the same conclusion.

"You have been here before?" he asked, looking at me carefully.

"No, sir. I am a waiter at the Pera Palace."

"Ah! of course. What is your name?"

"Chrysostomos, sir," I said. "We came to have dinner."

"Certainly, right this way gentlemen." We received a little extra attention—an unadvertised perk between waiters.

I could tell Costa had no idea what to do. After we were seated, I told him in Greek, "Costa, take the napkin and put it on your lap. Also, when the salad arrives, use the outside fork. It's a salad fork, and the outside spoon, the round one, is the soup spoon."

"Oh, yes, I see. A white table cloth! Well, we are certainly living well." Costa gazed at me, wide-eyed. "Thank you for bringing me here, big brother."

"Costa, you don't have to thank me!" I told him warmly. "Just enjoy your meal. I wanted to give you a special treat." That evening we certainly enjoyed our dinner. We had soup, tossed salad and veal, followed by strudel au pomme for dessert. Costa ate everything, including a second serving of bread. The foods were rich and new and well prepared—certainly a treat.

After dinner we walked along the Bosphorus for a few blocks. "Tomorrow morning I'll take you to Mr. Pappadopoulos at the Constantine School for Tailors. It's supposed to be one of the finest schools in Constantinople. Papa and I want you to have a trade so it won't be as difficult as it has been for me. I'm taking the morning off."

Costa couldn't thank me enough. "I don't know how I will ever repay you, Christo. What you are doing for me, I will never forget. One day I will make it up to you, I promise."

"You are my brother," I reassured him. "Brothers don't have to thank each other." I meant it, too. In fact, it was good to have Costa with me in Constantinople. It was the first time in years that I had some family around me. Costa was only five when I left for Samothráki Island, and except for two brief visits home, I had not spent any significant time with any of my family, except, perhaps, Katina. Over the next few weeks, despite our busy schedules, Costa and I got reacquainted with each other.

"Big brother," he said one day, "I don't know how you work so hard! You leave at dawn and you don't get back till ten o'clock at night, day after day after day. I truly don't know how you do it!"

I laughed. "It's not as bad as that," I told him. "I have half-days off on Sunday and one full day a month. Besides, next summer when you finish school I plan to take a week's holiday and go home with you."

"Still," he said, shaking his head, "the hours are so long—"

"Costa, the money is very good where I work, and we need the money—for school, for the family. It is not so hard when you have good reason to work." As I said it, I realized just how true it was. Somehow, knowing that others depended on you, needed you, inspired you to do more than enough to just get by. For me, there was little pleasure in leisure time doing nothing, and great pleasure in advancing myself, working for security, for myself and my family—no matter what the cost to my leisure time. It struck me suddenly as funny that leisure time to me was usually spent thinking of all the things I could or should be doing!

In the next sixteen months that Costa lived with me while becoming a tailor, I developed a deeper affection and appreciation for my little brother. We talked freely of the difficulties Mama and Papa experienced aging on the island under the Turks. The Turks had taken the town records, including the property deeds. It would be difficult, Costa told me, for Mama and Papa to verify their right to their property if the Turks ever contested their ownership. So far Papa, and a few of the old-timers who had deeper roots, had survived Turkish occupation, but it was not easy when so much of the population had been uprooted. Many properties were abandoned and had been converted to Turkish ownership without recompense to the rightful owners. These things I already knew, but until now I had been shielded by my family from the direct extent of the hardship. Nonetheless, I was powerless to do anything but work and be productive.

These concerns faded into a discussion of my longing to travel to America. Although I did not know how my dream would be realized, I knew it was my destiny.

9

The Work Battalions: Ameletaburu

Without a declaration of war and without warning or justification of any kind, civilians, including women and children, are being ruthlessly murdered... Nations claiming freedom for themselves deny it to others.

—Franklin D. Roosevelt
Congressional Record, App. 75 Congress, 2 Sess., pp. 20–21

By now I had been a waiter for over two years and even at twenty I was still the youngest waiter at the Pera Palace. Yet I was always assigned to prime stations, often requested by many of our best customers. My financial freedom was gratifying, but even as my personal future looked increasingly bright, storm clouds of war were brewing over Europe.

In the spring of 1938, Hitler "reunited" Austria with Germany. Great Britain's Prime Minister, Neville Chamberlain, in a misguided attempt to appease Hitler, signed the Munich Agreement later that year ceding the Sudatenland to Germany, while promising "peace in our time." As time passed, it was becoming apparent that Hitler was not likely to be contained by appeasement. Having created an unquenchable nationalistic fervor, Hitler was primed to invade his European neighbors in his quest to mimic the Roman Empire. Europe braced for war.

Although an ally of Germany in World War One, Turkey seemed committed to her neutrality this go around. In Constantinople, Costa had graduated from tailoring school and would soon return home to Imbroz. I would accompany him for my first visit in over three years. I had arranged to take my week's leave for the journey. For the past year I had paid all the expenses for both of us, including Costa's schooling. I had also sent money home and managed to save a few pounds. Before the trip I was able to buy gifts for Mama, Papa, and my sisters.

"Costa, soon you will be a tailor," I told him, "and will make a better living. You'll have a trade and one day, when I'm in America, I'll send for you. In America, a man is free to make out of himself as much or as little as he wishes. You will do well there, I know."

"Is America a Christian nation?"

"Yes, Costa."

"Good! No more Mohammedans," Costa smiled. "When you go to America and become rich and successful you will need a good tailor!" We both laughed. Suddenly, he turned serious. "Please send for me, Christo. Promise you won't forget me."

On a Monday morning that summer Costa and I boarded a cargo ship that made a brief stop at Gallipoli and then anchored offshore at Imbroz. There, once again, Captain Koutris picked us up and rowed us ashore. Once again, I saw the deep lines in Captain Koutris' leathery face that reflected the ravages of his long, hard life, a life made so much harder by the Turks.

The week passed uneventfully with none of the pomp or celebration of previous trips home.

My sisters greatly appreciated their presents. My parents, now in their mid-sixties, moved familiarly through days a little more slowly. The specter of war was taking a very heavy toll on Papa. He feared the Turks might use the war to revive the horrific Christian persecution. The lines in his face were the only evidence of the smile that used to come so quickly. Witnessing the toilsome, meager lives on Imbroz gave me a renewed resolve to move forward, away from the labored and numbing monotony of the Turkish occupation—such a sharp contrast to the robust pace I had thrived and matured in while serving in the Agatha Christie Ballroom. My departure from home was emotional and anxious. I began to realize that although my considerable energy could change much, there was nothing I could do to change Imbroz or my parents' plight. Nonetheless, what I could do I did without reservation. I had to move on.

* * * * *

In Constantinople, my busy schedule was shortened. Winter arrived early. The clouds of impending world conflict had significantly darkened horizons throughout Europe. Complacency was quickly becoming transfused with chaos and fear.

One night, I was summoned by the maitre d' and told to report to the head bellhop to assist in moving a newly arrived guest and his entourage into the hotel. Half-a-dozen limousines were out front along with two bellhops and myself to unload them. Then I saw him: Ahmet Zagu, otherwise known as King Zog, the King of the Albanians. The last Ottoman king, he had abdicated his throne for a handsome payment in gold bars by Mussolini. Even though the walk to the hotel safe was merely one hundred feet from the front door, it took the three of us almost two hours to unload the wealth of Albania to a vault. Never underestimate the price of an Ottoman king. Each trip with every bar we were accompanied by a bodyguard. When all the gold was safely stored, the King spoke to one of his aides, who then approached us giving each of us one Turkish pound. After all that gold, it seemed almost a pittance.

However, I felt I was participating in history. King Zog, a last artifact of the Ottoman era, his departure from Albania served as another reminder of the countless crimes and crises unfolding across Europe and spilling into the Balkans. King Zog was an anachronism, yet at the same time quite at home in modern Turkey. On April 7th, 1939, Mussolini declared Albania an Italian protectorate.

Although Zog fared well, the strengthening winds of war would soon come battering against my door. In the meantime, the Pera Palace sustained me. My waking hours were devoted to its smooth operation and my life revolved around it. I was immersed in a palace, serving the rich and famous of Constantinople, surrounded by a world of excessive poverty. I relied on diligent performance alone to keep myself from joining the growing masses of the impoverished and destitute. In my chosen field of serving others, I had become quite accomplished. The world around me, enveloped in lethargy, appeared inattentive.

In September of 1939, World War II erupted in the vicious overrun of Poland by the Nazis, and no one knew where they would strike next. Great fear and uncertainty gripped the people of Europe. Although Turkey would remain neutral, a compulsory draft was enacted among young Christians, and the Turkish Army had already called up some of the boys remaining on the island. The Christian inductees were placed in the infamous work battalions and treated most harshly by the Turkish army. Under the veil of the war, the work battalions served as concentration camps for young Christians, much the same fate of Jews and others in Germany.

The work battalions were operated in the genre of the Turkish military, under the Young Turks who, consistent with their Ottoman predecessors, had elevated Christian persecution to the level of extinction. Although distancing himself from the Christian slaughters, Atatürk had still formed the work battalions in the mid-1930's. Young Christian men and their families openly wept when they received the conscription notices to report to the battalions.

It was in the fall that a notice arrived from the Turkish government. With shaking hands, I read. It simply stated that I was to report to Ankara to serve in the Turkish Army. I knew what it meant. It meant the same as it did to thousands of other young Greek boys: conscription into the dreaded work battalions. By now, it was no secret that these camps were nearly equivalent to genocide, a convenient means to exterminate the young, healthy Christian male population. Papa's worst fears were about to become reality.

On the eve of my report to Ankara, I felt sullied by the realization that the ten years of working my way up to a decent standard of life for myself and my family were about to be dashed into oblivion. To bootstrap myself out of poverty and hardship now seemed nearly hopeless. I had been plucked from the solid security of the Pera Palace, and had regressed into the dark world of Christian persecution. As I went through the motions of my duties at the Pera, the glitter and passion I had always felt from its marble walls were gone, replaced now with a suffocating desolation so deep and black it had no beginning nor end.

I went through my duties that last evening at the Pera Palace like a robot, all life drawn from me—numb—my body simply going through the motions of living. Dinner service was finally over and only three parties remained in the ballroom. Andreas, the head waiter, beckoned me into a side dining room. I wearily crossed the room, with little curiosity about his purpose. There in the room stood most of the staff. Memet, Victor, Aristis, Andreas, even Theologos, a Greek from my island who had recently joined the staff as a busboy…they were all there.

"Christo, we wanted to show our support and let you know you will be missed by all of us," Aristis began.

Overwhelmed, I barely uttered 'thank you' when he went on, holding a shot of ouzo high above his head. "I propose a toast, wishing you luck and health and a speedy return to us!"

"Hear! Hear!" the entire staff shouted, their echoes merging into a murmur of personal well wishes.

Victor, the old French chef from whom I had learned so much, approached me. "You will be in my prayers, Christo. Take good care of yourself," he said earnestly.

"I will," I responded automatically.

Aristis, the waiter who had guided my "apprenticeship," tearfully embraced me. "God be with you!" he exclaimed.

After all of the embraces and handshakes, tears and words of support, we were parting company for probably the last time. The small group was dwindling as people headed for their homes, when Memet approached me. His eyes were bright as they held onto mine, and he silently extended his hand.

"Good-bye, Christo," he said softly. He grasped my hand for a very long minute, finally uttering, "I will keep your job. Please come back."

This was almost too much for me. The rest had been surreal, a round of good-byes, well-wishes, prayers for my safe return, much the same as any other job I had left. But this…Memet…my new reality came crashing down on me, this tempest that was now in control of my life. I would soon be dragged into the quicksand of Christian persecution, a world that would test my skills and ingenuity to the limit, a world from which many Christian young men would never return.

I don't even know if I said thank you to Memet. In a fog, yet composed, I bowed politely, arousing an echo of the small bow I had made to him on our first encounter years earlier. I don't even remember leaving the room, I only remember rushing outside to fill my lungs with the night air. I needed to breathe, just breathe and not think. I patted my forehead with a clean handkerchief and contemplated my uncertain twist of fate. Returning from my lost thought, I finally came back in from the dark, made arrangements with Theologos to send my final pay and a few valuables to my father, then went home for a last restless night.

I gathered my belongings the next morning, placed them outside the door, and took one last look at my apartment: the sink with running water, the private bathroom with plumbing, the electric light. I turned off the switch and closed the door. How quickly life can completely change, and all because of one letter.

* * * * *

With my relic coin pinned to my tee shirt and the rest of my belongings in a seaman's bag, I entered the military compound in Ankara. The Turks issued two shirts and two pairs of trousers. Army boots, however, were in short supply and the minorities seldom received them, even in northern Turkey where the temperatures often plunged to forty degrees below zero. The lack of boots was but a small part of a larger pattern of abuses inflicted on Christian minorities forced to serve in the Turkish work battalions as "soldiers." That was a joke…soldiers without boots, rations—not even weapons.

I presented my paperwork. A few minutes later, I was herded into a room with other inductees and in short order we went through the process of having our heads shaved, showering, delousing and dressing in army-issued shirts and pants. Shortly afterwards we were arranged in some semblance of formation and addressed by a Turkish gendarme.

"You are in the Turkish military," he shouted. "It doesn't matter where you came from, whether a village, an island or a city, you will serve the new Turkey. Any insubordination or treachery toward the Turkish government is punishable by death. Desertion is punishable by death. You will do what you are told for as long as you are told, no matter what you are told. Failure to carry out an order will be dealt with most harshly. Europe and much of the world is at war. Even though we are neutral, we have many enemies, and if need be, you will sacrifice yourself to defend our country."

Though we had all imagined the worst, no one among our group of inductees could imagine the difficulty of the ordeal before us. Over the following six weeks we would endure forced marches of 20, 30 and 40 miles, motionless sentry duty ten to twelve hours at a stretch, and physical beatings for any misstep. If a marcher collapsed, he would not be heard from again. We were also in the constant and slavish service of the Turkish "regulars" who, we had no doubt, would use the slightest infraction as excuse to shoot us dead.

After basic training, we were marched to the Russian border in northern Turkey, presumably to serve as "border guards." In reality we were forced to build roads with picks and shovels through the frozen mountainous border region. The march was over 200 miles and took almost three weeks over the rough terrain. To further complicate the difficulty, 1939 would soon see winter, and we were marching into its six-month-long teeth with wind chills as low as 40° below zero. All of us were inadequately dressed, and some even had shoes with holes in them, while the Turkish regulars had thick wool coats, fur hats, and sturdy boots. The fear and hardship I had known on Imbroz was nothing compared to the fear and misery I now lived every day. Those inadequately dressed died quickly from the harsh elements, while many others perished soon afterwards. It was a death march.

The reality was that we lived only to provide creature comforts and serve the Turkish regulars. Where I once served sumptuous meals to the rich and fashionable in luxurious surroundings, I now did the bidding of coarse men in brutal conditions, yet my waiter's skills served me well. Our battalion had about a half-dozen vehicles in which the Turks rode, while the Christians and other minorities marched on foot. At the end of each long day of marching, we would pitch pup tents and lay our tired, cold bodies onto the hard frozen ground. At dawn, we were aroused from a shivering sleep by the banging of a paddle on a steel pot. After a cup of strong Turkish coffee, we packed up the tents into our packs and continued the march. We bore the shovels and picks and saws, while the Turks bore the guns.

The Russian border is where I spent most of my enlistment; between the severe climate and the merciless Turkish regulars, survival itself was the principal daily chore. While World War II was raging throughout Europe, most of the casualties among Christian draftees assigned to the northern border were due to the conditions. Denied adequate shelter and clothing, Christian soldiers routinely froze to death at their posts guarding the border and the regulars' quarters. The Turkish regulars were housed in structures ranging from shanties to the near palatial, determined by rank and availability. No matter the accommodations, though, all the Turkish troops were provided with wood-burning stoves or fireplaces for warmth, and it was the minorities' toll to assure the daily supply of firewood. If someone has any questions about the Turks' civility, let him have joined the Turkish military to serve with the young Christian boys in the work battalions to know whether or not the Turks are truly barbarians.

While the Turks were relatively warm and comfortable, we lived in two-man pup tents with a shortage of blankets. We insulated them with dirt when we could chop through enough of the frozen crust, but more often with brush in a feeble attempt to provide some thermal retention. Over the course of time, these small tents frequently served as coffins for many of the young Christian conscripts.

For centuries the Turks had tormented the Christian population in Byzantium, yet nothing in time compared with the tortures wrought by the nihilistic Young Turks in the twentieth century. Religious intolerance in this region had been recorded in Christian blood for centuries, yet it was the Young Turks who systematically extinguished the Byzantine and Christian culture from Asia Minor. During the first quarter of the century, the Mohammedan Turks actively practiced ethnic cleansing of the Christian population. Though the genocide of Christians had stopped two decades earlier, during the Second World War the Turkish government still viewed young Christian conscripts with preferential malice as highly expendable. The days I spent in the far northern reaches of Turkey were the roughest of my life, but I had been prepared for hardship.

"That ought to do it, Christo. I've packed dirt on the outside. That should keep us warm."

"Yes, Gregory, I hope. I pray for us," I replied.

"You know, Christo, the Mohammedans kill dogs because they believe a dog revealed Mohammed's whereabouts. They also revere spiders because they believe a spider wove a web to protect Mohammed."

"I believe it," I responded, not at all surprised by any of their oddities.

My tent-mate was a young Greek conscript from Telenos, the island adjacent to my Imbroz. We were both twenty-one years old. He didn't have a pair of shoes when we began, and I had offered him my extra pair. They were too small for him, but they at least offered some protection throughout the winter.

Little progress on the road we were to build was ever actually made, but the Turks never seemed to really care. They only cared that we got up in the morning, marched to the construction site, and banged picks into the frozen ground all day and every day.

"It is so cold, Christo."

"I know. Let's hurry," I said to Gregory. "We can go to the fire and warm up."

"If they're able to get one going," he replied.

We worked quickly in the frozen ground of the tundra using the backs of our shovels as ineffective picks.

"Look! They got it going!" We hurried toward the fledgling flames on frostbitten toes with shivering breath. Although I was dressed better than most and wore socks, heavy shoes, gloves, army-issue jacket, shirt and pants, the frozen air and wind pierced my clothing, my flesh, like a thousand knives. I was one of the lucky ones. I had a thick wool scarf that Mama had made me that covered the lower portion of my face and ears, up to the army-issue cap that I pulled down over my ears. Many of the boys had no scarf, and they used whatever scraps of cloth they could find to wrap their faces and heads to keep them from cracking wide open.

"Look at that pot boil. What is this stuff they feed us? I think they put saw dust in it."

"I think it's oats, Gregory. I'll use my container, then give it to you."

Gregory nodded. I had a clean tin can that I would hold out to get my scoop of food.

"Next! Move along," called out George, the large cook. George looked Turkish, but was actually Greek. Usually at least one armed Turkish gendarme stood by watching. In a twisted perversion of justice and civility, the gendarme would shout out if it appeared that one minority soldier received more of the slop than another. No such protests were uttered if one of us was deprived of shoes or a jacket, or froze to death in our beds, however.

"Next...move along!" the cook droned on. Many of the boys held out their hands since they had no containers. I quickly ate the tasteless gruel, then washed my can and spoon with snow and gave them to Gregory.

"Thank you, Christo."

"Go quickly, before they pour out the rest of it," I urged.

Once packed inside our tent, we would often pull down the posts, allowing the tent to fall down on top of us for additional warmth then wish for snowfall to further insulate us from the frigid wind.

Much of the pre-dawn day before going to the road site was spent searching for wood and building fires in the Turkish quarters. Afterwards, we made the Turks tea and porridge. None of us minded this duty, which actually afforded the only time during a given twenty-four-hour period that we spent sheltered from the elements. Over time, because I was experienced at preparing and serving food, I was assigned to stand guard at the Pasha's—or general's—quarters, where, apart from the duty of actually guarding, I prepared breakfast and sometimes dinner for the general and other officers. This duty spared me from the farcical road construction detail and allowed me the luxury of two or three hours a day out of the elements. Sometimes, for appearance we were given an unloaded rifle. The Turks would not dare give a Christian conscript ammunition, for certainly he would shoot them. The rest of the time I spent caring for the livestock and trying to keep from freezing to death. It is very likely that the only reason I survived the Russian border was because I could prepare a tasty meal.

"Christo," my tent-mate Gregory said one bitter morning, "how can you get up? I'm so cold, I can hardly move." This was the second day of a blizzard that had stopped all roadwork and confined us to shelter.

Outside our tent the blizzard raged. I looked worriedly at Gregory, who huddled motionless under a thin blanket. I had noticed that Gregory was growing increasingly despondent of late, and I had seen too many others give up hope and succumb. Gregory was young and a good man with his whole life ahead of him. I just hoped it would be a long one. "I'll go up to the Pasha's house now and start his fire," I told my tent-mate. "You should come with me. It will be warmer there."

"I can't," Gregory replied. He peered at me from beneath his blanket, a scarf wrapped tightly around his head and ears. "I'm telling the truth," he said, "I'm too cold to move."

"If you stay here," I told him, "you'll freeze. Get up—you must keep moving."

"You go ahead," Gregory said, pulling his blanket completely over his head. "I'll come along later." He moved his legs a little to show me he would keep moving.

I knew there was little chance Gregory would make it to the Pasha's quarters without further prodding from me, yet my weakened intuition sent me to tend to my responsibilities. "I'll come back for you after I get the fire started," I told him as I wrapped a scarf around my own head and pushed out into the snow. My feet were numb as I struggled through the drifts. The howling wind buffeted me and snow whipped at my face, stinging my cheeks and eyes. The storm was so intense I could not even tell if dawn had broken.

I paused at the gate to the Pasha's quarters and felt around in the snow with my boot. The blizzard outside had extended the night's eerie darkness. Before the storm had struck two days before, I had made a stack of firewood and kindling and covered it with leaves to keep it dry. When the toe of my boot struck a log, I kicked away the snow and collected an armload of wood. I was so numb, I had lost feeling in my hands, feet and face; I was beyond shivering. In fact, shivering would probably have been welcome because it would force movement through my body. I carried the wood to the house and pushed open a side door. The execution of my chore would temporarily insure my survival.

"Who goes there?" a Turkish gendarme named Osmond barked from a bedroom.

"Ch-Christo, sir," I replied, forcing the words from my frozen lips. "I've come to light the fire."

"Well, come in, then. Hurry up and close the door!"

"Yes sir, right away," I answered quickly, hoping that the gendarme wouldn't notice that I was early and send me away. I wasn't sure that I could last another hour if I were forced back outside.

It was cold in the Pasha's house, but at least the walls cut the harsh wind. First, I sought out a kerosene lamp to light the darkness. Striking a match with frozen fingers was a time-consuming chore. I then knelt by the hearth and clumsily arranged the kindling, my hands so stiff I could barely make them work. The wood was frozen and the fire was difficult to start. Eventually, however, I coaxed a few flames into life and fed them more kindling until I had a nice blaze going.

"I will make some coffee," I called out to the stirring soldiers.

"Forget that," a voice bellowed from a back room. "Tend to the animals before you tend to the coffee." The voice belonged to a sergeant, a Kemalist with no love for young Christian conscripts.

My heart sank at the thought of going out again into the elements. "Yes sir." I paused before the fire for as long as I dared, maybe a minute, absorbing a final breath of warmth before heading back out into the blizzard. Feeling had just begun to return to my extremities when, stepping into the cold, I was slapped once again by piercing blasts of frigid air.

The animals were in a shed about two hundred feet from the Pasha's quarters. Beside the shed was a haystack, now so completely covered with snow that only the handle of the pitchfork appeared above the drifts. I kicked away the snow as best I could and forked some hay into a wheelbarrow, which I had stood on end next to the pitchfork so I could find it. Then I cleared a short path and dragged the wheelbarrow into the shed. I fed the animals—three or four sheep, a goat, a donkey, two horses and a half-dozen chickens—breaking the ice in their water trough with a shovel to allow them to drink. Then I headed back toward the quarters, taking a quick detour to my tent to check on my friend.

"Gregory," I called, "pushing open the tent flap. "Come on, get up. I've started a fire in the house and you can help me with the breakfast." Although not permitted, Gregory direly needed the warmth.

Inside the tent I was greeted with silence. "Come on, Gregory," I persisted. "You'll freeze if you stay here. Besides, I've got sentry duty today and I may not be able to get back here. You need to come with me now."

"You go on, Christo," Gregory told me, his voice so thin with cold I could barely hear him. Beneath his blanket I could see that he was trembling. I reached down and touched his shoulder.

"Please, Gregory," I pleaded one more time. The winter had already taken the lives of several men, their heads split open like coconuts by the cold.

"In a minute," Gregory said. "You go ahead...I'll be right behind you." He sounded calm, and I reluctantly agreed to go ahead again without him on his promise that he would follow straight away. I had already been gone too long and would be missed.

In the frigid interior of the tent I felt my own strength fading. Hesitantly, I patted Gregory's shoulder one last time and left the tent to make the hundred-yard trek back to the Pasha's quarters. By the time I reached the kitchen door, I had icicles on my eyes, mouth and nose. I slapped at my face with a numb hand, kicked the snow from my boots and entered the house where I stoked the fire and broke the thin film of ice that had formed on the buckets of water I had brought in the day before. That done, I filled the kettle with water and set about making coffee and the morning porridge. My limbs began to sting with a welcomed soreness. I realized suddenly that today was December 15, 1939, my twenty-second birthday, and I reflected that I had spent most of my working life preparing and serving food—for Papa, Uncle Russo, in the club, at the Pera Palace and now for the gendarmes. It had served me well, for here on the Russian front, it put me in a job that provided me with adequate sustenance and some shelter. Yet my overriding attention was directed to surviving to another birthday.

The Turkish officers and regulars were rising now. I served the regulars at a small table in the next room, then I prepared coffee, porridge and biscuits for the Pasha. When I was done, I loaded the food on a tray, which I handed to the gendarme Osmond to take to the Pasha's room. Gregory still had not arrived, and I was very concerned, but I had to finish my duties before I could check on him

Some minutes later while I was scrubbing pots, the Pasha called out to me from his room. "Christo, bring me more bread and some cheese!"

"Right away, sir." I turned away from the pots and sliced some cheese and bread, which I arranged on a plate and carried to the Pasha's room. I paused outside the door to knock, then entered and served the plate to the Pasha with a respectful half-bow.

"Who has first watch?" the Sergeant Osmond bellowed as I left the Pasha's room. Standing guard was another form of senseless torment.

"I do, sir," I told him, "but I would like to check on Gregory first as he is not feeling well."

"Nonsense!" Osmond snapped. "Finish your work and stand your watch."

I simply nodded, betraying no emotion. "Yes sir," I said, and retreated to the kitchen.

After the officers finished breakfast I cleaned up the dishes, fed the fire again and made my way through the snow to the front gate with an empty rifle. I had gotten warm while preparing the Pasha's breakfast, and the slug of frigid air that greeted me when I left the house cut through me with renewed impact. Instead of standing at attention by the gate, I marched back and forth—three steps to the left, turn, three steps to the right, over and over again, worrying about Gregory and trying, to no avail, to keep my extremities from going numb. My eight-hour shift was torturous. Halfway through I was permitted a half-hour break, during which I was allowed to stand in the side doorway where, partially screened from the wind, I could drink coffee and smoke a cigarette.

Afternoon finally arrived with no discernable change in temperature since dawn. I waited an hour past my time for relief, but there was no sign of Gregory, and Sergeant Osmond would not permit me to leave my post to check on him. After a second hour passed, I finally got permission to check on my friend. With all the haste I could muster, mixed with a large measure of dread, I made my frozen way through the snow to the tent.

Though fearing what I might find, and with severe frostbite myself, I did not hesitate to pull back the tent flap. As I approached his form, the hairs on the back of my neck stood on end, for I knew in my gut what I would find. "Gregory?" I whispered in vain as I pulled back the blanket and revealed his face wreathed with icicles, a pallid, waxy mask of death.

"Oh, Gregory," I sobbed and offered a prayer to God as I covered his lifeless face with the blanket.

I was so cold and tired myself, I thought I would be next. Surviving another hour was all that was on my mind. I barely made it back to the Pasha's quarters to report Gregory's death to the sergeant. With an unexpected show of compassion—perhaps due to his having lost a second man who could serve creature comforts—Osmond ordered me inside the house.

"You may fix dinner for the Pasha and his officers," he told me, "and one of the regulars will stand watch until a replacement is found for Gregory."

That evening while I prepared and served dinner, I was overcome with grief for Gregory. I think I felt that if I didn't grieve for him, no one would know or even care that he had passed away on the Russian border. He deserved so much more than that. As soon as I could, I slipped away to the tent and removed his body, literally frozen stiff, and placed it near the livestock shed. Because it was impossible for me to dig a grave, I covered him with leaves and dirt as best I could. I made a small cross from kindling, placed it at his feet, and said another prayer over my friend before returning to the Pasha's quarters to wash the dishes and thaw. This would have to do until the weather broke. No one noticed my absence and, even less, the death of my friend. I don't believe I have ever felt more sad or desolate or alone than I did the night my friend Gregory lay lifeless in a coffin of snow by that little woodpile in the middle of a vast border wasteland. The frozen tundra, the Turkish persecution, the senseless loss of lives tested my Christian faith to the limit.

When the dishes were done that night, I was allowed to remain for a while in the house. I nodded my thanks and made my way to the warmth of the kitchen fire. I wrote Gregory's family to tell them what had happened. Though having warmed a bit while indoors, I was still numb with sadness. Gregory was one of many young Christians who froze to death in the service of Atatürk's new Turkey. The sort of callous, shortsighted and insensitive treatment that led to Gregory's death was typical of Turkish attitudes and policy toward the Christian minorities. The harsh conditions the Germans would encounter during Hitler's battle for Stalingrad in 1943 were something the work battalions on the border had already experienced during 1939 and 1940. I was one of the survivors of those two terrible winters. I don't know whether it was due to my faith, heredity, motivation, or my cooking, but during my last three months I was promoted to corporal and issued a pair of boots— rather anticlimactic if I may say so myself.

* * * * *

In the early spring of 1941, one-and-a-half years after entering the Turkish military, I was discharged and sent back to the army base at Ankara where I was given back pay of three Turkish pounds, the rough equivalent of three dollars. I was clearly being robbed by the Turkish authorities, but I was happy to be out of the work battalions. I was also handed a dozen letters to my family that were never delivered to them and was told they were lacking in postage. Turkish humor was no less cruel than Turkish reason. I wrote my family immediately, telling them of my discharge and asking them to write to me at the Pera Palace in Constantinople until I found a place to stay. I also posted the letter I had written over a year earlier to Gregory's parents on Telenos Island, as I felt sure they had not received any news of their son's death. I enclosed his Christian cross.

I was frail, underweight and malnourished when I finally returned to Constantinople to pick up the pieces of my life. I didn't know where I would stay or if I even had a job—much had changed. Yet my relief, my spirits, my aspirations, my enthusiasm stood in sharp contrast to my material conditions. I went at once to the Pera Palace where Memet apologetically explained new waiters had taken my old station, but he offered me a smaller, less desirable position, which was fine. I was so pleased to be back—to be alive!—that I didn't care. I happily accepted his offer, and went off to shop for some suitable clothes and find a room to rent with a stipend he had forwarded me, fully knowing that as soon as an opportunity availed itself he would restore me to my previous station. Afterwards, I walked to the Patriarchate to pray. I thanked God for watching over me and protecting me during my military "tour." I prayed for Papa and Mama, for my sisters and brother, for the inhabitants of my small island, for all the young Greek soldiers who had frozen to death, and for those who were still alive. I could never understand how men like the Turks could treat other men so cruelly. Man's inhumanity to man is a great mystery of evil.

While I prayed, I clutched the coin that Papa had given me so long ago and which I still kept pinned inside my shirt next to my heart. Many a night on the harsh Russian border laying face down and shivering, hands clutched to my bosom, I had held Papa's relic coin and prayed. Our Lord had seen me through.

I was twenty-three years old, and although physically weak from my ordeal, my spirits were high. As I prayed in the Patriarchate that day, I realized just how fortunate I was to have survived such atrocity. To have returned at all was a blessing from God; to have returned with my health and a job still waiting for me was enough to make me weak with gratitude. I do not think at that time I fully realized how much the hardships of my past had given me the will and endurance to face the challenges that awaited me.

Now, as an old man, I believe I should have been thanking God for the many hard lessons I was fortunate enough to master and build upon. The cruel Turks, the frozen tundra and the senseless loss of life underscored the period as well as the continuation of the religious persecution. The ferocity of this persecution led to the deaths of tens of thousands of young Christian boys in the work battalions on the Russian border.

To this day I still have the three Turkish pounds issued upon my discharge—the hardest money I ever made.

10
Dare I Dream?

Military alliances, balance of powers, Leagues of Nations all in turn failed, leaving the only path to be by way of the crucible of war.... If we do not devise some greater and more equitable system, Armageddon will be at our door.

—Douglas MacArthur
Today the Guns Are Silent

In April of 1941, after conquering most of Europe, Hitler's army rampaged through Greece on the heels of Mussolini's bumbling and nearly disastrous (for the Italians) invasion in late 1940, thus bailing out his incompetent ally. The time the Germans spent conquering Yugoslavia and Greece, delaying their attack on the Soviet Union by a month, would turn out to cost them victory at the gates of Moscow. Another month's good weather for the German tanks before the Russian winter set in and Stalin would have been forced to surrender. The world would have been a very different place.

Since the Italian invasion of Greece in October 1940, Turkey had found it increasingly difficult to maintain her neutrality. Although Turkey favored Germany and the axis powers, she limited her participation in the struggle to a war of espionage, most of which was centered in the Pera section of Constantinople. During the Second World War, the Pera Palace, at the hub of where East meets West, became a natural magnet for cloak-and-dagger activity of all kinds. It had already been celebrated in fiction by Agatha Christie's *Murder on the Orient Express*, and again as the inspiration for Rick's Café Americain in the film *Casablanca*.

Once again waiting tables, much of my time was spent tending to the needs of guests in the Agatha Christie Ballroom. The old chef, Victor, had retired. In his place now was a man named Ogaleak. Despite the fact he was in his mid-fifties and thirty years my senior, we quickly became good friends. A Russian Orthodox and once a high-ranking officer in the White Army, Ogaleak had escaped to Constantinople in 1919 when the Bolsheviks took control. He had learned to cook while working in the restaurants in Constantinople and had become quite accomplished, though, truth be told, he lacked the delicate touch of his French predecessor.

I had also become a fast friend with a new busboy, Regas, who had come from a different village on my island of Imbroz. Regas was my age. It was so good to be back in Constantinople! I was rapidly regaining my strength, probably sparked mostly by my unconstrained high spirits.

"Christo!" Ogaleak called out in perfect French, "we will have cream of asparagus soup for luncheon today."

"Okay, Chef, I will let them know—Regas!" I called, walking into the ballroom.

"Yes, Chrysostomos?" he responded in Greek.

"Let me show you the proper fold in the napkin...like this...see?"

"Thank you, yes."

"Very well, finish the luncheon set up."

"Yes, of course, Chrysostomos." Hearing Regas speaking my name spoken in the Greek of my birthplace suddenly brought back the memory of my first job at the Pera Palace only a few short years before, yet it seemed a lifetime had passed and now the roles had reversed.

Despite the war that still stormed in Europe and Asia, the hotel was usually filled to capacity. Secrets were exchanged over morning coffee and tea, and clandestine political agendas were often hatched in the cocktail lounge in the evenings.

On occasion when the maitre d' was out, Memet would allow me to seat the guests. Although I was only 23 at the time, I looked older and I suppose my conduct and excellent French made me seem more mature than my years. I had been forced to grow quickly from a little child. I had worked at the Palace long enough to understand how to exude the manner appropriate to such an elegant establishment. As a result, I was fortunate to be highly sought after by the regular clientele and was often assigned to special guests. Then, an event occurred which, together with the retirement of Victor and increasing competition from the restaurant at the Park Hotel, plunged us into a decline.

The evening was March 11, 1941. The British had just begun landing troops in Greece on March 3 to assist the Greeks in their successful resistance against the Italian invaders. The British Ambassador, George Rendel, had arrived at the Pera Palace for a scheduled meeting with the Turks, hoping to gain assurances of their continued neutrality.

It was a typical evening at the Pera—the socialites in theater attire waiting for the taxi; a British gentleman enjoying a leisurely smoke on one of the overstuffed chairs in the lobby; a weary traveler speaking in two or three broken languages trying to communicate with a bellhop; and the ever-present staff, from the elegant concierge to the Pakistani boys and the bell captain, watering potted palms, sweeping carpets, emptying ashtrays and spittoons, and assisting guests. The familiar dance of glamour and service was in full, perfect step, a dance all the performers knew to absentminded perfection. The Ambassador was part of tonight's scene, another important guest whose needs were being served.

The Ambassador checked into his room and, after ascertaining that all was to his liking, he headed for the cocktail lounge. Suddenly, an ear-splitting blast shook the entire building, and the world as we knew it tilted slightly, altering our lives while a million shards of glass rained down on a stunned throng of patrons and peers. A split second of suspended animation preceded panicked screaming as thick black smoke rolled through the lobby, into the corridors and out onto the street.

I was in the dining room at the moment of the blast, and I felt the floor beneath my feet shake violently, while dishes and silver went crashing off trays and tables. After a stunned second, I ran into the lobby, but the police and hotel security had already descended on the scene and blocked off the area. A rubble of beams lay toppled with shreds of finery, silk and velvet; brass rails jutted from the top of splintered studs; dust and glass littered the remains of the heavy brocade draperies. Arriving medics rushed around to the injured, most of whom stared blankly in shock or wailed in uncontrollable outbursts. I felt strangely calm as I looked upon the surrealistic scene. I hurried to get clean linens and hand towels for the attendants to care for the injured until the ambulances arrived. The blast had killed six people—including a porter who was a friend of mine—and injured seventeen. The Ambassador, still in the cocktail lounge, was unharmed.

A few days after the bombing, food service continued with little interruption, but it took months to repair portions of the internal and external structures damaged by the explosion. After that, nothing was the same. The impermeable stronghold of the privileged had been touched by the violence of the war that surrounded it. Its aura as an oasis had been irreversibly destroyed.

* * * * *

The years of war were taking a toll that was visible everywhere; even the opulent Pera Palace was showing wear and tear. The grand finery of the 1930's was gone, only its ghost remaining as the partiers and socialites painted their faces, donned their slightly worn costumes and pretended life was still grand and gay. The Pera Palace had lost its glitter for me, her decline seeming to draw Memet with her, and soon, after thirty years of service, he retired.

The Rendel bombing had prompted Ogaleak and Regas to take jobs at the Park Hotel. In late 1943, I decided to join them. It was time for a change.

The Park overlooked both the Bosphorus and Sea of Marmara and was sleek and refined in a less opulent way than the Pera. An Armenian Christian owned it, and he wanted me to assist the maitre d'. Once again, I focused on my work, but thoughts and prayers also went with my brother, Costa, who had been recently conscripted in the Turkish military.

The complexion of the world conflict was slowly changing to favor the allies. Tens of thousands of German soldiers had frozen and starved to death on the frigid tundra of Russia around Stalingrad the previous winter, but not before killing a million Soviet soldiers in the battle. The Germans were finding the Russians to be a most difficult foe on their own soil. The German war machine had buckled under a frigid Russian winter that I knew only too well from my work battalion service on the Russian border. Also in 1943, the Allies won the battle for North Africa, Patton and Montgomery defeating Rommel and his vaunted Afrika Korps. In late 1943, the Allies landed on the European continent and slowly kicked the Germans up the Italian boot, knocking Italy out of the war. It seemed only a matter of time before Germany would be defeated, and in June of 1944, the Allies launched an all-out assault on the beaches of Normandy and began to drive toward Germany. All men who thirsted for freedom were heartened.

The world had begun to change in anticipation, even before Germany finally surrendered. New alliances were frantically being forged and the Americans reestablished diplomatic relations with Turkey. As Germany grew increasingly weak, communism became the new threat, and, bordering Russia, Turkey became a strategic ally overnight.

During the two years I spent working at the Park Restaurant, I met and served many wealthy and politically powerful people, among them Mr. Ragip Baydur, the newly appointed Turkish Ambassador to America. One evening in December of 1944, on the eve of my 27th birthday, what was for him simply a typical dinner at the Park Hotel was for me a life-changing event.

"Christo," he said after he had been served his appetizer, "you understand, don't you, that I've been appointed to go to America to open the Embassy in Washington? As the new Turkish Ambassador I will be taking some people with me. Would you like to accompany me as my aide? I have spoken to your boss requesting permission to ask you. You would be in charge of planning my meals and entertainment schedule...."

He was speaking so casually that the full import of his words at first escaped me.

"To America?" I gasped.

"Of course, to America," Mr. Ragip Baydur chuckled. "Where else would Washington be?"

"But, I am a Christian," I said. It was all so absurd! Our eyes met. I saw warm anticipation of my response. Mr. Ragip Baydur had chosen me to wait on him before. You wait and wish for something all of your life, without a clue how to achieve such a monumental feat, and then, out of the blue, someone just hands it to you in the easy flow of an ordinary day.

"I can take whomever I want," he was saying. "I am offering you an opportunity…."

I never even heard his next words. *America! America!* was all I could think. My father's words from my childhood were ringing in my head: "No matter how, you go to America where you can make a life for yourself. America—where a man can be free…free…free."

I was struck speechless. I remembered myself as a young boy with Papa before I had left over seventeen years ago. I heard him urging me to go to America, and I remembered how I promised him that someday I would. A chill ran up my spine and a lump swelled in my throat. I had been hit full force with the mighty blow of fortune.

"We will leave in two weeks," Mr. Ragip Baydur went on, so calmly, as if the entire significance and import of what he had just offered me was lost on him! "We will go first by plane to Cairo and then by ship to New York. From there we will take a train to Washington. There will be others in the group. A chef named Ogaleak will be my cook. You will assist my secretary with my itinerary and in coordinating my meals and functions." He paused, looking at me in some amusement. "I assume you wish to go?" he asked.

"Yes, sir!" I exclaimed, finally finding my voice and bowing respectfully. "Yes, I wish to go with you to America!" I said with a respectful half-bow.

"Good," he nodded, "then it's settled. The pay will be twenty pounds a month, and of course you will have room and board at the Embassy. Do you have any problem with that?"

"No, sir, none at all!" I replied hastily, shocked at the notion that anyone could possibly have a problem with such an offer. Suddenly I realized that I was staring wide-eyed at Mr. Ragip Baydur, an ear to ear grin splitting my face. My cheeks and face flushed, I glanced down, struggling to retain some composure. At long last my ticket to freedom had arrived. I was going to America!

It was almost too much to comprehend. Seventeen long years after leaving my island home at the age of ten, my dream was about to be realized. After years of six- and seven-day workweeks, harsh service in the Turkish military, and long, endless hours waiting tables, I was about to seek my fortune in America—the land of freedom and promise. My childhood dream was about to be realized.

* * * * *

My thoughts were focused on America when I met Captain Koutris on what would be my last visit home. "Greetings, Captain Koutris," I called out enthusiastically as I disembarked the steamer and scrambled into the Captain's little boat. "How have you been?"

The Captain was more haggard and worn than ever, his docile, reserved facade increasingly showing his age and reflecting the oppression on my island home. We all had aged, I mused. Ignoring his beleaguered, beaten spirit, I nostalgically surveyed him. He had become such a welcome part of the fabric of my past, always there to transport me back home. His chiseled features and detached solitude did not readily lend themselves to the feelings of warmth, family and home that he had always evoked in me.

"I'm all right, Chrysostomos," he responded pleasantly. "How is life in the big city?"

"Everything is fine," I smiled. "And what news do you have for me?"

"Nothing is the same, Chrysostomos. At the same time, nothing changes here either." he answered in a philosophical quandary. "My daughter and son left long ago for Greece. Once I knew every person in Panayia, but now there are just a few old-timers. All that is left on the island are the ghosts of memories past." So that explained why the light had faded from the depths of his eyes. His family was gone. He was alone.

"What is your news, Christo?" the Captain asked me, then added, "Look at you. You are a grown man...your parents are so proud of you."

149

"My parents...tell me, Captain Koutris," I asked, "how are Mama and Papa?"

"Your father and mother are fine, Chrysostomos. Your father is known and well thought of throughout all the villages on the island. He is a good man. You must know that."

"I do know."

"Yes, yes, indeed he is," the Captain continued. "Do you remember when I took you to stay with your aunt and uncle?" *Yes*, my eyes gleamed with recollection. "You were so tiny at the time. You slept on the floorboards under an old blanket. Soon you will be going to America, yet you have the same smile and those blue eyes. Sometimes you put me in mind of your father. You have made many people proud of you."

There was nothing I wanted more than to be like my father, and Captain Koutris' words were gratifying. He was a man of great virtue and integrity. I had written to my parents about the Ambassador's offer, and by the time I reached Imbroz the entire island had heard the news. Everyone, it seemed, was proud that one of their own would go to America, but no one would be as proud of me as Papa and Mama. At that moment I realized that to the few remaining souls on Imbroz, my journey to America was an uplifting, heartening event. It reflected their hopes for the future. I smiled my thanks, then my gaze slid beyond the Captain to the shore. There, on the distant dock, I could just make out the silhouettes of Mama, Papa, Katina and Sultana waiting, as they always had, to greet me one last time. To my surprise, Costa stood there, too.

In the seventeen years that had passed since Captain Koutris rowed me to Samothráki Island, the truth was that much had changed, yet much had stayed the same. The surging, painful anticipation of my last visit home fled upon my arrival. The picturesque shoreline of Imbroz, the worn and splintered dock at Castro, Captain Koutris, the vivid images of Mama and Papa, all unchanged in will and spirit yet worn through the passage of time, stood like a picture and would soon be reduced to memory. The pleasure of my return to Imbroz was marred by its brevity.

In this winter of 1944, World War II was nearing its end. In the cold air on the dock, my family and I embraced once again. I held Mama and Papa together for a long minute, fully realizing that my short visit would culminate in good-byes that might be forever.

Although Imbroz had been spared the German conquest, as a Turkish island its economy had never recovered from the Turkish occupation over twenty years before. Its traditional material and spiritual glitter had long since been eclipsed by the withered subsistence economy.

No matter how hard life seemed on Imbroz, it was wonderful to be back on my island to see my family again. Since Costa had returned from his stint of military service—at long last, Greek Christians were finally being issued boots—he had become an accomplished tailor. In late 1943, the work battalions had been disbanded. Although not a picnic, Costa had not faced the life-threatening challenges I had during my stint.

Although Katina had many opportunities to continue her education on Samothráki, she chose instead to return home to help Mama and Papa. Their livelihood still came mostly from sewing and tailoring clothing for the Turks, and was supplemented by farming and the money I sent home.

I would be home for a short week before leaving with the Ambassador from Ankara to Cairo on the first leg of our trip. Papa, of course, could not talk enough of America. As I had long ago as a boy, I promised him again that once I was settled there, I would send for everyone. "You and Mama and Katina, Sultana and Costa," I told him my first day home. "I will bring you all to America."

Just as he had years earlier, Papa shook his head. "No, Christo," he said, "don't worry about Mama and me. We are old and will spend what time is left to us here on Imbroz. I cannot, I will not, leave my island, but your sisters and your brother are a different matter. There is nothing here for young people anymore. It is them you must think of, not Mama and me. If you can, they are the ones you must bring to America." He paused for a moment and placed his hand on my shoulder as I pondered the same words he uttered long ago. "Chrysostomos, Mama and I are very proud of you," he said. "When you go to America you will have opportunity…the opportunity to start a family and live your life in freedom and peace in a Christian country. These are the things you have worked so hard for, my son."

I looked at my father with great fondness, a look he returned in kind. I remembered with a pang the dimmed eyes of Captain Koutris and could not bear to think of Mama and Papa like that. The years had aged Papa. His hair and moustache were shot through with white, although his compassionate eyes and warm smile remained as I had always remembered them. When I think of my father, it is his face at that moment that comes to my mind.

"How have you and Mama been?" I asked him gently.

"We are fine, my son. We mind our own business and the Turks mind theirs. It's as if we've declared a silent truce of sorts." He smiled, then changed the subject. "Nothing under the sun stays the same, Chrysostomos, not I nor Mama nor Imbroz." Although nothing could halt the passage of time, Papa's immutable will and spirit always called to me. "Your Mama and I want to celebrate your new life in America," he continued. "We have invited everyone to join us this Sunday. All our friends will be here with us, your Uncle Demetri and Bishop Iakovos as well. It will be a true celebration of your new appointment with the Ambassador in America!"

"Papa," I blushed. "I'm going to be his butler, more or less. I don't think it's worth all the commotion!"

"Nonsense, Chrysostomos," Papa said proudly. "You are going to be the Ambassador's butler in America and we are proud of you! You will have a chance to make a life for yourself. There is nothing for you here—there is nothing for any of the young people here—and this opportunity is what you have wished for and worked for so long and so hard. We must celebrate your success, Christo. Allow us, if not yourself, that pleasure."

Papa was right. This was something well worth celebrating. It was a momentous occasion in my life, and I was as proud and happy as he was. Katina was also full of happiness and pride for me.

"Chrysostomos," she said later that afternoon, "let's go for a walk."

"All right," I nodded, "where to?"

"You will see," she said mysteriously, wishing to keep her destination secret. "Sultana, come with Christo and me. We are going for a walk."

Sultana happily joined us and we walked through town toward the church. "Where are we going?" I inquired again.

"You'll see" was all she would say. The brisk walk took over thirty minutes. On a hill about a mile out of town was the little one-room schoolhouse we had attended as children. It had existed for over forty years, and although classes were no longer held there, the building was still standing. This is what Katina wanted me to see. We walked up to the small porch and looked in the window.

"Christo, remember when Mama and Papa would send you with me to school and Papa would give us a kiss and wave us off from the front door of his store?" Katina asked fondly. "Mama would have me hold your hand because you were so tiny and not yet six. She made us follow the older kids for the longest time. Remember, Christo?"

"Of course I remember," I told her. "It's hard to believe how many years have passed. You were always the best in school, Katina. I always wondered why you didn't stay with it."

For a moment Katina was silent. Then she said, "After the Turks came and Mama and Papa sent me to Samothráki Island, Aunt Cleo and Uncle Russo encouraged me to continue in school. They made sure both of us attended school on the island, do you remember? But you would have none of it—"

"No," I said, smiling ruefully. "I wanted to go to work, but you stayed on in school for a while."

"I did," Katina nodded. "And Aunt Cleo and Uncle Russo wanted to send me away for more schooling. But I just couldn't, Chrysostomos. I couldn't stay away with Mama and Papa here with the Turks. It just didn't seem right, and somehow I really felt I had to come back to help Mama and Papa. It was my way to contribute, just as working was your way.

I knew what she meant and nodded sympathetically.

"But what about you?" she went on. "Uncle Russo promised you your own store if you stayed and worked for him."

"Yes, Chrysostomos," Sultana chimed in, "why didn't you stay?"

"I just wanted to go out on my own," I told my sisters. "It was such a difficult time." In truth, I knew, somehow, that if I stayed on Samothráki, I would never get to America, and I felt I could earn more money, be of more help to my family, if I went to Constantinople.

"You know, Christo, there were times we could not have made it without your support. Papa has lost everything but his Greek pride, and your selfless support allowed him to keep his self-respect. And you brought Costa to Constantinople so that he would learn a trade! If you had not paid for it, it would not have happened. You have done so much for the family."

"It was nothing. I did what I could," I shrugged a little self-consciously. "And God willing, I will do more as long as you need me," I added softly. "When I get to America, I will be in a better position to help..." my voice trailed off into the distance. "And maybe one day I will need help and *you* will provide it!" I said, flashing a wide grin onto Katina.

"Perhaps," Katina smiled. Then she changed the subject. "Papa doesn't have many sheep left," she said. "You know that most of them were stolen, but he has slaughtered a lamb for Sunday and Mama said she will make *galatobouriko* (a custard-filled pastry in a paper-thin dough) just as you like it. We'll have fun, Christo, just like old times!"

"Yes, like old times!" Sultana echoed. Poor Sultana never really knew those old times.

"It is so good to see you, to see all of you," I told them. "Don't worry, my sisters. In time I will bring you to America to find your futures!"

"Well, you had better keep your promise," Katina teased lightly.

"I will," I told her seriously, "and you will write to me with all the news. Hold nothing back, I want to know everything."

"I will," she told me. "It's a promise we always make each other. I will write you and you will write me back. Life and fate have not allowed our family to be together for long, and have stolen our youth from us, yet somehow we have remained closer than most families…and we always have our letters," she added in a resigned tone.

"Now there, our lives are in front of us…just beginning," I responded. Katina's heartfelt speech moved me, but I was too embarrassed to let her see that. Instead, I teased her a little as we turned and headed home. "You are so melodramatic, Katina!" I told her lightly. "We may not be together as much as other families, but that's life, I guess. And as you say, we always have our letters!"

When we returned home, Mama had chicken and rice soup and spinach pie for us. It was wonderful to taste Mama's familiar cooking again. The food brought back memories of childhood, and for a brief moment I imagined myself back in the days when Papa still had his store. I felt so safe and secure in those days, as if wrapped in a warm, soft blanket.

Mama and Papa had spared no expense for my homecoming. In addition to all the food, Mama had knitted me a handsome sweater and Papa had taken out three bottles of his best aged wine that he kept for special occasions. Considering the economic status of the island, a supper such as this—not to mention the celebration planned for Sunday—was a great luxury for our family. Yet in Mama and Papa's view, it simply befitted the occasion.

After dinner, I took my sister aside. "Katina, take this," I said, handing her an envelope.

"What is it?" she asked in surprise.

"Open it and see," I told her, and watched as she lifted the flap and withdrew a sheaf of Turkish pounds.

"Christo!" she gasped. "So much!"

"I've saved some extra money since my release from the army," I told her. "I really have no need for it. Most of my expenses will be paid for at the Embassy. Use some of it to help Papa with the house. The rest you'll need for food and essentials."

Katina held the money out to me. "But Christo," she started to protest.

"No," I said, pushing the money away firmly. "Truly, I have no need of it, but the family will, especially through the winter. Take it. Use it for them, and when I get to America, I will send you more."

"Thank you, little brother." Katina's voice wavered with emotion, her eyes filled with trust, her look with affection. I had told her over and over through the years that if I ever got to America I would send for her, and I knew she believed me. Still, she wanted to be reassured. This is what she would cling to after my departure.

"Promise me," she said.

"I promise," I told her. "Just like always."

"Yes," she smiled, "just like always."

The next day Uncle Demetri came by and looked me over. I felt sadness that in a few fleeting moments I would be leaving once again. There was a knock at the door. It was the Bishop.

"Glad you could come!" Papa said while bowing to kiss his extended hand.

Bishop Iakovos moved toward me, "Chrysostomos...I have walked from Glyki to wish you the best and say my own farewell." His hair and beard had turned completely white. I bowed and touched his slightly gnarled yet scented hand to my lips.

"Thank you, Your Grace."

Papa handed out glasses of wine, and a moment later Bishop Iakovos offered a toast.

"To Chrysostomos, for his hard-earned and cherished opportunity in accompanying the Ambassador of Turkey to America. More so for being our ambassador from Imbroz and representing us well wherever he may go. Let God be with him and protect him and allow him the freedom and happiness that he has toiled so long to find. Let him rest assured that our prayers, our hopes and thoughts will be with him even though he will be far away."

My family and friends stood and raised their glasses. "To Chrysostomos!" they repeated.

The Bishop wasn't done. After a deep draught of wine, he continued. "I have something to say to all the young generation of which Christo is the most shining example." He paused and looked somewhere deep inside his soul. "My generation has failed you. During the first decades of your life we have unleashed the horrors of poverty, death, uprooting, destruction and unconscionable subjugation, a world in disarray. Yet, wherever you set down roots, remember us kindly for we have also passed to you intact the mantle of your heritage as Orthodox Christians. Hold your head high and forget the persecution and subjugation we have endured at the hands of these primitive people. Rise above them and make a good way for yourself. You have learned our ways and gained spiritual enrichment. This is not a fleeting thing, like material possessions. Your heritage is your legacy. This is our gift to your generation. It will be with you all of your days, and you will hand it down to the next generation as we have handed it down to you. God bless and protect you, Chrysostomos, and all the children of your generation. May God allow you to travel your time on earth in peace and remember your lessons well. With God at your side, you can achieve anything. Amen!"

"Amen!" the replies resounded.

"God bless this food of which we are about to partake. Allow it to give us physical strength as well as spiritual ardor."

The few family members and friends present embodied the true keepsakes of my short, intense life on my island home. The food completely covered the wooden tabletop like an artful tapestry. The aroma of the lamb, the rice pilaf, garden salad, oven warm bread, spinach pie and other food filled the air. We had just begun to eat when there came a loud repetitive knocking at the door.

"Yes, may we help you?" Papa called in Turkish as he and Mama both got up from their chairs. Papa peered past the door ajar and I could only make out the sleeve of an unfamiliar coat.

"We have come for the one called Bishop Iakovos," came the Turkish reply as the door was forced open and Papa jumped back. An armed Turkish soldier stood in the doorway, four other soldiers behind him, guns pointed.

The one in authority spoke again. "The one they call Bishop Iakovos, he must come with us," the cold, impassive eyes trolled the small company.

"But why?" asked Papa, his voice unusually shrill.

His searching eyes narrowed and fixed on Bishop Iakovos as he pushed Papa aside. "Certain bishops have been making subversive statements against the Turkish State. They are being taken into custody," he said as he strode purposefully toward the Bishop.

"He is a holy man!" cried Papa. "He is our spiritual leader! Of what possible threat can he be to the Turkish State?" Papa was visibly shaken and nervously tugging at the soldier's sleeve as he pleaded. I had never seen him like this.

Two of the other gendarmes had moved in and pointed their guns at Costa and me as we rose from our chairs, instinctively trying to shield Bishop Iakovos from the squad leader. Uncle Demetri was pushed aside as if he were nothing more than a pesky fly. We were clearly no match for five armed soldiers.

"There, there, Yanni," Iakovos spoke calmly. "I must go with these men. They will not harm me," he reassured Papa as he moved toward the one in charge. Bishop Iakovos was offering us comfort in a scene that was so bizarre it felt as if it were happening in a dream. None of us could move. We were helpless as we stood there while the leader roughly secured Bishop Iakovos' wrists with leather straps. "Bishop Iakovos, you are under arrest," he said as he tied.

"Yanni, you all must finish your dinner…and Chrysostomos, remember what was said." I gave him a slight nod of my head as the gendarme pushed him through the door.

The sound of Mama's voice startled me, "Five big Turkish soldiers to arrest one old man! My how brave you are!" she nearly sobbed the words out. They glared at Mama, and I leapt to my feet as one of them took a menacing step toward her.

"Be careful," he said through clenched teeth in a low growl. Uncle Demetri moved instinctively between them and Mama backed away. Another Turkish gendarme bent down to shackle the old man's feet, but the leader signaled him away with a wave and a tilt of his head. "Come with us," he ordered Iakovos.

"Oh, Your Grace," Mama sobbed.

"I will be fine. God bless you all," Bishop Iakovos said as they shoved him through the door. As he turned to leave, one of the soldiers grabbed a leg of lamb off the platter and bit off a large mouthful. "No sense letting it go to waste," he said through a laughing mouthful, his sinister eyes challenging any of us to protest. Then he turned and followed the rest out the door, the leg of lamb in hand.

Mama began to cry as they left, burying her head on Papa's shoulder as they stood with the heavy door between them and their dear friend. "Let's do as Iakovos wished and return to our dinner for Christo. There is nothing we can do for the Bishop," Papa said.

Still as if in a dream, we all moved back to the table and sat down. No one spoke, and we passed the rest of the meal in solemn silence. Yet the Bishop was in our prayers. What had been a joyous celebration was now a silent and somber meal. It hardened my view that the Turks were incorrigible barbarians. They had always been and still were. These views would have to be buried very deep within me, however, if I were to survive the trip to America as butler to the Ambassador of Turkey. What an irony that the ambassador of my oppressor would be the ticket to my freedom.

The arrest of the Bishop of Imbroz at the end of 1944, twenty-one years after the Young Turks had taken control of our island home, underscored the ongoing unchallenged persecution of Christianity.

The year 1945 would see the Allies win in both the European and Pacific theaters. The end of war was in sight, but the extreme discrimination that was endemic throughout Turkey was not.

My Photo Album

Archbishop Iakovos, Primate of the Americas

Papa Jon and
Mama Theopisti

Papa Jon and
daughter Katina

School in the second grade on Imbroz under Turkish rule. I'm second from the right in last row. Only two more years and I'm done with school!

Left to right: Sultana, Mama, Papa, Katina, and me crouching, at home on Imbroz before my going into a Turkish "work battalion."

Uncle Russo and Aunt Cleo with family and friends

Katina and Costa
in 1947

Katina, Papa and Sultana in 1947

Papa's dear friend, old Bishop Iakovos of Imbroz, was carted off by the Turks to a forced labor camp. Jimmy Coucouzes, who eventually became Primate of the Americas, took his name.

Ataturk's soldiers entering Smyrna in September of 1922

Smyrna burns

Smyrna destroyed

Destruction and looting
of Greek shops

The 13th century
monastery of Choras
is today a mosque

Greeks of Asia Minor
massacred by Turks
between 1915–22

Mourning the slain

Grandfather and grandson
slain together

The church of
Taxiarchis turned into a
liquor storehouse

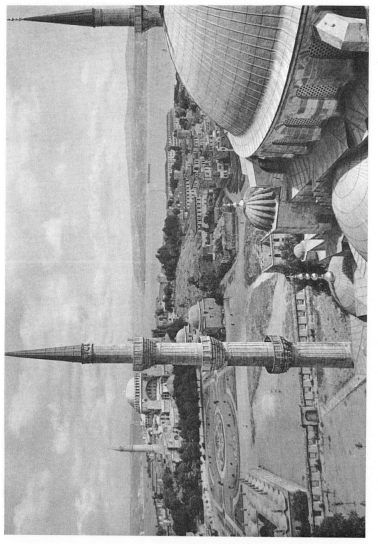

Constantinople: Hagia Sophia in distance faces the Blue Mosque of Sultan Ahmet in foreground. The direct opposition of Mohammedanism to Christianity can be stated no more clearly.

Elenitsa (left) and
Eugenia Spano in
Cumberland, Maryland,
just before the wedding

Bread Crumb

Our honeymoon in 1948 at Taki's and Sultana's apartment in New York

My Elenitsa and my first car, a Chrysler Windsor I bought from Vince Allan who
remained a friend and neighbor for over 45 years

Me (left) at the excellent Rive Gauche restaurant in Georgetown in Washington, D. C., 1956

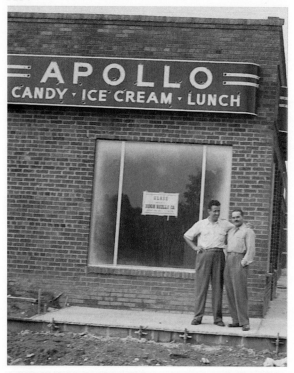

The Apollo, my first restaurant in America, signified, finally, freedom to do what I wanted.

(Left to right) Elenitsa's Uncle Chris; her father, Anton; Elenitsa; her Uncle Charlie; and in front my two little boys, Anthony and Jon, 1954

Elenitsa and the kids at the Tastee Freeze in Ocean City, Maryland, 1955

Here is the recipient of the Tastee Freeze award on his first vacation ever, and in Acapulco, Mexico, no less!

My friend and mentor, Ogaleak, and his new bride surrounded by my family and me. He was an officer in the White Russian Army, a great Christian and a great chef.

My childhood friend from my island of Imbroz, Primate of the Americas, Archbishop Iakovos, in 1991

Anthony's, my bread and butter and joy

Bernard, my employee for thirty-six years

Jon, my second eldest, continuing the tradition

Ianthe, my "Cookie," her husband, Steve Yeatras, and my little grand-daughter, Krislyn

A big catch for the little island boy

Showing my grandson, Brian, the ways of the sea

Fishing with my buds

My beautiful azaleas

My son, Anthony, his wife, Lee Ann, and their children (left to right),
Ashley, Brian and Katelyn in 1993

My slugger, Brian, with his grandpa

Grandpa with Ashley—"Let me squeeze the juice out of you."

Katelyn, my Miss America

The dining room table filled with family—what I live for!

The pilgrimage to Israel

Tracing the footsteps of Jesus at a Roman ruin in Israel

Sultana and Taki with Elenitsa and me 40 years after our honeymoon in New York—how time flies!

Bread Crumb

PART II
The New World

11
Flight to Freedom

In an age of fops and toys,
Wanting wisdom, void of right,
Who shall nerve heroic boys
To hazard all in Freedom's fight,—
Break sharply of their jolly games,
Forsake their comrades gay
And quit proud homes and youthful dames
For famine, toil and fray?
Yet on the nimble air benign
Speed nimbler messages,
That waft the breath of grace divine
To hearts in sloth and ease.
So nigh is grandeur to our dust,
So near is God to man,
When duty whispers low, Thou must,
The youth replies, I can.

—Ralph Waldo Emerson
"In an Age of Fops and Toys"

The time had arrived. In late February of 1945, the Ambassador's itinerary was set. Since returning to the mainland, I had been working with the Ambassador's entourage in preparation for our trip to America. We would depart Ankara by plane for Cairo where we would stay for ten days. Then we would board a passenger steamship bound for New York flying the flag of the Isthmian Steamship Company, and within a month we would be in the New World.

We had not had any news of Bishop Iakovos since his arrest, and we didn't know if he was alive or dead. Bishop Maxim, Metropolitan of Chakidonos had also been arrested, as well as two members of the Holy Synod, the ruling body of the Church at the Patriarchade. Rumor had it they had been imprisoned in Bursa.

News of the murder of another cleric, the desecration of another grave or the vandalization of another church, was by now commonplace, and had been ongoing throughout the century, varying only in degree of frequency or depravity. Even though the chaos of the world war was winding down, nothing seemed to bring civility to the Turks.

Our journey to America almost ended before it began when we encountered a potential calamity on the first leg of our trip. For the two-hour flight from Ankara to Cairo, Ambassador Husegyrn Ragip Baydur and his entourage boarded a twin-engine passenger plane that held about forty people.

It was my first trip on an airplane, and I watched in fascination as the ground fell away beneath us, clutching the arm rests of my seat, relaxing only when we reached our cruising altitude. After our ascent I noticed that my window was being showered as if it were raining. When I glanced at the porthole across the aisle, however, the window glass was dry. Could it be raining on one side of the plane and not on the other? I peered out a porthole three seats up on the same side of the plane as mine and saw no rain. Alarmed, I turned to Ogaleak, who sat across the aisle.

"Look at the rain on my window," I said, but his gaze showed he did not understand its significance.

"Oh, Christo," he responded, shaking his head. "I'm sure it's nothing—just a little moisture."

"I know that," I said impatiently. "But why just on a few windows?"

Then I realized that the rain-splattered windows were directly behind the right wing of the plane. It suddenly occurred to me that the droplets might not be water.

"Stewardess!" I called to the attendant who stood with her back to me several rows forward. "Madame, please!"

She turned and I gestured her closer. "See the rain hitting my window?" I asked.

"Yes," she nodded.

"Well, it's not rain. I believe it's gasoline."

"Oh, I don't think so, sir," she smiled.

"Look at the windows in front of the wing," I told her a little frantically. "And the ones across the aisle. They're dry, but the wet ones are behind the wing—where the fuel tanks are. Please, go tell the captain!"

She glanced at the windows where I was pointing. Then she nodded. "It's okay," she said, "just stay calm," but I noticed that her smile had disappeared and she moved rather quickly up the aisle toward the cockpit.

A few minutes later, an officer from the cockpit followed her down the aisle. "Excuse me," he said as he bent over me to peer out the window, then returned to the cockpit without a word to me. A moment later, the captain's voice came over the loudspeaker. "Your Excellency, ladies and gentlemen," he said in Turkish. "It has come to our attention that we must return to Ankara. Please remain calm. Thanks to an alert passenger, we are not in danger," he assured us, "it is just a minor fuel leak. We estimate our return time to be thirty minutes. Thank you for your patience."

No sooner had the captain made his announcement than I felt the plane veer to the right to begin a sharp descent. When the maneuver was completed the stewardess returned to my seat. "Sir, the captain has asked for your name," she said.

"Christo Chrysostomidis," I told her. Knowing the problem was solved, I did not feel nervous at all, and was still rather enjoying my first plane trip. I would not allow anything to thwart this, my long-awaited trip to America.

While waiting back in Ankara, Ogaleak talked about my life-saving discovery to anyone who would listen. Meanwhile, mechanics on the ground realized that the gas cap had been left off the tank in the right wing. The plane was refueled, the cap replaced, and we reboarded for another try at Cairo. Once we were airborne, the captain explained to the passengers that without a gas cap, fuel was profusely spraying from the tank. "Thanks to Mr. Christo Chrysostomidis' alert detection," he went on, "we avoided a serious problem."

"Bravo, Christo!" the passengers burst out in a unanimous cheer. Suddenly the entire plane, including the Ambassador, turned to face me. "Stand up, Christo," Ogaleak said, pulling on my arm. Embarrassed to the point of blushing I stood, smiling amidst rancorous clapping and cheers and offered my fellow passengers a brief bow of my head.

"See why I have him on my staff?" the Ambassador joked, and the passengers, in the exuberance that usually follows relief, laughed and chattered, continuing the celebration.

This time our flight to Cairo was uneventful. When we arrived, we were picked up at the airport and ferried to a downtown hotel. During our ten days in Cairo, the Ambassador and a few aides were scheduled to make a side trip to Portugal.

In the hotel after unpacking, I sat on the edge of my bed to reread my passport. "Chrysostomos Chrysostomidis," it said. "Not valid for more than one journey to the Unites States unless revalidated. Authorized by the Department of State, telegram no. 125, Jan. 27, 1945."

The Western Allied forces had driven across France and were nearing victory in Europe. There was a sense of exultation in the air and shortly I would become part of it. Like Europe, I would be free at last, liberated from the Turkish oppression I had known since I was five.

These exhilarating thoughts rushed through my mind while sitting on the corner of my bed in that Cairo hotel. I looked at the passport that would take me to a new and better life. "God bless America," I whispered softly. I had not yet set foot on American soil, but I had my passport and American visa in my hand and a lifetime of dreams and aspirations in my heart. Most importantly, I had the will to make them a reality.

During the next few days I accompanied the Ambassador to several receptions around Cairo. I also planned a function which we held in a room at the hotel for the Egyptian diplomatic corps, the American Ambassador to Egypt, and other assorted dignitaries. I planned the food and drink and Ogaleak prepared it. Later in the week I accompanied the Ambassador and a couple of his seasoned attachés on his brief state visit to Portugal. Back in Cairo we had a couple of days to relax before embarking for America. Ogaleak and I decided to see the Sphinx and the Pyramids.

Early one morning we took a cab to a stable on the outskirts of Cairo which housed donkeys and camels. The pyramids were a few miles beyond the city, and in those days the best way to sightsee in the desert was by camel. When we arrived at the stables at seven that morning, the temperature was already more than eighty degrees. Dressed in khaki pants and a white shirt, I was still uncomfortably warm.

Ogaleak and I quickly forgot the heat and promptly learned that riding a camel was very different than riding a horse, or in my case, a mule. Our legs quickly became very sore. It was our first and last ride on a camel. Even from miles away, the Pyramids appeared, against a backdrop of browns and blues, to be monolithic, lending a stark symmetry to the barren desert. The colossal formations loomed before us as we travelled toward them. To the side, the Sphinx sat almost life-like, staring at all who approached. These were two of the seven ancient wonders of the world.

"Christo, I am not a young man," Ogaleak said. "I, too, have known war and persecution in one form or another since 1917. I lost my family and a good part of my life to the Bolsheviks, just as you lost so much to the Ottomans. Yet I, like you, feel the excitement of a child when I contemplate my trip to America. For even at my age, the specter of freedom is exhilarating!"

"America, the land of freedom, will soon be our home," I told him.

"Yes, our home! We are a bit like vagabonds who have lived for a long time in exile in Istanbul," he laughed. "And now we will go, compliments of the Turks, to our new home. It is a bit more than ironic that the Turks are providing our passage to America, is it not?" We both chuckled at that.

The next morning was our last full day in Cairo and I had a number of things to do for the Ambassador. I rose at dawn, showered and dressed carefully, pinning my relic coin over my heart, and said my morning prayers to God, as was my habit. Then I packed my belongings and went downstairs. I had begun collecting stamps as well as menus during my years in Turkey, and before my workday began I wanted to purchase a few stamps for my collection. I found several interesting Egyptian stamps that I placed in my stamp book near the ones I recently acquired in Portugal. I then began the activities of the day, which included attending a farewell party for the Ambassador hosted at the American Embassy. That evening, porters carried our baggage in large cases to the dock for loading aboard ship.

The next morning we boarded the Isthmian steamship and began our journey to America. It was a large vessel with cabins for passengers on the three upper decks and cargo stowed deep in its holds. The Ambassador was berthed with two of his attachés on the main deck. Ogaleak and I shared a small cabin with bunk beds directly under the Ambassador's suite.

I had grown up close to the sea. I had fished in it, swum in it and boated across it, and never had been subject to seasickness. Poor Ogaleak was not so lucky. During our three weeks at sea he spent barely a day or two out of bed. Most days we ate in a galley below deck—or I did, at any rate. Ogaleak had little appetite. The galley food was palatable but unexciting which, under the circumstances, suited Ogaleak quite well. On two occasions the Ambassador invited us to the first class dining rooms which provided us a respite from the monotony of our usual fare.

During our third week at sea we ran into a nasty storm that pummeled us with squalls, gale-force winds and threatening swells. For over twelve hours the vessel rocked violently like a toy boat. Everyone was sick and stayed below deck. The captain turned the ship into the swells so that they broke over the bow, washing along the decks all the way to the stern. Everything that was loose had to be tied down. It was a northwesterly squall with the intensity of a hurricane. I wondered during the storm if the boat would hold together. When the storm finally abated we were off course by one day, yet we were only four days outside the harbor of New York. The calm sea and clear sky marked my passage from the tempest of my old life to the fair weather of promise before me. Ogaleak and I spent our last days aboard ship on deck playing tavoli—a popular board game in our part of the world, known as Backgammon in America—and absorbing all the sights and sounds.

The morning of our approach to New York Harbor, we were all on deck at dawn eagerly straining to see the Statue of Liberty. Ogaleak and I were so excited that we could barely talk. Gradually, the city's dramatic skyline appeared on the horizon and at the mouth of the harbor, luminous in the pearly light of sunrise, stood Lady Liberty. The sight took my breath away and sent chills of excitement up and down my entire body. I had heard that many thousands of immigrants had passed by the statue as they sought a better life, trading a lifetime of subjugation and sacrifice for a future of hope. Many were humbled by the sight of the statue welcoming them to their new country, and I was one of them. Like children, we anxiously awaited the gateway to better days.

Finally taking my eyes away from her, I glanced at Ogaleak who stood near me at the rail.

"She's beautiful, isn't she?" I murmured emotionally.

Ogaleak looked at me and smiled. "Yes, Christo, she is," he replied. A single tear dropped from a glazed eye and rolled down his face.

Also on deck that April morning was the couple who would assist Ogaleak in the Embassy kitchen, Elias Melas and his wife. They stood nearby, tearfully crossing themselves in whispered praise and humble homage to God. I quietly joined them, and I saw Ogaleak silently making a cross as we all stared silently at the New York skyline. The city of New York was immense! It filled the horizon and dwarfed anything I had ever before seen. At long last I had arrived in America.

Because we were part of the diplomatic corps, we were permitted to disembark directly and board a train bound for Union Station in Washington, D. C. In Washington we were greeted by a representative of President Truman from the State Department, then driven to the Turkish Embassy on Massachusetts Avenue. The city appeared to be very clean and manicured, standing in stark contrast to the filth and debris of Constantinople and the other old cities I had passed through. I was awestruck. My new home was more than I expected. It was not only free, but beautiful!

"Yes, Papa, at long last we are here," I whispered as I clutched the coin in my hand. I was overwhelmed with the feeling one gets upon coming home from a long journey, and I knew that the feeling would fill me for a lifetime.

12
The Butler and the Priest

The biggest power the President has is the power to persuade people to do what they ought to do without having been persuaded...and if the man who is President doesn't understand this, if he thinks he's too big...then he's in for big trouble, and so is the country.

—Harry Truman

The Turkish Embassy on Massachusetts Avenue had 48 luxuriously appointed rooms filled with marble floors and columns. Crystal chandeliers hung from the ceilings and fine Persian rugs covered many of the floors. I was one of the few on the staff who actually lived in the Embassy. My room had a full bathroom and my window overlooked Embassy Row. Although my wage was modest, I was quite literally living in luxury.

The Embassy had been closed for a number of years, but it had been carefully readied for our arrival. As soon as I unpacked I sat in the chair before the small desk in my room and began a letter home.

Dearest Katina,

Best regards to Papa, Mama, Costa and Sultana. After travelling through Europe and Africa we boarded a freighter for our three-week passage to America and entered the country by way of the tumultuous city of New York—a city of towering buildings that touch the sky and fill the horizon as far as the eye can see, a city whose entrance is guarded by an edifice we know as Lady Liberty. We travelled by train to Washington where representatives of President Truman himself met us! They escorted us to the Embassy where I am now, seated in my room writing you this note.

Each of the 48 rooms is the size of our small house, yet not one of them is as warm and beautiful as our home, which I miss dearly...

"Christo, Christo!" My writing was interrupted by the Ambassador who was quartered down the hall from me. The letter would wait. I promptly stood, slipped into my jacket and walked out into hall.

"Yes, your Excellency," I responded in Turkish, offering a slight bow.

"Tomorrow I will make a formal visit to the White House," the Ambassador informed me. "While I am gone you will prepare for the reception we will hold here at the Embassy the following day. We will receive guests in the ballroom and dining room; however, all rooms except for sleeping quarters will be open. Have Ogaleak prepare a full complement of hors d'ouvres and pastries. There will be many dignitaries among the guests, Christo." The Ambassador paused in his flurry of orders to look at me. "Even President Truman will attend," he said.

"Yes, your Excellency. I will attend to everything. What time would your Excellency care to dine tonight?"

"As soon as you can manage it, Christo," he told me. "Make it something small and light, and I will have it in my room."

"Perhaps some cream soup would be appealing," I suggested, "along with salad, a bit of cheese, some fresh bread, and a glass of red wine."

"That will be most satisfactory, Christo."

"With, perhaps, a little coffee and fresh baklava afterwards?"

"I would like that, Christo," he said with a satisfied smile and sigh.

I responded with another bow and hurried off to find Ogaleak. There was a great deal to be done for the Embassy reception and I spent the next couple of hours making plans. When I returned to my room, I finished my letter to Katina and went to bed. The next day would be filled with preparations. It would be the first day of my new duties in my new country, and it would include serving the new President of the United States!

The following evening as I was busy checking the preparations, guests began arriving, among them a small group of men escorting

President Truman. The Ambassador greeted them personally upon entering. As the President's gaze passed over me, our eyes met for a brief second. I saw in his face a serious and humble man who lacked the insecurities and superior airs of the Turkish leaders I had been accustomed to. I was filled with awe by the greatness reflected by the President.

The evening which celebrated the official opening of the Embassy was a success.

From the moment of my arrival in America I felt at home. America's struggle against tyranny in Europe and the Pacific paralleled my own efforts to achieve personal liberty in my journey to her shores. These heartfelt parallels between America and my life drew me closer to her. My service and commitment to the Ambassador was secondary to my primary agenda, which was to obtain freedom—freedom of choice, freedom to come and go as I pleased, freedom of opportunity, and, mostly, freedom to live my life in accordance with my traditions and beliefs. In America I knew I had found that freedom.

Germany surrendered unconditionally on May 8, 1945. Hitler was defeated and the western world was overwhelmed with joy. The entire staff, including the Ambassador, listened to the radio as President Truman and Prime Minister Churchill announced to the world the end of the war in Europe. The western world began an uncontained celebration of Hitler's defeat. Although a Greek Christian from Turkey, I celebrated right along. Truman had only been in office a month since President Roosevelt had died on April 12th. Although Roosevelt had many critics, he was generally viewed as a great man and his death was seen as an irreversible loss to the free world. It was sad to think that he did not live to see the victory he had worked so hard to achieve. Yet I was intrigued and pleased to learn that the new President had begun working as a haberdasher, much like my brother and family. It was evidence of the greatness of this country that a man could make his way from a clothing store to the Presidency of the United States of America. Such a man was now guiding the nation in the final months of war.

In the summer and fall of 1945, there were many diplomatic functions between Turkey and her new-found allies as talk of communism increased. The fact that Turkey shared its northern border with the Soviet Union and stood between the Soviets and a warm water port meant that she was of great interest to the Allies. Even before the surrender with Germany was ratified, the lines of the Cold War with Russia had been drawn.

The Ambassador represented the Turkish government in the negotiation of many matters. Toward this end there were many social and political functions, all requiring food and drink. The Embassy staff was very busy.

"Christo, the Ambassadors of France and England will join the representatives from the United States at supper tonight, so make sure the menu is Continental," the Ambassador advised me one morning.

"Yes, your Excellency," I replied, offering my trademark bow.

"Oh, and Christo, this letter came from your father," he added, placing the letter in my hand with a smile.

"Thank you sir!" Bowing, I slipped the letter into my pocket and hurried through the day's tasks so that I could retire to my room to read Papa's letter in leisure.

The letter, I discovered that evening, was dated April 11, 1945, more than two months earlier. My family had not received the letter I had written them when I had arrived in America late in April, and were responding to an earlier note I had written before boarding the ship.

Panayia

My Dearest Son Chrysostomos, We just received your letter and we are happy that you are in good health. Thank God, we too are in excellent health.

You ask if we are receiving the money on a regular basis. Yes, we are receiving 50 liras...and we are managing it exactly the way you instructed us to. Don't worry about it.

I kiss you and I pray that God will be with you always.... When a father is reaching the end of his days he calls his children together and gives them the following advice:

1) Manage your money. Your expenses should not exceed your income.

2) Never allow self-interest, no matter how important or unimportant, to separate you from your brothers and sisters.

3) If your country ever needs you, drop everything gladly and go to her aid. It's a patriotic duty.

4) No matter how high you succeed in life, never lose your humility and never abuse your power.

Rest assured that by doing this you will be loved by God and honored and respected by your fellow man; you will live a happy life.

Your Father,

I. Chrysostomidis

The letter was classic Papa. I felt like a child on our porch listening attentively to his wise words. Over the next few months I would write my family many letters and receive a number of replies from Mama and Papa, but mostly from Katina.

I had made new friends at the Embassy, including Elias and Anna Melas, the couple who had become essential assistants to Ogaleak. They were also Greeks from Turkey who shared my humble and deprived roots. From this base of common experience, a small circle of friendship grew, but it was Ogaleak who remained a tremendous influence on my life.

Meanwhile, my days at the Embassy were filled with protocol, scheduling, and arranging the work-a-day life of the Ambassador. A great weight had been lifted. The infectious mood of optimism and rebirth after Hitler's defeat was captivating. Along with the euphoria that summer came rumors of the super "doomsday" bomb that Truman planned to drop on the Japanese. Such a bomb, it was felt, would surely end the terrible fighting that still continued in the Pacific. The Atomic Age was about to dawn, which would alter the face of war, and its implications to mankind were as yet undreamed of.

The explosion of two atomic bombs in August would end hostilities in the Pacific in a gruesome display of man's destructive ability, unleashing the threat of future nuclear war. Man had developed a weapon that could bring an end to his very existence.

* * * * *

One day, I received an unexpected letter from Boston, Massachusetts. It was from Jimmy Coucouzes, my childhood friend. He had arrived in America four months before I had and was teaching at Boston's Holy Cross Greek Orthodox Seminary. Although I had not seen him for many years, I had kept in touch with him through my parents, but his arrival in America was news I had not yet received! As I held his letter in my hands I realized suddenly that I was no longer alone in America. Jimmy, my friend from Imbroz, was here with me!

On a morning in the first week of September, I was in the Embassy lobby when the doorbell rang. The secretary was nowhere to be seen so I crossed the lobby, swung open the door and gazed out into the sunlight. There before me stood a bearded, Orthodox priest in his mid-thirties. He was perhaps six feet tall and had brown curly hair. Both his hair and his beard, I noticed, were neatly combed. Around his white collar was a heavy gold chain, and hanging from it was a handsome gold Orthodox crucifix about three inches high.

For an instant the priest and I gazed blankly at each other. Then the priest smiled warmly.

"Chrysostomos, my friend—how are you?" he asked.

It was Jimmy Coucouzes. Astonished, I bowed and kissed his hand to show respect.

"Father," I said.

Jimmy pulled his hand from mine and chuckled. "Christo, don't you recognize me?"

"Of course I do, Father Coucouzes! Come in, please!" I said, ushering my old friend into the lobby. "But you are a priest now and I must show you respect!"

Jimmy clapped his hand on my back and smiled. "But we are friends first and always, Christo. My, it is good to see you!"

"And it is a wonderful surprise to see you," knowing my pleasure and bewilderment were evident on my face. "Although I must admit that I am surprised to see you here in Washington!"

"I came down from Boston on business, Christo, and I couldn't leave without seeing you. It has been a long time, my friend."

"It has been too long," I said enthusiastically.

Later that morning after introductions had been made and Jimmy and I had toured the Embassy, we settled in a small reception room where we visited for more than two hours. We talked comfortably about Imbroz and Turkey, our parents and families, and our journeys to America.

"I will continue my studies in Boston," Jimmy told me, then asked, "And how do you find your position at the Embassy? Do you like your new duties?"

"Very much," I assured him, "And I stay very busy. But I miss my family, of course. This may interest you, Father. Katina writes me to ask if I can find a husband for Sultana. I understand that Taki Hatzikiriakidis is here in America—do you remember Taki?"

The Hatzikiriakidis family was among our neighbors on Imbroz, although from Castro. Jimmy and I sometimes played with Taki.

"Of course I remember him," Jimmy told me. "Taki has been in America for quite some time, since before the war. I believe his entire family is in America now. You have heard, I suppose, that he is serving in the U. S. Navy, though I have no idea where he is stationed."

"Do you suppose you could get his address somehow?" I asked.

"Of course, Christo!" Jimmy laughed lightly. "I shall be pleased to assist you in a little matchmaking for Sultana! But tell me, what of Katina? How is she?"

"She is fine. You know, my parents are older now, and she is a great help." There was a time many years ago when I thought Jimmy had an interest in Katina, but the tumult of the Turkish conquest, then the war, placed all personal aspirations on the back burner.

To my delight Jimmy stayed to have lunch with me, and for dessert I made sure to serve him *loucomades*, a sweet doughball deep-fried then immersed in honey and sprinkled with cinnamon—his favorite pastry.

"Seeing you means so much to me," Jimmy told me over coffee. "I am reminded of our island home, our youth, our families and all that we hold dear. But I have kept you from your duties long enough," he added, pushing reluctantly away from the table, "and I have a train to catch to Boston."

We stood and Jimmy clasped my right shoulder. "I will not forget today," he told me.

"Nor will I, Father," I said, as I accompanied him back to the Embassy lobby. At the door he turned to face me.

"May God bless you, Christo, and always be with you."

"Thank you, Father," I bowed. "It has meant a great deal to see you again."

Our smiles, illuminated by the high noon sun, reflected our warm reunion. I watched as Jimmy descended the steps and caught a cab at the curb. For a brief time afterward my thoughts were with him and my mind flooded with rich memories of our island home.

Two weeks later I received a letter from Jimmy, in which he wrote: *I send heartfelt thanks for the happiness you gave me with your kindness and hospitality at the Embassy...You brought me a little bit of our home on Imbroz which I long so much to see...*

Try to come to New York on October 20th. What do you say? Write me. We will meet with some of our countrymen from Imbroz.

There was no mention of Taki's address, but I wrote Jimmy in reply that I would love to meet him in New York and that I planned to see him on the twentieth of October. Taki and Sultana had an innocent attraction as children that I now intended to exploit. I knew he was anxious to have me meet other Greek immigrants in America. A day or two later, another letter from Jimmy arrived at the Embassy.

My loving friend Chrysostomos, I hope you are adjusting to your new life in America and for the years you are here I wish you health and happiness.

I am unable to confirm the meeting on the twentieth with our countrymen, nonetheless I wish you would come. Don't worry about a place to stay; you will stay with me at the Kartz Hotel... Whatever you decide, write me.

Thank you for the newspapers from Greece and Turkey. Say hello to your parents for me when you write them.

With much love and good wishes,

Iakovos Coucouzes

It was strange to see Jimmy sign in the name of our old bishop on Imbroz, and I was not sure what to make of it. It must have been a way for Jimmy to honor him.

As it developed, there was too much work at the Embassy to permit me to visit New York. We were both disappointed, but we stayed in touch and I continued to send him Greek and Turkish newspapers which I acquired from the Embassy. Jimmy did not have much luck locating Taki or his family, but finally my old friend Theologos Regas—still back at the Park Hotel in Constantinople—located Taki's mother, Urania Hatzikiriakidis, and, through a friend in New York, eventually Taki's address was forwarded to me. Greek grapevines are quite extensive.

Throughout that year, the Embassy held over a dozen formal functions, which often meant long workdays for me. Planning for smaller, more casual events was also time-consuming because these so-called informal functions, though not as well attended, required nearly the same degree of preparation as the formal ones. They were usually attended by distinguished guests from around the world as well as dignitaries and diplomats from other embassies on Massachusetts Avenue.

I played my role in the matchmaking process successfully, for within a few months, Taki wrote my father asking if he could have permission to marry Sultana. His letter was short and to the point:

Dear Mr. Chrysostomidis,

My name is Taki Hatzikiriakidis. I believe you know my family. We are from the village of Castro. I am in good health and have a job with the U. S. Navy. I am writing to ask for permission to marry your daughter Sultana. I will love her and I have the wherewithal to care for her...

Working under the assumption that the match between Taki and Sultana would eventually take place, I began saving money to finance Sultana's passage and making arrangements with the Embassy for her visa. The whole process would be an expensive one, costing several hundred dollars, even if she travelled by sea instead of air. For better or worse, I was the only source of funds for my family, so Sultana's passage would be my responsibility. My mother was particularly anxious that Katina should come to America, too. It was my parents' wish to see both their daughters married and settled, but almost immediately another letter from home informed me that Katina would not come. She would stay behind to care for Mama and Papa.

Sending money from America to Imbroz was a complicated procedure. I sent money to friends at the Pera Palace Hotel who changed dollars to liras and sent it on to Imbroz, but keeping track of it sometimes grew cumbersome and difficult. Many of the letters I exchanged with my family during this time dealt with how much money I sent and when it arrived. In America, it was so easy to forget the difficulties involved for my family in even the simplest things, like the transfer of money. One evening after roughing out a menu for a small dinner party we were planning for the French Ambassador, I retired to my quarters and opened a letter I had received from Katina earlier that day. Amid our usual money concerns, I sensed her desire for her own life, tempered by her resignation to care for our aging parents.

My dearest brother Chrysostomos,

We are always delighted to hear from you and learn you are well...I can't get enough of looking at the photo you sent. You have gained weight and you look wonderful...

I also liked the photographs of the landscape...What a beautiful sight!... It carries you away...I want to see it with my own eyes someday.

Finally [your friend] sent us a letter. He said he received 500 liras from the Pera Hotel and will send them when we give him the name of a responsible party...we are anxious to find out what happened to the [rest of the] money that you sent us.

We have applied for Sultana's final papers and are told they will be received soon.

Please write. That is all the news. The weather here is cold and it is raining. Winter came early...I am awaiting a detailed letter...

Poor Katina, in those days everyone on our island discussed marriage, yet of the four of us she would remain home and tend to the needs of our parents. On Imbroz in those days there was no dating. Fathers watched their daughters very carefully and many marriages were arranged by parents and relatives. Although Katina was one of the prettiest and most intelligent of the young women on Imbroz, it would not be her destiny to engage in the romantic marriage she secretly desired. There was no one left at home to help our parents and Katina knew this. Mama and Papa came first.

Late in March 1946, I received a letter from Jimmy requesting that I assist him through the Embassy to obtain a visa for a brief visit to Turkey. In mid-August I heard from him again.

It has been awhile since I have corresponded with you [but] I have been sick. My illness caused me to cancel my earlier trip [to Turkey]...I may be in Washington and would like to visit you. Finally, could you please give me the full name of his excellency the Turkish Ambassador as well as, if possible, the American Ambassador in Ankara?

With my love,

Archimandrite Iakovos

Jimmy's new title reflected his advancement to a position above a priest but still below a bishop. Yet his appropriation of the name Iakovos had apparently become formalized.

Sometime after Jimmy's letter, Sultana and Taki Hatzikiriakidis—or Taki Hatzi, as he called himself in America— became officially engaged. Although they had not seen each other for years, the fact that our families were acquainted with each other—not to mention that Taki was now established in New York and could provide a good home for Sultana—meant that everyone was extremely pleased with the match. Religion and custom were most important to the families on our island, but after years of a difficult economic climate, financial considerations had to be considered in a marriage arrangement, the economic climate that had also determined my evolution into a butler. With the uncertain struggle of life and death in the Old World, arranged marriages were an effective and efficient method of matchmaking.

Papa soon wrote me of their reaction to the betrothal of my sister and Taki:

My Dearest Christo,

We are overjoyed about Sultana's engagement and we pray for her safe arrival in the United States.

We received your presents, shirts, socks and ties. We thank you very much. Although we are receiving the ten lira every month, we have yet to receive the 150 lira [you sent]...

I send you my love and I hope and pray that God will protect you always.

Around the same time, Mama also wrote to me. *I am so proud of you. You are doing so much for all of us. I hope God will repay you for all the great good you are doing and have done...I wish you joy and may God always be with you...Theologos Regas must be close to arriving...*

In the Old World, we helped each other if we could. I had been able to help Theologos (Ted as he would be called in America) to come to the U. S. Since he had waited tables with me at the Pera Palace and later at the Park, the Ambassador had agreed to permit him to work at the Embassy. Ted carried himself well and worked hard, and I believed he would be an asset to the Ambassador. It would be good to have him with me, and I was pleased the Ambassador had taken my recommendation.

Shortly after Mama's letter, I received a note from Katina. *We received the monies...your letter and photographs,"* she wrote. *Forgive me for writing in such a hurry...You will hear our news from Theologos...I kiss you sweetly...*

Letters were a lifeline to friends, families and homelands in those days before easy global communication. I wrote and received many, many letters during this time, and each letter I received from my island was as much of a treat as a long distance phone call is now. In one of his letters, my father talked about Taki's and Sultana's plans.

...You wrote that Taki wants to come to Imbroz. I strongly advise against it. He will be conscripted into the Turkish Army. If something like that happens we will jeopardize all our hopes and dreams for the future, what we have worked so hard for Taki and Sultana. It is best for all concerned that Sultana come to the United States [instead]. Because of the flight of young Greek boys to avoid conscription, the Turkish Army has instituted strict measures.

Shortly after Papa's letter, Regas arrived at the Embassy. It was a big event when someone from our small corner of the world made it to America. Mothers would burst with pride and fathers would boast in the coffeehouses. Villages would practically canonize the new Americans. The post-World War II group of immigrants appreciated the opportunities of America as much as any other immigrant group in America's history.

181

I greeted Theologos with real enthusiasm and satisfaction. It was rewarding to have an opportunity to share with a friend who had endured similar hardships. He was quick and bright and within days was performing his duties beautifully.

A few days after Regas' arrival, I was preparing a new menu in the kitchen with Ogaleak when I was called to the foyer of the Embassy. Waiting for me there was a pleasant surprise—a second unexpected visit from Jimmy Coucouzes!

"Greetings, my friend," he said as I bent to kiss his hand.

"What a pleasure!" I told him. "Will you stay for dinner with me?"

"I cannot," he replied regretfully. "I have a train to catch back to Boston. I could not leave Washington, however, without seeing you."

"Then perhaps you will share some coffee and *loucomades* with me?"

At the mention of his favorite pastry, Jimmy smiled playfully. "And how can I refuse such an offer?"

Within minutes, Ogaleak had prepared us coffee, and soon after the pastry treats were served. Jimmy and I retired to a quiet room to exchange news. We discussed our families and I told him about Papa's plan to send Sultana to America rather than risk Taki's conscription by the Turkish army should he travel there to get her. Jimmy heartily agreed. I also told him about Regas' arrival from Constantinople and for several minutes, as he consumed the tray of warm *loucomades*, he talked about other Greeks who had recently come to America.

"And what is your news?" I asked Jimmy finally.

"Chrysostomos, I am once again planning my trip home and I would like you to ask the Ambassador for assistance with my visa. As I have only my priestly possessions and very little money, I would ask if the Ambassador can mitigate or eliminate the fees involved, and in general allow me an uneventful passage and a timely arrival. Do you suppose he could do that?"

"I see...I will talk to him. When do you go?"

"I am uncertain of the date, but I will write you when I return to Boston. The point of my trip is to visit Constantinople and the

Patriarchate for sabbatical, but I will try to return to Imbroz for a while. Is there anything you would like me to tell your parents?"

"That I think of them and pray for them every day," I told him. "Now, let's have some more coffee and I'll ask Ogaleak and Regas to join us."

Moments later we were all together.

"Any news from home?" I asked Jimmy.

"After the arrest of Bishops Iakovos and Maxim a year ago, the Holy Mount and the Holy Monastery of Great Larva were taken over by Turkish settlers. All the elders who protested were exiled to Asia Minor. Recently, Iakovos and Maxim were released from prison," Jimmy solemnly told us.

"More property confiscations," I said.

Jimmy nodded, but the news of Bishop Iakovos' release was happily received.

"The Turks have stopped practicing wholesale genocide, so I guess you could say things have improved, but religious persecution is still a way of life for us few remaining Christians in Turkey."

Two hours later, after an afternoon of cordial talk and Turkish coffee, I reluctantly escorted Jimmy to a taxi. Before he turned to enter the cab, I pressed into his hands a bag filled with hot *loucomades* that I had asked Ogaleak to prepare.

Early in October, I received letters from Papa and Mama. In his letter Papa was concerned about some money I had sent the family which had never arrived. This time Papa worried that the funds had been misappropriated by someone in Constantinople. *Do what you think is best,* he advised me. *I kiss you and pray that God will be with you always.*

In her letter Mama wrote:

My Dearest Son,

First I would like to wish you health and happiness...and may God fulfill all your dreams. We are delighted with your every letter...

Regarding your question about Uncle Russo and Aunt Cleo, they regularly inquire about you. Uncle Russo...writes that [his business] is doing well...

Then late in December I received a long letter from Papa with well wishes for Christmas.

...I was recollecting days long past when you were children...before the Turkish occupation. Oh, what unforgettable childhood years!...

Regarding Sultana, when the time comes we will take her to Constantinople for her trip to America. Please write in detail exactly what we need to do. Sultana's papers still have not arrived...

...Regards to Theologos.

Papa's reminiscences of my childhood and Christmas underscored his outward optimism and confidence which continued to be gifts to all of us.

A few weeks later in January 1947, I received a letter from Jimmy telling me that he had seen Taki, and asking for the latest news regarding Sultana's arrival. Shortly after Jimmy wrote, I received another letter from Papa.

Dear Chrysostomos,

...We received Sultana's papers—the letters, immigration papers as well as the Ambassador's letter—for which we thank you very much. We also received the check for three hundred American dollars for Sultana's fare. Unfortunately, we have another problem and will require your further assistance.

On April 9th we brought Katina to Constantinople. She was in urgent need of an operation for her appendix. The operation was performed on April 10th. She was hospitalized for ten days. Afterwards, I took her to the Romana Hotel where we are staying.

I sent a telegram to Imbroz requesting that Sultana come to Constantinople and ready herself to embark for America...Katina has recovered...Please send [more money] to us in Constantinople as these events were unexpected.

With love,

Your father

Once again, I was reminded how easy it was in America to forget the difficulties of day-to-day life in the world I had left behind. The transfer of money was still a major challenge. It took a couple of weeks, but as soon as possible I sent Papa one hundred dollars.

Meanwhile, I had some concerns of my own. I wrote Jimmy telling him that I planned to leave the Embassy. I asked if he could obtain a birth certificate for me so that I could submit it along with my application for citizenship. My visa would expire if I left the Embassy, and there was nothing I wanted more than to be come a citizen of the United States.

Jimmy responded swiftly.

My Dearest Chrysostomos,

I read your letter with much care...Before you act you must gain knowledge. If you marry...marry an Orthodox Christian Greek girl born in the United States of Greek descent...I will gladly transcribe and translate your baptismal papers if that will assist you in obtaining citizenship.

With warm wishes that you will find everything in your life easy. Regards to Theologos and your other friends...

Marrying an American citizen was a near certain way to obtain citizenship. As much as I desired citizenship, though, I had no desire to pursue marriage for that purpose.

Later that week, I received a short note from Papa with information regarding Sultana's arrival. She would come in June aboard an American freighter docking in Norfolk, Virginia.

Taki and I made the trip together to meet her, and as soon as she cleared customs I called out to her. When she heard my voice she scanned the crowd, looking for me. "Christo!" she exclaimed in an excited squeal when she saw me. A moment later she threw her arms around my neck and kissed me. "I made it! I can't believe I'm here," she said breathlessly.

"Welcome to America!"

It took a minute, but eventually I calmed her down and performed the unusual duty of re-introducing her to her fiancé, who was standing awkwardly to one side, smiling nervously. "Sultana," I said easily, "you remember Taki..."

It had been nine years since Sultana and Taki had seen each other and for a moment they looked a little embarrassed, both wearing a shy, reserved blush. Then suddenly they greeted each other with all the joy of two people engaged to be married, yet with the reservation of two people who had barely laid eyes on each other. It was a happy day for everyone. I had finally brought my little sister to America, and she and Taki would soon be married.

"Hello, Sultana. We are going to take you to New York where you will stay with Urinia, my mother," Taki told her. In a shy but hopeful gesture, he took her hand in his.

"Okay, Taki," Sultana smiled warmly. I could see them both visibly relax, and we made our way through the bustling crowd to find a taxi.

Shortly after Sultana's arrival, I received another letter from Jimmy with news of his long-awaited trip.

This coming Friday, June 27th at 11:30 p. m., I am leaving by airplane for Constantinople...Maybe I will be able to go to Imbroz. My visa is for a return trip in September. Do you think that the Ambassador would give me letters so that I am not excessively charged by the Turkish officials upon disembarking with my possessions...icons, crosses...?

Should I see your parents, I will give them your warmest regards...

I had arranged a letter from the Ambassador for Father Coucouzes after his earlier request and I promptly mailed it.

It would be much longer than September before I heard from or saw Jimmy again, and then under conditions I would never have expected. The crisis period, which had persisted my entire life, was over. The dramatic changes from war and chaos to the light of order and productive improvement were everywhere. Soon I would be representing our family at Sultana's marriage to Taki. Then something would happen that would change my life forever.

13

A Lifelong Commitment

*I would like to counsel you regarding the
sacrament of marriage and married life...always
treat your wife with love and respect.... Both
should relate to the other with devotion,
temperance and tolerance. When you practice
these virtues in your lives, you can rest assured
you will have God's blessings and your fellow
man's respect.*

—Ioanni Chrysostomidis
from a letter to his son, Chrysostomos, 1947

It was June of 1947. The threats of war and crisis had receded.
Everything was making more sense. Once again, the world had
become rational and I finally felt in control of my destiny.
Freedom, dignity and a renewed value for life had replaced death,
destruction and disregard for the fragile human condition. A
boundless social appetite fostered enhanced individual welfare.
Opportunity replaced despair.

This sense of well-being was found as much in Imbroz as in
America. Letters from my family reflected a sense of peace and
optimism that had come with the war's end, a feeling that the
Turkish threat had subsided, even if economic development on our
island was still repressed by the Turkish regime. Turkey, for the
time being, had repressed her aggression, possibly wanting to keep
a low profile after aiding the Nazis during the war. Many of my
friends were getting married, a barometer of the island's improved
situation and mood, and my parents' letters were filled with details.
*Eranthia is coming to America as a tourist. It seems her aunt has
someone in mind to get her engaged to...* they wrote. *One of
Dimitriadis' daughters was engaged to Dimaria's brother,"* they
went on, and added, *"Katina Kouletbrianow is engaged to an*

187

Australian...a kind and good gentleman..." The list went on and on, cataloguing Greek marriages not only on Imbroz but in America, as well.

In the midst of this optimistic environment, Katina stood alone, dutifully devoting herself to our parents. Though she never complained, I knew her dedication was costing her the chance for marriage and a family of her own. While I increasingly empathized with her, my own life was becoming more and more rewarding.

Each ethnic group has its own gifts and talents. Generally speaking, Greeks are not known to be as financially sophisticated as, say, Jewish people, but when it comes to chit-chat and gossip, they are light-years ahead of all others. In the summer of 1947, this special Greek talent for building networks and grapevines proved enormously beneficial to me. Elias and Anna Melas, the older couple who worked at the Embassy, had a Greek friend in Altoona, Pennsylvania, a Mr. Mastos, who was, in turn, a close friend of a Mr. Anton Anthony in Cumberland, Maryland. Mr. Anthony had a daughter, Eleni Antonia, who was twenty-four and single. Through the Melas-Mastos grapevine, I was invited to dinner at the Anthony's in Cumberland. To make the situation less awkward, Mr. and Mrs. Melas, who had never met the Anthony's, were also invited, and the three of us planned to make the trip to Cumberland by train.

On the day of the dinner I was up, as always, at dawn. I showered and pinned my holy coin to a fresh new undershirt, said a brief prayer, and then dressed in a fine brown double-breasted suit. According to the Melases, who "had heard," Eleni was beautiful. She was a high school graduate with two years of secretarial school, and she worked for her father at his store.

The train from Union Station to Cumberland was slow, and the trip was long enough to make me slightly nervous about the mystery girl I was supposed to meet. When we finally pulled into the station in Cumberland, we were greeted by a middle-aged, bespectacled man, perhaps two inches shorter than my five-feet-eight inches, with brown receding hair.

"Good day," he called out in Greek as he spotted the three of us on the platform. "Greetings! I am Anton Anthony!" He extended his hand to Mr. Melas, acknowledged Mrs. Melas with a smile, and at the same time eyed me over.

"Greetings, Mr. Anthony," Mr. Melas replied. "And may I introduce you to Mr. Chrysostomos Chrysostomidis?"

Mr. Anthony turned to me and offered his hand. "Hello, young man. I have heard many good things about you."

I shook his hand. "The pleasure is mine," I said respectfully.

The four of us chatted briefly as Mr. Anthony herded us to his car. The drive to his house took us through the town where he owned and operated the Royal Confectionary. An energetic man, Mr. Anthony operated the Eat Well Grill during the summer season.

"I have worked hard all my life," he told us as we drove. "I usually take off a half-day on Sundays to take Alexandra and the kids to church. On Christmas and New Year's Day our store is closed. God willing, we are doing well, but it isn't easy."

"I imagine not," I said earnestly.

When we arrived at the house, we were met by Mr. and Mrs. Gus Mastos, who had come down from Altoona along with their daughter, and by Mrs. Anthony, a small woman about fifty years old who had difficulty walking due to arthritis.

"Come, Christo," Mrs. Anthony said. "Sit beside me on the sofa. You are from Turkey, are you not?"

"I am from Imbroz," I said, settling myself beside her.

The realization that I, too, had grown up under the shadow of the Turks, seemed to trigger a response in her, and she opened up to me. "I came with my mother from Rankia, Christo," she told me. "I am also from Turkey. I was a girl of fourteen when we left more than thirty years ago. Papa lifted my mother and me into a small boat with two other families. The Turks were trying to stop us, but Papa stood his ground. He stayed behind and pushed our boat off, protecting us even as the Turks grabbed him. He said, 'Go! Go!' The Turks beat my father, Christo. They hit him over and over. We were helpless.... I turned away for I could not bear to watch. When I finally did look back, I saw him floating, face down in the water. That was the last time I ever saw him." Her voice trailed off as she looked mournfully into the distance of time.

She turned to me and I saw that her eyes were glazed with tears. Even after thirty years, the anguish of losing her father was still fresh.

"I understand," I said softly, and I did as only a Christian from Turkey could have. She seemed comfortable with me.

A moment later my attention was drawn to Mr. Anthony who took me by the arm and led me to a sideboard in the dining room that was set up as a small bar opposite a small altar with an icon of the Virgin Mary, a crucifix and a bible. I watched as he plopped ice cubes from a silver ice bucket into a glass.

"What may I offer you to drink? " he asked hospitably. "Gin and tonic?"

"That would be fine," I told him.

He nodded and began mixing the drink. "You know, Chrysostomos," he said, handing me a glass, "I came to America in 1908. I was sixteen." He paused a moment, reflecting, I supposed, on that long ago time. "I am not educated," he went on abruptly. "I served in the U. S. Army during the Great War from 1915 to 1918. I was an immigrant who could barely speak English, but I was proud to serve my new country. In the twenties, I settled in Cumberland and I married Alexandra. In those days when I was starting I had a horse-drawn ice cream cart that I pulled all over town. I used dry ice to keep the ice cream cold." He eyed me seriously through the thick lenses of his glasses, which he removed from his nose and idly began cleaning with a handkerchief. "And then the thirties came. They were hard years. Many people lost everything, but we got by."

"You worked hard," I said.

Mr. Anthony liked that answer. "Yes, I worked hard. You know about hard work?" he asked, breaking into a smile.

"Yes," I told him, smiling in return. "I know about hard work." It is an immigrant's badge.

For a minute Mr. Anthony appeared to be studying me. Then he suddenly cleared his throat. "Come, Christo," he said, ushering me back toward the living room. "My daughter Eleni will be down shortly and I want to introduce you. She is a little sensitive," he confided a bit mysteriously, "but she is a good girl."

We were crossing the foyer when I saw her on the stairs. For an instant I almost stared, taking in her lovely long brown hair and soft brown eyes. Suddenly, I was lost.

Eleni saw me looking at her and smiled. She seemed to glide down the last few steps toward her father and me.

"Eleni!" Mr. Anthony called out affectionately. "Come! I wish you to meet my young friend here, Chrysostomos Chrysostomidis. Christo," he went on, turning to me, "my daughter Eleni."

Eleni extended her hand to me. "It is nice to meet you, Chrysostomos," she said in Greek.

I took her hand and bowed slightly over it. "It is a pleasure to meet you, Eleni," I said. "Please call me Christo."

"All right, Christo," she smiled, and it was a pleasure to hear her soft voice say my name.

In the next instant Mr. Anthony herded us toward some chairs in the living room and left us to our own devices. We sat facing each other and exchanged small talk until we were called to dinner. To this day, I have no idea what we talked about, for all I could do was watch the way her head tilted disarmingly as she spoke, the way her slim fingers waved and danced through the air while telling an amusing little story, or the way her brown eyes would soak deeply into mine as we passed the afternoon. I must have said something, I know I did, for I remember the sound of her sweet laughter as she laughed at something I said. Before we knew it, dinner was served.

I was so completely captivated by Eleni I nearly forgot to eat. "What's this, Christo?" Mr. Anthony teased me good-naturedly. "You don't like leg of lamb? What sort of Greek are you?"

I blushed and turned my attention to my plate, careful to eat plenty of everything we were served, from potatoes to pastries.

When dinner was over, we adjourned to the living room again. This time I sat on the sofa with Eleni and before I knew it I was singing, "You Have the Most Beautiful Eyes in the World," a popular Greek song, further proof that I had completely lost my mind. Eleni bestowed on me a pleased yet shy smile, and I was utterly smitten. "I will call you Elenitsa," I said softly to her when we were alone. *Elenitsa* is a nickname for Helen in Greek.

She smiled her approval.

"Christo," Mr. Anthony told me later that night as we were preparing to leave, "you are always welcome here. Please come and see us any weekend you wish."

He wouldn't have to ask me twice. On the trip home, I knew that I did want marriage and a family after all—with Elenitsa!

The next week I was busy with all my normal duties plus a few extra responsibilities. His Excellency was hosting three functions in the next two weeks and Regas was still relatively new and required time for training. Nonetheless, I telephoned Elenitsa often and before the month was out I had found time to visit her twice.

I had invited Elenitsa to come with me to Sultana's and Taki's wedding on July 20th and she had accepted. I would take a train to Cumberland and from there we would take another train to New York. Elenitsa would spend the night with Taki's mother and I would spend the night with one of Taki's friends.

A couple of days before we were scheduled to go, I called Elenitsa to finalize our plans. Her mother answered the phone and when I asked for Elenitsa she hesitated.

"Christo, Elenitsa is not feeling well," she said finally, giving me the impression that she was not telling me all she knew.

"Not feeling well?" I asked. "What is wrong?"

Alexandra had already handed the phone to her husband, and it was Anton's voice I heard next.

"Christo, Elenitsa had to go to the hospital...but she is fine. She will be okay."

"But what is wrong?" I asked again, nearly in a panic.

"Nothing, nothing!" Mr. Anthony tried to sound cheery. "The doctor says she just needs a little rest."

"Rest? In a hospital? I must see her!" Somehow, none of this was making sense to me.

"Yes, a little rest in the hospital. Unfortunately, she cannot have visitors and...well, Christo, she will not be able to go to your sister's wedding."

I was terribly disappointed, confused and worried, but I asked Mr. Anthony to convey my best to Elenitsa and hung up with her father's repeated assurances that she would be okay. I didn't understand what was happening, but I trusted Mr. Anthony, and I prayed to God that He would protect and restore Elenitsa's health.

That weekend I arrived in New York alone. I went straight to Mrs. Hatzi's home to visit Sultana before going out to spend the evening with Taki. The Hatzi family had been in New York since 1938, leaving behind large holdings of land on Imbroz for the safety of America. Taki had been 21 when his family left the island. He enlisted in the U. S. Navy to gain citizenship, served in the Pacific during the war, and had just recently been honorably discharged. We had a good time that evening, Taki and I, celebrating his last few bachelor hours by finishing off a bottle of ouzo, singing "Still One More Little Drink" to the wee hours of the morning. I had no doubt he would make Sultana a good husband.

Jimmy was still at the Patriarchade in Turkey, or he would most certainly have performed the service. Despite his absence, the wedding of Sultana and Taki the next day was a happy, beautiful occasion, filled with joy and optimism. I was proud to represent my family and delighted for my sister's good fortune. We celebrated the wedding with traditional Greek food, music and dancing that extended well beyond midnight. For a time it almost seemed as if we were all transported back to Imbroz. Yet somehow, through all the festivity and good cheer, I could not get Elenitsa off my mind. Knowing she had planned to come with me, several friends asked how she was. All I could tell them is what Mr. Anthony told me, that she would be fine, but his incomplete explanation kept playing over and over in my mind. Something was amiss, I was certain.

When I returned to Washington, I called Cumberland only to discover that Elenitsa was still in the hospital. This time, I learned from Mrs. Anthony that Elenitsa was being treated for "nerves," whatever that meant.

Katina knew that Elenitsa had planned to accompany me to Sultana's wedding. They had even exchanged a letter and my sister understood how serious our feelings had become for one another. Sometime after my return from New York, I received a letter from Katina full of excitement about the wedding that had occurred so far away. "...*you and you alone were allowed to attend that sacrament of marriage...Elenitsa represented me. I hope that your marriage will take place soon....* Often when a male let his family know of his feelings for a young lady, things progressed rapidly. Although I had not yet convinced Elenitsa, my feelings were firm and immutable, as was my family's support. This was the way romance occurred in my part of the world. Since I had informed my family of my feelings for Elenitsa, they had extended their love to her unconditionally and accepted her even though they had not met. This sort of blind acceptance was common on my island.

Katina went on to add an affectionate message for Elenitsa: *Elenitsa, you asked me to forgive you for misspelling some words [in your letter to me]. I found no misspellings at all. But between brothers and sisters such formalities should not exist...*

I sent cards and flowers to Cumberland, but still had no direct communication with Elenitsa. Eventually I obtained the phone number of the hospital where she was and spoke to a nurse on her floor who told me she was progressing nicely but did not tell me the particular ailment she had. In the process of making this call, however, I discovered that the hospital where she was admitted was called a "sanitarium," a word with which I was not familiar.

I immediately wrote a letter to my family regarding Elenitsa's illness and providing details of Sultana's wedding. Although I tried not to appear overly worried in my letter, the truth was that I was concerned about Elenitsa and simply did not know what to do.

Katina sent me a long letter about her concern for Elenitsa's health.

My Dear brother Chrysostomos,

Your letter just arrived and I am answering you immediately. You cannot imagine how sad we are about Elenitsa's illness. We hope and pray from the bottom of our hearts that when you receive our letter she will have completely recovered. Last night we went to the Monastery of the Saints Anargiroi to light candles for all of you. We are also sending you flowers from the icon of the Saints. In order to make an amulet you have to burn incense, get some flowers from the icon, use a little bit of garlic, and add some holy bread. The benefits from the amulet are great. She must wear it for forty days. After the forty days you have to take it away. She must not wear it forever. In addition, all of you have to fast from meat for forty days and then take holy communion. After you have

194

done all of the above, she will have a complete recovery. Also, don't forget to have her wear your amulet. It is made of wood from the Holy Cross and it cures everything.

Please write immediately because we are anxious to hear from you. We also promise a Divine Liturgy celebrated in honor of the Saints Anargiroi. We shall do that as soon as we hear from you...

I'll be waiting for an answer. Kiss Elenitsa for me. Give my regards to [her parents].

Kisses to Sultana and Taki. Tell Sultana to write to me.

With love, your sister,

Katina

Over the next two weeks Elenitsa remained in the sanitarium. It was September before she came home. She had recovered, although I was still uncertain what she had recovered from, and I made plans to go to Cumberland to see her the following weekend.

Despite the expectations of my family, Elenitsa and I had not actually discussed marriage. That weekend when I finally saw her, however, I was overwhelmed by feelings of relief to know she was finally well. She looked so lovely that I could not imagine a future without her, and I found myself asking how she felt about marriage.

Her answer surprised me. "I cannot marry," she told me. "I cannot have children—"

"That won't matter to me," I protested.

"It's unfair to you," she insisted. "Christo, a few years ago, I had peritonitis which required surgery. They ended up removing an ovary, Christo. I cannot give you or anyone children."

I would not let the subject rest. "Elenitsa, I will take care of you," I told her. "If we can't have children, it won't matter. We will have each other. I knew from the moment I met you, Elenitsa, that I wanted to spend my life with you."

I did not press her further. She knew how I felt and I understood that it would take some time for her to trust me. In the meantime I visited Cumberland every weekend I possibly could. My thoughts were focused on marriage to Elenitsa and, secretly, a family if we could have one. I wanted that above everything. It was my desire, my dream and my plan all at once.

I later learned that Elenitsa had had what they called a nervous breakdown. Although I didn't completely understand it, I was relieved. I had come from a harsh physical world where illness or injury often meant disability or death. In my world, we didn't have the luxury of non-physical ailments. I didn't know there was such a thing as emotional disability, or that it could be as debilitating. To me, it meant relief that her ailment was nothing more than emotional. It would be later that I would learn it had arisen from a plane crash she and her brother had been in a few years earlier. They were fortunate to be alive.

Marriage was not the only thing on my mind. I was still planning to leave the Embassy, and toward that end I began training Regas to take my place. If I had a family I would have to provide for them, and my embassy arrangement would be inadequate in that regard. I had recently been introduced by a mutual friend to a man named Blaze at the Place Vendôme, an exclusive French restaurant on M Street in fashionable Georgetown. With my experience in both French as well as fine dining, Blaze was anxious to have me work for him as a waiter, and I was confident it was a better opportunity than staying on at the Embassy. The upper class of Washington, as I understood it, were very good tippers. I knew the Ambassador valued my services highly, but I also knew that advancement was limited. Besides, it was my goal to one day have my own business, which would require capital. In order to accomplish that, plus the financial requirements to support a wife and assist my family on Imbroz, I would certainly need to improve my situation.

Traveling by train to Cumberland on weekends became my routine, and I got along well with Mr. and Mrs. Anthony. Because we both came from Asia Minor and lived under Turkish rule, Mrs. Anthony and I had a ready-made rapport. She and I would confide our stories to one another while Mr. Anthony boasted of his accomplishments and successes, which were the result of his Spartan work ethic. Although Anton didn't share my intellectual curiosity in politics and current affairs, he saw in me the same determination and seven-day-a-week work ethic that he embraced, and our relationship was filled with mutual respect and admiration.

One weekend Taki and Sultana came down to Cumberland by train. They were happy newlyweds, and Taki was proving to be a fine husband. He and Sultana had sent a hundred dollars to Mama and Papa; my parents were not the only ones who appreciated the gift. Having them meet me in Cumberland was a real pleasure and a good diversion for Elenitsa.

When they arrived, Elenitsa suggested we go to a drive-in theater that had just opened in town. This was a wonderful novelty for us. Imagine, watching a movie while sitting in your car! Afterwards, we went to the Royal Confectionary where Mr. Anthony treated us to ice cream floats and sundaes—although Taki and I would have preferred a cold beer. Even so, we had a thoroughly enjoyable time. Sultana was already pregnant and Elenitsa could not help but ask her numerous questions about her condition.

On another weekend I brought Regas with me, and Elenitsa invited Ann Theodor, a friend of hers, to join us. When we introduced them, another courtship began. My corner of America seemed to be full of Greek romances during those post-war years. Indeed, we were in the beginning of the American post-war baby boom.

Over the next few months Elenitsa and I talked about everything regarding her hospitalization. She had so many fears and concerns that surprised and perplexed me, though they were made more comprehensible considering her plane crash. She was so different from me, so fragile and delicate in her sensibilities. After all the physical hardship I had been through, her fears and concerns seemed small and manageable, but nonetheless, they were her concerns and therefore important to me. I did my best to support her through these difficulties to which I could not relate.

* * * * *

October 1947 began a very busy season for the Ambassador, with important functions scheduled monthly through the end of the year. Regas had learned my job sufficiently well so that, should I leave the Ambassador, the Embassy would be well served in my absence. I also had received my application for citizenship along

197

with my birth certificate and the baptismal documents Jimmy had helped me acquire. In short, I was prepared to submit all my paperwork for naturalization.

All was in order in my life, with one exception—and before the month was out, I even had that great piece in place. Elenitsa had agreed to marry me. I knew that she eventually would. She had fully recovered from her breakdown. Katina's amulet, along with our prayers, had helped for know. Her health and our happiness had been restored. Despite Elenitsa's concerns over her ability to bear children, there was no reason for us not to look to the future with joy. We had our health, we were in America, and for once in my life the world was at peace.

Now that Elenitsa had finally agreed to marry me, I gave the Ambassador notice that I would be leaving by the end of the year. He did not take it well, and his sober stare in return required me to give an explanation for my departure.

"I am getting married," I told him, "and I cannot devote as much time to the Embassy. I will have a family and responsibilities to meet—"

The Ambassador cut me off. "No, Christo. When you marry I will give you a suite of rooms. You may bring your wife here."

"Your Excellency, it wouldn't be fair to you. I may eventually have children and I would not be as available to you as I am now. There are others who can serve you better now. Regas knows my job and will serve you well."

The Ambassador was clearly annoyed. "Out of the question!" he said emphatically. "You know you are close to completing three years here and then will get an increase in pay that I am willing to accelerate. And since you will have a wife, I will see what I can do to sweeten your pay a little more. You think about it. Think about losing your diplomatic status, Christo. If you leave here, you will be deported." With that, he turned abruptly and left the room.

A day later I received a short letter from Mama and Papa assuring me of their health and thanking me for several newspapers I had sent them. At the end of the letter, however, Mama added some additional text about Elenitsa and my brother Costa, or Constantine, as she always called him.

We received a letter from Elenitsa's mother who informed us that Elenitsa is feeling better. Thank God for that...if you wish, send Constantine some [money] because we have run out. He will write you soon...right now he is carrying manure for your father...

That evening I wrote my parents back with the news of my engagement. I also enclosed some money for the upcoming Christmas holidays and asked Papa to give me an accounting of a small partnership interest I held in a business venture in Constantinople. I had invested in a small business with a couple of waiters before the war. This venture was intended to provide Papa with a small monthly stipend, and when I liquidated my share, I planned to give the proceeds to him.

I continued to be extremely busy, as the Ambassador's list of social functions grew to include three additional events during the month of December. We had not discussed my departure again, but I had arranged with Mr. Blaze to begin work in mid-January at the Place Vendôme, after my wedding and honeymoon. Meanwhile, every weekend I made my usual journey to Cumberland to see Elenitsa and help my soon-to-be father-in-law for a day and a half at the Royal Confectionary. I needed the extra money.

By the end of December, I had put a deposit on a room in a house in Falls Church, Virginia. It was one room and a bath—no kitchen. I was only renting, but it would be our first home. I would take possession on January 1, 1948, and Elenitsa and I would be married on the eleventh.

Two days before Christmas I received a note from Katina congratulating me on my engagement. I also heard from Papa with an accounting of my interest in the salami shop venture.

My Dearest Chrysostomos,

I am sending you greetings in Washington...We are delighted to learn that you are in excellent health...All of us are in excellent health also...We received a Christmas gift from Taki and Sultana of $100...We also wish you good health and great happiness during this Holy Season and a Happy New Year.

I am enclosing two statements of the partnership interest. I have multiplied each investment by the time that has passed, then divided it by the sum of the deposits to determine the share value of each of the four partners.

If you think I can help you, let me know...I kiss you...

Your Father,

I. Chrysostomos

I wrote Papa informing him that I wanted him to keep the proceeds for his and Mama's needs.

I spent Christmas with the Anthony's and Elenitsa. For the first time I met Elenitsa's younger brother, Gus, who was home on leave from the Air Force. He had enlisted at the end of the war and thus had not seen any action. Still, his service obligation had kept him away from home, so the holidays provided me with an opportunity to get to know him. Elenitsa was close to her brother, and for that reason he would have a place in our lives.

The final function I oversaw at the Embassy was on Thursday, January 8, 1948. For the past week I had also been working at the Place Vendôme and had discovered that with my training and experience at the Pera Palace I was well suited to work at one of Washington's best restaurants. The Ambassador's stance toward my deportation had softened somewhat. Though I had not intended to continue working at the Embassy after New Year's, the Ambassador asked me to oversee one final dinner because of its importance, and he was concerned that everything go well. With Ogaleak's help we served crème d'asperagus, rockfish with a special sauce, pilaf artichokes au gratin, and parfet tutti frutti and fruit for dessert. Because the Melases had taken the week off, I helped Ogaleak prepare while allowing Regas a free hand at organizing.

The evening went very well and the next day when the Melases returned, I moved out of the Embassy.

"Christo, are sure you must go?" the Ambassador implored me quietly.

"Your Excellency, it has been my privilege to serve you, and I have enjoyed serving you—but I cannot stay."

For a moment the Ambassador was silent. Then he cleared his throat. "I have checked the Anthony family and have found that they are well respected," he said formally.

"Thank you, Your Excellency, for your interest," I replied politely.

All the Ambassador's initial anger had been replaced with resignation and, I thought, a little sadness. Despite his earlier threats about my visa, he did not wish me any ill will and was pleased to know I had acquired residency papers. "Then I wish you well," he said, knowing that I would not change my mind.

I thanked him for his good wishes and bowed. In an uncharacteristic response, he offered me a bow in return and then embraced me. Although a Turk and thirty-five years my senior, I had developed an affection for him and was grateful for the enormous opportunity he had given me.

* * * * *

Elenitsa and I were married in a small, traditional Greek ceremony at the Church of Saints Constantine and Helen in downtown Washington. The ceremony was performed by Father Thomas Daniels, whose white hair and beard, glasses and general robust appearance bore a mild and reassuring resemblance to old bishop Iakovos, my childhood mentor in Panayia. Mr. Mastos, who had arranged my initial introduction to the Anthony family, was my best man. On my side, Ogaleak, Regas, Taki and Sultana, and the Melases attended; Elenitsa and her family had invited about thirty people.

After our wedding we had a honeymoon in New York, staying with Taki and Sultana, now six months pregnant and suffering with morning sickness. We spent our days touring the city, and our evenings with my sister and her husband. I was overjoyed to have married Elenitsa, to have her with me and to be able to care for her, and I thanked God every day.

After six days on our honeymoon, we returned to our little apartment and that evening I went to work. Soon, I was often working lunches as well as dinners, so I frequently left home at ten-thirty in the morning, not to return until one the following morning. There was a certain pleasure in these long hours because my work was a way of building my life with Elenitsa and laying a foundation for our future, unencumbered by Turks and their religious and

201

economic oppression. For the first time in my thirty-one years, the product of my service to others bore a residual which I could save.

Late one evening not long after we were married, I returned home to find a letter for me from my father. Elenitsa was asleep, so I put on my pajamas and sat down at a small table with a night light on to read Papa's letter. Papa was by now seventy years old.

My dearest children Chrysostomos and Elenitsa in the U. S. A.,

Greetings...we received your letter as well as the beautiful photographs which made us very happy. We are again sending you our heartfelt blessings for a long and happy life together with the arrival of little ones.

I would like to counsel you regarding the sacrament of marriage and married life. You are both entering a new stage in your life of mutual commitments. You, Christo, should always treat your wife with love and respect. You, my daughter Elenitsa, in your relationship with your husband, should be guided by the three virtues of obedience, patience, and attentiveness. Both should relate to each other with devotion, temperance and tolerance.

When you practice these virtues in your lives, you can rest assured you will have God's blessings and your fellow man's respect.

With love,

Papa

Papa's words of wisdom and counsel served again as a marker for the beginning of my new life in America with Elenitsa—a life my old family, although far away from us and unseen, fully shared in thought and spirit. Their contribution to my new life was reflected in Papa's words.

The post-World War II period continued to have a calming effect on the persecution of the Christian minority on Imbroz and throughout Turkey. The Turks were tenaciously courting the United States for aid as diplomatic relations expanded, and did not want to draw attention to their poor treatment of minorities. By 1949, elected committees of minorities were allowed to participate in local government for the first time in twenty-six years. The poor remnants of the minority population only wondered how long the gesture would last. Certainly, my aspirations and attention were far away from Imbroz or Turkey, as I enthusiastically planned my new life with Elenitsa, but the reminders of the Old World were burned indelibly in the consciousness of all who had endured, brutally forging us into what we had become.

14

Failure Is Not an Option

I fall, I stand still...I trudge on, I gain a little...I get more eager and climb higher and begin to see the widening horizon. Every struggle is a victory.

—Helen Keller

At one time, I would have had to draw a picture of a cow in order to get a glass of milk! Since the first day that America was to be my new home, though, I had set about teaching myself English, just as I had once made a project of French. From the beginning I had every intention of living a long and prosperous life in this country, so I made a point of speaking English constantly. I must confess that my undertaking was, if not perfect, largely successful. In later years, one of my hobbies would be to sit up late at night reading the *Encyclopedia Britannica.*

In April 1948, I received a notice from the Immigration and Naturalization Service with regard to my application for citizenship. It requested that I obtain a good conduct certificate from the police of my native country. Although the Turkish authorities had a keen understanding of obedience, I didn't think certificates of good standing for Christians were anything they would consider issuing.

The notice had been sent to my father-in-law's house, and I picked it up on a weekend visit. That afternoon, he took me aside so we could talk.

"Christo, now that you are married, what are your plans?" he asked.

"I'll stay in food service where I have some experience," I told him. "There are many possibilities..."

"Such as?"

"Such as owning my own business," I said with a conviction that surprised even me. "I won't work for someone else forever."

My father-in-law liked that answer. "When you find the right venture," he said, "I'd like to help you out, make you a loan." Then he smiled. "I believe it will be a very good investment." Anton was not wealthy, but over time he had saved a few thousand dollars.

His offer overwhelmed me. No one had ever offered me financial support before. As I stammered out my thanks I realized I was humbled not only by his kindness, but by his belief in me. It made me all the more determined to succeed.

I knew of a store that was available which I often passed near our rooming house. Around two thousand square feet in size, it would make a perfect restaurant. Within a week of my father-in-law's offer I had priced the store and all the necessary kitchen equipment and furnishings, even down to plates and silver. I also priced certain simple but necessary improvements to tailor the site for a restaurant and presented my proposal to my father-in-law, who immediately agreed to lend me $3,000. This was the first time anyone had invested in me, and I pledged to repay him with my word as my bond. In those days, it would have been impossible for an immigrant who had not been naturalized to obtain a conventional loan.

The night my father-in-law and I shook hands on our venture was the night Elenitsa told me she was carrying our baby. What unbelievable fortune from God! Elenitsa's peritonitis had cost her one ovary, but her remaining ovary was blessedly productive. Beaming with pride and overcome with joy, I folded her in my arms.

"Chris," she said, "if this is a boy, I would like to name him for my father." She looked at me. "Would that be okay?" Generally, the eldest son in a Greek family is named after his father's father, but if Elenitsa wanted to name our child Anthony after her father, that was fine with me.

"And if we have a second son," she promised, "we will name him John, for your father."

"One baby at a time!" I laughed.

Elenitsa lifted her eyes to mine. "Thank you, Christo," she said seriously. "My father will be so proud."

For an instant, I thought of Papa and Mama, my family and everyone back on Imbroz. A twinge of grief at our separation surfaced, which I immediately suppressed. I knew they were participating as observers from afar, but this joyful news of a new generation of Chrysostomides—the American generation—I suddenly wanted everyone to know! I immediately wrote them a proud, happy letter.

I was sure Papa would understand if we named the boy after my father-in-law, but I stopped in mid-sentence as another thought struck me. "Elenitsa, what if the child is a girl?"

She laughed at me. "No use talking more about it until we know."

Suddenly, I smiled. I was about to become a father and a restaurant owner all at once. It seemed God had removed Elenitsa's health problem and was allowing her to bear children. I would name the restaurant the Apollo for the Greek god of sunlight, prophecy, music and poetry.

* * * * *

Opening my restaurant required some creative financing. This was not unusual for any immigrant, Greek or otherwise, newly arrived in America and trying to start up a business. Most enterprises require a sizeable investment of capital and lots of elbow grease. Since I had very little capital, I knew I would have to increase the "elbow grease" investment and be extremely frugal with all expenses. This meant I had to personally supply any labor necessary wherever I could: waiter, cook, busboy, even janitor and maintenance man.

The building I found cost $10,000, and the stoves, grills, refrigerators, dishwasher, worktables, stainless steel counters and assorted other kitchen equipment totaled another $7,000. Improvements to the dining area, including counter and stools, booths, tables and chairs, floor tile and fixtures, were another $4,000. This seemed an enormous amount, especially in 1948 when the average income per year was $3,000 and the workweek could extend to 80 hours. A little financial creativity proved very helpful. The total investment was $21,000.

First, I leased the property with an option to buy for three years. Then I put down a little under $1,000 on equipment and furnishings, leaving me with a balance of around $6,000 which I financed over four years. After purchasing some needed kitchen utensils and equipment, I had about $800 left to open the restaurant, purchase the silverware, china, linens, detergents, cleaning supplies, and hire an assistant. My payments, including $100 to my father-in-law, came to $380 a month. I had no idea how I would afford all this, but I had faith.

Meanwhile, I was also wondering how I would also provide everything that Elenitsa and the baby would need.

"Chris, what if something happens? We hardly have any money as it is. If we lose our investment, we will have nothing! Then what?" Elenitsa began to worry.

"Nothing is going to happen, Elenitsa. It is an opportunity for us. For the first time, I will have a chance to create something. How happy it makes me that it will be for you and our family. Yes, I will have to work hard, but I have been doing that all my life. Don't you see, Elenitsa? This is our opportunity to make something better for our lives!"

"You will be just like Daddy—working all day, never around for me or the children. Why can't you get a regular job like everyone else?"

We never did see eye to eye on this issue, despite how hard each of us tried to get the other to understand our fears and desires. Elenitsa did not want to be left alone, this was clear. Although she understood creature comforts, she would never relate them to my long workdays, to the toil it cost me provide them. She never understood that success has its price. I wanted only to give her a comfortable life, the life of ease and security for my family that I had never had. Even years later, we would have the same circular arguments over my long hours, a source of contention that we never seemed to figure a way to resolve. I suppose every marriage has its issues, the ones that become broken records...so familiar that eventually the anger and passion behind them fade to an almost comfortable predictability. I wasn't there yet in my life, though, and we were still in the full force of emotions on the subject.

"How can I get a regular job like everyone else, when the restaurant business is all I know! Be sensible, Elenitsa, I'm doing this for you, for our family!" I could see the hurt in her face, and I immediately felt guilty. I could not bear to bring her any pain. I felt so helpless, so trapped. There was never an easy answer for an immigrant starting a business. Why couldn't she see the sense of what I was saying?

"Elenitsa," I said softly. "I love you. I love you more than any woman I have ever known. You know that." I pulled her to me. Though she was still resistant, I could feel her body soften as I held her against me, "Please trust me," I whispered into her hair.

"Chris," she sighed, "I just don't want to be alone."

"I know, but we're together now...let's not spend it fighting," and this time she yielded to my kiss. There was something to be said for the days of passionate argument.

After spending most of my adult life as an entrepreneur, I can say that successful business ventures are a function of three disparate yet requisite parts: hard work, experience and persistence. A little luck doesn't hurt either. Notwithstanding the financial risk and investment of time and labor, nothing excited me more over the years of my working life than the opportunity to own and operate my own business. After spending years powerless under the yoke of the Turks, I took enormous pleasure in the newfound control of my own fate. This was precisely why I had come to America! It was heady stuff, especially for an energetic, ambitious young man, for I had a chance at economic freedom. I had earned the right to risk, and, God willing, I would succeed!

Success is seldom easy, however, and usually involves enormous time, as well as periodic failure and setbacks. A week before the Apollo opened, I gave notice to Blaze at the Place Vendôme to reduce my hours significantly, but not completely severing the relationship. I then threw myself into the final preparations with unparalleled zeal. The preparations were unending, it seemed, and all consuming. By the end of that week, I was running on enthusiasm alone, for I am certain there was nothing left to keep me going. How I could even function without sleep, and with all the energy I poured into the effort, is a mystery to me, but it seemed that my energy was limitless!

The big morning arrived at last, the morning for which I had spent countless hours and seemingly vast amounts of money, plunging us deep into debt. The small restaurant had a long counter with stools and two four-seat and eight two-seat tables along the wall. To complete the set-up and closing tasks, I had to be there a half-hour before opening and leave about a half-hour after closing at 6:00 p. m. On Saturdays and Sundays, I would open at 8:00 a. m. and would stay open a little later on Saturdays.

Ready or not, opening day was here. I arrived well before dawn to begin the food preparation. Even though they were already polished to a high shine, I anxiously repolished the counters and floors, then opened the doors promptly at 6:00 a. m. to catch the morning rush hour. By 10:00, I had only one customer, and he ordered only toast and coffee.

My first day I took in a grand total of $2.80. My first week I earned $37.48. My first month I grossed $294. In the late 1940's, Falls Church was a growing suburb about ten miles outside Washington, D. C., but its true growth spurt would not begin until the second half of the next decade. A further complication was that business in general that summer was unusually slow. Still, I managed to pay a few dollars to all my creditors and buy some more time. The following month, business improved somewhat.

In a restaurant, even if there is only one customer, food set-up and preparation still must occur. As the days and weeks passed, a few more customers came in, and within three months I had thirty to forty customers a day, averaging about forty cents per sale. In order to pay bills, my evenings were spent waiting tables at the Place Vendôme while the restaurant continued to build business.

Though I was not yet breaking even, I decided to hire my first employee. Walter was a high school graduate, but had no knowledge of restaurants, nor did he appear inclined to gain any. Tall and thin, shuffling along on extraordinarily large feet, he moved with little urgency through his tasks and required constant guidance. I can say I learned one important lesson from Walter. I quickly learned that in your own business you have to do almost everything yourself. Often, it took longer to give instructions than to complete the task yourself.

"Excuse me, Walter."

"That's okay, Mr. Christ. A lot of people step on my feet," he drawled, turning with a slow smile.

"Walter, will you please clean the counter and watch for customers."

"Right away, Mr. Christ."

"I'll be in the kitchen preparing the specials. Call me if anyone comes in."

"I will," he smiled.

Walter was a likeable young man, though his duties never progressed beyond sweeping up, wiping counters and occasionally serving food. He lacked any motivation to better himself.

Walter was not my only concern. As Elenitsa's pregnancy progressed, it became apparent that our room in the boarding house, with barely enough space for us, was certainly not large enough for a baby. Elenitsa tried to be tolerant of our living arrangements, but in reality she was unhappy with the situation. We needed an apartment with a kitchen.

I felt that if we could stick it out in the rooming house for another year, the business would be doing well enough to support both the debt and an apartment. In addition, I was particularly anxious to repay Elenitsa's father as soon as I could. He was looking for a piece of property to purchase in Virginia, and, although he said nothing, I knew he would need his money back. Sometimes in life, actions are affected by the wishes of others. Elenitsa simply did not want to have our baby in what was little more than a boarding house room.

One day, after spilling soup while trying to heat it on the hot plate we used for cooking, she snapped. "Chris, we need a real apartment with a real kitchen and two real bedrooms!"

I knew her nerves were wearing thin, and she was uncomfortable in her pregnancy. Bless her, she was trying. If we could just manage for one more year. "I know dear," I said from behind her, putting my arms around her growing stomach. "Don't worry, Elenitsa, we will have one. One day soon. I won't let you down," I whispered into her hair.

"We can't have a baby in this room," she persisted, but I felt her relax a little against me, with more than a little resignation.

What else could I do? I had to take care of her. She depended on me, and I had to provide for her and the baby. The next day, I called Taki in New York. It was against my instincts to have a partner in business, but I knew Taki was looking for an opportunity for investment. He had saved money while in the Navy which he added to funds his family had managed to take with them when they had left Imbroz a decade earlier. Taki offered to invest ten thousand dollars in the Apollo in exchange for a fifty-fifty partnership. We sealed our agreement with a handshake. Nothing was put in writing, yet our partnership was no less real or committed for the lack of documents. Taki was from Imbroz where we stood by our word, and there were no contracts or lawyers.

Taki's investment in the Apollo allowed me to repay my father-in-law. It also gave us the funds to reduce our improvement loan by $2,000 and extend the balance for eighteen months. Equally important, I was now able to rent a two-bedroom apartment with a proper kitchen.

The apartment was just around the corner from the Apollo and the boarding house. Considering the long hours I worked, this proved to be very convenient. Taki came to work before lunch and stayed until closing. Finally, after six months, we were making adequate money to pay our debts and take home a meager wage. I would also occasionally work at the Place Vendôme to supplement my income.

* * * * *

In mid-August, my father-in-law forwarded a letter to me from the immigration authorities. The letter was brief.

Sir:

Please refer to our letter of April 29, 1948, and advise whether you have obtained a good conduct certificate from the police authorities of your native country...

The certificate of good standing was the only item in a long list of requirements that remained unfulfilled. I had requested the good conduct certificate from police headquarters in Turkey months ago, but it was unlikely I would ever receive a response. Personally, I questioned whether or not the Turks even knew what "good standing" was. Because of this lack of documentation, I had been served with a Warrant of Deportation, which was subsequently dismissed at a formal hearing. Though predictable, the lack of response from Turkish officials was frustrating and worrisome. My only hope seemed to be to persuade the Immigration and Naturalization Service to waive the requirement. In my reply to the Immigration authorities I detailed my efforts to obtain the requested paperwork and expressed my concerns that the Turkish authorities would not cooperate. Elenitsa wrote the letter for me.

Finally, after testimonials from American friends and much discussion, Immigration ultimately waived the requirement, and I was admitted to the Americanization School in Washington, D. C., where I attended class once a month until 1952 to satisfy my citizen requirements. It was the first formal school I had attended since fourth grade and I thoroughly enjoyed my four years there. I was very close to realizing a final step of my childhood dream to become a citizen of the United States.

That fall, with my immigration problems clearing up and a small income from the Apollo, I sent Mama and Papa fifty dollars. It was the first time since leaving the Embassy I had been able to send money home, and it felt good to be able to do so once again.

There were other developments that autumn. On November 1, 1948, Archbishop Athenogoras, a Greek from Turkey and Archbishop of the Americas since 1931, was elected Ecumenical Patriarch of Constantinople. He would be the 268th occupant of the Throne of Saint Andrew.

This was great news for the Greek community in America and for the Orthodox Church worldwide. At six feet, three inches, Athenogoras was very tall for a Greek, and stories of his leadership, wisdom and kindness had abounded for decades. As Archbishop of the Americas he had built the Orthodox Church into a vital and growing institution. Once, years before when he was Metropolitan of Corfu in the 1920's, an Italian fleet had entered the port at Corfu and, without warning, opened fire on the city resulting in scores of casualties. Athenogoras asked a fisherman to row him out to the flagship of the Italian fleet, where he confronted the commander and offered himself in exchange for the lives of the citizens. The Italian officers were so impressed with his courage and humanity that they ceased fire, came ashore, and offered indemnities.

Athenogoras, who was broadly respected by the leaders of the western world, was more importantly viewed by the rank and file as a servant of God and an ambassador for Orthodox Christians wherever he went. After many years serving the church in America, he would return to Constantinople. Upon hearing of his return, my thoughts went to Jimmy Coucouzes, who would be with him at the Patriarchade in Constantinople. Jimmy's planned short visit had obviously turned into a more permanent stay. I wondered how he was, what he was doing, and if he would ever return to the United States.

I wondered also at the ever-expanding needs of my immediate family. Although the Apollo was earning an income for us, its sales had flattened out. It soon became apparent that it wasn't earning enough to sustain the needs of a growing family. I continued waiting tables in downtown Washington, increasing it to two or three nights a week. The tips were excellent, but this part-time job, on top of my regular eighty-hour workweek, was tiring and created long, stressful days for me, and lonely nights for Elenitsa.

Elenitsa was now nearing full term. "Chris, I don't think I can manage it," she said tearfully one night. "We have to finish the baby's room, we still haven't even gotten a crib. At any time, I might have to go to the hospital and where will you be?" she lamented. "I have been all alone...It's so hard, Chris."

"Now, now, Elenitsa, don't you worry. I will be there when the time comes. You will call me, and I will be right there. Tomorrow, I will get the crib," I soothed.

I knew she didn't fully understand the business responsibilities and obligations that required my attention. In those days, men tended to business and women were homemakers. The roles of the two sexes were differentiated and rigid. This marital division was economically sound as well as practical in those days. The erosion of that division has brought disorder.

I was strongly committed to providing a good life for my family. I desperately wanted to spare them the deprivation, poverty and unrelenting adversity that I had endured as a youngster at the hands of the Turks. If I had to work an extra forty hours a week, so be it. It was part of what I believed I owed my family. Every day I mustered all my strength with humility and boundless enthusiasm.

A day and a half later, on March 30, 1949, Elenitsa gave birth to our son, Anthony Christopher. It was not an easy delivery, however, and Elenitsa remained in the hospital twelve days after the birth. The lengthy hospital stay was costly, creating yet another monthly debt and making it increasingly difficult to continue sending money to Imbroz, but my wife was safe, and we had a healthy son. There was much to be grateful for. I now had both a family and a business in America. My only problem was whom to pay when, and how much. The line of my creditors seemed never ending. Every morning at five-thirty when I pinned my relic coin to my tee shirt, I gave special thanks to God for my son and prayed that He would bless and watch over my new family. Responsibilities that might have seemed stressful were a breeze, given the extreme stress of my past. Yes, life in America was a far cry from the life-and-death struggle that was endemic to my first twenty years.

A month or two later Elenitsa and I called Father Daniels, who had performed our marriage ceremony, to schedule a baptism for our son. Elenitsa asked two of her close friends, Ted and Eleni Papadeas, to be godparents to Anthony, and I invited Ogaleak, Ted Regas and the Melases from the Embassy to attend. Taki and Sultana came with their small son, Peter, who was now almost a year old. Afterwards, our guests gathered at our apartment where we celebrated with hors d'oeuvres and drinks. Indeed, it seemed to me I had much to celebrate. After all, my son was born in America!

I continued to work long hours while Elenitsa took care of Anthony. By the time I got home from the Apollo, Anthony was usually asleep. Many late evenings, I simply stood by his crib and watched him. Before I knew it, we were buying a cake for his first birthday party. Most of the attendees were relatives and friends. Anton and Alexandra, my in-laws, were there. Christina Regas, a friend of Elenitsa's, and her mother were there. Sultana and her son Peter came to help us celebrate along with several kids from the neighborhood. Taki knew how important this day was to me and worked that afternoon to give me time at home. Anthony's birthday was another milestone in my life's journey, for it was the first time I had participated in the American tradition of a birthday celebration. In the old country, we celebrated name days of the saints, and I welcomed this new opportunity for Americanization.

A few days after Anthony's birthday I received an emotional letter from Katina. Some time before, I had broached to her the subject of her coming to the U. S. when she was no longer needed on Imbroz, but it was understood that our parents care remained of primary concern.

My dear brother Chrysostomos,

I was delighted to receive your letter, which I read carefully three times. Strong will power resembles water. Both of them, if allowed to flow, will open the way...These are our father's words.

You mention that there are two ways that I can come to the U. S.— as a tourist or through the Embassy. Do what you think is best. Do it by yourself... I truly believe you bring good luck to others! You possess the kindness, refinement, subtlety and, above all, the boldness. In all my life I have never met anyone with more courage than you...God only helps courageous people. With your charming personality and your gentleness of spirit everyone likes and admires you. In this world kindness is the most admired trait in a human being. The most superior type of person is the one who possesses gentleness. The greatest philosopher in the world who lacks gentleness is worthless.

When I arrive, six months on a visa is plenty of time to find someone...We must not let this year go by. This matter cannot wait.

I kiss you,

Katina

Poor Katina! The years had passed. She was thirty-six and unmarried. She longed for a husband and a life of her own. The post-war reawakening was touching everyone but her. Katina's duty to our parents would outweigh her youthful desire to marry and have a family. Poor, poor Katina. In fact, it would be many years before I would make good on my promise and bring Katina to America.

Her letter was the last one I received for some time. Neither she nor Mama and Papa wished to worry me with their needs, and they tried to discourage me from sending money. They knew I had a family to support and with it came added financial responsibilities.

In fact, my new family was growing. By the end of 1950, Elenitsa gave birth to our second son, Jon, named after my beloved father, Ioanni. Within three months after Jon's birth, I had finished paying medical bills for the baby's delivery, and resumed sending about $50 a month to Imbroz. Sultana and Taki also did what they could.

The early fifties, although difficult, were manageable and rewarding. By the middle of 1952 both my sons were walking and talking. Business at the Apollo had increased and I was successfully paying down our debts. At the age of thirty-five, I had developed a stoic tolerance for the unexpected. I hoped things continued to go smoothly. If there were no unpleasant surprises, I would finally be able to save a little money and get ahead. Yet financial surprises seemed to emerge from thin air and there were never enough hours to do my day's work.

"You know, Christo, some nights we hardly do any business," Taki casually observed with a shrug, indicating he had no explanation for it. It was just one of those things.

"I know, Taki. Maybe next week will be better. We'll see." On the weeks that we didn't take in enough to cover our expenses, we would not take any pay for ourselves.

"This week was a holiday. Next week things should be back to normal," Taki said.

For some reason, as I looked at him, it became clear to me that one day, we would sell the business, and I would buy my own. Taki, too, was restless and wished to return to New York with his family, where he now owned two townhouses.

In that year, I finally completed my naturalization classes. This was also the year I followed my first presidential election campaign in the United States. I had arrived in America three years before Truman's 1948 election, but I was not yet eligible to vote. I observed the process with abundant curiosity. This time, as a prospective American citizen, I took a keen interest in the upcoming elections. President Truman decided not to run for re-election, and Adlai Stevenson was defeated by the Republican candidate, Dwight D. Eisenhower. Eisenhower had enjoyed great popularity for his command of allied armies in Europe in World War II. Meanwhile, back on Imbroz, local Christians were allowed to serve on administrative committees, and Greek Christian schools were reopened in 1952, after 29 years. In its own small way, my island was participating in the rebirth of optimism.

On the evening of my citizenship ceremony, Elenitsa approached me with an unusual request. She wanted to shorten our surname.

"What would you like it to be?" I asked, trying not to sound surprised.

"Something easier for the children to say—and everyone else, for that matter. Most people can't even say Chrysostomidis, let alone spell it."

"It's hard, Daddy," little Anthony chimed in, "too hard for me to say!"

I looked from my son to my wife and thought about it. A moment later I had an idea.

"How about Christ?…as in Christmas," I suggested.

"That may work," Elenitsa nodded thoughtfully.

Anthony was more enthusiastic. "Yes, Daddy, make it Christ!"

Chrysostomidis is a fine old Greek Christian name, but if my wife and children wished, we would shorten it to Christ. "All right," I told my family, "Christ it is, then."

That evening in District Court in Alexandria, Virginia, I swore allegiance to the United States of America along with others who had been in my naturalization class. The odyssey that began with a ten-year-old's dream in 1927 found me a quarter of a century later a citizen in America. As I somberly stood on the steps of the courthouse, I thought of Papa's words to me on our sunny porch so many years ago. "Go to America, Christo," he said. "Go to America." It had been Papa's dream as well as mine, a goal we shared, and now I had truly fulfilled it. "Papa, we did it. I am an American and here for good," I whispered under my breath.

I received my citizenship certificate on December 10, 1952, five days before my thirty-fifth birthday. No longer was I Chrysostomos Ioanni Chrysostomidis of Imbroz. I was now Chris John Christ, an American citizen. I did it! How proud I was!

The next weekend I purchased a used DeSoto, obtained my driver's license and proudly drove my family to church. It was almost Christmas and we drove to the new Greek Orthodox cathedral, St. Sophia, on Massachusetts Avenue in Washington. Built in the Byzantine style, it is a beautiful church and brings to mind the lovely architecture of the churches in Constantinople and Imbroz, although most had been desecrated.

The priest at St. Sophia was Father Lalousis. He was a likeable man with a brilliant voice, and his chants resonated throughout the cathedral, echoing childhood memories of melodious chants from long ago on my island home. After church we introduced ourselves to him. For the next few years, I brought my family to St. Sophia regularly. "This was the church of my youth," I told them. "It may be new, but it resembles the churches I grew up with." It was my duty as a father to pass this tradition to my children. The Church had stood strong for me in my youth, and I felt compelled to stand strong for her now in my prosperity.

After our first visit to St. Sophia, we drove the DeSoto home where I made a lamb and rice pilaf dinner for my family. I had begun preparations the night before by soaking long grained rice in tap water to remove the starch, boiling chickens with carrots, onions and celery to make broth, and trimming a fresh-cut leg of lamb, then inserting a clove of garlic beneath the skin to take away the taste of mutton. On Sunday after church, I sautéed the rice briefly in butter, then poured the chicken broth over it and allowed it to simmer while the leg of lamb roasted in the oven.

So began a tradition of preparing this meal for my family on Sundays and holidays. Over time, traditional meals can cement familial bonds, and of course I always prepared it with Elenitsa's help. As the years passed and the generations grew, it became a favorite with my children's families as well. There were many meals Elenitsa and I prepared for our family, but my lamb and rice pilaf, along with Elenitsa's spinach pie, was always a special get-together feast for us. That Sunday, we all ate heartily. Then, at four o'clock, I went to the Apollo to work the dinner shift, relieve Taki, and close up the restaurant for the night.

* * * * *

In 1953, my father-in-law sold his house and business in Cumberland and bought a piece of property in Warrenton, Virginia, where he constructed a nineteen-room motel which he named The Jefferson. As a first-generation immigrant, Anton may not have known much about Thomas Jefferson, but he respected him as a symbol of America. Later that year he built a small ice cream store for his son, Gus, who had just gotten out of the Air Force. Gus seemed a self-absorbed man who put effort into obtaining title and position in life at the expense of substance.

"Chris," he later said to me, "I am associated with some gentlemen and may obtain the regional franchise for Tastee Freeze. That's something you should look at."

"We'll see, maybe later," I told him.

Gus obtained a Tastee Freeze franchise and sold ice cream, hot dogs, hamburgers, sodas and french-fries. His first wife had run out on him leaving him with a young son, Ronnie, who was raised mostly by Elenitsa's parents. Ronnie was a small boy who was born premature. Anthony was six months younger, but by the time he was four years old he was already a head taller. I had been small as a young boy myself, and my size had been the subject of good-natured teasing. I was both proud and relieved that Anthony was big enough to be spared that.

Although I was a partner in a restaurant, by this time I had come to realize that the Apollo was not where I wanted to stay. Taki was a good man and a fine friend, but the partnership seemed to inhibit my energy and I knew I needed to be on my own. I began keeping an eye out for different opportunities, but there was something important I wanted to do before I left the Apollo. Elenitsa and I wanted to buy a house.

In the summer of 1953, I found a house about a mile and a half away from the Apollo. It was a thousand-square-foot rambler on a quarter-acre lot with a full basement. The asking price was $17,500, but I haggled it down to $17,000. I was 36 years old and I had paid rent all of my life, from Constantinople to America. It was time to buy a home and pay a mortgage instead. After years of hard work, I finally had enough money for the minimum down payment of $1,700. Only in America could you borrow to buy your home with ten percent down.

Of all the things I've done, buying my first home was one of my proudest moments. Elenitsa, the boys and I moved in later that summer. Anthony was four and a half and Jon was three. It was important to me that they grow up in a house their family owned. It was a goal, another milestone I had reached.

God had been good to me. I had become a citizen of the country of my dreams and now I had a home for my family. When I think of the opportunities America offered me, they stand in sharp contrast to the way of life in Turkey. Almost without interruption this land afforded me the opportunity to advance and to care for my family. One can never fully appreciate this country's freedom of choice unless one has lived without it. For that, the uncivilized Turks had a special place in my life: to heighten my appreciation for my newly adopted land.

Most of the houses in our neighborhood were ramblers with young couples and children like us. Elenitsa exchanged baked goods, Christmas cards and birthday presents for the kids with the other moms, but my work schedule kept my relationship with my neighbors to a few polite greetings on the rare occasions our paths crossed during the thirteen years we lived there. An exception was Anthony's fifth birthday party, which we held on a Sunday afternoon. This was one of the few opportunities I had had to actually get to know them.

Everyone was busy raising their children, paying their bills and earning a living. Still, most of the husbands had time in the evenings and on weekends to spend with their families and to get to know their neighbors. My failure in this regard further stirred Elenitsa's desire to have me at home more.

"Chris, why can't you work like Leo or Bud Brandt? They're always home in the evenings," she would say with tears in her eyes.

"They have different sorts of jobs," I would point out. "I have no formal education." The restaurant business was my vocation. That is what I knew. Unfortunately, it demanded long, thankless hours. On the other hand, it offered an income that permitted us to do things for our children. When Elenitsa wanted to enroll Anthony in the Humpty Dumpty Nursery School, we were able to afford the fee. Elenitsa thought the school would be fun for Anthony.

"They have a pony there for the children to ride," she said. "And he'll learn his numbers and ABC's."

"Isn't he a little young for school?" I asked.

"He'll be five in March," Elenitsa replied. "He's ready. He's more than ready. And he'll like it so much."

So we enrolled Anthony in the Humpty Dumpty Nursery School, and I gladly paid the tuition. Elenitsa, Anthony and Jon were constant sources of motivation for me. I derived a great deal of pleasure and fulfillment from giving them the things they needed and wanted. It was my hope that one day, that would include a college education.

* * * * *

Since Katina's rather lengthy letter over four years earlier, there had been no mention of coming to America, and I knew my sister was torn between duty to our parents and a desire for a life of her own. I would support whatever decision she made, but I knew Katina well, and I knew she would never leave Imbroz as long as Mama and Papa were alive. As the older children bore the weight of responsibility, Katina and I took care of family before ourselves. Katina felt an obligation to care for our parents in their advancing years just as I felt an obligation to send money home every month. We each did what we had to, but the day would come when Katina could look to her own needs, and when that time arrived, I would bring her here.

That winter Elenitsa's brother Gus spoke to me again about opening my own Tastee Freeze franchise.

"It may be an opportunity for you to have your own business, Chris," he told me. "It would cost about $2,000 for a location. If something turns up, would you be interested?"

The truth was I was very interested, and told him so. For a year or so I had thought about leaving the Apollo, but something—

a house, a birth, hospital bills—always came up to deplete my savings. Maybe it was time to go out on my own. Gus told me he would keep an eye out for me, and for a while I thought no more about it.

One day he called and said he had found a location for a Tastee Freeze franchise that he thought I'd be interested in.

"It's a small store at a resort," he told me. "Ocean City, in Maryland. I'd like to take you to see it, Chris. It's a good location and if you like it I can help you arrange the purchase."

Gus was brimming with a salesman's excitement. "If you want, we could go now!" he suggested.

"Now?" I laughed. "I've got your sister and two small boys with me, and it's a five-to-six-hour drive, Gus!" His enthusiasm was contagious. "All right," I told him. "If you think it's that good, then I suppose we'd better go have a look, but not now."

Two weeks later I took a whirlwind trip to Ocean City with Gus. It took an hour and a half to reach the Chesapeake Bay and the ferry ride across the Bay to the Eastern Shore took almost two hours more. From the ferry we could see the pilings that were being built to support the new five-mile-long suspension bridge that was under construction, called Bay Bridge, which would eliminate the long ferry crossing.

After we disembarked, we had another two-hour drive to Ocean City. We checked into a small motel a half-mile before the bridge that crossed the bay separating Ocean City and its peninsula from the rest of the Eastern Shore. From the time I first saw the island with Gus, I thought it was beautiful with its fresh air and ocean breezes. It reminded me of my island home. That year, the stretch of 17th Street where the store was located was undeveloped, but I felt certain that people would see what I saw, and, over time, would come. The blue skies, white sands and cool ocean breezes were soothing yet stimulating. I was sold. Upon returning home, Elenitsa didn't share my enthusiasm, but she supported my decision to start a business there. I hoped she would come to love it as I did.

Meanwhile, my family had increasing demands. In 1954, cowboys and Indians were all the rage and my boys wanted cowboy hats and six shooters for Christmas. As the holidays approached, Elenitsa picked out not only hats and guns but shirts and pants as well. It was fun to see the boys wound up with anticipation, wondering what Santa would bring them. It felt so American!

A few days before Christmas, our happy scene was disrupted when Anthony developed a severe stomach ache and Elenitsa took him to the doctor. He was diagnosed with stomach flu and was prescribed some medicine to calm his stomach. Anthony seemed to improve, and on Christmas day, he and Jon were beside themselves with excitement. They spent nearly the entire day in their cowboy-and-Indian attire, firing caps from their six shooters.

All of a sudden, Anthony doubled up in pain. I bolted across the room and scooped him up.

"What's wrong, son?" I asked, cradling him against me.

"I hurt," he whispered, gritting the words out through clenched teeth. "My tummy really hurts."

"Perhaps he needs more medicine, Chris," Elenitsa said, her brow creased with worry.

Before I could reply, Anthony shook his head. "No," he said. "It doesn't help. Besides, I'll feel better in a little while."

"Maybe so," I said, "but you'll take your medicine anyway."

After a bit Anthony did seem to feel better, but we still remained concerned. I checked on him before I went to work the next day, and I called home several times during the morning. Anthony seemed to be fine, and Elenitsa agreed there was no more pain. The next day at work, she called distraught.

"Chris," she said, "Anthony began having more pain, worse this time, much worse. I didn't know what to do so I called Dr. Retsina and he told me to call an ambulance. He wants us at the hospital in Arlington right away."

I drove as fast as I could. Anthony had been taken immediately in the ambulance, and Elenitsa, Jon and I followed in the car. When we arrived, he was already being seen by a Dr. Moses, the surgeon on duty. Elenitsa and I waited anxiously outside the examining room door until Dr. Moses came out.

"Anthony has an appendix that has to come out right away," Dr. Moses told us, and from his serious expression and tone of voice I knew he was very concerned. Within minutes, Anthony was in surgery, but his appendix had already ruptured, leaving him seriously ill with peritonitis. Elenitsa and I visited every evening and prayed every day for our little boy. He looked so small and sick lying there in the stark hospital surroundings. It was a full two weeks before he recovered, and we knew what a close call it had been. Our Christmas present that year was to have our little boy safely home again.

Much of our savings went to pay the hospital bills, paying every month for a year against the balance, but the hospital stay took a greater toll than money. Elenitsa, already stressed by caring for two rambunctious boys, was almost overwhelmed by Anthony's illness, and many of her usual tasks became too much for her. Some months later she suffered a nervous breakdown and was hospitalized for almost a month.

I was worried and distraught. Elenitsa's mother had two brothers, Mike and George. George's wife Anna May was not Greek, but knowing we were in need she came to us immediately. Her presence was a godsend. She cared for the boys, freeing me to return to my strenuous work schedule and cope with Elenitsa's illness.

Elenitsa, the doctor told me, was suffering from depression. In those days doctors discouraged family visits, which made the situation even harder for me. Throughout my life I have had as little to do with doctors as possible, but I took very seriously the advice they gave me about my family. If a doctor said Anthony's appendix should come out, it came out. If a doctor advised me not to visit my wife while she was ill, I stayed home. So when Elenitsa's doctor suggested electric shock for treatment of her depression, I agreed, but it frightened me terribly. It appeared to be successful, or so the doctor said. Two weeks later, I was able to bring her home.

The hospital bill was very large. I paid a fraction of it and arranged to pay the rest over the next year. We had no hospitalization insurance in those days and the expenses were becoming terribly burdensome. Fortunately, hospitals extended credit. This all came after I had committed my available money to my brother-in-law to become a franchisee in the Ocean City store.

After Elenitsa's return home, things were different. Elenitsa had a hard time recalling things and she seemed disconnected.

"Chris, I don't remember so much," she said wistfully.

"Don't worry, I have enough memory for both of us," I would tease her.

Even in the best of health Elenitsa was always worried about things and needed a lot of reassurance from me—reassurance I gladly gave. My naturally positive outlook on life was helpful to Elenitsa. I told her how much we had missed her and urged her not to focus on the day-to-day details of life. That Sunday all of us, including Anna May, went to the Cathedral of St. Sophia where I thanked God for bringing my Elenitsa home and restoring her to health. The next day Anna May, who had been such an enormous help to us, went home, refusing to accept anything from me other than my thanks. I took her to the train station and when she wasn't looking slipped fifty dollars into her purse.

We decided it was time for the boys to start attending Sunday school. Anthony was almost six and Jon was turning four, so every Sunday morning I took the boys to Sunday school and Elenitsa stayed home to have some time to herself. Then we all went to church, and afterwards we had our big traditional Sunday dinner of lamb and rice pilaf that we prepared together.

One Sunday, Ogaleak and Regas came to our family dinner. We had seen very little of them since Anthony's baptism. Seeing my old friends put me in mind of our early days in this country and gave me an opportunity to speak a little French and Turkish. We all ate and drank a little too much that day. After polishing off a bottle of ouzo, our discussions got loud and raucous.

Ogaleak had not a hair on his head and my sons stood in awe of his Yul Brenner appearance. On the rare occasions we would see him, they sat quietly and attentively near him, which was out of character. To them he may have seemed exotic, and much to my amusement they hung on his every word, whether in French, Turkish or English. Although unmistakably authoritarian, Ogaleak, though he had none of his own, was a soft touch when it came to children. It was so good to see my old friends in my new country, in my own home.

* * * * *

In early spring, Elenitsa received a letter from two of her great-uncles, Uncle Chris and Uncle Charlie, who had come to the United States as young men in the 1890's. They had sold their place in Wheeling, West Virginia, and bought a 200-acre farm outside Newport News, Virginia, some years ago. Neither had ever married.

Letter in hand, Elenitsa turned to me. "You know, Chris, one of these days I'd love to visit my great uncles."

I knew what was coming. "Which 'one day' would you like to go?" I asked, and made Elenitsa laugh.

The uncles had lived alone together for all their lives yet they were as different as night and day. Chris, who was extremely religious and supportive of the church, could not stand cigarette smoke. Charlie was a chain smoker and was quietly rumored to have been a gigolo in the Greek community some time ago.

So one Sunday morning when Taki was opening the restaurant, I took Elenitsa and the boys to Newport News to see her old uncles. When we got to the farm, we turned onto a dirt road that curved through the woods for about half a mile before ending at an old farmhouse with a sweep of lawn, a barn, and an old 1940's Plymouth parked nearby. This property revealed a beautiful expansive view of the James River as it emptied into Hampton Roads, the site of the famous *Monitor* vs. *Merrimac* ironclad naval battle of the American Civil War. The farmhouse was a speck in the bucolic splendor of the tidewater, marshes and fields humming with wildlife. A couple of dogs ran up to bark at our car but fled when we opened the doors, much to the boys' dismay. Chris and Charlie stood on the front porch to greet us. Charlie was tall and thin with a thick head of hair and a mustache. Chris, on the other hand, was short, heavy, and bald.

"Uncle Chris, Charlie!" Elenitsa cried as she ran to her great uncles and embraced them warmly. She linked each of them on her arms and introduced us. The house had few modern improvements. The old gentlemen cooked and heated by wood stove and drew water from a well, but their simple life seemed to suit them. They served us a light lunch and presented Elenitsa with two paintings done by their mother, her great-great-aunt.

"She always wanted someone to have them who would love them. Now we pass them to you." One was of a dog and the other of men by a campfire. They would become rustic heirlooms for our growing family.

Later in the summer, as a treat for the boys and to lighten Elenitsa's load for a few days, we drove to Warrenton to leave Anthony and Jon with their grandparents for a week.

At that time, I spoke with Gus about my Ocean City franchise. Although I had paid Gus the franchise fee, Taki and I were still trying to sell the Apollo. Gus mentioned three other locations that were available, but Ocean City most interested me. I was certain people would travel to the beach. One day the town, and my business, would be very popular. Although my family would have to remain in Falls Church most of the year, I felt confident that this was the opportunity I had waited so long and worked so hard for. It was a chance to provide well for my family and to own a business that was completely mine.

Going to Ocean City was a risk. It was a seasonal business and I had a wife, two children, a mortgage, and a family on Imbroz. I also had doubts about the Tastee Freeze menu that my brother-in-law so avidly endorsed. I was thirty-six years old and I could not afford a misstep. I once again found myself gripping the object of my heritage, my relic coin, as I heard whispers from across the oceans I had crossed, through time, dreams, hopes and losses. The present challenge was upon me. *I will not fail,* I whispered to my father as I kissed the sacred coin and tucked it securely in its resting place against my breast. The appeal of blue skies and sandy beaches had lured me to a new frontier, a new challenge as I prepared to go to Ocean City to start a new business in the spring of 1954.

A couple of good Greeks, both named George, finally agreed to buy the Apollo and the next few weeks were spent finalizing the sale. At long last, Taki and I were free. We decided to take Elenitsa, Sultana and the kids to nearby Glen Echo Park for a picnic. The park overlooks Little Falls on the Potomac River a couple of miles west of Washington, D. C. Aside from a campground, there was an amusement park with swings and an old-fashioned carousel. The children had fun reaching for the ever-elusive brass ring, hoping to win the coveted free ride. After several attempts at it, they contented themselves with the swings, urging the adults to push them higher and higher, soaring to views of the world they seldom glimpsed. Taki's little girl, Theope, was five, about the same age as my younger son, Jon, and the two of them giggled and played happily in the crisp autumn sunshine.

Being in the food business, and all of us from a deprived background, we tended toward excessive picnic baskets. We all took our fill of food, fresh air, and probably a little too much drink for Taki and me. As we rode back in Taki's old Plymouth, we broke out in our favorite song, *Still one more drink, still one more song...*

"Taki, please keep your eyes on the road!" Sultana pleaded. Taki had a habit when he was singing or talking to turn around and look at the people in the back seat.

"Taki, the road!" which only seemed to further his amusement, and we continued with our song.

Still another drink.
Still another tune.
Bringing desire into one's mind
And anything I want to,
I can see it through...

Even without the drink, a picnic in America with our most cherished possession, our family, was intoxicating for two island boys from Imbroz. So ended another day of enchantment in our land of opportunity.

Taki and Sultana returned with their children to his mother's house in Brooklyn. My brother-in-law, Gus, had sent the papers for my purchase of the Tastee Freeze. He had already opened almost ten stores by himself. I was aware that Gus' primary motivation was to lease another Tastee Freeze store, but I couldn't forget the sunny seaside beach and I put aside my reservations about dealing with family. Certainly, over time, people would come to vacation there and the store would thrive. I could see it, feel it and taste it.

My beach store included complete financing on all equipment as well as a lease from Mr. Charlie Holland, who owned the property and the building. Charlie was a man about ten years older than I was who owned a lot of property in Ocean City, property that was both inherited and accumulated over a generation. He and his wife Myrtle owned and operated Maridel Realty, as well as two motels elsewhere in town. Although Charlie's holdings went well beyond two motels and a real estate company, he always dressed in jeans and a plaid shirt. In the forty years I knew him, I nearly always saw him driving up, casually dressed, in his red pick-up with a rusty Golden Retriever sitting next to him in the cab.

In April of 1954, when I had first met with Charlie to discuss the lease, it was he who suggested I have an attorney go over it for me. "Chris, I'll lease the building to you as is for $2,500 a year, to start off," Charlie told me. "It's a five year lease and it will go up a hundred dollars a year with a five year option. You will be responsible for all utilities, taxes and upkeep." He squinted at me intently—an unsettling characteristic I eventually grew accustomed to. Mark Williams, my attorney, was a mild-mannered, intelligent man, reasonable in his fees. He explained the lease to me clearly and in careful detail, and I liked his way of doing business. I would see Mark for legal advice for many years to come.

Equipping the store and paying the franchise fee to Gus took all my available funds, including the proceeds from the sale of the Apollo, plus a little more. There was a certain way the people at Tastee Freeze wanted things done, and Gus schooled me carefully in the preparation and presentation of the menu, which was very basic: hamburgers, hot dogs, french-fries, sodas, milkshakes and, of course, soft ice cream. Although elementary for a person of my food background, I was polite and attentive to my brother-in-law's presentation. Handling the soft ice cream and sterilizing the ice cream machine, which had to be washed daily, were the only things new to me. Fries and meat were bought only through the Tastee Freeze corporation and arrived frozen and ready to cook. The food was unimaginative and tasteless, but I followed the program to the letter, down to the white-paper Tastee Freeze hat.

I stayed in Ocean City long enough to complete all the paperwork pertaining to the lease and the franchise before returning home to Falls Church, where I filled up the refrigerator and gave Elenitsa a hundred dollars to keep the children fed. Then I packed up some clothes and headed back to Ocean City to open up the store for the summer.

In the spring of 1955, Elenitsa gave birth to a baby girl whom we named Ianthe, a Greek word for "flower." With a third child, my responsibilities had expanded yet again. The Tastee Freeze store was bleeding my resources dry, and my creditors continued to pile up. Undaunted, I managed to keep my faith, my focus and my positive attitude, determined to stay the course. As each problem required attention and resolution, my purposeful action was empowered and renewed daily.

15

A New Archbishop

The Church is in bondage to capitalism.
Capitalism...is a faith and a way of life. On the
basis of this idolatry, it develops a morality in
which economic worth becomes the standard by
which to measure all other values... The
bondage of the Church to nationalism...regards
the nation as the supreme value...it breeds an
unlimited lust for national power and
expansion...the result is conflict, war and
destruction... The Church has become
entangled with...these systems of worldliness.

—H. Richard Webehr
The Church against the World

Life's cycles of success and failure are intermittent and of
varying intensity. Even in a neutral environment, the pleasures of
success are blemished and, at the same time, enhanced by random
failure. In twentieth century Constantinople, the environment was
decidedly hostile for the Christian community. Small successes
garnered great satisfaction. In 1955, the fragile veil of religious
civility that had prevailed for a decade was torn. For a three-day
period in early September, Moslem mobs, at the encouragement of
the Turkish government, once again unleashed destruction against
the Christian minority. The news took me back into the dark
Mohammedan world I had struggled so long and hard in.

The riots were triggered by the report of a bomb that exploded
outside of Atatürk's birth place in the Turkish consulate in
Salonika, Greece. The truth later came out that the bomb had
broken only two windows and was detonated by a Moslem law
student of the University of Thessaloniki named Oktayi, but the
incident was used to spark riots against Christians. The press

showed graphic pictures of manic crowds, fire, and billowing smoke, yet they were agonizingly bereft of detail. In snapshots, the horror of Christian persecution unfolded anew.

A month later, I received a call from Ogaleak, who was still working at the Embassy, telling me they had received a letter for me from Constantinople. A couple of days later, I met Ogaleak at a small bar off M Street to pick up my mail.

"Good to see you, Christo!" he said with a broad smile and a hearty slap on my back.

"It's wonderful to see you, too," I replied. "How is the Ambassador?"

"Oh, he is the same, Christo." He pushed an envelope across the bar toward me. "Here is your letter. I believe it is from the Patriarchade."

"Yes, so it is." I took the letter and opened it, hungry for any news from the Old World.

"Dear Chrysostomos," it began. *"I am a bishop serving Athenagoros, our Patriarch. I understand you have married and have a family. When I left, I never expected to be in Constantinople this long. I imagine you heard about the riots. The reality was much worse than the accounts reported by the western media. Chrysostomos, not a day has passed during my forty-five years when I did not feel powerless to end our people's religious persecution…"* I looked up at Ogaleak.

"It's Jimmy," I told him. "He's writing about the riots last month." Ogaleak nodded while handing me a shot glass full of anisette.

"Cheers," he said, raising the glass. "To health, happiness and children."

"Yes, thank you," I mumbled as I read on.

We estimate the destruction from the riots as follows: 4,500 shops, 1,000 homes, 110 hotels, 26 schools and 73 churches were looted and destroyed. Countless graveyards have been defiled. A Greek Orthodox priest was murdered, along with fourteen other victims. It was officially reported that 200 Christian women were raped, though over 2,000 women were actually treated and examined for rape.

In short, the riots have been successful in uprooting most of the remaining Christians of Constantinople. A mass exodus of Christians has reduced the minority population from 300,000 to less than 100,000 and rapidly declining. Homes and businesses have been confiscated by the Turks without recompense. The riots concealed the unconscionable and illegal property transfers, violently taken during the uprooting. Those of us who remain have no choice. The Church must go on. One day, I will see you again in America. May God bless you and your family.

Your Countryman,...

"Iakovos," I sighed.

"What did you say?" asked Ogaleak.

"Jimmy has taken the name Iakovos, after the old bishop on our island, and he himself has become a bishop. He wrote to tell me about the severity of the religious riots that occurred last month."

Ogaleak nodded, and we talked of the atrocities, both old and new. The rest of our time together was spent talking about my family and the Embassy. It was good to see my old friend again. At that moment, I felt a strange feeling of homesickness. I suppose one never loses that, no matter how good the times are. We longed for a simpler past to reflect upon. However, mine certainly was not. Perhaps the memory of challenges overcome and contests won is more pleasurable to look upon than the uneventful passage of time. At any rate, the remainder of our afternoon was spent in comfortable cheer and camaraderie, and it was with genuine sadness that I said farewell to my good friend.

That winter, I worked hard waiting tables at Place Vendôme and paying down debt. When it came time to return to the beach, I was recharged. That third season in Ocean City, I was determined to bring my family down, despite the financial strain. A couple of blocks from where the boardwalk met Talbot Street was a rooming house called the Nordica. It was owned by Gus Jones, shortened from Jonakakis, an Albanian Greek who came to America before the Iron Curtain fell. He had a bad back that resulted in an unusual, rigid walk, and prevented him from bending or lifting, as well as from looking side to side without turning his body. He gave me a room at a reasonable rate in the basement of the Nordica, and we agreed to negotiate for a larger room when Elenitsa and the kids came down for the summer.

Every morning I rose at dawn, pinning my relic coin to my T-shirt and saying my morning prayer. I never forgot to thank God for each new day, always asking Him to watch over my family and grant me the strength to succeed in my new store. On my way to work, it was my habit to stand for a moment, gazing eastward across the boardwalk and the white sandy beach to the ocean glittering in the morning sun. It was God's grace and this tranquil sight of the sun rising over the sea, reminiscent of my island home, that sustained me through many years of hard work. It endeared this tiny island to me, evoking emotions that I had not felt since leaving Imbroz many years before. The sight of dazzling ivory sand caressed by the sunlit sea, the touch of fresh ocean breezes on my face, the view of a clean, blue April sky...these things refreshed and filled me with peace, placing a new perspective on the events of my life. The chess game of violence, power and upheaval conducted by demagogues such as Atatürk and Hitler melted away over the waves of the timeless sea. Everything seemed insignificant when compared to the serene sounds and cool breeze over the expanse and ancient, cosmic rhythm of the sea. These impressions would stay with me without requiring my presence, for although I worked a block from the Atlantic for many years, I rarely had sufficient time to actually see it.

My first few weeks at Ocean City that third year were busy ones preparing for the summer season. Each morning I drove nineteen blocks north to my store. I dealt with the utility companies, cleaned and scrubbed the store, installed equipment, and purchased supplies and food. Every cent I had was invested or spent in my venture, this small, fourteen-hundred-square-foot operation, and its success or failure would rest solely with me. Since my boyhood I had served many of the basic needs of others. I would bear the pain of failure, or endure the price of prosperity.

Finally, on a Thursday at the end of April, I opened up for business. That morning I set up the soft-ice-cream machine, turned on the grill and deep fryer, set up the stations, and waited for customers. I made $2.68. By the end of the week I had taken in less than $25. Elenitsa called and needed more money. Since she didn't drive and couldn't make it to the bank, I wrapped a twenty-dollar bill in paper and mailed it to her with a note. At the end of a month, my revenues totaled only $200. My third season was starting out no better than the first two. The height of the summer season was just beginning, however, and I had high hopes that business would improve.

"The season" at Ocean City ran from June through August, with a step up in the spring and around Labor Day. Basically, I had six months, from April through October, to make gross revenues of $12,000, the minimum I would need to meet expenses and stay in business.

When school let out, I brought my family down to join me. As soon as we arrived in Ocean City we went to the Nordica where I introduced them to our landlord. Gus' stiff posture and bald head gave him a stern, serious manner, but he was friendly with children. As soon as he saw my three, he exclaimed, "Here they are! Here they are!" over and over until the children smiled with delight. Then he led us up one flight of stairs and down a narrow hall to a worn room, rustic in appearance with two lumpy double beds, a refrigerator, sink and window crammed into a ten-by-twelve-foot space and a window that faced the adjacent building. I brought our suitcases up, kissed Elenitsa, hugged the children and left to open the store. It was 9:30 in the morning. The arrival of my family served to charge my energy and outlook toward this third season at the beach. Twelve hours later I would close up shop and return to our room for a few hours of sleep, the pattern of my summer routine. On weekends I kept the store opened until midnight, and during the six-month season, my store remained open seven days a week.

Running a restaurant is hard, but particularly hard when you're not making money. The hours are long and the work is tedious and taxing. In the beginning, to save on expenses, I hired no full-time help and shouldered all the work myself. Later, I hired a young girl, Barbara, part time, who was introduced to me by Mark Williams, my attorney. Business improved that summer, but before it drew to a close it became apparent that despite all my hard work, sales would fall far short of what I needed. There was no turning back, though, so every morning I pinned on my coin, said a brief prayer and headed out to work. Each month I reliably paid the Tastee Freeze fee, because that was what I had agreed to do. I was beginning to feel, however, that the Tastee Freeze menu was not the right one for my store. We limped along through the end of the summer, with only mild business increases, and I somehow managed to remain optimistic.

Late that August I packed up Elenitsa and the kids and prepared to take them home. We left Ocean City at 5:00 a. m. on the Tuesday before Labor Day, leaving Barbara to open the store. As soon as we got home, I stocked the refrigerator with food, just as I had before I had left in the spring. Although she could easily walk the few blocks to the store, I wanted to spare her as much of that as I could. She would have her hands full as it was, since Anthony would be entering first grade and Jon kindergarten in less than a week. I left her money for new trousers, shirts and school shoes for the boys, grabbed a stack of mail to take back with me, and kissed everyone goodbye. Then I turned around and headed off to Ocean City, arriving at the Tastee Freeze by mid-afternoon.

That night back in my room I flipped through the mail, sorting out bills, most of which would receive partial payment, when I came across a letter from Mama.

Dear Chrysostomos,

Papa, Katina and I are all well and hope the same for Elenitsa and the children. Costa is working in Constantinople but we see him often. By next year he should have his visa completed to come to America...

The Turks leave us alone but things are worsening. They have closed the Greek schools again. Thank God for Katina, she does so much for us.

Regards from your Uncle Demetri.

With all my love,

Your Mother

"They have closed the Greek schools again" struck an ominous chord inside me. Immediately I wrote a response and purchased a money order for a hundred dollars to place in the letter. As pressing as my obligations remained, I knew there was greater need than mine. Time had compounded the circumstances to insure that their needs would be chronic.

At the end of the season I paid Gus for my room, but I was unable to pay my rent to Mr. Holland in full. Fortunately, Charlie was a fair and reasonable man and trusted me to pay the balance as soon as I was able. Certainly my first three years in business were much slower than I had thought they would be, but I still believed I would make a success of the store. I had no choice.

While getting ready to close and winterize the store, I got a call from Elenitsa. I knew immediately from her voice that something was wrong. Little did I know I would be soon jumping from the proverbial financial frying pan into the fire.

"Chris, the children are fine," she reassured me immediately. "But I'm not well." She paused. "When can you come home?"

"Elenitsa, what is it?"

"It's…it's my nerves, Chris. I saw the doctor."

"What did he say?"

"He wants me to go to the hospital," she said softly. "He told me…" She broke off and started again. "Sometimes, things are just too much for me, Chris. The doctor said I need to rest."

"There, there, don't worry, everything will be fine," I responded keeping my voice positive.

We had all been under great stress with the demands of the new business, and Elenitsa, who worried terribly over everything, felt it keenly. I tried to soothe her, promising I'd call every night and be home as soon as I could.

I had planned to remain open another couple of weeks, but over the next two days I rushed through closing and winterizing the store. By Wednesday I was done. After calling to check in, I grabbed my bags and headed home. The boys were not yet home from school when I arrived, and Elenitsa was in bed. Moments later I was talking on the phone with her doctor.

"Mr. Christ, your wife is suffering with depression," he told me, "and I believe it can be best treated in a hospital." He went on to explain that there were many ways to treat depression, but that recovery would take time. Having been through this before, the doctor's speech seemed eerily familiar.

"Will she be all right?" I asked.

"I believe, with proper treatment, that she will recover," the doctor said carefully, "but delaying treatment will work against her.

I would like to have her at the hospital tomorrow. Will you be able to bring her?"

"Of course," I said. "Of course I will bring her. We will do whatever is best for her."

Elenitsa was suffering her second breakdown. The timing of her illness was difficult. The hospital would want an immediate deposit, which, on top of a slow summer, would cause great financial difficulty. My biggest worry was for the children, who would have to do without their mother for a while. So as soon as I hung up from the doctor, I called Elenitsa's Thea Anna May.

To my relief, Anna May agreed to come and stay with us once again. Next I placed a call to my old friend Blaze, the owner of the Place Vendôme in Georgetown. When I first decided on the Ocean City venture, I knew I would need a source of income during the off-season, so I kept the arrangement to work for Blaze during the winter. Now, with Elenitsa entering the hospital and my finances so terribly extended in my new venture, I could not afford to wait. Thankfully, neither, apparently, could Blaze. He was short staffed and asked if I could come into work that night.

I worked until nearly midnight. The next morning I got the boys off to school, packed up Elenitsa and Cookie, as I affectionately called Ianthe, and drove to the hospital. That evening Christine Regas came over to watch the children while I worked.

The next morning after Anna May arrived and was settled, I hurried to Georgetown and waited tables for lunch and dinner. For the next several weeks, my time was torn between double shifts at the Place Vendôme and caring for the children at home.

Waiting tables worked well for me. The tips were excellent—good enough to support my family and make my mortgage and car payments. Just as important, summer was a slow season for the restaurant business in Washington, and no one cared if I took leave to operate my Tastee Freeze store in Ocean City. Waiting tables was a perfect solution to the problem of supporting my family until my store got going.

Elenitsa was hospitalized for six long weeks. The boys seemed to handle their mother's absence with few problems, but it was hard on the baby. Cookie simply wanted her mother, and often neither

Anna May nor I could console her. My financial obligations compelled me to work double shifts at the restaurant, often remaining downtown between shifts, which placed a heavy burden on Anna May and meant I saw the children less often than I wished. Still, I was there each morning before they left for school, and on Sunday I took them to Sunday school and prepared a traditional Greek dinner for everyone before going to work at five. Anna May was a godsend and she managed to keep my little family running in Elenitsa's absence. Even so, the weeks were hard. We all missed Elenitsa.

I had regular consultations with the doctor, who assured me Elenitsa was progressing and that her twenty-eight treatments with electric shock therapy were progressing. The treatments, he said, would affect her memory. "At first, she will seem to have forgotten commonplace things and events," he told me, "but over time, her memory will come back."

"Yes, I remember the same things from before."

Finally, the day came when I brought Elenitsa home, and we began her long, slow recovery together. I was realizing that her condition was more serious than what I had thought after her earlier treatment.

The $3,000 bill compounded my financial fracture. I paid the hospital $100 down and agreed to pay a hundred dollars a month toward the balance. I didn't even want to think how long it would take me to pay it off, but was happy that they accepted my plan of payment.

Elenitsa was better, however, and even though we were having some rough times, I was steadily employed, paying a mortgage on a house I owned, and investing in a small business. Most importantly, I was a free citizen of the United States of America. God gave me energy and my country gave me the freedom to exercise it. I greeted each morning with prayer and optimism, and my certain belief in God and myself would carry me through all adversities. My current problems paled in comparison to the circumstances of my youth, yet much of my inner strength derived from those hard and hungry times. I knew I could do it. I remembered my father when the Turks stole from his store, the lack of medicine and food, the struggle for employment as a young teen, the forced conscription on the Russian border. Certainly if God saw me through those times, he would see us through our current problems.

Elenitsa was quiet and withdrawn when I drove her home from the hospital that day, but nothing prepared me for the shock I was about to receive. For several miles I made idle chatter but Elenitsa did not seem to hear me. Finally I brought up the subject of the children, thinking that would pique her interest. At last, in a slow, flat, toneless voice she spoke.

"I don't think I remember their names."

Not remember their names! My mind jolted. Then I remembered what the doctor had said about the effect of the shock treatment on her memory. He had told me she would seem "forgetful." Forgetful! I was dumbfounded. I think it hit me for the first time, just how sick my poor Elenitsa was. So for the rest of the journey home I talked to her about our family, being careful to repeat everyone's name. As I talked, Elenitsa gazed distantly out the car window, a detached smile playing about her lips, but I knew she was listening. I would have to try harder by providing more support at home. Where would I find the time, I wondered.

* * * * *

The holidays came and went. I continued to work double shifts. Tips were good and my finances slowly improved. We were barely treading water, however, and would never get ahead unless the small store in Ocean City became successful.

That winter Elenitsa, much recovered, wanted to get a dog for the children. Although I had no affection for dogs, I wanted Elenitsa to have everything she wanted, so a little half beagle, half terrier puppy joined our family, and we named him Toby. He arrived in time for Anthony's eighth birthday in March, and on my insistence he slept in the basement. Almost every evening, I brought him scraps from the restaurant—usually filet mignon. Within no time at all he was the best fed little mutt in Northern Virginia, if not in the whole world.

Come summer in Ocean City, little Toby had a hard time readjusting to dog food. Even after working the entire winter at the

Place Vendôme, I was still not finished paying last year's rent to Charlie Holland. Business that summer was better than the previous three, but it still fell short of what I needed and in order to stay current on our mortgage I fell behind on my payments to the hospital. Gus Jones, knowing my difficulties, insisted I hold off in paying my room rent at the Nordica, God bless him. On the morning of June 1, I began a novena to the Virgin Mary to please grant me the strength and show me the way to make a success of my store. All along, Elenitsa and the children remained unaware that our finances were so tight.

My novena must have worked, for that month I began to realize and deal with my chief problems with the business. My brother-in-law, Gus, owned the Eastern Shore Tastee Freeze franchise, and he wanted us to buy our supplies and groceries from a commissary he was establishing. I had spent the better part of twenty-five years in the food service business and I knew that in order to be successful, the quality of the supplies had to remain high. The commissary, I knew, could not provide that quality. On top of that, the Tastee Freeze menu, with its limited offering of hamburgers, hot dogs and french-fries, lacked diversity, as well as quality. As a novice Tastee Freeze franchisee, I had thought it improper to challenge or change the Tastee Freeze menu, and therefore was saddled with the same bland fare.

Now, however, it was different. The lack of a tasteful, well-rounded menu was hurting my small store's chance of success and I knew at that time there was no choice. I would have to change it if we were to survive. I had the experience to do it successfully, but it was something I would need to plan.

During the next few years, I would work regularly at the Place Vendôme, and later, in the early 1960's, Blaze and I moved to the Rive Gauche. Washington's crème de la crème dined at these two restaurants where I served the wealthy and well-known, much as I had at the Pera Palace and the Park Hotel years before in Constantinople. One of my regular customers at the Rive Gauche was a young woman who later became First Lady of the United States, a lovely woman named Jacqueline Kennedy. Another of my notable customers was a gentleman dressed in a suit with an open collar shirt and a top hat. From under his hat wild curly hair stood out around his head. When I bowed and pulled out his chair for him to sit, he smiled and bowed back. Puzzled, I repeated my bow and gestured for him to sit down. He grinned and bowed back. Again I bowed and indicated that he sit, and again he mimicked my motions.

"Please, sir," I laughed, placing my hand on his shoulder and gently guiding him into his seat. Later I learned that my playful customer—and, as it developed, my biggest tipper—was Harpo Marx. Over the next two years, Mr. Marx made several trips to Washington, returning twice more to the Rive Gauche where I was his waiter. We always seemed to enjoy each other.

* * * * *

In early 1958, Costa arrived in America. He stayed for a while with Taki and Sultana in New York and arrived at our house in Virginia in time to join us for Thanksgiving dinner. When I met him at Union Station, I was surprised to see he was wearing a hat to cover his balding head. I remembered him as a small boy running down the dock to hug me farewell when I left for Constantinople, and later, as a young teen arriving in the big city to study tailoring. When I finally held him at arm's length I realized that, apart from his baldness, he had changed very little. With much excitement I ushered him to the car. The sight of Costa brought me, for a moment, close to Mama and Papa.

Costa had lots of affection to pass around to Elenitsa and the children, and my family greeted him with joy. At Thanksgiving dinner that afternoon, we were joined by Elenitsa's parents who came in from Warrenton. There was something uniquely wonderful about having my family members around me in America. For a moment all my financial woes seemed to fade when I considered my great and humbling assets of freedom and family. When we sat down I said a special grace, in honor of the reunion with my brother, my past: "Thank you God for protecting us and allowing us to be together for another year," I prayed. "We also thank You for the possessions You have given us and for the food on our table. And we offer You our greatest thanks for bringing Costa to us safely from Imbroz to share this special day. Amen."

"Amen," everyone echoed softly. Then we shared a traditional American Thanksgiving dinner of moist, tender turkey served with a special rice, raisin and nut stuffing and Greek sweet bread. The tablecloth was obscured by the various savory concoctions Elenitsa and I had prepared in honor of the holiday. Even though my debts were huge, there had always been plenty of food since the day I arrived in America.

Costa stayed the week, spending time with our children, the nieces and nephews he had never met, before returning to New York where he had already found a job. His plan was to earn enough to put some savings down on a townhouse in Brooklyn. The brief week with Costa was exciting for all of us. For that brief week, I opened the window to my past, and, through my little brother, connected with it. I hoped he would be able to visit us for a longer stay before his six-month visa expired, but that was not to be. He would return to America as soon as he was able to obtain a permanent visa.

Shortly thereafter, my good friend Ogaleak, who was still at the Embassy, announced he was marrying a Russian Orthodox woman about thirty-five years old—thirty years his junior. Patience is often well-rewarded. They would marry at the Russian Orthodox Saint Nicholas Cathedral on Massachusetts Avenue, diagonally across from Saint Sophia. The whole family was invited, and he insisted that I bring the kids. That week Elenitsa and I went shopping for the wedding, and bought white jackets and blue pants for the boys and a little white dress for Ianthe.

The wedding service, the icons and the priest's vestments, were identical to our Greek service in every respect, except it was in Russian. After the ceremony, we went to Ogaleak's two-bedroom apartment downtown for a small reception. Theologas and Elias and Anna Melas were there, along with a couple of his Russian friends, and Ogaleak and I drank a bottle of Metaxa on top of shots of ouzo. It had been years since I had left the Embassy and the four of us had much to catch up on. I introduced my family to everyone and spent the balance of the day and into the evening drinking and swapping old stories with my friends.

After Christmas, another memorable event occurred. Elenitsa's great-uncles came to visit. They had sold their farm in Newport News to the DuPont family for a rumored two hundred thousand dollars—a huge sum. Both men were now into their eighties, and Elenitsa had asked me if they could stay on with us for a while. It turned out to be quite a while. Uncle Chris drove an old DeSoto so slowly that one day he was given a ticket for obstruction of traffic. They were indeed a couple of characters and kept our winter quite unpredictable. Chris still carried a crucifix in one hand and worry beads in the other, working them constantly in his palm. Charlie still chain-smoked non-filtered Camels. I think he did it mostly to irritate his brother, who fussed and nagged him about the habit constantly.

In the spring they received a letter from their niece in Greece and promptly departed overseas with barely a thanks for our extended hospitality. Before they left, I told Chris that when God took him to give me a sign from heaven.

"Don't forget," I told him.

Chris nodded in agreement.

After they went to Greece we heard they made a significant financial contribution to the building of a church, and most likely to their nieces. The next we heard was that Uncle Chris, the clean-living non-smoker, was dead. Three months later, Uncle Charlie died as well. The two paintings they had given Elenitsa would remain our only reminder of two colorful, very elderly gentlemen who lived three decades in the nineteenth century. No sign from Heaven ever arrived.

* * * * *

Later that year, I drove to the post office to mail some bills and asked the postmaster to show me the new 1958 issue stamps. I bought ten three-cent stamps and three four-cent stamps for a total of forty-two cents. Stamps were so beautiful I never lost my interest in the hobby. The 1958 Overland Mail stamp and the Noah Webster, Gunston Hall and Minnesota Statehood stamps were all beautifully detailed and colorful.

I had collected stamps from all over the globe for over twenty years, and I still had the ones collected long ago in Turkey, Egypt and other places I had passed through. Over time I came to realize that independent of a country's wealth or form of government, stamps were unique imprints of each country's optimism. In my hectic, hard-working life, stamp collecting offered a few fleeting minutes of diversion and relaxation. It was, perhaps, one of my few indulgences.

The summer of 1958 turned into another struggle for my business. By the end of the season I had implemented many menu changes and was now thoroughly committed to completely changing the menu. I had planned all through the winter and when I arrived in Ocean City in the spring of 1959, I was finally ready. The first thing I did was to call Dale Truit at Swift and Company and order the best grades of meats and cheese in every category. From now on, I would serve no frozen foods in my shop; everything would be fresh and prepared with great care. I kept my focus on reasonable price, speed of service and variety of choice. My gourmet background in food served me well, apparently, for as soon as the menu was in place my sales jumped. I now offered chicken, ham, and submarines.

Early one morning I was out cleaning my asphalt parking lot with a hose when a muscular young black man rode up on a bicycle. The bike had elevated handlebars, two saddlebags, a multitude of reflectors, a large horn, a headlight still shining in the early daylight, and a foxtail hanging off the back. Without a doubt, it was the most unforgettable two-wheeled vehicle I had ever seen.

This was my first sight of Bernard. With slow, thoughtful speech and impeccable manners, he introduced himself and told me he was twenty-five years old. "Since my mama died this winter I don't have anyone to take care of me," he said, "and I wonder if you know where I can find a job." Bernard was different from other people. He was simple. Today, we have all kinds of words for people with such disabilities: intellectually impaired, challenged, learning-disabled and the like. I am not sure what Bernard's specific difficulty was because we did not have such labels back then, but, plainly put, Bernard was simple. He was a good man and he deserved the same respect as any other man. I knew people teased and ridiculed him, maybe even feared him, but I saw his dignity and I respected him. I gave him a job, and I demanded the best from him, as well.

"Bernard, see what I'm doing with the hose?" I was moving the hose slowly across the blacktop parking lot from left to right, pushing a line of sand, dirt, cups, paper and bags in front. "You see, Bernard?" his eyes focusing on the line of water. "Hold your thumb over the water like this, you see?" I showed him how to limit the water to force it out faster.

"Yes, sir, Mr. Christ."

"All right, you take over and I will go inside to prepare for today."

"Yes, sir. I'll take care of it!" he said.

I watched Bernard for another minute. "No, no Bernard, look down while cleaning, look down."

"Bernard," I said a few minutes later. "When you finish you can have your breakfast. Afterwards, we have a lot of work to do."

"Yes sir, Mr. Christ," he said.

"You come inside and I'll fix you a sandwich." I gestured toward the back door.

"Yes sir, Mr. Christ. I will," he repeated.

This was how Bernard's first day with me began. Bernard lived in Berlin, a town six miles away, in the house he had once shared with his mother. As the summer progressed he became a regular employee, arriving early every morning on his fabulous bicycle. Cleaning was Bernard's primary duty, which was very important in the food service business. He worked hard to keep the store clean exactly as I wanted it, an increasing need as business improved. Over time I showed him how to become a good preparations man, as well, cutting and slicing vegetables, meats and cheese. Eventually, he would routinely help me paint the store before we opened each spring. Like Papa thirty-five years earlier, we painted it white, inside and out, and—yes—the trim was blue. Bernard was reliable and honest and stayed with me for many years. To this day, in his sixties, I believe he still rides a flashy bike.

We were very busy that summer. Our hamburgers were lean beef, pattied fresh every day from ten-pound bags of premium fresh ground beef. Our french-fries were cut from Idaho longs, peeled, sliced and fried in peanut oil. They were always served fresh and hot. Our hoagies were made of Italian sausage, sliced ham, baloney and Provolone cheese on a bed of lettuce and sliced tomato, with a generous helping of mayonnaise—all ingredients, of course, fresh. As our new menu grew in popularity, so did my receipts. It was not until the summer of 1959 when I was 42 years old—32 years to the day after I had left home, that I felt I had finally made it. During that June, my sales doubled! Although the numbers were still small, my small store had begun to thrive.

It was that same summer that I waited on a young man with a full beard who ordered a Coke and a hamburger with onions and catsup. I served him and after he had eaten, he approached me and asked if I needed help. I looked at him and thought a moment. The truth was that business was good enough to support more help. I told him to report to work at six o'clock the next morning, and that the beard would have to go.

The young man's name was Vassilli (Bill) Moschonas. He was a 23-year-old Greek immigrant who was at that time a bit of a drifter, but he had an intensity of manner and was properly respectful. The next morning when I arrived at work, he had been standing at the back door for some time, cleanly shaven and clad in a white shirt and tie. He worked hard with me for over three years, becoming my first manager of sorts, before moving on to open his own store in the Maryland suburbs. Vassilli was the first of many young men over a twenty-year span who worked with me, and went on to start their own businesses. So it seems, just as success had found me, others in pursuit of their success sought me out.

Summer was winding down when I received a call at the store from Ted Regas at the Turkish Embassy.

"Hello, my friend," I greeted him enthusiastically. "How are you?"

"Fine, Christo, I am fine. And you and your family?"

We went on this way for a while, exchanging polite greetings and inquiries. "To what do I owe the pleasure of your call?" I asked finally.

Almost at once, he lowered his voice conspiratorially. "Christo, have you heard the news that Archbishop Michael has died?"

I hadn't. "Well," he continued, "His Eminence Patriarch Athenagoras, along with the bishops in Constantinople, has appointed a new Archbishop of the Americas." He paused dramatically.

"And that new Archbishop would be...?" I prompted.

"Iakovos!" he exclaimed triumphantly. "Iakovos has been chosen as our new Archbishop!"

"Iakovos?" I repeated, a bit dazed. "Iakovos!" It took a minute for me to realize that Jimmy Coucouzes, my childhood friend from Imbroz, had been chosen to be the new Archbishop of the Americas. Archbishop Iakovos! For the rest of his life Jimmy would be addressed as Archbishop Iakovos! Suddenly I was filled with joy.

"God bless him! God bless my old friend Jimmy," I repeated. "It's a miracle!"

From the ash of Turkish genocide and persecution, a religious leader for the Christian Orthodox faithful of the Americas had risen, my childhood friend.

16
Nick Anthony and the Roast Beef Sandwich

For this is wisdom; to love, to live,
To take what Fate, or the Gods, may give,
Speed passion's ebb as you greet its flow,—
To have,—to hold,—and,—in time,—let go!

—Lawrence Hope
"For This Is Wisdom"

In the fall of 1959, the Greek community in Washington was preparing to attend Saint Sophia Cathedral for the first formal visit of Iakovos, the new Archbishop of the Americas. It was the end of my sixth year of operation in Ocean City. My new menu had really taken off and for the first time in my life I was almost caught up on all my bills. By the time I returned from Ocean City late in October to begin my winter work at the Rive Gauche, I even had a little money in the bank. I bought a Plymouth station wagon for transporting family and supplies between Northern Virginia and Ocean City. From that point on, a station wagon became a mainstay for me. If the following summer proved as profitable as this past one had been, I would talk to Charlie Holland about buying the Ocean City property.

The contrast between our Archbishop and my new station wagon underscored the material distance I had traversed which was satisfying, yet my mind and spirit were never far from my poor island roots.

A week before the Archbishop arrived, I took the boys out and bought them new suits. Ianthe was also fitted in a new dress. Although they would outgrow them in a year, it was imperative that they look their best for the new Archbishop. That Sunday morning

Elenitsa's parents joined us for the drive to the cathedral. Anton's health had remained good through the twelve years I had known him. In fact, his energy and appearance seemed unchanged. Even though he was in his late sixties, his hair was still jet black and he continued to work tirelessly fourteen hours a day, six to seven days a weeks at his new Jefferson Motel in Warrenton, which was becoming a success.

Alexandra's health was not as good. Although she was ten years younger than her husband, arthritis had practically destroyed her knees, and her legs were bowed and brittle. Over the years she deteriorated from using a cane to relying on a walker to get about. It was hard on her, but she found solace in her faith and increased support from her family—especially Elenitsa. I thought of my sister, back home, taking care of our parents, and was always supportive of Elenitsa's desire to take care of hers.

I loaded my family—wife, children, and in-laws—into the station wagon and headed off to church. The cathedral was packed with the faithful who had come to welcome their new Archbishop. I was lucky to find seats in the front for my in-laws, Elenitsa and Ianthe, but the boys and I stood in the aisle. It wasn't until Father Laloussis signaled for the congregation to sit down that I saw the new Archbishop. Even in his imposing vestments and headdress, even with the staff of an archbishop in his hands and his longer beard and hair salted with grey, I could see he was my childhood friend Jimmy Coucouzes. How far he had come since Imbroz! As for that, how far had I come as well. I bowed my head and crossed myself three times. "May God bless you and protect you," I whispered.

Both Father Laloussis and the Archbishop had resounding voices and, backed by the marvelous choir, they filled the church with Byzantine chants. The crowded cathedral was illuminated by shafts of tinted sunlight pouring through a rainbow of stained glass, showering the incensed interior with a thousand glimmers. For a moment, the sound and spectacle of this service to God transported me back to the days of my childhood, sending shivers of reverence, community and history through my heart.

Certain faded images of old Bishop Iakovos conducting services in Imbroz were reflected in Jimmy. Now, almost four decades later, an archbishop from that same childhood setting stood before us, thousands of miles and events from that church on Imbroz. It was an eerie sense of connectedness, of unity and passage.

At the end of the service we joined a long line waiting patiently to receive the blessed bread, which the priests pass out to the parishioners before they leave the church. When we entered the line, I arranged my family in front of me so that I was last and could assist my mother-in-law, who walked slowly with a cane. Though her legs pained her terribly, Alexandra was not about to sit this out. She was devout in her beliefs, and she wanted very much to receive His Eminence's blessing.

As we approached the head of the line, he saw me immediately. His eyes lit up and he motioned to me excitedly.

"Chrysostomos, come to me!" he said in a loud Greek whisper that drew the attention of all around. A minute later, with a broad smile and a reverent bow, I introduced my family to my friend, then bowed again and kissed his hand which he then placed on my shoulder. Though dressed in the imposing regalia of the archbishop, it was Jimmy's eyes that twinkled.

"Come see me downstairs when I'm done," he invited. "Will you do that?"

I nodded. "Of course, Your Eminence, I will," I responded with a respectful bow.

After we had been received, I sent my family outside and headed downstairs to the crowded auditorium, as the Archbishop had requested. When I entered the room, a bishop on Iakovos' staff noticed me and asked that I follow him. He led me through a suite of offices to a quiet room where Jimmy sat waiting for me. As soon as I entered, the Archbishop stood and gestured the bishop out.

"Your Eminence," I said, bowing once again.

"Christo, it is so good to see you! Here, sit. You must tell me about your parents, your sisters, your brother. Is everyone well? And, of course, your new family in America."

He settled me in a chair across from him and for several moments I recited the news of my family, old and new.

251

"Well, not much news on my parents, your Eminence. You know Katina is still dutifully taking care of them. Yes, my family in America! I have three children. Anthony my oldest, you see how large he is, and he is only ten years old! Jon, named after Papa, of course, and my little flower, Ianthe. Of course my Elenitsa, whose mother is from Rankia, Turkey."

"I saw your parents about five years ago," he told me. "I was only able to go to Imbroz twice during my years in Constantinople, but I made it a point to see your family, and Bishop Iakovos who is doing fine. The last you saw of him was when he was arrested before serving eighteen months in prison. Everyone is growing old, Chrysostomos. The last time I saw Bishop Iakovos, he and your father were discussing politics as in the old days. It was as if the clock had been turned back, and I was still a child, standing quietly listening to the grown-ups talk among themselves! Remember?" he laughed exuberantly, drawing surreptitious glances from the two bishops nearby, who knew his eminence as normally pensive and measured in speech and behavior.

"Yes, I remember!" I laughed.

"I have kept up on news about you," he continued. "I heard you have your own store now, is that so? You're quite the entrepreneur."

"Yes, Your Eminence," I said, and proceeded to tell him all about Ocean City and my Tastee Freeze store.

"You are like your father, Christo."

The comparison pleased me, and I nodded. "And how are things in Turkey?" I asked.

Iakovos shook his head. "The Turks are still mistreating the remaining Christians. Bishops are still assaulted, graves desecrated, and the few remaining holy relics are one by one being destroyed." He looked at me sadly. "In many respects, nothing has changed, but we make do and get by. The Church will survive and Our Lord will find a way."

Suddenly, he changed the subject. "Come see me at the Archdiocese in New York," he said warmly. "Promise me that you will."

"You must promise to come as a guest to my home for dinner," I invited. "It would mean much to my family and me."

"I'd like that, Christo."

Before we parted, we embraced.

On the way home Anthony turned to me and said, "The Archbishop was from your island, wasn't he, Dad? Did you know him?"

"Yes, I knew him, Anthony." I smiled. "I knew him quite well."

* * * * *

During the winter of 1959, Elenitsa and I were approached by a group of Greek families to join them in forming a new Orthodox church in Northern Virginia—Saint Katherine's. Originally there were thirty founding families in the congregation. For two years we held services in the Sunday school room of a small Presbyterian church. Eventually, after many functions and fundraisers, for which I usually prepared and donated the food, we purchased a suitable piece of property and built a church.

Even though St. Katherine's was closer to our home in the Virginia suburbs, I would periodically return to St. Sophia. Its soaring, Byzantine structure, icons, mosaics and stained glass, were close to my heart. I never entered its doors without being captivated by the Byzantine architecture and thinking of the graceful church edifices of Constantinople in my youth.

The next summer, I went down to Ocean City early. Jerry Moutzalias came to teach me to prepare a steamship round of beef. Jerry was the chef at Blackie's House of Beef, a popular Washington restaurant so large that it took up nearly an entire city block. Blackie's had created a roast beef sandwich that was incredibly popular in Washington and had obtained success of legendary proportions among Greek restaurant entrepreneurs. I wanted to introduce the roast beef sandwich to Ocean City and welcomed instruction in its preparation.

"This is going to be the best sandwich you can imagine, Chris!" I watched as he trimmed the beef and ran a rod through the length of the roast next to the bone. Then he added salt, pepper and onions and cooked it at 550 degrees for three hours, pouring a little water over the beef every fifteen to twenty minutes. Finally he lowered the heat to 375 for another two hours. "Very simple, but also very, very good," Jerry humbly boasted.

I wholeheartedly agreed. After my lesson from Jerry in the making of a steamship round, I arranged three steam table pans in the front window in plain view of my customers, with heat lamps hanging over them. On the right I displayed my specially seasoned oven-baked chicken, and on the left was our Virginia sugar-cured ham. In the center, dominating the display, was a seventy-pound steamship round, au jus. Over time, I made changes to the spices and other minor modifications, but didn't tamper too much with success.

All our sandwiches were popular, but Jerry's recipe helped us create the most popular sandwich on the beach. Our steamship round was thinly sliced and served on a Kaiser roll, seasoned with salt and pepper. It was a wonderful sandwich, the top of the roll dipped in the hot juice of the beef. People came from all over the beach to buy one and before long we were selling almost an entire steamship round every day for 75 cents per sandwich.

I had turned a corner in my business, for we were now strongly in the black. My fisherman's patience and years of work were paying off. Last year's success had carried over, and with the new beef sandwich added to my menu, my receipts continued to grow. The next step would be to buy the property from Charlie Holland.

One morning in mid-July, while Bernard was busy cleaning the floors inside, I took over his usual task of cleaning the parking lot with a hose. While I was working, a gentleman almost twenty years my senior walked up to me.

"Are you Chris Christ?" he asked.

I acknowledged that I was and asked if I could help him.

"My name is Nick Anthony," he said, extending his hand with a smile. "Someone said to look you up if I needed a job."

Nick was an inch or so taller than I, with a sweep of white hair and trusting eyes magnified through thick spectacles. He wore a short-sleeved white shirt and khaki pants, which, although I never imposed it, was my preferred work attire. Nick was clearly down-and-out and in need of work and a second chance.

"Do you have any experience?" I asked.

"I was in the restaurant business for thirty years."

"And you're not any longer?"

Nick's reply turned into a story. He had lost his restaurant in a poker game, and he had a wife and two young children to support. He seemed genuinely repentant. I took a long, appraising look at him and felt that he was honest, though perhaps a little misguided. With my growing business I could use more help. If nothing else, Nick had experience and I needed someone responsible to close the store. I decided to take a chance on this man who had gambled away his livelihood.

It was a decision I never regretted. Nick proved indeed to be reliable and honest, and before long he became my right-hand man. In the first few months that I made him my night manager, which allowed me to leave at six or seven each evening, cutting my workdays from sixteen or eighteen hours to a mere twelve or thirteen. The addition of food professionals (Vasili and Nick) and the improved quality of the menu boosted the business upward.

Nick carved countless hundreds of seventy-pound steamship rounds, serving numerous customers continuously, year in and year out. During the thirteen years he worked for me, he never missed a day of work and was often visible in the showcase window slicing a steamship round. Over time, he became well known to our regular customers.

One morning in August, I looked up into the face of a tall man with short-cropped hair and a handlebar mustache. It was Max, the chef at the Rive Gauche, who had come down at my invitation to show us a recipe for a fresh tomato sauce for pizza, which we planned to add to our menu. My oldest son, Anthony, eleven now, was working for me part time. Although too young to wait on customers, I told him to assist Max in the back.

"Max, my son Anthony will help you," I said placing my hand on the boy's shoulder.

"Okay, then, Anthony, let's begin," Max said as he moved into the kitchen.

Max boiled fresh tomatoes in a big, stainless steel pot, then rinsed them under cold running water, peeled them, and squeezed them into another pot. Next he added sugar, salt, pepper, bay leaves, garlic, oregano and pure olive oil. He allowed the mixture to simmer over a slow fire for two hours, then cool for three hours before serving it up on freshly kneaded pizza dough.

The sauce was excellent, but Max's dough left something to be desired. We postponed the introduction of pizza for a week or two while we modified the dough recipe and trained Anthony in the art of pizza making. Finally, our pizza made its debut. Although it wasn't as popular as our sandwiches, it made its contribution to our growing business. As the demand for pizzas grew over time, we abandoned the time-consuming task of boiling tomatoes and shifted to canned sauce, which we enhanced. The store was growing by leaps and bounds.

To complement the new menu, I decided it was time for a new name.

"Elenitsa, let's call our store 'Anthony's Carryout,'" after my father-in-law, who had given me my first chance, and after my son. I still kept the Tastee Freeze sign up, though, and continued to pay the franchise fee to Gus.

* * * * *

The next summer proved to be even busier than the last. Even with Nick, Vasili and Bernard to assist me in the kitchen, we simply needed more help. That was the summer Willa Mae Hobbs joined us at the restaurant. She was a local girl who promptly eased the workload in the kitchen. A black woman with six children and a husband named Theofalos, Mae eventually became an invaluable asset. Every Sunday morning, her entire family would come in to give the store and parking lot a thorough cleaning after the Saturday night rush, which often lasted until 4:00 a. m.

It was also the summer my orders placed with Swift, my food supplier, grew so large that the sales manager there, Dale Truitt, offered me credit. Credit is a twin-edged sword. When money can be leveraged to a productive use, it's a blessing. When applied to consumption, however, it creates cascading debt. In my case, it allowed me to bootstrap up. Dale had been coming by the shop three mornings a week to make deliveries and take the next day's order for a few years now. In essence, this meant my business was prospering. It was a marvelous asset to me, permitting me to place a month's worth of orders before being billed, which in turn allowed my daily receipts to build up at the bank and accrue interest—you guessed it—making me creditworthy at the bank. No one had offered me credit of this sort before, and I viewed it as a turning point in my life. I had done well enough to be invested in by a big wholesaler like Swift.

Swift was not the only wholesaler I dealt with. Our baked and fried chicken sandwiches were so popular that I also kept Frank Perdue, my chicken wholesaler, well supplied with orders. In those days, before his company became famous, Frank was always hustling business himself. He often stuck his head in the back door of my store, calling out my name and leaving an iced case of fresh chickens in the kitchen with a bill tucked in. With that small, beaked face and thin neck bobbing in at the back door, we had to smile to ourselves. Frank not only sold chickens, he even looked like one. Later, of course, he would make Perdue Chickens a household name, but in the 1960's, he was working hard to build a business, just as we were.

My day was an unending series of purposeful, repetitive tasks, from morning to night, to ensure the quality of our food. Swift in those days represented high-quality, fresh meats and cheeses, and I was always alert to maintain the highest standards. Everything in my life trained me for what I was doing, and tending to these details provided me unending joy. Mae would call out to me, asking how many subs she was to make. Bernard would stick his head in the door, wondering whether he was to hose down the building or just clean the parking lot. No sooner would I answer those questions than Nick would call for help on the grill. Suppliers brought their wares daily—chickens, beef, potatoes, produce, bread, each a separate negotiation involving quantity, quality and price.

One day, my brother-in-law Gus came in with Byron, his youngest, and asked if I would give him a job. Poor Byron had had a hard life, mostly without a mother. He could not work in the front part of the store since he was only eleven, so I put him to work making hamburger patties. I tried to help him with his life; I helped so many, the least I could do was help my nephew. He stayed with me five years and learned a lot about business.

Meanwhile, customers streamed in and out, meat was sliced, vegetables chopped, another rack of chickens set out to roast or fry. There was inventory and bookkeeping and payroll and bills, and a great deal of planning and organization just to get through the day successfully. It was an enormous amount of work, and looking back, I wonder where I ever found the patience. It was a privilege and an unending source of satisfaction to have the problems of a successful store. A busy store meant good money, so I liked it busy, but there was always too much to do and not enough time.

Charlie Holland often came by in the early morning for coffee and a ham and egg sandwich. Casually dressed as usual, his southern accent gave him a disarming manner, but behind the slow, easy manner was a smart, shrewd businessman. I had been thinking hard about exercising my option to buy rather than just renegotiating the lease, and I was sure he was approachable. One day in late summer, I exercised my option and, on a payment plan, bought my small store. My future payments would now create equity for me instead of for someone else. Charlie was a good man and gave me a fair deal.

Nick arrived every afternoon around 3:30, and he worked until long after midnight. Ninety percent of our conversations were held in the few minutes after his arrival at the store, as he sat with a cigarette and a cup of coffee while I performed my tasks.

"Nick, you're going to be very busy tonight. I have a second top round in the oven."

"Okay, Chris."

I placed a steaming tray in front of him and lifted the cover.

"See these meatballs? They can't be overcooked."

Nick poked a toothpick into one and popped it into his mouth. A smile lit his face. "They're delicious!" he said, reaching for another. Another successful addition to the menu!

Even though Nick was a number of years older than I, he had married a younger woman and had children the age of mine. "I started a family late," he told me once, and he worried about supporting his children as he got older. When he started with me, I paid him about $125 a week, and by the time he retired in 1972 he was earning $250 a week. I also gave him a generous bonus at the end of each season, and in later years I sent him additional money every Christmas. He was dedicated to his work, an asset to the business and a tremendous help to me. I counted on him and trusted him implicitly.

Through Nick's white shirt, you could see the outline of an Orthodox crucifix with its wide and ornately carved form. He always wore glasses and a smile on his good-natured face. In the afternoons as he drank his coffee, I would watch him take long, quiet drags of his non-filtered Camel cigarettes. His hand, resting on the lip of the stainless steel work table, revealed yellow nicotine stains on the inside of his index and middle fingers, the only tarnish to his otherwise impeccable appearance.

Many times I would leave Nick in front to wait on customers while I did preparation in the back—so much so, that over time many customers came to believe he was the owner. In all the years Nick was with me, he never allowed anyone else to slice the steamship round. After trimming the beef, Nick would cut it in thin and regular slices around the bone parallel to the floor. His rhythmic stroke and thin, symmetrical slices became his trademark. He had the hands of a surgeon. Each slice rested on the flat of his knife, supported by the serving fork, and was added to a generous pile on a fresh kaiser roll until each sandwich weighed a bit over a quarter of a pound. It took two people to carry a fresh round from the oven to the front window where it would sit upright under the heat lamp for everyone to see. Nick usually made a dozen sandwiches at a time, shaking a mixture of one-third salt and two-thirds pepper over the meat before spearing the tops of the rolls and dipping them, one by one, into the hot "au jus" of the beef. Finally, he placed the tops on the sandwiches and wrapped each individually in wax paper.

The roast beef sandwich continued to be our most popular sandwich in the summer of 1961. Within three years, we would be selling more than three seventy-pound rounds a day.

* * * * *

In March of 1962, America put its first man in orbit around the earth. The astronaut was John Glenn, and the U. S. was stepping up its race with Russia to land a man on the moon. America never ceased to amaze me with her scientific abilities, and I had no doubt that the race to the moon was a race America would win. A month after John Glenn orbited the earth, a man approached me as I was opening my store one morning.

"Are you Mr. Christ?" he asked.

"Yes, sir, what can I do for you?"

"My name is Jack Selby and Charlie Holland said you might need some signs."

"Yes, I do!" I said enthusiastically. The store was a cinderblock building painted white with glass panes in the front and a big Tastee Freeze sign on the roof. Not wishing to offend my brother-in-law who had found the store for me, I had left it all this time as it originally was. Nonetheless, aside from the soft custard ice cream, the store had expanded into many items and recipes that were not related to the franchise. It was time, I thought, to advertise what we did best. People needed to know that we were not just a Tastee Freeze store, but offered much more.

Within a week, Selby submitted several sketches to me. He proposed that the main sign run the length of the store. It was to be illuminated by lights and would read "Anthony's Carryout," replacing a smaller, wooden one. Interestingly, as Anthony was Nick's last name, it was another reason for tourists to believe it was his store. This didn't bother me at all; the locals knew better, and as long as they kept coming back, what difference did it make? Because Coastal Highway was now a four-lane thoroughfare that ran the length of the island paralleling the beach, our sign was clearly visible to thousands of passers-by.

Selby proposed numerous additional signs. For the southern corner of the building he sketched a billboard showing a tub of chicken. He also created a pizza sign, featuring a little pizza man which I later used as a logo. There were menu board signs to hang above the counter inside and a giant submarine sign. Each was done with artistic skill to illustrate the menu and convey the idea of delicious, well-prepared food to the customer, as well as affordable price.

Initially I bought the internal menu signs, which Selby painted on the white block walls of the restaurant, and over time he added the others. Within three years, though, they were all proudly displayed. No one mistook my restaurant for a simple Tastee Freeze anymore. Out of respect to Gus, I kept the Tastee Freeze sign and paid the franchise and royalty fees for a decade, until the franchise ultimately folded.

This was the summer I found an apartment on 15th Street, two blocks from the store. That ended seven years of residency at the Nordica and cut seventeen blocks off my commute. The apartment had a kitchen and two bedrooms and was not only a convenient walk to the store, but spacious enough for my family. Bill Moschonas, the Greek immigrant I had taken on three years before, was no longer with us, and in his place I hired Tony Russo, a twenty-two year old Italian boy from Baltimore. He was a hard working, responsible man with a heavy accent. He only stayed with us two years. Over time he founded Tony's Pizza and became a very successful businessman. His success never surprised me. In fact, at the time I hired him, he reminded me of myself as a young man.

This was our seventh year of business. Mae and Bernard were in charge of preparation and cleanup, Tony did the pizzas, and Nick, of course, was in charge of the steamship round. I supplemented this core of employees with about twelve to fourteen summer hirelings who were college and high school students. The cooking load had also reached a point where I hired a chef. This began an eleven-year odyssey with nearly as many chefs.

Chefs—glorified cooks—admittedly have a hard job. That said, they generally seem to have a higher opinion of their culinary ability than deserved, often don't show up on time, and generally pick a time you are swamped and short-handed to walk out. Vito was my first chef. During the month of June, which was the slowest of the three summer months, I acquainted him with his chores and recipes. One weekend after July Fourth, he asked me if he could take his dinner break at the Seascape to have a bowl of soup, and I told him I would wait until he returned before I left for the evening. I am still waiting...

The rest of the summer, my eleven- and twelve-year old sons took over the position, with supervision. I was so proud.

This was also the summer that Nick brought his family down from Baltimore to spend the season with him. He had been concerned about leaving his wife and children for weeks on end every summer, and when I suggested the obvious solution of bringing them to Ocean City, he seized on the idea immediately. I paid the cost for the larger apartment that they would need.

A week later, Elenitsa and the kids were going to spend a day at the beach with our neighbors, when Elenitsa brought a letter to give me at the store. It was from Katina. Since Costa had come to the United States permanently in 1958 to work as a tailor in New York, Katina was the only one of my siblings left behind. In our apartment that evening as I opened her letter, I thought of Imbroz, so distant, so different from my new life in America. Katina's letter was dated April 20th, 1962.

Dear Chrysostomos,

I hope you are in good health. Give my love and kisses to Elenitsa, the children and Sultana and Costa.

Papa is so happy with your success. Uncle Demetri, Uncle Russo and Aunt Cleo also send regards and are very proud...

Chrysostomos, we have grown old, you in America and I on Imbroz. Papa is in his mid-eighties and Mama is not so far behind. To date, they have both retained their health. Last year I sold our fields to the Turks because we are unable to work them any more. We are still tailoring clothes, however, and have our property in Panayia.

Things have grown progressively worse since the riots in Constantinople. Boycotts of our businesses and deportations have resumed. A couple of months ago the Turks formed a penal colony here on Imbroz in Schinoudi, where they have moved the most hardened of criminals. Although the criminals were supposed to stay in Schinoudi, they roam the island. After forty years of occupation, the Turks have now populated our tiny island with criminals to drive the few of us that remain away from our homes... I never thought I would say it, but after forty years of occupation, I don't know how much longer we can survive.

I look forward to seeing you one day. We are fine. Thank you for the money you have so generously sent. Loving regards to Elenitsa and the children.

Don't forget your promise.

Your sister,

Katina

I still held Katina's letter in my hands when a voice piped up from behind me. "Hi, Dad!" Anthony greeted me.

"Anthony! What are you up to, son?"

"Mom's going to take us to the ocean again tomorrow," he told me, then added, "If that's all right with you."

"Ah, yes, that will be fun. You go and enjoy yourself."

"You don't need me to work, do you?"

"No, go to the beach. Take your days off before you start work. Enjoy yourself!" Through my children's adolescent leisure I captured moments of the youth I was denied.

Reassured that his day at the beach was not just permissible but actually justified, Anthony smiled and changed the subject. "What have you got there, Dad? What are you doing?"

"It's a letter," I told him, "from your aunt in Imbroz. Now go to bed, son. You've got a big day tomorrow."

I turned back to Katina's letter, lost in thought. Katina was right, we were beginning to grow old, and for Katina, who had put her entire life on hold, it was especially hard. My thoughts were running along this vein when Elenitsa came to sit beside me. She had finished putting Jon and Ianthe to bed. I could see she had something she wanted to talk to me about.

I put aside my sister's letter and smiled at her.

"Chris, it's good to be here," she said. She had been down for two weeks.

"Yes." I patted her hand. "I have missed you."

"And we have missed you. You are never home, always working, and it is hard raising the children without you. Even now, when we are all here, we hardly see each other."

This was an old complaint and I tried to comfort her. "Now, now, Elenitsa. It's not all that bad, is it? We do what we must to earn a living—"

"The children hardly know their father," she broke in. "It's not healthy. I have taken Anthony and Jon to a psychologist because they are always fighting, did you know that? They need their father, Chris."

I didn't know about the psychologist. I didn't know the boys were fighting that much. I knew it was hard on Elenitsa raising the children while I was working, but it was my work that would open opportunities for them I had never had. It was my work that would provide an education for them and a future that I had never had. The business I had worked so hard to create now formed responsibilities that bound me. I *had* to work. What else could I do? I imagined it had been hard for Elenitsa, but I was committed to promote my family out of the deprivation and poverty I had known growing up—all else seemed more readily reversible or fixable once security was established.

I was too tired to go into this with Elenitsa. Instead, I squeezed her hand and rose from my chair. "Elenitsa, it's late and I have to get up early," I told her. "We will talk, but for now let's go to bed."

The next morning I was up at 4:45 as usual. I went through my morning ritual of pinning my relic coin to my tee shirt and praying to God for strength and guidance. Then I set off to work feeling refreshed and full of energy, moving quietly so as not to awaken anyone. I knew that Elenitsa and I would never really reconcile my obligations with her need to have me with her more often, but I also knew I was doing all I could to care for my family. I knew too well how harsh the world could be, and while I was alive and able, I would shield my family from it. Now I had a growing business and the promise of greater security, and I had purchased the building where my business was housed.

* * * * *

My father-in-law became ill. This was completely unexpected, as Anton had always seemed very robust. Alexandra, who was a devout Orthodox Christian, well versed in the nuances of the faith, had a deep respect for all forms of Christianity. That, coupled by the constant pain of her osteoarthritis, fostered her strong interest in Oral Roberts, a TV evangelist who claimed to have God-given powers to heal. Desperate for a cure, Alexandra persuaded Anton to take her when Oral Roberts had a tent show in Cambridge, Maryland on the Eastern Shore. The lines of people waiting to be healed were long and slow, so to spare his wife, Anton stood in line in the sweltering heat while Alexandra sat with her walker. Anton, who at 74 years of age boasted of never having had a sick day, collapsed with a stroke. Unfortunately, the 150-mile drive to Cambridge from Warrenton, combined with the heat and the long wait in line, took a sadly ironic toll on him that neither Oral Roberts nor his ministry could reverse.

I was at work when I got word of this. I had a quick conversation with Nick and then I flew out the door. It was late in August and Anthony was at Scout camp that week, so I picked up Elenitsa, Ianthe and Jon at the apartment in Ocean City and drove the 60 miles to Cambridge. When we arrived, Alexandra was in the waiting room. She was distraught over the thought that while she was trying to find a cure for herself, Anton had become so ill.

"He's going to die!" she wailed, close to hysterics. "I just know it! I rode with him in the ambulance and he never woke up, not once! He is going to die, Chris! He is going to die...." her voice trailed off to a weeping moan.

There was little we could do to comfort Alexandra. Anton was moved to the hospital at Salisbury, Maryland, and a week later, still critical, he was moved by ambulance to Fairfax Hospital, just outside of Washington, D. C. I brought Elenitsa and the kids home two weeks early so that she might be with her father. The next day he was examined by Dr. Kakaviatos, a heart specialist, and that afternoon as we gathered by Anton's bedside, Dr. Kakaviatos delivered his prognosis. He was very sorry, he said, but Anton wasn't going to live. Upon hearing the doctor's words, Alexandra began wailing uncontrollably, and Elenitsa's eyes teared up. There had been no improvement since his stroke three days earlier, and that was an especially bad sign.

Chaos broke out in Anton's hospital room. Everyone was weeping all at once. I tried to question the doctor, while Alexandra sobbed and implored Elenitsa to call a priest. In the middle of all this uproar, Anton, who had been drifting in and out of consciousness, awoke just in time to hear his own prognosis.

"What do you mean I'm going to die?" he demanded irritably. "I'm not dead, damnit! Why, that no good S. O. B. of a doctor!" he exclaimed. Dr. Kakaviatos was stunned by Anton's articulate utterance.

Hearing the forecast of his death seemed to revive Anton, and while recovering for the next three weeks, he continued to take issue with Dr. Kakaviatos. Finally, he was released from the hospital and Elenitsa brought him home to our house, but the stroke had taken its toll. His left arm was paralyzed and his left leg was stiff. His vision had also been affected. Gus, who managed Anton's assets, was now in a second tumultuous marriage and left his father's care to us. Meanwhile, I made arrangements to have Anton's car moved back from Cambridge where it had been left following his collapse, and I partially paid the hospital and the ambulance fees.

Throughout the next few weeks I shuttled back and forth between Ocean City and Northern Virginia, leaving Nick to work double shifts. Anton, who had been active all his life, now lay partially paralyzed, and the forced inactivity was wearing on him.

"Dad, what will happen to Popi's motel?" Anthony asked me.

"Your Uncle Gus is handling it," I told him. The truth was, Gus was visibly helping himself to his father's assets while Elenitsa was preoccupied with her parents' care. I was disappointed in my brother-in-law, but felt it was not my business. I could only hope for the best.

Meanwhile, I returned to Ocean City to close up the store for the winter. There was a lot on the corner of 33rd and Philadelphia Streets, with a beer and wine carryout and a one-room apartment above, which had captured my attention. It was for sale and I was interested in purchasing it. Business in the beach town had grown so much that the season was extended. I now remained open more than six months a year—much to Elenitsa's chagrin—and I felt the property with the carryout on it was just what I needed to expand. I also added 150 square feet to the south side of my store.

When I returned to Northern Virginia I knew this would be the last winter I would wait tables. My business was taking up too much of my time now, and I was doing well enough that for the first time I didn't need to work for anyone else. There was another advantage to this: I would have more time to spend with the children, which would please Elenitsa. That winter, my last at the Rive Gauche, I cut back some of my hours. The idea of having time during the winter to spend with them pleased me enormously.

Yet my wintertime would soon be applied to another venture. My in-laws stayed with us so Elenitsa and I could take care of them. Over the winter my father-in-law slowly improved and, eventually, he and Alexandra returned home to Warrenton where they were able to stay with the assistance of a live-in maid. Anton's days working at his beloved Jefferson Motel, however, were over.

* * * * *

Early that spring, I returned to Ocean City to prepare for the season. As the weeks of familiar preparations passed, it seemed particularly hard to be away from my family. The time spent over the winter had been so special, and heretofore so rare, that it accentuated the loneliness of my preparations. On Father's Day, I received a card from Elenitsa and one from Cookie, who was now almost eight. "Daddy, I miss you," she wrote. "Please come home soon," and I could not keep from swallowing hard. This was an emotional side I hid well from all who knew me. The thought that it wouldn't be too long before my family would join me at Ocean City cheered me.

I hired a Greek man, another Vasili, who spoke no English at all and had no experience in food service, but I desperately needed help. At the time he came to work for me, the only notable thing about him were his eyes. He had a thyroid condition which caused his eyes to protrude in a startling manner. Small children were sometimes afraid of him, but I knew this immigrant dockworker was a good and decent man.

I sometimes chuckle recalling the image of Vasili with his big bulging eyes turning over his first English words with his heavy Greek tongue, "Howt doag?...Hampbairgair?"

Vasili stayed with me for three years and soon became, through sheer perseverance and hard work, my manager. He eventually opened his Prima pizzeria in Northern Virginia.

The hardest part of running a restaurant, provided you know the business, is finding good people. It is an ongoing, unrelenting challenge. Since the restaurant provides easy access into the labor market, its only requirement being a willingness to work, it attracts the bottom of the labor pool. Language and experience are a distant second requirement. This was further complicated by the fact that my store was located at a seasonal resort. The beach atmosphere fostered an already high worker turnover. Nonetheless, our employees ate free and were treated well.

We were busier that summer than we had ever been. Many Greeks from the church communities in the Baltimore-Washington area, even if just acquaintances, would pass by the store and pay their respects to Chris from Ocean City, or, "Ocean City Chris," as I was often called. We had twenty-five positions open that summer, but, with the season's turnover, I had to hire a total of 60 employees to fill them, for most of the kids only wanted to work part time to finance their fun in a sunny summer resort.

At the end of the summer my friend Dale Truitt with Swift's came by to take an order from me and to have a cup of coffee. "Hey, Chris," he said. "Do you know you use more roast beef than any other place on the island? In fact, you're my biggest customer."

"Drink your coffee, Dale, before it gets cold," I responded, pausing for a moment to reflect on how far we had come.

* * * * *

That fall I had done so well that I paid all my seasonal obligations, had money in the bank, and was able to give Nick an extra bonus and a raise. After the holidays, I would even buy Elenitsa a car. There was a new development, as well. A doctor from Fairfax who frequented my store that summer asked me if I would be interested in operating a luncheonette in the newly built Seven Corners Medical Building. I accepted the invitation, obtained financing, and opened the Fairfax Inn in mid-October of 1963, planning to run it during the winter. The luncheonette kept me busy, but it also meant, to my great pleasure, that I was home by seven in the evening with Elenitsa and the kids.

In February of 1964, I bought Elenitsa a white Olds Cutlass Supreme. She had gotten her license the year before and I knew the car would give her more freedom and make her feel less isolated.

One afternoon just before Thanksgiving, as I was working at the Inn, I heard news that stopped me in my tracks and overtook me with an eerie lightheadedness—a lightheadedness that prevented me from realizing the words I had just heard. "President Kennedy has been fatally shot today in Dallas, Texas..." In an instant all my achievements paled in the face of this great national tragedy. For several suffocating moments, I was anachronistically taken by the memories of the dreary life I had left decades ago. I thought of his poor widow, Jacqueline, the charming young woman I had waited on some years before.

As the days following the tragedy unfolded, there was something reaffirming in the dignified way our grieving nation responded. While people wept, the government moved smoothly to install Lyndon Johnson as President. There was no rioting in the streets, no uprising or revolution. The mechanics of my new country's democracy had been so grandly conceived and carefully thought out, that it weathered calamity with strength, calm and purpose.

The President was buried, the nation quietly grieved, and the holidays and the year's end were anticlimactic and uneventful. Elenitsa's parents joined us for the holidays. Anton was still limited in his mobility from his stroke, but he and Alexandra were managing pretty well on their own with the help of the maid. After such a tragic autumn, there was added meaning in having everyone gather together for Christmas dinner. John Kennedy was my age and had my father's name. His loss underscored for me the fragility of life itself.

Several weeks later after an evening meal and clean up, I was relaxing in my chair when the phone rang.

"Hello, Christo, Merry Christmas!" It was Nick calling from Baltimore.

"Why Nick, how was your holiday?"

"Pleasant, Chris, very pleasant. Christo..."

"Yes Nick?"

There was a pause as he seemed to search for words.

"I can't thank you enough," he finally simply said. How hard we had worked, side by side, throughout the summer. He was my right-hand man. Now he was miles away at the other end of a phone line at Christmastime, full of gratitude.

"Merry Christmas, Nick. I'll see you in May,"

"Yes....see you in May," his voice quivered with emotion.

* * * * *

Although the money I sent was an important part of their livelihood, I remained unable to bring real change to my parents' and sister's daily struggle. The living conditions had significantly worsened since the riots of 1955, and the deportation of Christians resumed in 1964, especially those in Constantinople. All property held by deportees, except one suitcase, reverted to the state. The deportations made survival of the few remaining Christians quite tenuous. Christian culture there was now nearly at an end.

Following the violent and tragic loss of President Kennedy to an assassin, nature dealt a blow much closer to home. In March of 1964, a nor'easter pummeled Ocean City during a lunar high tide, flooding the island for more than two days. Churning offshore, the hurricane-force storm blew high swells across Ocean City tearing out the pier and boardwalk along with many buildings that lined the shore. Properties everywhere suffered tremendous water damage as the island sank under four to five feet of sea. I closed the Fairfax Inn early that Friday and drove to Ocean City to survey the damage with my sons, Jon and Anthony, and my nephew, Gus' eldest son, Ronnie. When we arrived, the National Guard was there, allowing only property owners onto the island. It became known as the Storm of March.

"Dad, look!" Anthony exclaimed when we arrived. "There's no boardwalk!"

In fact, the damage was so extensive that I couldn't speak. The pier on the south end of the island was gone, the white sandy beaches had been washed away, the roads were covered with sand, debris and water. From about 4th Street northward, where the beach was narrower, the damage was greater. Almost all commercial and hotel structures had been either severely damaged or completely washed away.

With a feeling of dread rising from my stomach and consuming me, we headed toward 17th Street, negotiating the washed-out roads with care. We arrived to see a waist-high water line along the walls, but the store was intact. We had a lot of cleaning up to do, so we rolled up our sleeves and began what would turn out to be two days of hard labor.

The first day we took a brief break from our restorations and drove north. We were stunned by what we saw. Whole blocks had been swept clean of houses and structures, and debris was everywhere. I saw one man tearfully surveying what looked like a slab of cement that had been upended in the sand. On top of the slab was a commode.

I approached the man to ask if he needed help, but he only shook his head and pointed to the sculpture of debris. "This is my commode," he said, red-eyed. Poor fellow. It was all he had left of his house that had been swept away.

The damage from the nor'easter of '64 was a huge setback that summer. In fact, it took many years for the town to recover from the storm. Many businesses never reopened and many homes were never rebuilt. Still, even if the summer of 1964 saw a costly decline in tourism, it was a busy season for residents and business people as everyone who could struggled to clean up, rebuild and recover. I spent much of the summer hearing the stories of loss, feeling thankful for my own good fortune and praying for my less fortunate neighbors. Anthony's Carryout sustained only minimal damage and people still seemed to need sandwiches. My business held its own.

That summer I received a particularly upsetting letter from Katina.

Dear Chrysostomos,

We received the pictures of the kids, Elenitsa and you at Christmas. They are so beautiful, we thank you so much. Mama and Papa look at them every day. Sometimes Papa will just hold them and stare for what seems to be long periods of time, always with a smile.

My dearest brother, the news that I will share is not good. Papa is over ninety and Mama well in her eighties and, of course,

Uncle Demitri is older than Papa. I don't know how much longer we can hang on.

In March of '64, the Turks moved another 600 long-term convicts from the mainland to Schinoudi. They are allowed to roam free, terrorizing, destroying property and worse. We are overrun.

A commission of elders complained to the Turkish authorities who installed an army legion between Clyky and our village. The soldiers have destroyed farmhouses, chapels, openly stolen from the Christians, beating and terrorizing the residents. In short, they are indistinguishable from the convicts.

After 40 years of occupation, the Turks are no longer subtle or covert about their agenda. They are driving us from our properties to turn them over to future Turkish settlers.

Thank you for your generous gifts and God bless you. We have all taken great pride in your success.

Love, Katina

No sooner had I set down the letter than I took up my pen to plead to my remaining family to come to America. I used all my powers of persuasion and felt the strength of my words as they poured from my pen. Filled with triumph and resolve, I hurried to the post office and posted the letter. No sooner had the letter fallen through the slot, however, than did I know my words were useless, my efforts wasted. Papa's stubbornness had not diminished with the years. I knew he would never leave Imbroz and allow the Turks to take his home.

That Christmas, Elenitsa's parents joined us once again, and with Elenitsa's help I prepared a festive Greek dinner. When the table was covered with dishes, my family seated and grace said, I found myself reflecting back over the events of the last few years. We had been so fortunate, and many good things had happened to us. How fleeting everything sometimes seemed! As my family dined merrily on the same foods I remembered from childhood, I once again felt close to my parents, imagining they were sharing in the holiday feast and celebration with us. I prayed for our new Archbishop that he might be strong in leading us, and thanked the Lord for allowing our paths to cross in America. I prayed that He would give us strength to face with courage and faith whatever the future may bring, and please watch over my family both here and abroad—realizing more fully than ever that each moment should be savored. My material accomplishments stood in sharp contrast to my family's difficulties on Imbroz, which I was largely powerless to influence.

17

A Terrible Loss and a Traditional Dinner

And where our strength and determination are clear, our words need merely to convey conviction—not belligerence. If we are strong, our strength will speak for itself. If we are weak, words will not help.

—John F. Kennedy
from his undelivered Dallas speech, November 22, 1963

The devastation of the storm of 1964 underscored how fleeting and fragile our lives truly are. To see concrete edifices swept away in one rush by nature is humbling. These natural losses were but a precursor to the permanent losses I would face over the second half of the sixties.

After the storm, I purchased the property with the beer and wine carryout. It was a boxy building with a garage-door front on 33rd Street, sixteen short blocks north of Anthony's. It was my third business operation.

Increased financial security came with increased responsibility. The restaurant business owned me, not vice versa, its daily hours leaving precious few for my family. I began to encourage my children to seek other lines of work for their careers. With a good education, they could obtain a job with regular hours. I wanted my children to be successful—more so than I had become, and at a lesser price.

Looking back, I realize my absence added to problems my children experienced. My memories are a mix of pride and guilt over their strides and missteps. Frankly, at the time, from my background of adversity, I viewed the problems as small in the overall scheme of life. The truth would prove to be, however, that they were not so much small as they were hidden.

* * * * *

Costa had purchased a townhouse in Brooklyn and was pretty well established in New York. He returned to Imbroz to find a wife, joining Katina who was still dutifully tending to Mama and Papa. Uncle Demetri, Uncle Russo and Aunt Cleo had also grown old, and the burden of caring for them all was increasing. In the spring of 1965, I received a letter from Papa. Although his body might be failing him, I was pleased to see his mind was as sharp as ever.

Dear Chrysostomos,

It has been twenty years since Mama and I last saw you yet barely a day goes by when we don't proudly reflect on you, Elenitsa and the children. Your success in America has been the light of our lives.

Remember our teachings and our ways so that you may pass them to your children. And although we have been apart for so long, don't forget that Mama and I will always be with you.

Please watch out for your older sister, Katina. God will not forget the material help you have provided us over the years.

God bless you, Elenitsa and the children.

Your Father and Mother

I took a deep breath after reading Papa's letter. It was difficult for me to imagine that I had not seen my parents since the party they had held in my honor to see me off to America. The fact that two decades had passed was incredible—and sad. I wrapped a $100 bill in two pieces of blank paper, wrote a brief note of love and blessings, and as I tucked it into the envelope I said a tearful prayer for them all. I didn't know what else to do. My success and my prayers were all I had to share with them, but it never seemed enough. My eyes had not seen them nor my arms hugged them for so many years, and I dreaded the thought of my parents' inevitable passing. I prayed for their continued good health.

Elenitsa and I were still helping with her parents. We moved them into a two-bedroom garden apartment near us that spring, and a caretaker moved in with them. Meanwhile, things were not going well between Gus and his father.

"Christo," my mother-in-law implored, "what are we to do? Gus has sold our house in Warrenton and we have never seen a cent from the sale!" She turned and gestured to my father-in-law. "Look at Anton! All he does is sit and stare, Christo! I just don't know what to do!"

"You have the apartment," I said, trying to soothe my in-laws. "And Elenitsa is close by to care for you. Enjoy your life and perhaps the other problems will seem less important. Sometimes, they even resolve themselves in unexpected ways. Just trust in God and live in happiness for today."

After his stroke, Anton had turned much of the management of his assets over to his son, and it saddened me to see that he was depressed over their mismanagement. I wished I could help Anton regain some control over his finances, but this was a private family matter. Elenitsa adored her brother and I adored her. I didn't want to cause additional anxiety in her life by raising questions about his activities, so I remained silent. Again, I felt helpless in caring for our family.

It was now the fall of 1965, and I found a new manager for the Fairfax Inn, a Mr. Merkezas, a Greek from Cyprus, then headed off to Ocean City to open up the shop. This was also the spring I bought a two-bedroom townhouse on the bay six blocks north of my store. We had come a long way from our little room at the Nordica.

God willing, we expected a strong summer, stronger than the storm year, anyway. Population at Ocean City increased almost 20 percent each year. My pizza chef, Tony Russo, had left us and I had a hard time filling the position. I finally hired a young man from California, who arrived with his own surfboard and announced that he was a "hippie." I didn't care what he was so long as he worked hard and was honest. His name was Brian Tara and he stayed with us for five years, never once missing a single day. He was a very good pizza man.

My sons were also of considerable help that year. Anthony only worked about half the summer, since his athletic schedule was so demanding. He spent a week in wrestling camp and then the month of August training for football. Fortunately for me, Jon spent the entire summer at the store helping out wherever he could. Jon was the quiet one of the two, hard-working and earnest.

In fact, I had things running so well that, despite the fact it was a very busy season, by autumn I had managed a routine that allowed me to go fishing every morning at 5:00 during weekdays. It was serene and peaceful at that hour, reminding me of youthful summer days fishing on Imbroz. How I love the sea. It was as though the salty air and ceaseless surf rolled through my veins.

That fall, I think I began for the first time to feel my age creeping up on me. After closing up the store in Ocean City, I headed to the Fairfax Inn. The kids returned to school, and I began to realize how much in the moment I lived. I rarely spoke to my children about my life in the Old World, or the events of my past. I always believed in living for today, not dwelling in the past. What's done is done, and there's no going back and changing it. Why dwell on fear and pain and suffering? As a result, though, I realized that my children were being deprived of knowing their grandparents, their heritage, the courage and spirit with which they had survived atrocities. Knowledge of these experiences may prove, in many ways, more valuable than any material possessions or accomplishments. Most importantly, this selective knowledge was not the whole truth. I thought about my children more and more, perhaps because I was watching them grow up and become young adults, working beside me as I had with my father and Uncle Russo so many years before. They had taught me much, and I hoped I was giving my children what my father had given me. I suppose it was the realization that time was running out for me to give them everything I wanted to give them. I had given them financial security, but was that enough?

During Thanksgiving week I received a letter from Katina. For some reason—perhaps I was busy with the Inn—I put it aside unopened and did not remember it until Sunday morning. I suppose I chose to ignore the letter, perhaps fearing what it might say.

In the back of my mind I guess I expected to receive this letter someday. Nonetheless, my sister's words hit me hard. There is a chasm between expectation and acceptance. My knees gave way, and I sat heavily on the edge of my bed. I read the letter through twice as if I could not comprehend her words, as if by rereading it I could find the "catch," the words I had missed that would make it not so.

Dear Chrysostomos,

It is with a heavy heart that I bring you news of our parents. On August 5th Mama grew ill. She could not keep anything down, and the doctor was away. During the night of August 6th, our Mama passed away. I only became aware of it in the early morning when Papa called. She was still warm and I ran to get the doctor, but nothing could be done. When we buried Mama, Uncle Demetri, Uncle Russo and Aunt Cleo attended with Papa and me. At Papa's request, Bishop Iakovos performed the service.

On November 8th I fixed Papa dinner and we sat down to eat. He told me it was his fiftieth wedding anniversary and after dinner he went to bed early. About midnight he called out for me and when I went to him he was sitting up in bed. As soon as he saw me he sighed and went limp. I ran out into the street screaming for help, but it was too late. Papa was gone.

Uncle Demetri and I buried Papa and many people came to the funeral. Bishop Iakovos cried during the service.

I am sorry to bring you such sad news. God bless and protect you and your family.

With all my love,

Katina

Katina would tell me later that Papa weakened greatly soon after Mama's death, which is why she waited to write.

When Elenitsa found me, tears were streaming down my face and my hands were shaking. She had never seen me in such a state, and she tried to console me as I sobbed openly for my parents, my beloved Mama and Papa, who had survived everything, it seemed. They had been my inspiration, and now they were gone. I had not seen them in twenty years, and now this deadly sheet of paper had robbed me of them. Poor stubborn Papa. He lived under Turkish rule for forty years rather than leave his beloved island, and now these cruel strokes of ink in a single letter pronounced him dead. I wept uncontrollably with grief. Never had I been in such pain.

My tears brought my children into the bedroom filled with worry and concern. "Your Dad has received some bad news," Elenitsa told them as she tried to usher them out, but Anthony wouldn't budge. "What news?" he demanded. "Tell me!"

"Your Aunt Katina wrote," she said. "Papou and Yiayia in the old country have passed away," steering Anthony toward the door. "Now please give your father some privacy. That's how you can help him. You can give him a little time to himself, okay?"

When Anthony had gone, Elenitsa turned to me. "They have never seen you cry," she said gently. "Neither have I." In fact, it was the only time in all my adult life that I had ever cried.

Although death is part of life, I don't believe anyone ever entirely gets over the death of his parents. I am not a person to harbor regrets, but my regret at not having seen Mama and Papa before they died has never left me. They had always been there! How could they be taken away before I was ready? It saddens me to think how little I spoke of my parents to my children. Mama and Papa were strangers to their American grandchildren. Even Katina was little more than a letter's passage and a holiday mention to my children. They simply had no understanding of her sacrifice for their grandparents. How could they? They had been sheltered from the Old World and my past.

* * * * *

Of course, I can point to a number of times when I was there for my children—as I often did to Elenitsa. Anthony would spend whole summers working at my side at the carryout. He had become quite skilled with food preparation. While he was pursuing his athletics, Jon was at my side. Anthony had made the varsity wrestling team. During his junior year, I planned to attend one of his matches for the first time. It was a regional tournament in 1966. Prior to the event, I hosted a training meal at the Fairfax Inn. Anthony coached me on the time and particulars. "The weigh-in is at 2:30 and the team will get to the restaurant around four," he said. "There will be fourteen of us. It's a training meal, Dad, so don't fix too much."

"And the match?" I asked. "When does that start?"

"At seven," Anthony told me, then added, "The coach is dressing two extra guys, but I'm sure I'll be wrestling tonight."

When Anthony left for the weigh-in I turned my attention to my preparations. A few minutes after four the team arrived to a dinner of seven-ounce Delmonico steaks, mashed potatoes, peas, rolls and iced tea. For dessert I served some of my good rice pudding. Wrestlers diet carefully to maintain their weight and these kids, weary of various food restrictions, fell on the meal like they were starving. They were nice boys, polite and disciplined. One by one, they thanked me for the meal. I was pleased Anthony was on the team, and it was my pleasure to prepare the meal for them.

The match that night surprised me. I began the evening sitting quietly on the front corner of the bleachers, but soon I was caught up in the excitement. Mrs. Godfrey, mother of Anthony's friend Dennis, erupted in a screaming frenzy. Spectators all around me were shouting and jumping out of their seats. It was exhilarating and infectious, made even more intense because it was my son they were all screaming for! I had never in my life experienced anything like it.

It was the first of several matches I would see during the next two years. By his senior year, Anthony was the top-seated wrestler in his weight division in the state. Much to my delight, my younger son, Jon, made the wrestling team as well.

The night after that first match, I made a special dinner—shish kebab with beef tenderloin and rice pilaf. It was not often I could have dinner with my family. My meticulous food preparation was one way I demonstrated my love for my family and it gave me great pleasure to prepare special treats.

I was still fussing with the *spanakopita* when they all began teasing me.

"Dad, get in here and eat with us! You're so busy cooking, you won't even know how good it is!"

"Shhh! Keep quiet, there'll be more for the rest of us!" teased Jon.

Everyone was in good spirits and it felt warm and comfortable, all of us together sharing a good meal. After dinner that night I played backgammon with the boys while a Redskins football game played on the television. For a while we were the family Elenitsa had always wanted us to be, a family with Papa home for the evening. It was an evening that gave me just as much happiness as it did her, and after all these years I still recall it.

While I was recovering from the death of my parents, I went to watch Anthony wrestle three or four times. Sitting in the bleachers watching my son compete, I realized that only from a picture had my parents ever seen their grandchildren. They would have been so proud of them. To most of the spectators, the match was probably much the same as any other. The exhilaration and excitement was familiar, but for me it was not diminished by repetition. My excitement for the game and pride in my son's performance was beyond words. When he won a close match to a tough foe, I pranced, proud as a peacock. This was partly due to what had had to happen in my life to bring me to watch Anthony wrestle. The joy in my heart was from the satisfaction of seeing my endless hours of hard work enabling Anthony this opportunity I had never had. He was a contender for the state wrestling championship. The price was high and I knew it, Elenitsa knew it. It had come at the cost of great pain, from the ashes of a world destroyed.

That winter President Johnson was talking about the Great Society, a world where all people would work only twenty hours a week. This notion was unimaginable to me, and undesirable. For much of my life I had worked seventeen hours a *day*. Only now, after years of labor, was I able to cut back a bit on my hours. During the winter, when the Fairfax Inn claimed my attention, I only worked twelve hours a day Monday through Friday, and a mere nine hours on Saturday. In Ocean City my workday had fallen to no more than fourteen hours—5 a. m. to 7 p. m.—during the season, although I still maintained a seven-day workweek.

* * * * *

It was just before the holidays and I sent Katina and Uncle Demetri, who was now living with her, a long letter and some money. With our parents now gone, I could finally bring Katina to America and fulfill my promise of so long ago. I made all the arrangements for her journey. At about the same time, my brother Costa returned with his new bride from Imbroz, Afrodite. At the age of 44, he was a U. S. citizen, no longer on a visa, married, and ready to settle down in his adopted country. My family's migration to America was nearly complete.

"Costa!" I said, embracing him for what seemed longer than normal.

"Big Brother!" he responded, just as he had for years. It was comforting now more than ever to have that bond, as the patriarchal mantle passed to us from Papa. He turned to introduce me to his wife.

"It is so good to meet you, Christo," she said. "I have heard many good things about you from Costa and others back home. Your parents were fine and wonderful people, and I am very sorry for your loss."

Her words touched me. I thanked her and welcomed her to our home and family. When they first arrived in Virginia, Costa and Afrodite stayed in a room in our basement for a month or so, then they rented a garden apartment not far from Elenitsa's parents. Although they required daily care, Anton's condition had stabilized. His pride and independence compelled him to move to a nearby first floor garden apartment. Later, I lent Costa money for a down payment to buy a small house within two miles of mine. Costa found a job as a tailor for Lord and Taylor, a well-known and respected local department store, where, a decade later, he would win an award for outstanding employee for not missing a single day of work. Within thirteen years, he and his bride would have four beautiful children.

After the death of my parents, I refocused my attentions on my family, my business and the future. I remained active in the Church, frequently volunteering my labor and contributing food and time to fundraisers. I drew up plans to revamp the beer and wine store I had purchased two years earlier and finalized plans to build six new stores adjacent to the beer and wine to lease out. I also opened a small carryout next to the beer and wine on the eastward side.

The next year, after I had constructed the six stores, I rented two of the stores to Peter Panayotedis, who had worked as a bus boy at the Park twenty years earlier when I had come over with the Ambassador. One morning during Easter, I found the door open and red-dyed eggs everywhere—dozens of eggs and no Peter! Three days later, he was found drunk in his car on Route 50 between Ocean City and Washington. Peter had simply abandoned his store, and I don't know what happened to him after that. Ironically, I would then rent his store to a Turk named Adil from Constantinople. My first two tenants were a Greek and a Turk from, of all places, Constantinople. What a small world!

Earlier that year, Harry Jagoda, a friend of mine from the Apollo, had visited me with his friend, Lincoln Vance. The two were partners in a development where they were building nice, spacious homes on half-acre lots, and they urged me to buy one. I had been thinking of moving my family to a larger house for some time, and Harry and Lincoln's advice intrigued me. A month later, I took them up on their suggestion and picked out a lot on a hillside cul-de-sac. It amazed me to think that I could trade my thousand square foot rambler for a 4,800-square-foot, center-hall colonial. My dream home would cost $66,000. I was so proud of my home. I would borrow $55,000 at four-and-a-half percent interest for thirty years.

By the end of the year, we were happily settled in our new house. That Christmas was especially festive. Elenitsa's parents were with us, and Costa and Afrodite were over for our Christmas meal, when Costa announced that they were expecting their first child. The prospect of a new baby in the family was exciting, and Elenitsa was delighting in helping Afrodite.

Costa's hair had receded to the point of baldness and his voice was a raspy baritone, considerably lower than mine. He spoke English with a heavy accent and was an instant center of attention for my two sons who spent the afternoon playing tavoli, our form of backgammon, with him. I taught the boys the game on our Sunday dinner get-togethers when they were barely ten and eight years old.

Indeed, we had a lot to be thankful for, and my prayer was an old one, though no less heartfelt, as we sat down to Christmas dinner in our new home: "God bless and watch over us. Thank You for the food You have given us. Thank You for allowing us to be together and for bringing Costa and Afrodite to us. Please deliver Katina safely to America and allow Mama and Papa to rest in peace. Amen."

"Amen," my family replied.

*　*　*　*　*

After spending nearly all of thirty-nine years apart, I finally had my little brother close to me. It wasn't that I expected to see him every day, but the thought of him living nearby was pleasing. It was a bridge of continuity connecting my past life in the Old World with the present.

After the holidays I sold the Fairfax Inn for about the same price it had cost me to open it a few years earlier. My time had to be freed for my increasing Ocean City business, which had grown to become year-round. A few weeks later I was at the beach readying my store for the upcoming season. The procession of cooks through my store continued. One cook named Phil picked the peak hour to show his dissatisfaction with his job by leaving without a word to anyone simply to let us know he would be missed. Then came Jean Pierre. He was a good man and actually stayed with us for two years.

That summer would not stand out remarkably in my mind except for the day a call came from my sister Sultana in New York. "Christo," she said gaily, "I have someone with me who wants to speak to you!" A moment later I heard another voice, tentative and soft.

"Chrysostomos?"

"Katina!" I exclaimed. Even after twenty-four years I knew her voice. "I cannot believe you are here already! Was it a good trip?"

"Yes it was, very good—"

"You must come to see us!" I interrupted.

"Of course I will," she said. "I'll wait for your call and then I'll—"

"And Uncle Demetri," I said, interrupting again. "What of Uncle Demetri?"

"Christo, he has no one since Papa died. His goddaughter found him a room in an old folks home in Constantinople. We must send him money, Christo. He has no one, nothing."

"Yes," I agreed, a tinge of regret clouding my joy. "Don't worry, we'll do that, I promise."

Suddenly I heard my sister's youthful chuckle. "I can't believe I'm here, in America!" she said.

"Of course you are here!" I told her happily with a chuckle in return.

In mid-June Elenitsa and the kids had arrived for the summer and, with the store fully staffed, I was able to resume what I had come to look forward to with great relish, my joyous sunrise fishing expeditions. They were food for my soul, almost mystical experiences that soothed and calmed the frenetic pace of serving the summer tourists. My fishing excursions also kept my spirit in touch with my roots. It was after returning from one such morning, wisps of misty meditations still clinging to me, when I saw rising before me an apparition, right there in the sliding glass doors of my shop. I must have dropped the cooler full of sea bass and trout, for I heard a loud crash beside me. My first thought was that I had stayed in the sun too long and was still caught in my musings of Imbroz. I rubbed my eyes to shake off the spirits and bring me back to the present, but there still stood before me the apparition—Katina!

Her arrival was an unexpected surprise and we rushed into a long, happy embrace without a word. "Forty years ago as a child on Imbroz you would go fishing—and now, forty years later, what do I find you doing? Still fishing! Nothing has changed!" she teased me happily.

We talked long into the night, too excited to sleep and so much to talk about!

Before she left Imbroz, Katina had been forced to sell Papa's property to the Turks. I was angry and saddened to learn of the "sale," but I realized she had little choice considering the great pressures the Turks had exerted through their unjust laws. There would no longer be any material evidence remaining of the many generations our family had lived on Imbroz. Papa and Mama had been the last stronghold, and that was difficult for me to accept. Their lives, the store, the fields, their toil…all were gone now.

Katina did not stay with us long in Ocean City. She shyly revealed to me that she had met a man, a widower named Nick Pananis, who wanted to marry her. Katina was fifty-one years old, but she had wasted little time after arriving in New York to begin living her new life! I heartily encouraged her to marry and have a home of her own. She was anxious to return to her fiancé, but before she left she said, "You are truly a good man, Christo. You have brought us all here. You have kept the promise you made to me many years ago in Imbroz, the promise to bring me to America."

"Of course I did, Katina. How could I ever forget such an important thing as that?"

"Papa was so proud of you," she told me. "A day hardly passed that he would not boast of your accomplishments as if they were his own. We all lived your successes. You see, even though we have not been close, we have all gained strength from you."

"Katina, it is you who has shown strength and honor beyond reason…you sacrificed so much. So much more than money could ever buy."

My sister smiled and kissed my forehead. "May god bless you and always be with you," she said, and departed for the bus to New York. These few short days had satisfied a life-long promise.

Five months later we received an invitation to the January 1968 wedding of Nickos Pananis and Katina Chrysostomidis. The ceremony was to be performed by the Archbishop of the Americas, Iakovos.

Anthony was away at the College of William and Mary in Williamsburg, Virginia, one of the finest and oldest colleges in the country. Jon was busy with his senior year of high school, so Elenitsa, Ianthe and I decided to drive up to New York by ourselves for Katina's wedding. Katina had no father to give her away, and she had no dowry, traditional for a Greek bride. She had sacrificed her childbearing years to tend to our parents' needs. She was now marrying for companionship. Costa, who had a second baby on the way, had to work that weekend and could not drive up to the wedding with us. I would stand in for my father and give

Katina away, and I arranged to give them a generous present that would help them get started.

It was a small wedding. Taki and Sultana were present, of course, as were Nickos' daughter and son by his first marriage. Before the service, Iakovos called Katina and me to join him behind the altar. A moment of silence passed as we all looked at each other. The Archbishop was 56, Katina was 51 and I was 50. It had been over forty years since the three of us played in the grassy field across from my parents' house in our little village. Each of us had travelled very different roads, displaced by decades and thousands of miles and circumstances. As we stood together again at last, for that moment before Katina's wedding, the years melted away from our aging bodies as our memories travelled back together, to those moments of our youth, our innocence. Yes, our bodies had aged, but our eyes saw the silent, still frames of our youth.

Finally, Iakovos spoke. "Katina, you look as beautiful as ever," he said. "And Christo, my friend, we are growing old in America. I prayed for your parents this morning as I have so many times over the years. Let us go out now and join the others. We have a wedding to celebrate!"

During the ceremony Katina beamed with youthful happiness. It was as if she had recaptured time. I had worked hard over the years to attain a degree of material success so that I might care for my family, but the sacrifice of her youth to care for our parents was perhaps a greater, more selfless, gift. As Iakovos performed the marriage ceremony, I wished her every happiness. She had given much, and now she deserved much in return. Her sacrifice seemed to have been rewarded abundantly.

* * * * *

When John Kennedy had been assassinated, it had deeply scarred the heart and soul of the nation, yet the country picked up the pieces and continued on. We would not be so lucky during the spring and summer of 1968. Martin Luther King, Jr., was gunned down by an assassin as he stood on a hotel balcony. Across the nation, cities erupted into a contagious violence that spread from coast to coast. In Washington, D. C., whole blocks of the city burned and looting was widespread. Smoke rising from the nation's capital stirred memories of Turkish invasions. I was swept by an overwhelming sense of sadness for my adopted country, a land of freedom. In the wrong hands, boundless freedom also leads to chaos.

Only a few weeks later, just as suddenly and dramatically, Robert Kennedy was assassinated in a hotel kitchen in Los Angeles, California. The country, stunned by the violence that had followed King's death, was crushed by grief. As I watched the events of the summer unfold, I realized that America had lost a part of her innocence and seemed to be drifting, rudderless. I wondered if we would ever recover; but just as strong individuals survive devastating tragedies, so can great nations, all through the resiliency that God gives them.

That summer, I received a great personal shock. Anthony came to see me in Ocean City, but when he arrived I almost didn't recognize him. He had been president of his high school class and earned eight varsity letters in high school athletics. A little over a year earlier he had qualified for the final Olympic trials in wrestling in the 198-pound weight class. Now he stood before me with a beard and shaggy hair, announcing he would not be returning to college that fall. It seemed America's problems had now become my own.

"I'm not getting anything out of school," he told me, "and besides, my draft number is high enough—189—that I don't think I will be called."

I was speechless. When I finally found my voice I asked him what he intended to do.

"Hitch-hike up to Dartmouth," he said, "to visit Ken Bruntel."

Ken was a high school friend of Anthony's who had worked for us in Ocean City for two summers as a short-order cook.

"I see," I nodded, trying to appear calm. "Do you have a few dollars?"

"Yeah, thanks Dad, I'm fine."

Even so, I managed to press some money on him for my own peace of mind. Anthony had always made his own decisions and I would not interfere now—aside from a few helpful suggestions. I stood by silently and watched him go, full of grave concern.

I was spending more and more time tending to business in Ocean City, but I managed to get home for a while late in September. While I was there, I passed the remnants of "Resurrection City" on the Mall in Washington. Resurrection City was an encampment of black Americans who were protesting for civil rights. Having grown up under Turkish rule, I knew what real oppression was, and the contrast between their oppression in America and the oppression under the Turks was like day and night. There seemed to be, with the terrible assassinations and subsequent unrest, a sense of dissatisfaction in the land which I found difficult to understand, even artificially imposed. I thought back to the words of President Johnson and his "Great Society" of 20-hour workweeks. Didn't people realize how lucky they were to be in America? Again in the backdrop of social unrest—indeed, upheaval—I felt, more than ever, out of step with society. It was as if so many here in the land of opportunity had lost sight of those opportunities, those blessings, placed right at their feet. If only they would stop trampling them and put their energy into using them wisely!

In November of that year Richard Nixon was elected President and the problems of the Vietnam War were approaching a peak. America was a confused and divided nation. I had always taught my sons that if their country ever called them, they should drop everything and run to her aid. I believed deeply and passionately that this was an unconditional obligation, a responsibility that those who live in a free society must always be willing to meet. Still, one of the many thoughts that went through my mind that autumn was Anthony's vulnerability to the draft. I knew his draft lottery number was high enough to make it unlikely he would be called, but if he were called, I knew he would go. The prospect of my son or anyone else's son fighting a terrible war so far from home saddened me, but freedom costs dearly. To my great relief, however, Anthony decided to return to school at William and Mary that summer and Jon, who was attending the prestigious University of Virginia, managed the beer and wine carryout.

Early in the summer of 1969, I wrote to my old friend, Archbishop Iakovos, and asked him to join us for dinner sometime after the summer season when I was at leisure to return home. One evening after Labor Day, Elenitsa called to say she had received a letter from the archdiocese in New York stating that the Archbishop would be in Washington in mid-October and wanted to know if that would be a good time to take me up on my dinner invitation.

It would be a wonderful time, I replied by letter to the Archbishop. Two weeks before his visit, we began receiving requests from various priests in the Washington-Baltimore area, most of whom we even knew, to attend the dinner we were hosting. In the end, though wishing we could repay this sudden popularity, we invited only three priests to join us. I spent the entire day before the Archbishop's visit cooking and preparing. Elenitsa assisted me.

Promptly at four o'clock in the afternoon of the event, a long black limousine pulled up in front of our home. Instantly, there was pandemonium inside the house. Our visiting priests jumped to their feet and rushed into the hall, carefully collecting themselves in ecclesiastical pecking order to form a receiving line. Meanwhile, Ianthe bounced excitedly in front of the window.

"He's here, Daddy, he's here!" she squealed.

"Oh my goodness!" Elenitsa gasped, her hands smoothing the front of her dress.

Katina, who had come from New York for the event, tightly clasped Elenitsa's trembling hands.

"Okay, okay," I said, trying to calm everyone, myself included. "Everything's ready, everything's fine. I'll get the door. Everyone relax!"

Before I went to the door, I paused at the bay window that looked out into the street. There, surrounded by the golds, reds and greens of autumn foliage, I saw two bishops clad in black helping the Archbishop from the limousine. Like the priests, he was also clad in black. He wore a black headdress and a long white beard, and he carried a staff in his right hand. I watched as he moved up the walkway, then I went to the door and opened it.

"Welcome to my home, Your Eminence," I said, bowing deeply with a broad smile.

The Archbishop smiled and gave a sidewise glance to the bishops flanking him on his right and left. Instantly they bowed and retreated to the limousine, which then drove quietly off, leaving the Archbishop with his old friend from Imbroz.

"You have done quite well for yourself in America, Chris Christ," he said, placing heavy emphasis on the shortened, American version of my name.

"Thank you, I am doing my best, your Eminence." As soon as he entered the foyer, the three priests who had been waiting inside snapped to attention and descended upon him like excited children, falling all over themselves in their eagerness to show respect.

It is traditional in the Greek Orthodox Church for lay people to bow and kiss the hand of their priest, and the same custom is practiced by priests to show respect to their superiors. This kissing of hands might explain why many Orthodox priests of all levels walk with their hands folded before them—to discourage kisses from the faithful. The day Archbishop Iakovos came to dinner at my house was no different.

They mingled briefly in the living room, chatting politely and sipping drinks, while I was busy working in the kitchen. I shooed Elenitsa out of the kitchen, assuring her I could handle it, so she could entertain our guests. When dinner was ready, I placed the Bishop at the head of the table and Anthony on his right. Father Ted, our local priest, sat on his left. I sat at the opposite end with Elenitsa and Katina on either side of me, and Fathers John and George were seated next to them. There was not enough room at the dinner table, so I had delegated Ianthe and Jon to act as servers. Along the length of the table were goblets of wine and water, dishes of feta cheese and olives, and baskets of freshly baked bread.

Conversation ceased as the Archbishop, followed by the rest of us, sat down. Then Iakovos lifted his clasped hands and lowered his forehead, offering up a nearly inaudible prayer followed by a melodious Amen. Dinner had begun, and Ianthe and Jon began serving us. The Archbishop reached to his left for a basket of bread, and as he extended his hand, Father Ted, either intending to show respect or mistaking Iakovos' intention, greeted the Archbishop's hand with an unsolicited kiss. Abruptly, the Archbishop withdrew his hand and fixed the poor priest with a cold, disapproving stare.

"I am sorry, Your Eminence, I am sorry." Mortified, Father Ted repeated his apologies over and over, accompanied by equally ineffective head bows. Iakovos responded with silence and focused his attention on the bread tray.

Apart from that little episode, dinner went well. Jon and Ianthe served all the courses with encouragement and help from me. I received liberal kudos from all regarding my food preparation. Afterwards I escorted the Archbishop to the living room for an after-dinner drink.

"It has been many years, Bread Crumb," he said, calling me by the nickname he had bestowed on me so long ago, a personal connection between us.

"So it has, Your Eminence," I agreed, exchanging a smile with him.

"Christo, you have a family, you have become successful. Tell me, how have you found life in America?"

"Very busy, Your Eminence," I replied honestly.

The Archbishop chuckled.

"As long as a man is not afraid of work, there is more to do than time to do it in America," I continued.

"That is so," he said.

I excused myself to assist Elenitsa in clearing the table. When I returned, Anthony was engaged in conversation with the Archbishop.

"The war in Vietnam doesn't have a clear purpose," my son was saying. "I doubt very much that our country should even be involved in this conflict."

I stood quietly watching my son, who was six feet tall and probably 220 pounds, as he sat next to the Archbishop of the Americas and discussed one controversial subject after another. Both my son, the hippie, and the Archbishop shared full beards.

"And what about the poor people in America?" Anthony asked when at length the topic moved from war to world poverty. "What has the Church done to help them?"

"Let me tell you a story," the Archbishop said. "When the Patriarch first dispatched me to America, I found a building for the leadership's use in New York around 150th Street. It had electricity, it had indoor plumbing and running water. The building was five stories high and made of stone and mortar. I thanked God for allowing us to have such a fine building. It was not until some years later that I learned that the building we were in was in Harlem, considered one of the poorest areas of the city. To many, it was called a ghetto. To us, it was called a godsend."

His story was simple, but the point was profound. In the eyes of much of the world, poverty in America wasn't poverty at all.

It was time, I thought, to move on to dessert, and an instant later Elenitsa and I began serving pastries, including the Archbishop's favorite, *loucomades*. The mood had lightened and everyone was relaxed. I reached for my camera and tried to take pictures, but to my great disappointment, on this once-in-a-lifetime occasion, my camera wouldn't work. A few minutes later the limousine returned and my old friend was gone.

The next day, I took Elenitsa, Katina and Ianthe to church where the Archbishop was the centerpiece of the service. When we advanced in a line to accept the blessed bread from him after the service, he called us to join him, then signaled for someone on his staff to take a photograph. Remembering my disappointment with the camera the night before, this was his gift to us. I was touched.

* * * * *

I had reached an interesting point in my life. I had accepted the responsibility of Elenitsa's handicapped parents, suffered the painful loss of my own parents, realized my business ambitions, and discovered that my oldest son had become a hippie.

Jon was now a serious young man, and with more of his mother's temperament, he had always helped me with the family business. At the University of Virginia, he was majoring in history and wrestled, as well. By cooking for his fraternity, he received free room and board. His study of the American Civil War would remain a lifelong interest.

Ianthe, my Cookie, had no shortage of admirers. From a very early age she wanted to be a teacher. She was active in youth ministry at church and was always teaching the younger children. She was the light of my eyes and I couldn't spoil her enough. At sixteen, she was first runner-up in the Miss Greek Independence Day beauty contest. I had to bolt the door to keep the boys away, but she just didn't seem to be interested in dating, not with all her other activities.

One late autumn day in 1969, I looked down at the sacred coin my father had given me. I had worn it faithfully every day for almost forty years. The coin was a reminder of my youth, my father, and all that he had taught me. It was a symbol of my life, my beliefs. In an instant of time I stood, a middle-aged man, gazing at the unchangeable coin that had helped me keep my faith as a small boy. Life was not perfect, and there were many hard things I simply could not change, but as I stood in my bedroom that afternoon, half a world from Imbroz, I pressed the coin to my heart thanking God for His gifts and praying that He continue to watch over us.

18
A Belated Vacation

I never saw a moor,
I never saw the sea;
Yet know I how the heather looks,
And what a wave must be.
I never spoke with God,
Nor visited in heaven;
Yet certain am I of the spot
As if the chart were given.

—Emily Dickinson
"Chartless"

Although his letters always inquired of our welfare, never complaining, poor Uncle Demetri's uprooting from Imbroz when Katina left marked the first time in countless generations that a family member had not inhabited the little island. Elderly members of my family had always been cared for by relatives at home, but now there had been no one left on Imbroz to care for Demetri. In fact, at the time Uncle Demetri had left for Constantinople, there were only three hundred elderly Greek Christians left on the island and most of the property had been confiscated by the Turks or abandoned.

By God's good grace I had been allowed to establish myself in America and build a life and security for my family, but Uncle Demetri's resignation to a Turkish nursing home remained an unspoken grief. The meager material conditions he faced were a reminder of the sharp contrasts in my life. Yes, even my material success couldn't alter a moment of reality for my favorite uncle.

The Turkish presence on Imbroz had assumed many forms over the years. Since 1965, the penal colony that was established in the once cheerful and bustling village of Schinoudi had unleashed one horror after another on the little island's inhabitants. Violent criminals roaming freely and terrorizing towns and villages proved too much for the few remaining Greeks.

Yet, if I closed my eyes I could still see the windmills of Castro turning in the breeze, just as I remembered them from childhood— Castro, the island's oldest village, dating back before Christ. Though many things lived on in my memories, much of our cultural heritage was rapidly vanishing. Like Uncle Demetri, it had been condemned to the past. Its loss went beyond the loss of relics and artifacts. It was a loss of people and a way of life, surviving only in the memories of a few sad tales told by a few old souls.

* * * * *

At the post office one day in January, I looked over the 1970 commemorative stamps and purchased four sheets. Over the years, I remained fascinated by their artistic beauty and symbolism, and the collection I had started as a youth in Constantinople had continued to grow through the years. Elenitsa laughed at me, saying that in life there were four things that gave me pleasure: feeling the tautness in my fishing line when a sea bass struck the bait, watching my azalea garden bloom in the spring, admiring my beautiful stamps, and helping my beloved children.

In fact, I spent many evenings studying my stamp albums open in my lap and a magnifying glass in my hand. This was what I was doing one evening that January when Elenitsa's brother, Gus, called.

"You think you and Elenitsa can make it to a Tastee Freeze convention in March? The president's going to present you with an award."

"Really?" I said with surprise. "Where's it being held this year?"

"Acapulco," he replied. "Beautiful, sunny Acapulco."

"Well, we'll have to see, Gus. Maybe we will."

After I hung up, Elenitsa called to me from the kitchen. "Who was on the phone, Chris?"

"Your brother," I said. "He sent his regards."

Elenitsa came out of the kitchen, wiping her hands on a towel. "He didn't want to speak with me?"

"He wants us to go to Acapulco," I told her casually. "I'm supposed to get some sort of an award."

For a moment Elenitsa stared at me. "Chris, let's go!" she said finally. "We've never had a real vacation. I would love to go to Acapulco! Wouldn't you?"

"Yes, we can go," I said slowly, remembering the many years Elenitsa bemoaned my long work hours and the limited time I spent with my family, but only because there were always things to do and responsibilities to tend. Perhaps it was time to relax a little. The thought of arranging the responsibilities of all the stores in my absence, especially a prolonged one, was unsettling to say the least, yet life was passing us by, and my torturous schedule had finally evolved into something I could control.

"Yes," I repeated, much to Elenitsa's delight. "Yes, we will go."

Late in March we departed for four sunny days in Acapulco. We spent much of our time wandering happily around like the tourists that we were, buying souvenirs: tee shirts for the kids, some jewelry for Elenitsa, and, for me, a three-foot detailed replica of a pirate ship complete with orange sails. When we weren't shopping, we lay on the beach under a warm sun, and in the evenings we drank daiquiris and listened to Calypso bands.

The last evening in Acapulco was the night of the big, formal Tastee Freeze banquet, and Mr. Leo Moraine, founder of Tastee Freeze, addressed the audience. When he came to the words, "I would like to award this plaque to Chris Christ of Ocean City, Maryland," I was surprised how nervous I was as I rose and he placed the award in my hands. "For selling more ice cream during the past summer than anyone else in his region," he went on. I thought it was funny that I had had no idea I was selling so much ice cream!

I glanced down at the plaque inscribed with my name and the words, "Eastern Region Production Leader." Then I realized that everyone was applauding. Smiling, I thanked Mr. Morany, bowed, then returned to my seat next to Elenitsa, who squeezed my hand. She was proud of me, but I was a little embarrassed. Still, I placed the plaque between us on the table, and during the evening I would steal a glance at it from time to time.

A few weeks later my vacation was a pleasant memory and I opened the Anthony's for the season. Nick came down to join me a couple of days later. He was seventy-one years old now, and I knew he was beginning to feel his age. I asked after his health and he asked about my vacation. As I poured him a cup of coffee, I began feeling my age, too.

"Well, Nick," I said after a thoughtful pause, "we are getting old. Nothing under the sun stays the same." He looked up with the same innocent, naïve stare that had always been so intriguing. "We have a lot of work to do. Drink your cup of coffee and let's get going."

"Yep, you're right."

With that, the summer of 1970 began. The vibrant economy of the sixties left a legacy in the excessive structures that would be erected in the early seventies. This became apparent in government as well as the private sector. Little did we know, however, that the extended post-World War II growth cycle was about to come to an end.

During that spring and summer, the cultural revolution erupting among the youth of the country became increasingly noticeable to me. Still, I wasn't really aware how widespread the movement had become, nor was I prepared for my son's immersion in it. Shortly after we opened the store, Anthony, accompanied by a friend of his from school named Charlie, drove up in Charlie's MG Midget. Anthony was now in his junior year at William and Mary.

"Dad, I'm going with Charlie to play in a chess tournament in California," he told me. "We're plotting a course out to the West Coast."

Charlie, a graduate math student, was the Armed Services' chess champion. I could only wonder if Anthony's studies were progressing along with his skill at chess. This was not my idea of how to productively spend a summer, but on the other hand, I reasoned, the experience might be good for Anthony, even though I could have used his help.

"You'll need some money," I said, reaching for my wallet, "and a gasoline card might not hurt either."

Anthony accepted the cash and gas credit card with appreciation and thanks, then headed off to the townhouse to get his belongings and say goodbye to his mother. "Take care of yourself," I said. Watching him go, I had misgivings regarding the course of his life, offset by an overwhelming swell of pride at the sight of him. He had been a successful kid, clean cut and focused, but now he seemed unsettled and directionless, and it worried me, as did most of the youth I was seeing. Not for the first time, I hoped he wasn't on drugs. Flamboyant youth paraded a defiant condescending air in opposition to our culture, teachings and work ethic. It was a hollow defiance rooted in intellectual relativism and excessive materialism. Values had been widely abandoned in favor of chaotic rebelliousness. I was glad that Jon was with me at this time, for he was considerably more stable, and Cookie was thankfully unaffected.

I had a local clientele that came in for breakfast sandwiches every day, along with the fishermen who had me make sandwiches to take with them. Like my lunch sandwiches, my breakfast sandwiches were well known, and my store was busy from morning to night. During the day, the local crowd would look for me just as the vacationers would seek out Nick at night. I was in my fifteenth season. Ocean City boasted clean white beaches, sunny skies and beautiful water, though I saw little of them until the fall, after the season had passed.

One August morning, as I was hosing the parking lot, two men approached me on the south side of my small store, Leo Vondes and his father Anthony. Leo was an assistant principal, working a summer job as a police officer, and I was on his beat.

"Mr. Christ, this is my father," Leo said. "Papa, this is Mr. Christ, the man we've been talking about."

"How do you do?" I said in English. Then in Greek, "What is your name?"

"Anthony Vondes," he responded in a stern yet polite manner. He stood about my height. His Greek face had the look of a hard life, an old country look. His hands were worn from work like my own and he had a mild discoloration in one eye.

"My name is Christo Chrysostomidis," I said, "but I've shortened it to Christ. Where do you come from?" I inquired, still in Greek.

"Albania."

"Albania?" I repeated—another Greek who had survived under the Ottomans, and later the communists. Like so many who had found their way to America, Anthony Vondes was a good, hardworking man. "Won't you come inside, and we'll have something to eat together."

We talked about the Ottomans, King Zog, the Christian Holocaust, the Pera Palace Hotel, and finally the food business. Anthony Vondes had a restaurant in Seat Pleasant, Maryland.

"My family was burned out during the first Balkan War in 1912. We went to the islands and stayed with an uncle. Later I went to seminary for two years and finally ended up working in the hotels in Athens," he told me. We were two old Greeks who had just met, but we were bound, nonetheless, by a lifetime of parallel experiences.

* * * * *

After the first five years, the beer and wine store was very busy. Jon, still a student at the University of Virginia, was now managing that plus the six other stores. I had also made changes to my carryout store, installing a new fifteen-foot counter and two service windows. In June we had plenty of help, but in August, when our business was at its heaviest, half the staff left to catch a couple of weeks of fun and sun before heading back to school. This ritual was repeated every year for over twenty years. It was usually a scramble, but we somehow managed to keep things together and to serve our customers to their satisfaction.

Nick's health that summer was not good. He was having difficulty breathing, and it would only be a matter of time before his coughing would develop into deadly emphysema—the result of smoking two packs of unfiltered Camels every day for decades. During the eleven years Nick had worked for me, he had never missed a single minute of work, but I knew this could not continue. I was fifty-three, eighteen years younger than Nick and in much better health. Even so, I too was feeling some wear and tear, the result of a lifetime of hard work, and I knew Nick had to feel it even more. I wondered if this would be his last summer.

That month, Anthony returned from his trip out west and worked for two weeks before heading back to school. It was good to see him safe, and he arrived right at a time when I was terribly shorthanded, but he seemed just as unsettled as he had before he left. It appeared to me that the trip, which I had hoped would help him mature a little, had gained him nothing. I still had no idea what was bothering him. In the end I realized that although I could guide him, I would have to allow him to use his own judgement to work out his problems.

The intense pace of the summer withered with the leaves of fall as the sun-bleached sand cooled under the autumn sky. That winter I ordered a stamp book on United States First Day Covers from the Postal Commemorative Society, and subscribed to the series. Each cover was personally addressed to me and bore at least one colorful eight-cent stamp. The commemoratives were beautiful, but I felt terribly extravagant in my purchase, though they would presumably appreciate in value. Twenty of these little covers, however, cost nearly fifty dollars; I would not be so extravagant in the future.

In February of 1971, Anthony was runner-up in the Wilkes-Barre, Pa., Wrestling Tournament, which was a national event, and he seemed to be more settled than he had been of late. I told myself that there would always be problems to solve and so much work to do, and not to worry beyond the difficulties of today. Within a few months, though, Anthony's grades fell off. He then admitted himself to a mental hospital in Williamsburg, Virginia. When Elenitsa learned of this, she fell apart.

"He's there because you were never home when he was growing up!" she told me bitterly. "I told you there would be problems! I told you over and over! I've told you for years, and you never paid attention!"

Anthony's admission to Eastern State Hospital seemed to validate all her concerns, and perhaps she was right. Thus began a period when I would be devoting an increasing amount of attention to my troubled son. I had worked hard over the years and had spent much time away from my family, but self-reproach wouldn't help Anthony now. The fact remained that we were both very concerned. Anthony was our eldest son. Like many a papa I could vividly remember the moment I first set eyes on him. I could recall standing quietly by his crib watching him sleep, a reward I looked forward to each night when I came home. When he was small I could take care of him and keep him safe. I felt helpless now as I witnessed his turmoil. I struggled to overcome my dismay and renewed my belief that there was a solution to these problems, and, God willing, I would help him find it.

Meanwhile, 1971 was a difficult season for me in Ocean City. I was worried about Anthony, and even though Nick came back that year, his health was still declining. With Anthony in the hospital and Jon working full time at the beer and wine carryout, I found myself short-handed all summer. I had always encouraged my children to go to college, get an education and find another way to make a living, yet I still needed their help sometimes in the family business. That summer I seemed to lose a step. My usual high intensity had diminished and I missed my sons keenly. Perhaps it was the cumulative toll of years of work just wearing on me prematurely, but my energy was lower than it had ever been.

Somehow Nick and I made it through another busy season, and that fall Anthony came home from Eastern State. Although Dr. Schmidt pronounced him "recovered," he sat in his room all day and did nothing. Elenitsa insisted we take him to Tony Tsitos, a Greek psychiatrist from Constantinople whom I knew from church and whom Elenitsa had seen for several years. I have to admit that with all the problems and needs in the world, I really did not understand what psychiatry solved. Tony Tsitos was some fifteen years my junior, perhaps an inch shorter than I was, and his receding hairline and large thick glasses made him look like a college professor.

After two or three sessions, Dr. Tsitos called me.

"Chris, Anthony is very ill. He shows symptoms of manic depression."

"What does that mean, Tony?"

"It means that he needs medication and much therapy. I've prescribed him Thorazine, which he needs to take regularly. Without medication and ongoing therapy, his symptoms could become chronic, Chris. He could be hospitalized for a prolonged period of time. I suspect that this was all brought on by his use of drugs."

"I see," I said nodding acknowledgement, but not truly believing it. "So he must use more drugs to cure the use of drugs?"

I sensed Tony's hesitation on the other end of the line. "It could be a life-long illness, Chris," he told me finally.

"Help him, Tony," I said. "He's a young man with his life ahead of him. Do whatever you can to help him."

* * * * *

For a number of months Anthony continued under Dr. Tsitos' care. "He is a good man," I told my son, trying to convince myself of the doctor's effectiveness. "He's married and has three children. Such a lovely family..."

"He's seeing his secretary," was Anthony's response.

"What?"

"Dr. Tsitos is seeing his secretary, Pam. He thinks no one knows. I know."

In fact, Tony Tsitos eventually did divorce his wife and marry his secretary, but at the time I was more concerned about my son's mental health than about the doctor's extramarital affairs.

As a young Greek Christian, I had survived Atatürk and his regime of oppression and persecution. I had learned to survive under extreme adversity. I could not believe that my son had become crazy simply because he had experimented with drugs, nor could I believe that my absence was entirely responsible for this alleged mental illness. The fact was, I could neither understand how Anthony became ill nor the nature of his illness—therefore I rejected the whole notion of his illness. I believed in my heart that if and when he made up his mind, it would be easily overcome. In the meantime, however, I was willing to let the doctors try what they thought best, and stood by to encourage any positive action. Anthony's illness was more a product of a world bent on self-gratification and pleasure rather than the simple life of work and survival I had known. I could never understand these mental problems in a land that offered so much when so many in the world were starving.

Late in January 1972, I took my son to Ocean City and put him to work in the store. I felt inactivity was not the solution; indeed, I felt it promoted despondency. His attention and concentration improved, and over the winter he slowly responded. That summer, he even obtained a job as an undercover police officer in Ocean City. Apparently, his stint with drugs and his hospitalization had motivated him to formally oppose illegal drugs. Although not my choice of a career for my son, I think it helped him feel like he was doing something positive and undoing the things he regretted. It seemed for a while that Anthony had once again turned a corner.

He hadn't, though. Ultimately, he resigned from the police force in Ocean City and was admitted once again to a psychiatric hospital in Virginia. Not long afterwards, I had another brief conference with Tsitos, who told me that Anthony was suffering from paranoia.

"Paranoia?" I repeated, startled. "But a year ago you told me it was 'manic depression.'"

"Chris, psychosis can take many forms," he told me. "Very likely, Anthony's health problems are inherited from Elenitsa. The form of his problems may have changed, however—schizophrenia and bouts of depression coupled with paranoia may produce psychosis in the child…psychosis that is not manifested until the patient is in his late teens or early twenties."

"I see," I said. However, this rambling explanation made absolutely no sense to me. "Well, whatever this mysterious illness is," I told him, "it hasn't affected his appetite."

Dr. Tsitos blinked. "Excuse me?"

"Look, Tony, I intend no disrespect, but I cannot see a cause for this so-called illness. Compared to the Turks, how can anything my son has experienced be so bad as to cause all this? He used to be so strong, so full of energy and purpose, and now he's…" I shook my head. "Now you would have me believe he's chronically ill? My family survived torture, starvation, uprooting and countless atrocities…I cannot believe he is afflicted with anything that can't be cured through faith, strength and, frankly, a job. Anthony had that before, and he can find it again. Keeping busy is what sustained me all those years under Turkish rule—perhaps it would sustain Anthony."

"Perhaps it's better not to compare—" Tsitos interrupted.

"*Perhaps*," I said, cutting him off, "what Anthony needs is a swift kick in the ass."

Dumbfounded, Tony Tsitos stared at me wordlessly.

"Tony, I sometimes wonder what it is you are practicing—sorcery or science?" With that, I left his office, more convinced than ever that this period would pass and my son would regain his strength. With all this heavy, depressing stuff these doctors were convincing their patients they had, no wonder they were depressed and despondent! Where was hope and encouragement and faith and joy in all their mumbo-jumbo?

In spite of my great reluctance, however, I relented to a doctor's help for my son. Shortly after my conference with Dr. Tsitos, I placed my son in the care of another physician at Sheppard Pratt Hospital, a private psychiatric facility in Baltimore. It was expensive, but I felt it was his best chance for a permanent recovery, and I did not want him to stay in a public institution.

Meanwhile, my own health was in jeopardy. That winter, as I was shoveling snow from the driveway at home, I felt a warm pressure in my chest. Even after I finished shoveling, the pressure persisted. When I went inside I discovered I was perspiring, and a minute or two later my stomach was upset.

"Chris, are you okay?" Elenitsa asked.

"I think I have a little cold," I said, waving her off, but for five days I had a chronic low-grade fever and couldn't hold any food down. The numbness in my chess persisted.

"Chris, please call the doctor," Elenitsa repeated almost daily. "This could be something serious." I didn't have time, so much to do.

"It's the flu," I told her. "I'll be fine." It took two weeks, though, for the fever to subside, and a month later I still wasn't feeling myself.

Finally, at Elenitsa's insistence, I went to see a doctor. After an examination and a number of tests, the doctor sat down to talk with me. "You've had a bad heart attack," he said, looking grave. "A large part of your heart muscle has been damaged. Why did you take so long to seek help?"

I couldn't answer that. I had always avoided doctors, believing that whatever was wrong, my body would heal itself. This time, however, I had pushed myself too hard. Now there was damage that would never completely heal, damage that couldn't be fixed.

"It is critical," he said, "that you learn to take it easy. You've simply got to reduce your workload and eat lighter...curtail your red meat consumption."

Even as he said the words I knew it would be a difficult undertaking. I had made work a lifetime habit, and old habits are hard to break. Nonetheless, I would discipline myself to a new diet and shortly thereafter to a substantial reduction in my workload. I would compensate. There were too many things to do; it was not yet my time.

* * * * *

By summertime I was feeling slightly better. This was my nineteenth year of business in Ocean City and Nick's thirteenth year with me, but the summer had a somber tone. Nick looked very ill and although he continued to work day after day, his breathing was quick with a shallow wheezing and he had developed a limp. His weakened condition last year had become chronic. It would steadily worsen throughout the day and when Nick came to relieve me, he would lean on the stainless steel worktable for support, then out the doorway to the counter and customers. In fact, his health was clearly terrible and mine wasn't a great deal better. He was such a good employee and friend, yet hardly able to work. My children were gone and not available to help that summer, and aside from Nick, Bernard and Mae, help was unreliable.

I had told no one about my heart attack the previous winter, and although I had improved over the months, I still had not recovered my usual vigor and strength. Our maladies went unnoticed to our customers, friends and family, as I put in my usual long days. Each evening when I went home to prepare dinner with Elenitsa, she urged me to retire, obsessing on her fear that I would drop dead. Although I was only fifty-five, she was concerned that the work that I loved so much might kill me.

In the autumn Anthony was discharged from Sheppard Pratt. His doctor was a very nice man with a ponytail. He explained to me that after all my son's treatment and therapy, the biggest job that remained was to convince Anthony that he was all right. This was music to my ears! I figured one way to do that was to bring him to Ocean City to work for me until it was time to close the store for the winter. We needed each other. Prior to Anthony's miraculous recovery, he had been diagnosed with every psychosis known to psychiatry. I was confirmed in my belief that his problems were rooted in opinion rather then fact.

The demands of the season had exhausted me. Work that normally invigorated me left me tired and drained, and for the first time in my life, I sometimes struggled to get through the day. I knew Elenitsa and the doctor were right; I could not continue to work at my accustomed pace.

Late in that summer of 1973, not only Nick and I had slowed and worn down, the economy had begun to sputter and dwindle. For the first season in twenty years, sales had remained flat. As the season wound to a close, I finally came to a decision. This would be my last summer in Ocean City.

When I told Nick, he gave me a solemn smile. "Chris, I have just turned seventy-five. If this is to be my last year with you, I take nothing but good feelings with me. You're the best boss and kindest man I've known in my life, and it's been a pleasure to work with you."

The words of my loyal employee and friend meant a great deal to me. The last few months had been enormously difficult for all of us, not only in regard to my health, but in respect to Anthony as well. I had come to accept Elenitsa's view that my commitment to my work had negatively impacted on my children. Anthony was twenty-four years old; at six feet tall and over 200 pounds he towered over me, yet he needed my help. Although I did not completely understand how I had hurt him, I would do all I could to make it right.

The last day Nick and I were at the store, we shared a cup of coffee together. Fall was upon us and the sun-soaked island resort was penetrated by a cool, constant breeze. I thanked Nick for all his years of service and friendship, gave him a large bonus, then called a cab to take him the fifteen blocks to the Trailways station where he would catch a bus home to Baltimore for the last time.

"Nick, if you need me, call," I told him.

Nick nodded his thanks and shook my hand. He looked old and frail standing there on the sidewalk—but the truth was he was almost as proud as I was of the job we had done over the years. I sometimes thought it was the carnival atmosphere of the friendly beach crowds that partially sustained him, and I wondered sadly how well he would fare in retirement at home in Baltimore. I never had a desire to retire and only prayed for the energy to perform the daily tasks in front of me.

Nick's departure in the cab that afternoon marked the close of twenty glorious years at my small Ocean City store—tedious, taxing, repetitive toil that I was good at and loved so much. It was time to move on, to turn my energies to other things.

* * * * *

That same fall, a full-blown recession plagued the nation's economy. Obligations from both liberal political reform and the Vietnam War had sunk our economy. Though perhaps not the best time to retire, I had already set that course in motion. I could no longer oppose the wishes of my wife and children. A man named John Simms, in partnership with two other men, agreed to lease my sandwich store beginning the following summer. The income from the carryout and the rental stores I had built was enough to pay my mortgages and bills, and still leave a little extra for my children's tuition and emergencies.

Ianthe was now at Lynchburg College; Jon, after graduating from the University of Virginia in 1972, was living in Ocean City and managing the beer and wine store; and Elenitsa, Anthony and I were at home. Saint Catherine's, the church we helped to form years earlier, consulted me on most of their food functions and often enlisted my services on a volunteer basis. We saw a lot of Father Ted, who was a fixture at Saint Catherine's. He was its first priest, appointed by Archbishop Iakovos, and was as at ease eating a hot dog in Yankee Stadium as he was chanting in ancient Greek in front of his parishioners. Father John, the priest of St. Sophia Cathedral on Massachusetts Avenue, often came to visit us with his wife, Harriet, Elenitsa's second cousin. Slowly, I began to build a new life focusing on my family, friends, and community.

If retiring meant an end to old routines, it also meant an end to forty-five years of grinding, unending workdays, and the beginning of new routines and activities that were more voluntary. I was about to begin an extended vacation, complete with normal working hours alternating with bouts of outright leisure.

Early in the spring I returned to Ocean City, not to open the store, but to meet with the group who wished to lease it. Although I would come to regret my decision to sell the business during the ensuing economic recession, I never regretted my decision to rent my store to John Simms. He had a wife and small children and was just starting out in business. Most importantly, he had an enthusiasm and energy I respected. It would take energy and attitude to run the store. I liked him at once.

Although over time John made numerous small changes in the operation, some of which I didn't agree with, he kept the menu that had served the public so well. I spent a few weeks with him and his partners acquainting them with the business, and then in April I left for Baltimore. Quite frankly, watching each of my tasks being performed, I moved more toward a resolution. When I walked out of the store that last time, I felt a tremendous sense of sadness mixed with a surprisingly deep relief.

The point of my trip to Baltimore was to visit Nick, who had been admitted to Baltimore General Hospital. When I entered the room I greeted his wife and then moved to his bedside. I noticed that his breathing was labored, but he was conscious and lucid.

"Nick," I said. "It's me, Christo."

Nick raised his hand in acknowledgement, then moved it to the small side table, fumbling for his glasses. Then he removed the oxygen mask so that he was able to speak.

"Christo," he greeted me in Greek, his voice raspy. "How are you? How is your health?"

"Improving," I replied in Greek. "And you?"

"I am having a hard time breathing, but don't worry, Christo— in a month I will be fine," he reassured me. "In June I will come to the store and be ready to work."

"Nick," I said quietly. "I leased the store, remember? You and I have no more store to return to."

"Ah," Nick shook his head sadly. "So you really did it, eh? I had thought that over the winter you might talk yourself out of it."

"And so I would have, my friend, but my family would not allow it. No, the store is leased, and now you have plenty of time to rest and get well again."

Nick closed his eyes, and for a moment I thought he was asleep. Then he spoke, "Chris, my time with you was the best. I meant what I told you last summer. You are a good man, Chris Christ, the best I ever worked for. The work was hard, but so what? The store was my joy; my every moment feeding the crowds was my paradise. You know, Chris, I always watched after the store as if it was mine."

"I know, Nick," I said.

A few moments later, Nick drifted off to sleep. I turned to his wife and pressed a check for five hundred dollars in her hand.

"No, Chris," she protested, "I can't take this…"

"Take it for Nick," I urged. "He earned it. And there will be more as you need it."

"I don't know what to say," she stammered, turning so that I wouldn't see the tears welling in her proud eyes.

"You don't need to say a word," I smiled. "Just take care of my friend."

19
Lost at Sea

The answer is to rely on youth—not a time of life but a state of mind, a temper of the will, a quality of imagination, a predominance of courage over timidity, of the appetite for adventure over the love of ease.

—Robert F. Kennedy
from his speech to the youth of South Africa, 1966

Life is an uneven administrator, apportioning grief and joy disproportionately in time. The same is true of loss and gain. Although I was no longer operating the sandwich store, Elenitsa and I still spent the summer at our Ocean City townhouse. That season I managed my rental stores, helped my son Jon at the beer and wine carryout, attended bank board meetings and fished. Since Jon was managing the carryout, I didn't go to work until 8:30 in the morning and I usually left by 3:30 in the afternoon. I was still working seven days a week, but this was the lightest schedule I had ever had. I was, after all, retired, and so I tried my best to act like it.

I had a young visitor that summer of 1974, a little seven-year-old boy. In the evenings he used to nudge open the sliding screen door to our townhouse and play with the toys my children had long outgrown. His name was John and he was the youngest of Dr. and Mrs. Caroll's five kids. The Caroll's owned the townhouse next door. I would lecture John on philosophy and life in general, much as I might have my own children in years long gone.

In August, Richard Nixon resigned from the Presidency under threat of impeachment. That fall the nation faced a gasoline shortage, the economy was in the throes of a recession, bankruptcies were on the rise and we were evacuating our troops from Vietnam. It seemed as if the social and economic fabric of our nation was being torn to pieces. The legacy of Johnson's Great Society had smothered the economy like a blanket. The only bright news was that Anthony's stay at Sheppard Pratt—all thirty thousand dollars of it—seemed to have done him some genuine good. Since his release, I had been urging him to concentrate on the life he had before him, to work on his problems and to have faith in the future. "You're young, you can do what you want to do," I told him, and in fact he seemed more balanced and focused than I had seen him in a long time. Moreover, he continued to work and eventually moved into his own apartment in Arlington, Virginia.

Late in September, I returned to Baltimore one last time, to attend the funeral of my longtime friend. Nick was sadly now a part of my past, a memory of my success. He would be sorely missed, but it was God's will and his time had come. Through his final illness I had sent checks to his family, and on this visit I pressed a final, generous check into his widow's hand. Nick had always been loyal to me and had worked hard. He was always there when I needed him. Easing his family's loss seemed the least I could do.

Aside from Nick's death, the fall and winter of 1974-75 were uneventful for me, but the nation was still reeling from a severe economic slowdown, compounded by a significant increase in oil prices and interest rates. This was a time for me to do the things I never had before, little things that many people take for granted, such as getting to know the neighbors. Mike and Elizabeth Pappas had lived near me for years, and yet I had never known that both had worked hard in their photography business. Mike, who was an airborne marine in World War II, had started driving school buses after the war and taking wedding pictures. Eventually photography turned into a full-time occupation. Mike was about six feet tall weighing about two hundred and eighty pounds, and Elizabeth was petite, barely a hundred pounds. He and Elizabeth had no children and Mike often volunteered to mow the church lawn. Although big and gruff in appearance, he had a gentle side.

* * * * *

Elenitsa's parents were living with us again. We had fixed up a downstairs room for them, and Anton—who at eighty-eight was ten years older than Alexandra—sat in a chair most of the day ceaselessly fingering his worry beads. One January evening after dinner, I sat with him a while and showed him my new Bicentennial commemorative stamps. Anton's eyesight was nearly gone, and so I described each stamp to him in detail.

"They are beautiful, Christo," he said, "just beautiful." Suddenly he added: "Thank you, Christo, for your help." His dim eyes locked onto mine and in the silent moment that passed between us, a mutual understanding was expressed.

"You once helped me, a young man with few prospects," I told him. "You lent me money and believed in me. If it had not been for you, I may not be where I am today. It is only right that I do what I can for you now."

At the end of February, Anton had a blackout and, worried about his health, we moved him to a nursing home nearby. Anthony visited his grandfather a few weeks after he was settled in and introduced him to his new girlfriend, Lee Ann. Later that evening, Anton lay in bed clutching his crucifix and cursing his son, Gus, for taking his money. It must have been a terrible blow to him, the belief that his own flesh and blood, a son he had loved and raised, had betrayed him. Just a few hours later, he was dead.

My father-in-law was a remarkable man. In many ways he had had a successful life, but it saddened me to think that his last years were marred by his son's dishonesty and a paralyzing stroke. I found out just before Anton died that he had left one dollar in his will to Gus so that he could buy a bullet and kill himself. Though unbelievable, it is true and shows how terribly bitter their relationship had became.

After Anton's death, Alexandra continued to live with us. Her health was very poor and, crippled by severe and painful arthritis, she was confined to a wheelchair.

I often prayed to God that when my time came, He would take me with my mental and physical faculties intact. My great fear in life was that I would be disabled physically or debilitated mentally, that I would be constrained in any manner from living the life I was living. For the last ten years my in-laws had had severe health problems, and as their primary caregivers, Elenitsa and I had witnessed their deterioration with painful clarity. This was not how I wanted to end my life.

In late 1977 Ianthe, now graduated from college, became a public schoolteacher in Fredericksburg, Virginia, some fifty miles south of us. Jon continued to manage the beer and wine carryout, and Anthony, who was making a strong recovery, began work as a bricklayer's apprentice while taking college classes at night.

That Christmas we had Taki's and Sultana's son Peter and his wife Cathy, who was also from Imbroz, over for dinner. It was a pleasant, festive evening and I prepared my traditional leg of lamb and rice pilaf. All my family was together again and my enthusiasm over the event released surges of energy as I set about my preparations. I had served and waited on people all of my life, the rich, the famous, the powerful, and now it was my pleasure to serve the most important people of all, my family.

The following summer, my brother Costa came to Ocean City with Afrodite and their four children. His children had all learned Greek before they learned English, and I found them delightful. They called me Theo Christo, and would kiss my hand and offer me respectful bows. They were also very bright kids. Some years before, Afrodite methodically and patiently had worked with each child during their pre-school years, thus largely explaining their wonderful academic success. By the time they began formal schooling, her children were not only bilingual, but their mathematical skills were quite advanced.

One morning during their Ocean City visit, I excused myself from my obligations with Jon at the beer and wine carryout and took my little brother Costa fishing in the ocean on my small, twenty-foot runabout.

"Big Brother," Costa said, using his life-long nickname for me, "perhaps you should slow down a little." He sat clutching the rail with a white-knuckled grip, his feet firmly planted against the bulkhead, as we rounded a point and hit the whitewater in the inlet where the ocean met the bay.

My mind drifted back on the difficulties of our past then propelled me forward to the present. We were indeed two fortunate men. God's light had shined on our lives.

Costa must have been thinking along the same lines as he idly fingered the reel in his hand. "And so, from Greece to America," he continued at last, "from an old life to a new one...and we are still fishing!"

Suddenly his line snapped tautly. "I think I have something, Big Brother!"

"Yes, I think you do!" I exclaimed. "Bring it in slowly, Costa. Slow and steady."

Minutes later we had a nice four-pound sea trout onboard and a very pleased Costa.

"Here, Costa, have a beer," I said as I snapped a pop tab on a can of Budweiser.

Costa grinned his thanks.

During the afternoon we pulled in more fish, and that evening everyone dined on our catch.

"Costa, eat the head, too," I said, pointing at a nice little trout on his plate. "It's very tasty."

"Ah, so it is, Big Brother," Costa announced, his mouth full of fish, and all the kids followed suit.

Although infrequent, the times we had together seemed to almost makeup for all the time we had spent apart. .

* * * * *

The following year, in mid-March 1974, Costa suffered a massive and unexpected heart attack. He died in the ambulance on the way to the hospital, leaving behind Afrodite and his four children, ages six through twelve. It was a tragedy every bit as severe as any I had witnessed.

That morning when I arrived at the house, Costa's children surrounded me crying out, "Theo Christo...Theo Christo...Theo Christo!" I reached out my arms and drew them close to me, then released them to embrace their mother.

"I've lost Costa," Afrodite sobbed. "I've lost Costa!"

I shared Afrodite's shock and sense of sudden loss. It was as incomprehensible to me as it was to her. We had survived so much together, Costa and me. How could he be gone—just like that, without a warning, without a word...without a goodbye? Costa was my little brother, the small boy who had followed me around our island home, the youth I had brought to Constantinople, the man I had helped come to America after years of separation. He was only fifty-five and still my little brother! It underscored in the sharpest of ways how fragile and precious our lives are.

God had given us thirteen years to be reunited. What was denied us in the Old Country we shared in America. Yes, Costa was gone, but the fulfillment and gentle love he felt and freely gave to his wife and four children would live on. In comforting Costa's family, I also comforted myself. In the days that followed, I helped Afrodite arrange for Costa's burial, and then I handled his estate. I immediately sold his second home and used the proceeds to pay off the mortgage on his first home. What remained was about ten thousand dollars, which we put into a certificate of deposit. Without a mortgage to pay, Afrodite was essentially debt-free, but she and the children would have to live on Costa's social security. Lord and Taylor sent a note of sympathy and a check for five hundred dollars.

At the time of Costa's death, Anthony was attending night school working on a new major to complete his degree. The evenings he wasn't in class he usually spent with Afrodite and the children, offering a sense of security to the grieving family. Taki's and Sultana's son, Peter Hatzi, who lived close by, often came by on Saturdays. With time, I knew the family would heal. In those first few years, it was primarily Anthony and Peter who spent time with Afrodite and the children.

That fall, Katina called me to say that Uncle Demetri had died in the nursing home in Constantinople where he had spent the last fifteen years. Demetri had never married and his only remaining family were his nieces and nephews thousands of miles away in America. Apart from his goddaughter he was alone, and his only support was the money and small gifts we sent him. I had so many vivid memories of him from my childhood. He was Papa's younger brother and my favorite uncle, and although we weren't entirely certain of his age, we believed he was a hundred and one. The pain of not having shared his company and wisdom in America struck me the same as it had upon my parents' demise.

"Christo," Katina said, "Demetri was a good man and his mind remained sharp up to the end. He last wrote me six months ago and he always asked after you and your family."

"Yes," I agreed soberly. "He was a fine man, the last of our family in that part of the world."

"That is true," Katina acknowledged. "And such a good Christian, too."

"God rest his soul." Our parents' generation had now all but disappeared. The fragility of life was only overshadowed by the quickened passage of time. It was quite a year of loss. The passage of all these important people, first my parents, then Nick Anthony and Anton, Costa, and now Uncle Demetri, gave an urgency to my desire to spend more time with family and friends. My life was passing before me with increasing speed. I would not waste one precious moment of my time remaining on earth. The loss of loved ones in a brief time can only be mitigated by the easing of pain over a long time.

* * * * *

Finally, Elenitsa and I received some long-awaited good news. As the decade drew to a close, Anthony, who was still working in construction and attending night school, became engaged to Lee Ann, the girl he had been dating for quite some time. I liked Lee Ann and felt from the beginning of their relationship that she was good for my son. I welcomed their engagement with an open heart.

At a dinner Elenitsa and I held for them in early December 1979, I turned to Lee Ann and said, "You can't continue calling me Mr. Christ any more."

Lee Ann smiled. "What would you like me to call you?" she asked.

"You are marrying my son," I told her. "That makes you my daughter, so I think you had better call me 'Dad.'"

"And me, 'Mother,'" chimed in Elenitsa.

On the day Anthony and Lee Ann married, I looked at my son with satisfaction and affection. He had had his own personal struggles early in life and had overcome them. His dark eyes and hair belonged to his mother, but his smiling expression was the same as my own. For a brief moment I saw myself in his eyes.

As she stood next to my son, Lee Ann's light Scandinavian features and blue eyes made a striking contrast. She and Anthony were, I thought proudly, a handsome couple. As the wedding ceremony commenced, I reflected briefly on the past decade. I had committed myself to helping Anthony. I had faith that he would recover, and I let him know I had confidence in him. As I watched him exchange vows with Lee Ann, I offered God a prayer of thanks. However I may have failed my son in his childhood, it had all worked out now and I was a proud father.

My children surrounded me in the chapel where Anthony married Lee Ann. We had faced tragedy and loss over the past decade, and a wedding was what we needed. Anthony's marriage I could turn my attention to other matters…like getting my daughter married.

* * * * *

Late in August of 1980, I arranged a fishing excursion on my new boat with my friend and first mate Paul Yeonas, a successful homebuilder in Northern Virginia. I was up at the crack of dawn, readied the boat, then came in for coffee and a toasted muffin while waiting for Paul. There was a heavy fog over the bay that reduced visibility to 30 feet, but Paul thought it should lift as the morning unfolded.

"Captain Christ!" an earthy, somewhat nasal voice blasted out in greeting through the crack in the sliding front door. "Captain Christ!"

"Come in, Paul, come in," I exclaimed, walking toward the door as it slid open.

"What can I do to help get ready, Captain Christ?" he asked with typical enthusiasm.

"First, relax, Paul. Sit down and have your coffee." I gestured with a nod while pouring him a freshly brewed cup and refilling mine.

Within a few minutes, we had embarked and were in the channel headed toward the inlet at twelve knots, enveloped in the heavy fog. The fog was eerie and stifling, but on sheer instinct I found the boating lane through the bay and we would be at the inlet in fifteen minutes. I never carried a compass or a two-way radio, relying instead on the sun, stars, experience and judgment to navigate. This intuitive reliance enhanced our isolation as we motored through the thick fog.

"Paul, keep an eye peeled for the jetties."

"Aye, aye, Captain...ever seen anything like this?"

The blanket of white mist wasn't accompanied by any signs of whether the calm sea of the inlet would turn to chop. Within minutes, though, swirling three-foot swells of tepid bay water abutted the ocean brine. We were in the crosscurrents of the Ocean City inlet. Whitecaps sprayed us as the small 22' vessel rode the jagged swish of choppy water.

"Captain Christ, I can't see the jetty."

The inlet was about 600 feet wide and cut through the rock jetty of Ocean City to the north and a sister jetty off Assateague Island to the south.

"Don't worry, Paul. We will be in the ocean soon," I said as we both strained to see through the white curtain.

"What do you make of it?" he asked as we motored from the inlet's tempest to the more rhythmic ocean swells.

"It's early yet...only 7:30. Let's see if it lifts in an hour," I responded, though I had noticed its blanketing chill as I turned northeast, heading for the ten-mile buoy. We arrived about 45 minutes later, then fished for an hour. We only managed to catch a single three-pound hardhead. The fog had not lifted a bit.

"Paul, pull up the anchor. We're heading out to the fifteen-mile buoy."

"Okay, Captain!" Paul promptly responded. About 30 minutes later, we were at the second fishing marker. Over the last five years, I had frequented these fishing spots so often, I could literally navigate to them blindfolded. When we reached the bobbing buoy bell, our engine sputtered, then failed. Neither Paul, the builder, nor I, the cook, knew much of anything about engines. After a few minutes of vain attempts, we dropped anchor and began to fish the becalmed sea.

"Here, Paul, have a beer," I said popping open a can.

"Thanks, Captain, believe I will," he responded. Within an hour, we had eaten the cold cuts I had prepared and drank all but two of the beers we had brought. By mid-afternoon, we had caught three more fish and had intermittently attempted to restart the engine, to no avail.

Gradually, the weather had begun to change. The small, slow rhythmic swells were hastening and losing cadence. The chill of early evening air roused a breeze stirring white caps and swells that rocked the little boat, ushering in the specter of worsening weather. The rocking of an anchored boat in harsh weather follows no rhythmic movement or pattern and is quite unsettling.

Paul was the first to voice concern. "Captain, we have some weather coming in."

"I know Paul. Get some rest. It will be dark soon."

Seated in my captain's chair, jacket zipped up to my chin, I spent a restless night while we tossed and turned on inclement seas. Paul lay in the back quadrant of the deck, crouched in a fetal position.

"Captain Christ, what are we going to do?" he asked in a raspy whisper.

"We are going to wait, Paul. I'm sure they are looking for us...we are going to wait. Good night."

"Good night, Captain Christ," he echoed.

The next morning, the weather worsened, intensifying our fears. The cloudy cover remained, the wind quickening with intermittent gusts. The swells were foamy and ominous. A weather front was definitely moving in. Vulnerable and subdued, we sat on our boat in the wash and spray of increasingly savage seas.

My hand found its way to my sacred keepsake as I silently prayed. Paul put our fears into spoken words. "Captain, it looks like a squall is moving in—as the weather worsens, they won't be able to rescue us."

"When the weather worsens, rescue will be the least of our problems. Don't worry, Paul, Captain Reed will find us...he must be on the way."

Captain Reed, a judge from Baltimore, was a meticulous, consummate fishing chum. He sat atop a powerful 26' vessel, usually sporting a crew of three. Pipe clamped in his jaws, his worn countenance presented a potent profile.

By late afternoon, the weather had significantly worsened, and I was really beginning to fear our small craft would succumb to the battering waves. I knew that any search expeditions would quit at nightfall, and I dreaded the prospect of another night in the storm. We had hoped that the increased wind and tide would push off the fog, but visibility had only improved to 50 feet, not much on the open sea. There was nothing to do but peer into the fog, desperately seeking a glimpse of another human being hopefully in search of two desperate fishermen.

Suddenly, from somewhere in the fog came a faint voice, "Captain Christ? Captain Christ?"

We looked at each other with joy and relief. "Over here!" we screamed in the direction of the barely audible voice, "over here!" It was the voice of Hawk O'Brien, Captain Reed's brother-in-law! Within moments, we were under tow toward safe harbor.

When we had safely docked, our families and extended families gave us a resounding chorus of applause in excited relief. It was at that time that Captain Reed shared an oddity of divine proportion with me.

"Chris, when I left the inlet, my ship held unalterably on a course of 36°. I have been boating for over 30 years now, and I have never had anything like that happen. When you're steering at sea, you know how hard it is to hold a course. Yet, every time I turned the wheel, it would return to 36° and hold! You realize you were nine miles off the coast of Bethany Beach? If you had not dropped anchor, you would have been off the Jersey Coast. I tell you, it was the hand of God guiding my vessel.

I nodded my acknowledgement with a broad smile of gratitude. At that moment, lightning cracked nearby and torrents of rain angled through the slicing gusts, chasing us from our dock to the shelter of our townhouses. A nor'easter unleashed its fury. It pummeled the beach and closed the port throughout the night, as well as the entire next day.

The following week, largely due to my family's insistence—they had not slept nor stopped worrying during our seafaring absence—I bought a two-way radio. Neither Paul nor I was a world-class boatsman. What I never admitted was that, in this new boat, we didn't know how to flip on the second gas tank. We had run out of gas, and all it would have taken to avoid the dramatics was a flip of a switch. Chalk one up to experience!

20

The Fishermen

Everything about him was old except his eyes and they were the same color as the sea and were cheerful and undefeated.

—**Ernest Hemingway**
The Old Man and the Sea

Recession continued to plague the new decade. With the economy at a standstill, I had a number of vacancies among my rental stores and my income was sharply curtailed. If I had worked a few more years, I could have cleared off more debt. With the explosion of interest rates, the economy recessed once again, and I found it necessary to borrow to cover the gap between income and my family's expenses. Nevertheless, I was thankful for my family's health and welfare and for the assets I had built over time. In spite of the economic downturn, I still managed to provide adequately for my family.

By the end of 1982, President Reagan had reduced taxes and interest rates began to subside from their previous record high. This stimulated the economy and rekindled productive growth. It seemed that the mood of the country brightened in response after nearly a decade of stagnation. In September of that year Anthony and Lee Ann had their first child, a little boy they named Brian Anthony.

To become a grandfather is a momentous occasion for any man. A grandson gives a feeling of extension beyond our own lives, a reach into the future, a glowing light after we have gone. It was especially joyful for me in view of Anthony and his past troubles, which now seemed to be far behind us. Elenitsa may have been right regarding the effect on him of my absence during his childhood, but I spent a great deal of time with him during his early

323

twenties. I nurtured and cared for my son, coaxing him through his difficulties longer than many other parents would have done, yet I was rewarded many times over by the return of the healthy, stable son. Now I had a beautiful grandson.

Anthony had received his bachelor's degree the year before and by the end of the year he received his master's degree in economics with high honors. The fact that it was a decade late did not diminish his accomplishment. He was the first person in our family to obtain a master's degree and we were tremendously proud of him. In fact, after seeing how well Anthony was doing, Dr. Tsitos, his psychiatrist, would later admit that he had misdiagnosed my son. Anthony was subsequently accepted into a Ph. D. program, but left his studies a year later to begin work as a stockbroker.

Jon had now settled in Ocean City where, besides running the beer and wine carryout during the season, he worked part time in real estate during the off-season. Jon would receive and forward my mail from Ocean City when I was back in Falls Church. He maintained this routine throughout the seventies and into the eighties. Although I encouraged him to find a girl and get married, I was more concerned with my daughter Ianthe.

Since becoming a kindergarten teacher in Fredericksburg, she had achieved teaching awards and seemed happy, but was approaching thirty and remained unmarried. She had had scores of boys interested in her since high school, but nothing ever seemed to develop into anything serious. It was difficult for me to understand why a young woman was not more interested in settling down and marrying. This was not the Old Country nor the old days, and I had a certain awareness that American women held different attitudes, but I still could not understand such behavior.

* * * * *

Nearly every day in the spring and fall when weather permitted—and sometimes when it didn't—I would routinely start my boat and round the southern tip of Ocean City where the bay met the sea. The inlet was always choppy and often downright dangerous, with squalls blowing in at a moment's notice, and swells reaching ten feet or more. Most of the vessels that cruised the channel were larger pleasure boats and commercial fishing vessels, but my little runabout always made it safely out to sea. This test with the elements became almost a religious experience to me, invigorating and uplifting. Traversing the inlet was always exhilarating...although sometimes my guests couldn't quite stomach the excitement, proving themselves a little unseaworthy.

One day in early June, my neighbor Mike Pappas called and said he and Father Theodore Chelpon, the priest at Saint Catherine's and a New York Yankees fan educated in Brookline, Massachusetts, were coming to Ocean City, so I invited them to go fishing. I included on this fishing outing two other friends of mine: Dr. Economous, a successful Washington surgical internist, and Paul Yeonas, my first mate. Dr. Economous sounded interested in the invitation, but admitted he had no boating experience. Aside from Paul, I was uncertain if anyone the group had deep-sea fishing experience.

The next evening after work I readied the boat for a dawn departure. Early the following morning Paul and Dr. Economous arrived promptly at the dock. Paul was a tall man, about six feet two inches, and like me he was in his mid-sixties. He wore thick glasses and had a full head of white hair. There was a rugged quality about his appearance that was confirmed by his hands, which were worn and rough from his years in construction. His rugged exterior contrasted sharply with his personality, which, though firm, was kind and gentle.

Paul and I were dressed in shorts, knit short sleeved shirts, baseball caps and tennis shoes. Dr. Economous, on the other hand, looked as if he had stepped from the pages of a fashion magazine. In his early sixties and bespectacled, the doctor was perhaps my height—five feet ten, but that's where the similarity ended. From his stylish tan fisherman's cap to his handsome tan deck shoes, he was color coordinated and expensively dressed in "fishing attire" that no sane fisherman, mindful of the effects of baiting hooks and cleaning fish—let alone the turbulent tides—would ever wear. That is, if he had any experience.

While we waited for Mike and Father Ted to arrive, Paul barked out in his raspy voice, "What can we do to help, Cap'n?"

"Finish your coffee, then let's load up the supplies," I responded and nodded toward the coolers lined up on the dock, one containing squid for bait, a second one containing sodas and beer, and the third packed with sandwiches and chips. Paul and the doctor dutifully hefted the coolers and placed them aboard while I carefully lifted the fishing gear propped against a deck railing—three deep sea rods and two spin reels, each with two hooks threaded into cork for safety—and stowed them away carefully.

By this time Mike and Father Ted had arrived. Father Ted was a sturdy looking man with a receding hairline. He had a broad face and a short neck that made his head appear as if it were set directly atop his thick broad shoulders. He was about the same height as I was, and almost as wide as he was tall. Though three inches taller, Mike carried sixty pounds more than the stately priest, bearing no resemblance whatever to the recon paratrooper he had been during World War II. Both men were about ten years younger than the rest of us. With curly black hair running down their arms and forearms, they resembled two sizes of the same stout black bear.

Mike was dressed in long pants and a white shirt, which he wore with the tails out so that it stretched over his extended middle and rear, the tails covering his ample thighs. Father Ted was dressed in traditional black priest's garb complete with white clerical collar. Both men wore black dress shoes, which were highly unsuitable for boating. We were a rather comical group of "fishermen."

"Hello Father, Mike," I greeted them. "You sure you'll be comfortable dressed like that?"

"I don't plan on getting wet, Chris," Father Ted responded.

"Oh really!" I chided.

I nodded, thinking how unsuspecting they both were. Looking up, I caught Paul shaking his head in disbelief. Then, as was my habit, I spelled out the rules of the boat for everyone before I allowed them to board.

"Keep your hands and feet inside the boat," I instructed them, "and remain seated while the boat is moving. As we pass through the inlet you may want to hang on tightly—there's a stiff, intermittent breeze and I expect the ride may be a little bumpy. We will cruise out to the ten-mile buoy, fish, and we should return by one o'clock." I paused to survey my passengers, then added, "And we're not coming back early for anyone—for any reason." Having survived the rigors of paratrooping in the Second World War, Mike thought my admonishment was highly amusing.

When we boarded, I took the seat behind the wheel and Paul sat next to me. Mike and Father Ted, both big men, could not be seated on the same side of the boat, so I assigned Father Ted the seat behind me and seated Doctor Economous behind Paul. Mike sat on the back bench a bit forward from the outboard motor. It was the only place I could seat such a heavy man. Even so, his weight made the stern of the boat ride noticeably low, angling the bow up out of the water.

When my passengers were settled, I slipped the boat from its mooring and headed into the channel. While cruising down the bay toward the inlet, I noticed that the wind-driven chop had intensified. Mini white-capped swells speckled the expanse of bay water around us. About twenty minutes later as we rounded the corner to the inlet where bay and ocean met, the breeze intensified and I noticed that the chop was significantly higher than usual. With every swell, spray broke over the bow and hit the windshield. A stiff headwind whipped up five-to-seven-foot seas, and the pitch and roll of the boat were worsened by Mike's weight in the stern. Although it served as ballast, his weight lowered the plane of the stern, allowing spray and splash to wash aboard. Even with a warm morning sun in a cloudless blue sky, the chill from the breeze and surf would add to the discomfort of my passengers. In a worsening tempest, the chill of wind and water left a shiver to the bone that was not reduced by the morning sun, but was somewhat controlled by continuous movement.

For several long minutes my attention was focused on navigating the treacherous inlet. Finally, I risked a glance toward the stern.

"Mike, you okay?" I called.

In reply, Mike offered me a fish-eye stare. His usual smiling, ruddy face looked clammy and nearly colorless, and his shirt and trousers were drenched with spray. With white knuckles he clutched at the boat rails on either side. If I had to guess, I would bet that Mike was anything but okay, yet controlling our small vessel was much more important.

I turned my attention back to the water, but a moment later I heard a loud, unpleasant belch and a spray of vomit splattered across the floor to my left. It was Mike, the paratrooper who had been so amused at the idea of seasickness. I navigated a series of swells, then turned and saw Mike slithered off the seat and lying crumpled on the floor, his back propped against the bench and his face blanched white with misery and vertigo. He vomited again, this time less dramatically, staining his shirt and pants.

My eyes travelled from Mike to Father Ted, who was, I noticed, turning the same suspicious shade of pale white. With his index finger firmly pressed against his thumb, he reverently crossed himself. "Holy Father, please watch over and protect us in our time of need," he muttered over and over.

"We're almost through the inlet," I announced cheerfully to my passengers as a swell slapped up against the bow, drenching us with spray.

"It's a little rough out today, Captain Chris," Paul commented nonchalantly.

"A bit," I agreed.

A minute later, just as we rode out the last of the inlet swells and broke into the open ocean, I heard a groan over my right shoulder. It was Father Ted. Grasping the wheel firmly I leaned hard to the left to avoid what I knew was coming, but I wasn't quite quick enough. My right hand became the victim of the Father's unseemly eruption. A half-dozen eruptions later, the priest had slipped from his seat to the wet floor, his forehead resting against the railing behind me. Poor Father Ted. He was so stricken he was incapable of either crossing himself or praying, but rather lay panting and listless in another pile on the deck.

"We may be through the inlet, Captain," Paul observed, "but the seas are still running high. The fish won't be biting in these conditions. It looks like rough seas all day."

"Let's see what we find at the ten mile marker," I said.

When we reached the buoy about 9:45, the sea, although still rough, had calmed somewhat, but we were still buffeted by a stiff breeze that whipped the swells into three- to five-foot whitecaps.

Paul and I readied the poles with bait, our windbreakers zipped to the neckline, while Mike and Father Ted sat on the floor covered with vomit and salty wash. I gave each of them a towel. Father Ted buried his face in his, while Mike tied his bib-fashion around his neck to catch the salty drool from his chin. Mercifully for the rest of us, their stomachs were practically empty, but the persistent rocking of the small vessel did nothing to alleviate their misery, resulting in intermittent dry heaves.

I handed the Doctor a baited pole. "How are you doing?" I asked.

"Not bad, Christo," he said unconvincingly.

"Cast your line over to the left," I instructed. He took the pole hesitantly, and I helped him cast his line. "If we don't get any bites here, we will troll for a while."

"Right," he said, and swung the rod back for a cast. I could almost read his mind: Now he had something to do to take his mind off the rocking, repetitive vertigo of the sea that negatively affected so many.

The first hour of fishing produced nothing beyond a few nibbles, so we began to troll. Almost immediately, Dr. Economous had a strike and his face lit up.

"What do I do, Chris?" he called excitedly.

"First you set the hook," I told him, grinning. "Then you reel it in, like this," and I demonstrated the motions

A moment later he brought a three-pound sea bass alongside the boat. I helped him land it and removed the hook. A while later Paul caught a somewhat larger bass and I caught a small sea trout. By this time Father Ted had recovered sufficiently enough to hold a pole weakly over the side, but poor, big Mike could barely hold up his head. He lay sprawled in the stern, clutching at the floor for support with one hand while the other rested across his distended abdomen.

"Hey, Chris, how about a beer?" Paul asked.

"A little early, isn't it?"

"Nah, it's eleven o'clock—almost noon!" he protested, and we both laughed.

"So what do you think of this surf, Captain Chris?" Paul asked as I handed him a beer.

"It's starting to kick up again," I told him, keeping my voice low. "And there are some dark clouds to the southeast. I don't like the looks of it. Let's hook up the two-way radio and see what we can find out."

I cut the engine and stopped trolling, then channeled on an open frequency for a few minutes until I caught the Coast Guard in the middle of issuing a warning. The loud, gusty wind rocked the stilled boat with sea and shrill, muffling the Coast Guard warning while at the same time serving to intensify its meaning.

"Storm approaching from the southeast," a tinny voice crackled across the airways through a buzz of static. "All small craft head immediately for port. Larger vessels head to sea. Possible gale force winds, landfall within less than an hour…"

The message was repeated several times, but I didn't need to be told twice. "Paul," I said quickly, "let's pull in the lines. We've trolled about three miles beyond the buoy, I would guess, so it's going to take at least forty-five minutes to reach the inlet."

"Aye, Aye," Paul said as he moved toward the lines, seasoned from his lost-at-sea escapade.

I ordered our passengers into life jackets. Mike groaned and the doctor paled. Father Ted once again began praying. "Protect and guide us back to port, O Holy Father," he intoned over and over, until the increasing pitch and roll of the boat upset his stomach again and silenced him.

As soon as the poles were reeled in and secured, I turned southwest and headed full steam for the inlet. Gusts were reaching 35 knots and wind-driven swells were frosted with breaking white caps as they smacked the side of our small craft and rushed over the low gunwales of the boat. The seas were running about five feet, the swells frequent and increasing. Because the storm was moving in a northerly direction, I had to face into the wind, travelling in a southwesterly direction instead of directly westward. This would lengthen the trip, but it lessened our chances of being swamped or capsized by the high seas.

Within thirty minutes the swells had increased to six or seven feet, and gusts had risen to forty knots. A dark wall of storm clouds was rapidly closing in on us as we cut through the wind and waves, yet the inlet still wasn't in sight.

Father Ted had sunk back to the floor where he muttered intermittent prayers punctuated by moans. Mike lay moribund in the stern and Doctor Economous gripped the rails, all color drained from his face. Beside me, Paul watched the sea with interest.

"Cap'n, this is really something!"

In fact, there was a dark beauty to the scene. The sea rumbled about us in fury and the sky hung low with angry black clouds. We cut doggedly through the heavy swells, drenched by spray. Ahead of us a bolt of lightning lit the horizon.

"Paul, how are the passengers doing?" I yelled into the wind.

"Not too good, Captain," Paul replied, grinning. "We have two hugging the floor, and the Doctor and his elegant attire look a little worse for wear."

"Everybody in life jackets, Paul?"

"Aye, aye, Cap'n." He paused. "You think we'll be able to make it through the inlet?"

As he spoke, the rain finally caught us and a huge swell smashed into the bow.

"This is pretty bad, Paul," I told him. "The squall has forced us south of the inlet. We've got to turn to the northwest to make port, putting the swells on our stern."

"You're the boss, captain."

Actually, I couldn't see where we had much choice. As I made the change in course a call came over the radio from the Coast Guard, instructing small craft to tune to frequency 640 immediately. As I navigated the seas, Paul found the frequency. Through wind and static we heard, "Small craft needing assistance entering the inlet should contact the Coast Guard cutter at the head of the inlet upon approach." The alert was repeated several times.

Finally, after fighting wind and sea for over an hour, we reached the inlet. Paul surveyed the churning waters and turned to me. "I don't think we can make it, Captain."

"Yes, we can," I told him, "God willing." The truth was that although I had navigated my way through several squalls in the past, I had never encountered anything quite like this. Towering swells swept through the inlet tossing a 120-foot commercial fishing vessel around like a child's bathtub toy, then smashing into the rock pier and overflowing white foam deep into the parking lot.

"Paul, make sure everyone has his life vest securely fastened."

"Will do, Captain."

"Then prepare to hang on."

"Will do."

As Paul checked our passengers, the Coast Guard cutter hailed me. "Small vessel, this is Coast Guard cutter four-four-three-five-oh. Do you require a tow through the inlet?"

"No, thank you," I radioed back, "no tow needed."

"Small vessel, follow our lead and keep your bow to the swells," the cutter instructed me. Moments later it had pulled about a hundred yards in front of us, its wake lost in the pounding sea.

The inlet between Assateague Island to the south and Ocean City to the north was about three hundred yards wide. Jetties extending into the sea abutted both landmasses from each side of the inlet, arresting the sifting sands to keep the inlet open. On a dead calm day the inlet was rough. During hurricanes, the sea would swamp the inlet and wash over both islands, with swells sometimes approaching thirty feet. At any time the inlet was dangerous and unpredictable, and as we entered the channel in the wake of the cutter, the gale whipped the water into a wild froth and spray.

Near exhaustion, I braced myself against the wheel and watched as the cutter, now in the middle of the channel, tossed about on the waves. Winds were gusting to sixty knots and sheets of hard rain pelted down, making visibility difficult. The pounding from the ten-foot swells tossed us about violently. We edged further and further into the inlet, swells breaking all around us and washing over our bow. Suddenly, the two-way crackled to life.

"Small vessel, you are clear ahead to safe harbor."

"Aye, Aye," I responded, "and thank you, four-four-three-five-oh."

A moment later in the relative calm of the sheltered bay, I turned to my passengers just in time to see Dr. Economous, white-faced and purple-lipped, vomit onto Paul Yeonas' back and promptly wilt to the floor where he joined Mike and Father Ted.

"Three down," Paul said, stripping off his soaked shirt.

We slipped carefully through the white caps of the bay and twenty minutes later, in wind and rain, we tied up at the dock.

"Paul," I called out, "Leave some slack in those lines."

"Yes sir, Captain Chris," Paul replied cheerily. "That was a hell of a ride, Captain. I've never been through anything like it!"

"It was a little rough, wasn't it?" I said with a weak laugh and a smile.

"A little!" Paul laughed at my understatement. "Nothing gets you in a flap, does it?"

As I grinned back at Paul, I touched the medallion pinned to my tee shirt and offered up a silent prayer of thanksgiving to God. "Give me a hand with the good Father, will you, Paul? Grab his right arm, I'll take his left."

With a little effort we dragged Father Ted from the boat and put him on the dock where he collapsed all over again muttering, "Praise the Lord, Praise the Lord..." Then we hauled the doctor out and put him down beside the priest. Mike, big as he was, posed more difficulty. When we got his upper half on the dock, he managed to pull the rest of himself out. Groaning, he crawled on all fours past the inert bodies of Father Ted and Dr. Economous, down the dock to the sidewalk and onto the porch of the townhouse, leaving Paul and me to unload the gear.

Watching his friend's slow progress down the dock, Paul turned to me and said, "Cap'n, today was something I'll never forget."

"Yes," I agreed, heaving a cooler onto the dock, "and I don't care to repeat it, either."

Paul tipped his head toward the dock. "I don't guess those three will be going fishing again any time soon."

I paused, looked at the bodies lying on the dock and at Mike's retreating backside.

"You know, Paul...I think you're probably right."

We broke out in hearty laughter.

21

A Pilgrimage to Jerusalem

Then doth thy sweet and quiet eye
Look through its fringes to the sky,
Blue—blue—as if that sky let fall
A flower from its cerulean wall.
I would that thus, when I shall see
The hour of death draw near to me,
Hope, blossoming within my heart,
May look to heaven as I depart.

—William Cullen Bryant
"To the Fringed Gentian"

The excitement of a stormy fishing trip would prove to be a precursor of a more distant trip, a rather unsettling return to the Old World.

I passed the balance of the summer helping Jon prepare food for the delicatessen spread at his beer and wine carryout. He was now managing it on his own and doing well. I rose each morning at 6:00 and had coffee and toast.

"Chris, don't forget Father John and my cousin Harriet will be here for dinner," Elenitsa reminded me one morning over breakfast.

I nodded, while spreading jelly preserves on my piece of toast. "Yes, I remember. I'll be home early to prepare."

"What shall we have?"

I shrugged absently.

"Chris," Elenitsa looked at me over the rim of her coffee cup, "they want us to go with them on a trip to the Holy Land." She paused. "Please, Chris…can we go?"

I took a bite of toast and chewed thoughtfully. "We'll see…we'll see," I said slowly, then changed the subject. "I'll be home by 2:30. We'll make lamb and rice pilaf. That's Father

John's favorite, and I've already trimmed the lamb and seasoned it."

"And I'll make my *spanakopita*."

"That's fine," I told her, carefully brushing toast crumbs from my white knit shirt and checking my khaki pants. I rose from the table, bent to give her a kiss, and headed out the door. As I walked down the quiet bayside street our townhouse was on, I was greeted by the familiar ocean breeze that had graced my summer mornings for almost thirty years. I enjoyed these mornings and looked forward to my nine-block walk to work.

When I arrived at Jon's carryout, Bernard was in the parking lot sweeping, just as he had countless mornings at my sandwich shop.

"Bernard, good morning!" I called out.

"Morning, Mr. Christ. I'll be through here in just a bit."

I smiled and headed toward the kitchen in back of the store where I began preparing salads. I boiled potatoes, macaroni and pasta, cooked chickens and prepared fresh tuna fish. A moment later Bernard came in, his chores outside accomplished, and we set about cleaning up the kitchen. That done, I finished preparing the salads, chatted a few minutes with my son, and headed home. It was only 1:30, a short six-hour workday, but I had to prepare for our dinner guests.

Father John and his wife Harriet arrived promptly at 5:45. Dinner that evening was pleasant and relaxed, except for some concerns of Father John's.

"Things are not going well at the cathedral, Chris," Father John mentioned as I carved the leg of lamb.

"Oh?" Since I had been at Ocean City all summer, I was not up on the latest at Saint Sophia.

"There's a group of parishioners, some of whom are on the board, who are...well, not happy with me."

It was not unusual for Father John to seek advice from me, and often my counsel consisted of basic common sense. "Just ignore them," I suggested, "and see how much of this dries up on its own." I turned to Harriet. "I'm going to give you a slice from the end."

"Looks delicious, Chris," Harriet smiled. My lamb and pilaf was Harriet's and Father John's favorite.

"But Chris, it's not that simple," Father John interrupted. "You see, they've tried to implement significant changes. They could get control of the board this fall."

"Then it's important for everybody to vote…Father, would you like some more?"

"Yes, please," he told me, then added, "This group, Chris…they would change the service—and possibly even the priest!"

I paused in my carving and looked at him. "I'm sure it will not come to that, Father. Another piece?" I figured that this resistance group would not gain the momentum Father John feared. Sure enough, some months later, the group would seem to fade much as I had predicted, and Father John relaxed.

Eventually the conversation turned to other topics and we left the issue of church politics behind. Dinner was excellent and Father John and Harriet complimented us heartily. The leg of lamb was fresh and perfectly cooked, they said, and Elenitsa's fresh crab cakes and *spanakopita* (spinach pie) were excellent. As we chatted around the table during dessert, Harriet turned to me.

"Chris, Father and I both want you and Elenitsa to join us on our trip next month. It's not too late to go, and it should only take ten days to receive your passports."

Elenitsa looked at me expectantly. "Do you think we could, Chris?"

"It would be a long overdue homecoming of sorts," Father John added, placing a brochure in my hand.

"Chris, please let's go," Elenitsa repeated.

I knew when I was outnumbered. "All right," I said, "We'll see," both of us knowing full well that meant we were going.

Later that evening when Elenitsa and I were alone, I put on my reading glasses and glanced at the Holy Land brochure. It was titled *Pilgrimage to the Holy Land,* and what caught my attention was the itinerary. Cathedrals, mosques, images all blurred in a religious tapestry of conflict, which, when stripped away, revealed a further harsh territorial, economic struggle over scarce resources.

September 12th—Arrive Heathrow Airport
September 13th—Arrive Ben Gurion Airport
  Bus trip to Jerusalem

September 14th—Enter old Jerusalem via Dung Gate, visit Wailing Wall

September 15th—Temple Mount, El-Aksa Mosque...visit Dome of the Rock, Pool of Bethesda and Via Dolorosa...Church of the Holy Sepulchre on the site of the Crucifixion...Church of the Nativity

September 16th—The Holocaust Museum, Chapel of the Ascension, Monastery of John the Baptist...

I had mixed emotions about returning to that part of the world almost forty years after leaving Constantinople, and the more I looked at the schedule, the more convinced I was that I did not wish to go. Israel was not Byzantium, of course, but the Holy Land stirred many familiar sights and sounds of the Old Country where I had struggled so long and fought so hard to gain freedom. Although I felt I was a religious man, I had no tolerance for zealots of any persuasion. The Holy Land was a cauldron of religious extremes, something I knew so well from the past. Unfortunately, I had committed myself. It was a journey that beckoned me in a strange way. It was a journey I knew I would have to take.

A few weeks later, we had Anthony's family over for a family celebration. It was Sunday, September 11th, the day before we were to leave for the Holy Land. Elenitsa had baked a small cake for our grandson Brian's first birthday, which would occur on September 16th.

"Dad, he's walking and talking!" Anthony announced proudly. "Look, Brian, here's your granddad!"

The small fry looked up. "Papa," he said.

I was amazed. I hadn't heard the word since my Papa had died.

"No, honey," Elenitsa said, "he is your Papouli!"

"Let him call me Granddad," I said.

"Well, I want him to call me Yiayia—the Greek version," said Elenitsa.

I watched as Anthony and Lee Ann settled Brian in his walker. He smiled at them, a sweet smile that made his eyes dance.

"Come here, Brian, come to Granddad," I coaxed.

The baby gazed at me from his walker, then launched himself in my direction. I picked him up and put him in my lap. "You're a big boy," I crooned. "Yes, a big boy."

The child laughed as I bounced him on my knee. "Aye, aye, aye, aye," he babbled in time to the rhythm of my knee. "Aye, aye, aye, aye."

A little later, looking wide-eyed from his mother's arms, he was serenaded with a chorus of "Happy Birthday." He seemed pleased with the proceedings and intrigued with his gifts, but the pleasure we gave him was small compared to the joy he gave to us.

I would soon be sixty-five and my grandson was only one year old. As I watched him that afternoon, I wondered what those innocent eyes would see in the decades after I departed this earth. I prayed that God would watch over him and grant him health. I prayed that God would protect him during his life as he had me during mine. I felt I could make a contribution to his future, and, God willing, he would have a life full of opportunity in America. Ah, what would his eyes see in the decades ahead, during his life? Will he face a crisis? God only knew.

* * * * *

The next day Elenitsa and I left for the Holy Land—with trepidation and reluctance on my part. The group of twenty-six met that morning at Dulles International Airport outside Washington, D. C., but our departure was delayed four hours due to a storm. As we milled around waiting for our flight to be announced, I surveyed my fellow travellers. We were middle-aged and older, and most of the group was active in church affairs at the cathedral in Washington. Seated in a chair nearby was Steve Yeonas, the older brother of my first mate, Paul. Steve was a mild-mannered man who was, at six feet one, the tallest in the group—Greeks not being known for their height. Beside him were our good friends Gus and Mary Bochanos, who were about ten years younger than Elenitsa and I; Dorothy Manatos, who was a friend of Presvetera Harriet, Father John's wife; and Elenitsa Stikas, who was a good friend of Elenitsa's. Elenitsa's husband, Gus, one of my good friends, was unfortunately not feeling well enough to make the trip.

Sitting a little apart from the others was Dr. John Nassau, who sang in the church choir. Ten years younger and an inch or two shorter than me, Dr. Nassau walked with a pronounced stoop that made him appear to be hump-backed. He had an intelligent, likeable face that beamed from behind a pair of thick glasses, making one forget his diminutive, almost handicapped, appearance. He was devoutly religious with a positive outlook on life that immediately endeared him to me as a kindred spirit. Next to him was his wife, Mary, plump with a round, pleasant face, and beside her were George and Ethel Chaguras. A retired government worker, George was tall and lean with white, receding hair and a mustache. Ethel, who was short and stout with white hair that matched her husband's, did administrative work for the Sunday school at St. Sophia. Across from them sat Pete and Cleo Kasandra, a pleasant couple about the same age as Elenitsa and I. Cleo was also an active volunteer for the Church.

I imagine there were different reasons for this group of devout Christians to make this journey to the Holy Land. Some may have gone for recreation, others out of an interest in history, but most of the travellers probably felt that visiting the holy places in and around Jerusalem would enhance them spiritually and bring them closer to God as they journeyed toward the twilight of their lives.

Although I had attended church services, celebrated the tradition and volunteered my time, during the course of my life my religious inspiration was mostly private. I knew my work habits struck some people as excessive, but truthfully, in my beliefs and personality I was not a person of extremes. On the other hand, as a religious center for Christians, Jews and Mohammedans, the Holy Land attracted a fair number of religious extremists who routinely expressed their beliefs through violence. I had experienced that in another part of the Old World years before Israel was founded and spent a good deal of my youth trying to escape it. Of course, Israel was not Turkey, but they both existed in a climate of fanaticism where zealots sacrificed the freedom of others toward their own political and economic end, where Old World justice was determined solely by numerical strength and economic superiority.

I was not anxious to revisit old memories of repression and violence, but absent the zealots, the Holy Land was where Jesus was born, lived and died. The thought of seeing the sites where Christ lived and taught and healed presented a powerful attraction to me on this journey to a world I once had left behind.

As we arrived at Heathrow Airport in England at the end of the first leg of our journey, I sensed genuine religious excitement building among members of our group, yet felt none myself, just a quiet void of emotions. Certainly, I was void of the tempest of emotions I would soon confront and, ultimately, embrace.

We waited on the ground at Heathrow another four hours before boarding a plane bound for Tel Aviv. We arrived in Jerusalem and checked into the Hotel Senesta. The next afternoon we entered the Jewish section of Old Jerusalem through the Dung Gate. There, in the shadow of Mount Olive, we visited the Wailing Wall. Finally, among the sharply contrasting sectors and structures, I saw shades of the Old Country I had struggled in for so long. I felt a chill wash over my skin, a lump rise in my throat, and an overwhelming heat sear my heart.

The following day was quite memorable. We entered the old city again, this time through the Lion's Gate, and followed Christ's path along the Via Dolorosa, His Way of the Cross. Next we saw the caves where Christ and Barrabas were imprisoned, and then entered the Church of the Holy Sepulchre, erected over the site of the crucifixion, burial and resurrection of Jesus. Greek Orthodox clergy maintained an altar in the church, and we prayed there for some time.

Although much of what I saw called up mixed emotions for me, I was genuinely moved by the tiny chamber enclosing the stone shelf on which Christ's body was laid. With my right hand I clutched my relic coin and with my left I firmly held Elenitsa's hand. She smiled as she viewed Christ's resting place, yet tears streamed down her face. The presence of the shelf somehow underscored the enduring fragility of life on a seamless Christian tapestry.

Before we left the Church of the Holy Sepulchre, we gathered in the Greek Orthodox chapel for a group picture. Then we travelled on to Bethlehem to visit the Church of the Nativity. One of the oldest churches in the world, the Church of the Nativity is built over the site of the stable where Christ was born. We spent considerable time exploring this remarkable place and other nearby holy sites before finally returning, exhausted, to our hotel.

The next morning we visited the Holocaust Museum. While viewing the artifacts and memorabilia of the Jewish holocaust, a rush of childhood memories swept over me. I recalled the unspoken holocaust, the violent uprooting of so many, the starvation and plague of atrocities that were the Christian Holocaust, the events that shaped and defined my childhood. Persecution of a minority is nothing new, and certainly not unique. The deliberate and calculated extermination of Christians and the annihilation of Byzantium by the Young Turks were the hidden holocaust of my youth. Like snapshots, a slide show of images flashed before my eyes. The early slaughters in Salonika of Bulgars, Serbs and Greeks brought on the First Balkan War of 1912, followed by the Massacre of Phocea and the Armenians in 1914. The extermination continued for a decade as a mass slaughter, then continued sporadically until Turkey had virtually purged itself of Christians. Though we were looking at pictures of the Jewish holocaust, I could have been looking at pictures of my childhood.

The images I had for so long repressed, never even spoke of, rose up fiercely now as if I were living it all over again. The haunting images that had lived these many, many years as mere whispers at the back of my mind now consumed me in huge, horrible living color, so palpable I felt I could touch them. Suddenly the room was spinning around me and my knees went weak. I felt helpless to move or speak as I stood frozen, transfixed by my silent horror.

"Chris, Chris! Are you all right?"

It was Elenitsa. She was looking into my face and gently shaking my shoulder, a look of genuine concern on her face, and I was once again standing in a museum in Israel, Elenitsa by my side.

"I'm...I'm fine," I said, managing what I hoped was a reassuring smile. She smiled hesitantly in return and we headed for the rest of the group. I held her hand tightly the rest of the tour.

It was ironic to me that the Young Turks, by opposing the religious zealots of the Ottoman Empire, were credited with creating the modern state of Turkey when in fact they were annihilators who were bent on destroying the Christian population.

Many of these new, secular Turks had migrated from Salonika back to Turkey and Asia Minor when the territory was returned to Greece after the first Balkan War in 1912. In a brief decade they proved more barbarous than the Ottomans had been during their four centuries of rule. The Young Turks from Salonika, led by Talaat, Enver, Jamal, Mustafa Atatürk and others, were nihilists who not only destroyed and uprooted Christian populations, but seized their wealth—the product of generations of toil—transferring it to their cronies and themselves.

This was the silent holocaust, the forgotten holocaust, the Christian Holocaust, whose ghostly museum is all of Anatolia—the one nobody attends or remembers…if they ever even knew about it at all.

When we left the museum that day we faced a troop of young Jewish boys strutting about with Uzis resting menacingly on their shoulders. How ironic, I thought. The Jews, once victims of persecution themselves and alleged champions of human rights, now carry the instruments of repression over the Palestinians they displaced. I simply could not understand how they could live in such hypocrisy.

The next day, we visited an underground market where Palestinians bought their food. The market was impressively large with rows and rows of stands displaying a bounty of goods. The Palestinian vendors stood proudly over their wares armed with donkey tails to swat at the swarms of flies. Each sweep of the donkey tail dispersed a multitude of flies, but within seconds they returned. For most of us, the flies spoiled what would have been a handsome presentation of food, but not for Father John. As we travelled through the market he purchased sample after sample, suffering no ill effects whatever.

"Give me one baklava," he called out to a vendor, using the international language of pointing fingers. "So tasty…and—" he pointed again "—an order of meatballs. Delicious!" he said, turning to Dr. Nassau.

"Er…yes," the doctor smiled.

"Have one?" asked Father John, generously extending the meatballs.

The Doctor surveyed the clouds of flies that swarmed around us and politely shook his head.

By two o'clock that afternoon the city was preparing for the celebration of Yom Kippur. Hasidic Jews who normally wear black were dressed in white for the holiday. We had an early dinner and returned to our hotel. By sundown the city appeared deserted and the following day the entire city was shut down since it was not only Yom Kippur, but an Arabic holiday as well. Although we were Christians on a pilgrimage, we had no choice but to observe Yom Kippur. All service, including transportation and food, ceased for the day. There was no staff to be found in the kitchen, since nothing was to be cooked during the holiday, but we came upon a note directing us to some cold boiled eggs and bread. Five years later, I would recall this forced observance when my daughter, Ianthe, an elementary school teacher, told me that the Lord's Prayer had been removed from the classroom.

Late that evening we walked to the Church of the Holy Sepulchre to attend a midnight service in the Orthodox chapel. When the service started, something quite special occurred. The voices of a dozen Russian Orthodox nuns filled the air with beautiful, melodious chants. A Greek bishop celebrated the liturgy, chanting in the company of the nuns.

"Come let us worship God our king," he sang. *"Come let us worship and fall down before Christ our king and our God. Come let us worship and fall down before Christ Himself our king and our God...*

The lovely, mesmerizing sound of priest and choir filled the air for a captivating ninety minutes. At the close of the service we took Holy Communion and made our way back to the hotel, the sound of the nuns lingering in the quiet night air like a heavenly lullaby. It was something none of us would ever forget.

The next morning, Sunday, we began what would be a busy day by visiting the Tomb of Lazarus. A priest of the monastery there took us to his residence and offered us Greek cookies called *kolurias*. Afterwards, as we continued on our way to Jericho in the Jordan Valley, we saw the Dead Sea from a distance. From Jericho we drove to the Mount of Temptation in the wilderness where

Christ was tempted, and visited the Monastery of Temptation where no more than half a dozen monks resided.

After our visit to the Monastery of Temptation we returned to Jerusalem, visiting Mount Olive and viewing the Garden of Gethsemane where Christ prayed before he was arrested. Nine olive trees are still standing. Afterwards we visited the Church of All Nations, built on the site of Byzantine and Crusader ruins. Within the church is a nine-foot square area with a large rock where Christ spent his last night before his arrest.

From the Church of All Nations we walked to the Tomb of the Virgin Mary. The story goes that the Virgin was laid to rest here, then taken to heaven by angels. The area was profusely and elaborately decorated and attended by a Russian nun. Finally, after an event-filled day, we stopped at the Israeli Museum to view the Dead Sea scrolls, the documents that revealed some of the life of Christ.

On Monday, we visited the Greek Orthodox Patriarchate and had an audience with the Patriarch Diodoros. Before granting the certificates attesting to our pilgrimage, the Patriarch made a few comments. He stressed the role of the Greek Orthodox Church in Jerusalem in guarding the Holy Places. Were it not for the small presence of the Christian Church, the Holy Places might be lost forever. The Franciscans, too, have preserved the Holy Sites for over 600 years. He appealed for our support and for the support of the Greek-American community back home.

The balance of the day we visited a deserted Russian Orthodox church. Then we drove to the Church of Saint George, the patron saint of Palestine. Finally, we returned to the hotel to pass our last night in Jerusalem.

On Tuesday morning we left Jerusalem and drove through the West Bank, stopping briefly at the site of Jacob's Well where a Samaritan woman gave Jesus Christ water. There is a Greek Orthodox church at the site, and we learned about the many violent historic attacks against the church and its worshippers. Travelling further north, we visited the Church of the Annunciation and the Church of the First Miracle, where Jesus turned water into wine.

Then we continued our trip toward Tiberias, where we had our first glimpse of the blue Sea of Galilee. After lunch in Tiberias, we traveled on to the site of the Sermon on the Mount, where we had a beautiful view of the Sea of Galilee. Here, facing northeast, Father John held a brief service. As we prayed, I realized that only a few hundred miles away lay my beloved island home, and suddenly I was filled with longing. I could almost feel its presence in the distance, yet I knew that the only Imbroz I would ever see again was the one I carried in my heart.

I was still gazing solemnly across the distant sea when John Nassau walked up beside me.

"In the distance is Turkey, Chris."

"Yes, John," I nodded, and stood awhile longer in silent reflection. *Only I know what Turkey has done to the Greeks, and our culture*, I thought. *Only I know...*

* * * * *

When I made my pilgrimage to the Holy Land I was sixty-five years old, a retired man travelling with a church group to learn more about our Christian roots. Yet for me the trip was more than that, for it brought me back to the Old World, the world of my youth, after thirty-eight years in America. Although Jerusalem was neither Constantinople nor my island home of Imbroz, the cultural and architectural similarities were striking. It stirred feelings I had not experienced for a long, long time. The climate in Jerusalem was hotter and drier than in my native land, but many of the old portions of the city were Byzantine and therefore seemed very familiar to me. The religious conflicts of the Arabs, Christians and Jews, sown far in the past, may have differed on the surface from the conflicts which pitted against each other the Young Turks, the Jews and Christians in Turkey a half-century earlier, yet underlying fanaticism and zealotry remained constant.

Oddly, the presence of religious tension in Jerusalem was hardly noticed by most of our party. The hostile images—like that of the Uzi-armed Jewish boys—were fleeting, but they stirred memories of the Turkish gendarmes of my youth, partially repressed by the passage of years. I was sensitive to what I saw there, and to the violence that lay so near the surface, because I had known violence in a similar context. I had witnessed uprisings and bloody repressions and knew the signs only too well. These stark images, like ghosts revisiting from the distant past, were no less menacing than the soldiers of my youth.

My pilgrimage to show reverence and humility to my Savior and God unleashed ghosts of the past. Along with its rich memories of my roots, I saw the same persecution reflected in the faces of poor Palestinians. Man's inhumanity to man never seems to change.

22
Dinner with the Patriarch

The tattered outlaw of the earth,
Of ancient crooked will;
Starve, scourge, deride me: I am dumb,
I keep my secret still.
Fools! For I also had my hour;
One far fierce hour and sweet:
There was a shout about my ears,
And palms before my feet.

—G. K. Chesterton
"The Donkey"

My consuming interest was in my family. By 1985, my sons were approaching middle age. Anthony was almost thirty-six and Jon was thirty-four. Ianthe, the youngest, was just turning thirty. Possibly some part of my attention to my grown children was compensation for my absence during their childhood, but mostly I simply wanted to give them the support and security that I had always lacked. Unquestionably, the pleasure I derived from assisting my children, either by performing tasks for them or by providing financial assistance, was the knowledge that I could protect them from some of the adversity that plagued my own early life.

During the summer season, I continued to help Jon by working the register in the gourmet deli we opened. As part of my morning routine in Ocean City, I would visit my old sandwich shop some sixteen blocks away, stopping on my way to Jon's to have a cup of coffee with John Simms who had purchased my old business. Each time I walked into my small store, a feeling that I should start working would overcome me. I enjoyed a comfortable, pleasant relationship with John, and I enjoyed my morning visits with him. He still maintained the store pretty much as I had, which I found gratifying, and his family helped him run it. He was a good man, strong and organized enough to successfully run the store.

I spent my mornings slicing fruit and preparing assorted salads in Jon's deli, but even those chores were somewhat relaxed in the absence of the full weight of responsibility. I was now sixty-eight years of age and could still outwork most younger people, but the deli was something I did to pass my time and help my younger son, who was running the business. A day of work at the deli was a breeze, and I simply enjoyed the work and being with Jon.

One morning when Jon was gone, the day manager, Mike Herr, reported that the air-conditioning was out. He fussed with the equipment to no avail, then poked his head in the kitchen.

"It's hot," he announced irritably.

These kids had not known a days' work without the air conditioner. Jon's staff worked at a slower pace than I was accustomed to, but this was a different era, and the crisis caused by the broken air conditioner, almost laughable to me, was paramount to Mike.

"Really?" I raised an eyebrow at him, then busied myself with a knife and a cucumber. A minute later I emerged from the kitchen with a slice of cucumber on my forehead.

"You see, boys," I announced to the staff, "put a slice of cucumber on your forehead, like this, and it will cool you off." Within moments, all five of us had a cool slice of cucumber stuck to our foreheads. Air conditioning? For much of my life I didn't even know what it was, let alone have it where I worked or lived. Even in all the years I had the sandwich shop—all those long, hot Ocean City summers—I never had air-conditioning. Yet in a far less labor-intensive deli, paralysis set in when the air conditioner stopped. I couldn't help but think of all the creature comforts that had made America go as soft as my ice cream.

Another routine I developed was to hop in the station wagon after work and drive down past the bridge to Tony's Fruit Stand. Tony was an Italian and I frequented his fruit stand for more than two decades. Tanned, sinewy and hardworking, Tony was about five years older than I was. He was a stickler for the quality of his fruit, which was unfailingly beautiful, fragrant and fresh. Often I would haggle with him over cost and quality, but I was fond of the man and it was a European performance of bicker and babble we both enjoyed. I particularly enjoyed sweet, cool, fresh fruit on a summer day.

One important project of mine in retirement was to help my daughter find a mate. Coming from the Old Country, it was difficult for me to explain the anxiety I felt on this point. As time passed, I found the subject more and more pressing. My daughter would remain my concern and responsibility until she married. With each passing year, the pool of eligible men got smaller and smaller. Although society had changed a great deal in the way it viewed the sexes, one precept remained constant: Older men found it easier to marry than did older women. It was clear, however, that I was a good deal more concerned with this issue than Ianthe was, although I seldom let my concern be known.

I was better at catching fish than catching husbands for my daughter. Because of my heart problems I ate extravagant meals no more than half a dozen times a year, sustaining myself mostly on lentils, beans and fish. To relieve the monotony, I also had a chicken recipe I particularly liked with carrots, garlic, onion and a touch of tomato, which was economic as well as healthful, but fish was the mainstay of my diet. Besides, it gave me an excuse to spend many hours in search of solitude on the open water.

There were many people who accompanied me on my fishing trips. After my earlier experience, I preferred that my fishing companions be experienced in both fishing and boating. I had purchased a new boat that was three feet longer than my old one and had two outboard motors. It was beautiful, fast and powerful, perfect for getting through the inlet and out to my favorite fishing spots.

* * * * *

As time passed and I moved toward my seventieth birthday, the seasons of my life seemed to change more quickly. Still, I retained my energy and enthusiasm for life and I thanked God daily for that blessing. I was always interested in what went on around me—the world, country, my church—and in the activities of my family, including my nieces and nephews. As a result, I was enormously pleased with the achievements of my brother Costa's children. Little John, Costa's eldest son, was valedictorian of his high school class and was accepted at Harvard. In 1986 and 1988, his daughter Mary and youngest son Tommy were also accepted at Harvard. Their father, God bless him, would have been proud of them—and of Afrodite, who raised the children so well.

My varied interests in life also helped me to stay physically active. I loved to garden and I did all my own yard work with the exception of cleaning gutters and trimming trees. In fact, my yard work was medicinal, and on clear, warm spring and autumn days, I spent hours trimming my azaleas and tying up my rhododendrons. I worked hard to winterize my plants, and in the spring they would reward me with their lovely blossoms. It was something I always looked forward to. Each spring, my garden was reborn in beauty.

* * * * *

Time marched on. Late in January 1986, I received my thirteenth set of commemorative stamps. There within the first two pages was the commemorative stamp for the lady who had greeted me when I first arrived on these shores thirty-one years earlier. It was the hundred year commemorative for the Statue of Liberty, and as I gazed at the lovely stamps, I recalled with some emotion my entry into New York Harbor so long ago. The commemorative stamp series gave me a historical sense of so many places, events and people—of my adopted country. Not only were people like T. S. Elliot, James Canfield and Sojourner Truth commemorated, but even my friends the fish had their own artistic stamps. Cod, bass, tuna, catfish…they were all there.

Gazing at the stamps late in January, admiring the careful, detailed rendering of tuna and catfish, brought me memories of pleasant autumn days aboard my boat. Usually there were five or ten days each spring and fall that presented the perfect combination of temperature, wind and current for fishing. During the 1980's, Russian trawlers would deplete the enormous bounty of fish by extensive trolling with nets, but I still returned with some fine catches which I cleaned and froze. Trout, sea bass, croakers and blues were always served.

My love of seafood came with a cost, a bout or two of gout, and late in February 1986 I made an appointment with Dr. Mandes. It was not my first attack of gout, and Dr. Mandes prescribed the usual medication. On this occasion, however, it gave me little relief. For a week I took the medication religiously, yet I grew increasingly uncomfortable. Although I did not notice, something else was happening as well. It soon became apparent that what was going on was definitely not the gout.

"Dad, you're jaundiced!"

It was my daughter-in-law, Lee Ann, who had just stopped by for a quick visit. I greeted her with pleasure and gave her a fatherly hug.

"I have a bit of a cold," I told her.

Lee Ann, a nurse, shook her head. "No, Dad, you're yellow," she exclaimed. "Dad, you need to get this checked out right away."

It was true. My skin had turned a pasty yellow. Lee Ann was persistent and eventually I called Dr. Mandes who sent me to the hospital, where it was determined that my gall bladder had to be removed. However, it took the doctors three days of prodding and testing to come to that conclusion, during which time I was very uncomfortable and ran a low-grade fever. The surgery itself was uneventful, although afterwards the soreness in my side grew to feel like a hot, searing coal. Unfortunately, the doctors mistakenly prescribed the wrong medication. My fever shot up to a hundred and four degrees and the area surrounding the incision reddened and swelled. One week dragged into two with only modest improvement.

Through all this my children visited regularly and in shifts.

"Dad, how are you feeling tonight?"

I opened my eyes and saw Anthony bending over me.

"Okay, thank you Anthony."

"Hello, Dad," came another voice.

I turned my head slightly and saw Lee Ann.

"Do you feel better since they stopped the gout medicine?" she asked.

"Yes, a little," I said, nodding.

"Dad, did you know Dr. Mandes was restricted from practicing at Fairfax Hospital?" Anthony asked me. "I think you should get another doctor before he kills you."

Anthony's bluntness made me smile. Still, Tom Mandes was my doctor. I liked him, and I was loyal. Anthony could chide me all he wanted, but I wouldn't change doctors, and he knew it.

"We'll see, Anthony," I said to placate him.

"He doesn't like the food," Elenitsa told the others, "so I brought him something from home." She recited an inventory of the food she brought while Lee Ann studied my chart.

"You know, Dad, your fever is down to a hundred." She looked at me and smiled. "That's much better."

"This was supposed to be a straightforward gall bladder operation," Anthony persisted. "And now you've been here over two weeks. You sure you don't want a second opinion?"

My son was concerned, and rightly so. I shook my head and tried to smile. "No, Anthony, that won't be necessary. I will be fine. I'm really getting better, Lee Ann just said so."

"I only said your temperature was down, Dad. Anthony's right...a second opinion—"

"No," I waved my hand, cutting her off. "Everyone worries too much. I'll be fine."

At that moment a fast-moving nurse named Fran bustled into the room and shooed everyone out to the hall. She was there to take some blood and give me my medication, and as she worked I reflected on my hospital stay. Despite surgery and medication, I still had a pressing feeling in my side. I still had gout, I was still mildly discolored, and no one seemed to know why my condition was lingering. The experience reinforced a life-long conviction: Except for social occasions, you should stay away from doctors. Elenitsa was just the opposite. She couldn't go a month without seeing one doctor or another. We were so different...I guess that's why we fit together so well after all these years.

Three days later with the same bland dinner mush in front of me, I made a decision. I had to get out of this place. If I stayed any longer, the combination of doctor, food and hospital might really kill me.

I watched as Dr. Mandes bustled into my room, efficiently herding my family out into the hall. We exchanged pleasantries as he examined my chart, and then we got down to business.

"Chris," he said, probing and examining me, "you still have a low grade fever and a little redness around the drainage tubes at the site of your incision."

"Hmmm," I commented noncommittally.

"So we'll need to keep you through the weekend," he went on. "Then next week, we'll see..."

It was only Thursday. At that moment, three more days seemed interminable, and I knew I'd never survive another weekend in this place.

"You're the doctor," I said with deceptive complaisance.

Dr. Mandes smiled and retreated to the hall where he fell into a muffled conversation with my family. A moment later the doctor departed and my family trooped into the room.

"Daddy, Dr. Mandes says you'll be here for a few more days," Ianthe said gently. "He says you're getting better. You should listen to the doctor."

"Whatever he thinks is best," I told her agreeably.

"You do look better tonight, Dad," Lee Ann observed. "You really do."

I smiled. Unwittingly, Lee Ann had just reinforced my escape plan. If I *looked* better, then I was well enough to go home.

Momentarily, everyone began making motions to leave. Ianthe leaned over to give me a kiss and Lee Ann patted my shoulder.

"Goodbye, girls," I told them.

"Bye, Granddad!" Brian said in his sweet childhood voice, while little Katelyn, Anthony's eight-month-old daughter, fixed me with an innocent wide-eyed stare.

"Goodbye, Brian. Goodbye, Katelyn." I watched as my family began to file out.

"Good night, Dad!"

"Good night, Anthony."

"G'nite, Dad," Jon said as he headed toward the door. "See you tomorrow."

"Oh, Jon...before you go..." I said casually.

Jon stuck his head back into the room. "Yeah, Dad?"

I waited a minute until everyone was safely down the hall, then I cleared my throat. "Jon, would you get my clothes for me please? I believe you'll find them in the closet."

Jon looked puzzled. "Do you need something, something in one of your pockets?"

"What I need is to get out of here," I told him calmly.

"But...you can't do that!" Jon exclaimed, clearly aghast. "What about your fever? What about the tube?"

"Just get the clothes," I told him firmly. "I'll take care of the tube."

"But Dad..."

"No arguments," I said.

"You need more rest, you need medicine, you need..."

"To go home!" I cut him off. "I *need* to leave this place and *you* need to get my clothes! Now don't argue with me...please!"

For a moment Jon hesitated, then moved reluctantly to the closet. The instant his back was turned I slipped my hand to my right side. Just below where my gall bladder used to be was a plastic tube that exited from the surgical site. It was taped to my side and descended to a jar on the floor that collected fluid draining from my wound. Suddenly I grasped the tube, said a quick prayer, and yanked, pulling about eight inches of tubing from my side.

I paused to survey the damage. There was still more tubing to come out, but surprisingly the only discomfort I felt was a mild burning around the opening. I took a breath, pulled again, and the last few inches of tubing came free. With some degree of pride, I held the end of the tube aloft and looked at it.

"Dad!"

I looked up to see my son gazing at me in horror.

"You shouldn't have done that!" he gasped, looking a little pale and weak-kneed.

I shrugged, holding the gown to my side where the tube had exited.

"This simply isn't wise," he admonished me as he deposited my clothes into my outstretched hands. "You could get infected. You could end up back in the hospital, you could—"

"Go to the Safeway—" interrupting his objections.

"What?"

"I want you to go to the Safeway," I repeated carefully, "and get me some chicken legs and lemons. Then go home and start preparing them. I'll be there shortly."

Jon tried to dissuade me one last time, but with no real conviction, having already accepted defeat. "Dad, you're being foolish. I really wish you wouldn't do this."

"Now don't argue with me," I told him. "I cannot stay here one more day with this food or I will surely die. Now go on…Go! I'm fine, don't worry." I shooed him out of the room with my hand. "I'll see you at home."

Knowing he was defeated, Jon departed without another word and a minute later I was out of bed. I peeled off the adhesive that held the tube to my side and replaced it with two Band-Aids from the bathroom cabinet. Then I dressed, found my keys and walked cheerfully past the nursing station and out the door. No one noticed. Since I had driven myself to the hospital, my car was exactly where I had left it in the parking lot. The mild breeze and warm sun of a chilly spring evening invigorated me. I climbed in, unsure for a moment if it would start, turned the key and headed home where, in a few minutes, the familiar aroma of chicken baking with lemon and oregano greeted me from the kitchen. For the first time in almost three weeks, I had an appetite.

Elenitsa, of course, was waiting for me, her hands on her hips. "Chris!" she said sharply. "The hospital called. They want to know where you are!"

"I'm here, that's where I am," I told her, stating the obvious, patting her arm and giving her a peck on the cheek.

Elenitsa stared at me in exasperation. "You know, you're being very foolish!"

"I've already told him that," Jon said as he turned the chicken baking in the oven. "But he didn't pay any attention."

Elenitsa's eyes went from our son and back to me. "Are you crazy? What possible reason could you have for not listening to the doctors!" A note of hysteria was creeping into her voice.

"My reason is my health," I said mildly, opening the refrigerator door and taking out a cold beer. "If I had stayed there any longer I would have died."

"You must go back!" she said, "Go back this minute!"

"Yes, Elenitsa," I said, already preoccupied with the garden salad I was preparing. I eyed the chicken in the oven, grabbed my beer, and sat contentedly at my kitchen table taking in the comforting, familiar smells that surrounded me. I was famished. For several long minutes I sat quietly, eyes closed, and basked in the pleasures of my kitchen—until I felt Elenitsa's disapproving gaze upon me. I blinked my eyes open.

"Chris," she said, pointing a finger emphatically at my chest. "For the last time, call Dr. Mandes!"

* * * * *

In a brief time I fully recovered from the damage I had sustained by doctors and hospitals. Later that year a tragedy struck my friends and neighbors from Ocean City, the Carroll's. Their youngest son Johnny, the little boy who had spent many summer evenings during his childhood visiting me on my patio listening to my ruminations on life, was injured in a serious motorcycle accident. Johnny was paralyzed from the waist down, a young man struck severely in the prime of youth. My heart ached for him, but I never let him feel pitied. I treated him as if nothing had changed. His life lay in front of him and he had to carry on and live it, independent of his handicaps. It would be tough, I knew—we both knew—but what Johnny needed most was not sympathy, but strength. Strength derived from people who believed he was a member of humanity, the same as anyone else.

Johnny's accident put into perspective my little brush with hospitals and doctors, and I was not a young man.

That winter my commemorative stamps arrived on time. Among them were four state-issued stamps and a commemorative of William Faulkner, who once described himself as "just a farmer who loves to tell stories." Reviewing my commemoratives at the beginning of the year was a habit—a ritual, really—that brought me great joy. Each year, I would carefully place them with the preceding years' collection and carefully review them. I still to this day cannot explain the pleasure I derive, nor the fascination I hold for them.

* * * * *

In March of 1988 my good friend and first mate Paul Yeonas died. I saw him shortly before his death and was deeply saddened by how ill he looked. A big man, the cancer that was eating him up had reduced him to a shadow of his former self. Although in much pain, he never complained.

"Hello, Paul," I greeted him that day.

"Hello, Cap'n," he replied.

"How are you feeling, old friend?"

"It's rough, Cap'n. Rough."

I put my arm on his shoulder, and we said nothing further. Those peaceful dawns and exhilarating ocean excursions that comprised our fishing adventures were behind us. His passing was a loss to all his family and friends, but we also knew he had been released from his lingering suffering and pain. Death, for him, I could only see as a blessing.

That summer, Anthony left his brokering job to straighten out a deli he had acquired with a partner in downtown Washington, D. C. His partner had managed the business and had now left it in debt. Bookkeeping was a mess and bills were unpaid, including a bank note that bore both their signatures. I told him that if he walked into the restaurant he might have to stay, and he did...for three years. Elenitsa and I preferred that he use his education—but there he was, back in the restaurant business. This meant that whenever a cashier or kitchen helper failed to show up, he was responsible...or more correctly, I would get a call to help—and I did. I couldn't complain, though. I enjoyed work, always had, and I liked to help my kids, even at 73.

"That'll be $3.95 please," money changing hands, as I placed a sandwich in a bag along with napkin and plastic fork. Ah, the good old days! Such familiar routine. So Anthony's detour back into the food service business gave me plenty to do off and on through the winters for the next few years.

Early in 1989, I received a special treat. In addition to my commemoratives that year I had ordered a set of the *Encyclopedia Britannica* for the house. Ostensibly, I bought it for the house, for the kids and grandchildren, but actually, owning a set of the

Britannica had been a secret desire of mine since the late fifties when I had sold the *World Book Encyclopedia* part time door to door. *Britannicas* were the finest, and all my life I had wanted a set for our house.

The evening my set of the *Britannica* arrived, I sat down with the first volume and started leafing through the pages, struck with the depth and detail of the content. I had bought a new glass-fronted case to house the set, and over the next three or four years hardly a winter evening went by that I didn't read from its pages. Having only gone to school through the fourth grade, encyclopedias gave me a way to learn much of what my childhood circumstances had prevented me from learning.

After three years at the deli, Anthony was a little worn out. In the restaurant business in Washington, the help situation is very difficult and Anthony was working long hours, filling in for absent employees. He and Lee Ann now had a third child, Ashley Elisabeth, and Elenitsa felt they needed a vacation. So I obliged by looking after the deli for a week while Anthony and Lee Ann drove the kids to Disney World in Orlando during Christmas break that winter. Of course, it was hard for Anthony to leave behind the day-to-day details of the business, and he briefed me over and over. Did he know whom he was talking to for goodness sake? I had to laugh, for I knew the feeling all too well.

"Dad, you only need to prepare the deposit. Don't make that trip to the bank. Just give it to Jose and he'll take it over after lunch. Oh, and here are the catering orders we have for the week. Alex and Janie will prepare them and Miguel will make the deliveries."

"We'll manage fine," I told him. "Don't you worry."

"And here's a list of our suppliers," Anthony went on as if he hadn't heard me. "The deliveries are all set but if you find you need—"

"I will be okay, Anthony," I said, interrupting him. "I know what to do. Go, enjoy yourself!"

Eventually I managed to get Anthony out of the deli and off on his vacation. The deli was a busy place with long lines at lunch and at least five different daily specials, but I had the right background for it, and even though I was seventy-three, it hardly ruffled a feather. I stayed busy that week and somehow, doing this to allow my son and daughter-in-law some time to themselves, made up in part to Elenitsa for all the vacations we had missed with the kids. The week went very fast.

The truth is, as long as I had the time and health, helping my children first, and then other people in general, was something I enjoyed. It seemed to me the full essence of life.

* * * * *

That spring my azaleas were especially lovely. Often times I awoke long before Elenitsa. With the kids grown and moved away, the house was quiet and empty except for holidays. Soon it would be Easter and my holiday preparations would bring them all home. In the soft light of dawn, breathing the crisp morning air, I walked among my azaleas and admired their brilliant colors. The blossoms, heavy with dew, glittered jewel-like in the morning sun. Mornings like these, with my flowers in bloom and alive with light and color, were truly a gift from God.

Depending on the ferocity and duration of winter, my azaleas usually began blooming in March April, a feat they repeated faithfully every year. Their blossoms heralded the arrival and warmth of spring and to me symbolized renewal and life. The beauty of nature, whether in a garden like mine or in an unspoiled wilderness, gives special meaning to human existence, and the buds and blossoms of my garden became my own springtime Byzantine temple.

By 1990 Ianthe was dating a Greek man, Steve Yeatras, and I became a big and enthusiastic supporter of this relationship. The urgency regarding a suitable marriage for my unwed daughter had increased. Ianthe was thirty-four, and more than anything I did not want to see her become an "old maid." Perhaps I was overly occupied with it as a result of some guilt I may have felt over my sister's own sacrifice caring for our parents. I don't know. I just knew I wanted her to be happy, and to me, that meant married. I watched as her relationship with Steve progressed, nudging it along whenever I thought it was not moving fast enough. I was not a modern papa and I did not see any charm in a woman leading a single life. For my peace of mind if not hers, Ianthe needed to be married and have a family of her own, and that was that. To me, Steve was an excellent candidate.

That summer a special dinner was held in Washington. For the first time in America's history, a patriarch of the Orthodox Christian Church of Constantinople would visit America. To Orthodox Christians, this was a very special event. The Patriarch would be honored at a dinner and accompanied by his bishops and archbishops, including my friend, Iakovos, Archbishop of the Americas. I had not visited with the Archbishop for many years, though I had followed his career with interest. He had prayed at Presidential inaugurations and was credited for building up the Orthodox Church in America. I could not let pass this opportunity to see him—who knows when our paths would cross again?

As a result, I bought tickets to the Patriarch's dinner for my entire family—including Ianthe and Steve Yeatras. Time was racing by, and I made every effort to get all the kids there for what I knew would be a special night. As we arrived at the Sheraton in Washington, D. C., an entourage of bishops passed directly in front of us dressed in black gowns and impressive headdresses. A moment later Patriarch Demetrious appeared. An old man in his mid-eighties, he was of slight stature—my height, but almost emaciated—and with a beard that extended to his waist. Although he was born on the island of Imbroz, he was ten years older than I was and I never knew him. As he passed me, I bowed my head and crossed myself in reverent respect.

The ballroom at the Sheraton was packed with dignitaries and the faithful. Since this was the first trip by an Ecumenical Patriarch to the United States, many of the Orthodox faithful had travelled far to attend. Even President Bush was there to give the keynote address, although he departed with his security detail shortly afterward, leaving the head table and the black-garbed, bearded bishops. The main attraction for the Orthodox faithful, though, was the Ecumenical Patriarch himself, leader of three hundred million Orthodox Christians. My friend the Archbishop was sitting at the Patriarch's right and a bishop from Constantinople was on his left. When the Patriarch rose from his seat to address the crowd, I wondered if he would say anything about the problems, past or present, that the Church encountered at the hands of the Turks. It was a longstanding habit, for reasons I did not fully appreciate, to keep the mistreatment of the Church by the Turks out of public attention. The Patriarch's speech was conciliatory, appreciative and short, failing to mention, even in passing, the lengthy persecution of the Christians of Asia Minor. It was not lost on me that the Patriarch and his bishop would have to return to Turkey after the function.

After dinner the Patriarch, Archbishop and bishops remained seated at the head table while the guests moved about and mingled. I signaled to Anthony and began moving from the back of the ballroom to the head table of bishops. As we approached, Archbishop Iakovos caught my eye and motioned to me.

"Chrysostomos, my friend!" he exclaimed. "Come!" He gestured for us to go around the table and join him, and a minute later he welcomed us with open arms.

"Chrysostomos, it has been years since I've seen you!"

An affectionate smile adorned a warm facade while his eyes surveyed me in a slow, nostalgic stare. Yes, it had been a long time. Our keen memories allowed us to embrace our childhood excitement once more.

"Too long, your Eminence," I replied, bowing. Then I brought Anthony forward and added, "Do you remember my son?"

Anthony bowed as the Archbishop replied, "Yes, Anthony—of course I remember him." Then he smiled. "When last I saw you, Anthony, you were a young man full of ideas and a little righteous anger."

"I remember all too well, your Eminence," Anthony smiled, blushing.

In that moment of conversation, I surveyed the Archbishop. Though the color of his hair had faded to pure white, the glow in his eyes had not faded a bit. We were two old men now, reunited for a brief moment in the twilight of our lives.

"Chrysostomos," the Archbishop said, turning his attention back to me, "allow me to present you to our Patriarch." With that he placed a hand on my shoulder and moved me toward Demetrious.

"Your All Holiness," he addressed the Patriarch, "may I present Chrysostomos Chrysostomidis. He is from Imbroz. His father was Ioanni Chrysostomidis."

"Ioanni…" the Patriarch mused. "Ioanni Chrysostomidis from Panayia? Yes, I knew your father, Chrysostomos. He was a good man. Come closer," he beckoned.

"Yes, your All Holiness. My pleasure," I said, bowing deeply and kissing his hand.

The patriarch placed his hands gently on my shoulders and righted me. "Let me see you," he said as I rose. "Yes, it has been many years but you look like your father. May God be with you, Chrysostomos."

Deeply gratified by this small reference to my father, I murmured my thanks. Then the Patriarch turned to a bishop in his mid-fifties behind him. "May I introduce Bishop Demetrios Arhondonis? He is also from Imbroz. Demetrios, this is Chrysostomos Chrysostomidis, from Imbroz."

"My pleasure," the bishop responded. "Where on Imbroz are you from?"

"Panayia," I replied.

"I am from Theodora," he smiled. "Chrysostomidis…your sisters babysat me when I was small." I nodded my surprise and acknowledgement.

Little did I know that two years later, when Patriarch Demetrious died, Demetrios Arhondonis would take the name Bartholomew and become the next Patriarch of the Orthodox Christian faith, yet another patriarch from Imbroz.

As I moved to leave the table, the Archbishop turned to me. The light was shining on him in a way that seemed to create a halo on the snow-white hair and beard that flowed beneath the large, impressive headdress, and it glinted off the jewel-studded gold cross and staff. He looked dignified in his ethereal splendor. His wizened face was impassive and documented his years of experience, hardship, kindness…years spent contemplating pious thoughts in a realm above and apart from other men, thoughts of humanity and its relationship to God, but when our eyes met again, I saw for a brief moment the boy I befriended over sixty years ago.

"Chrysostomos, my friend, it is so good to see you."

"The pleasure, your Eminence, is all mine." At that moment, the thought occurred to me that this might well be our last meeting. I think he sensed it too, and our eyes exchanged this knowledge with a simple, poignant acceptance. For a moment, he placed his arm on my shoulder, then our eyes disengaged.

I turned and left the table. My brief interlude with the past and my childhood on Imbroz vividly refreshed me. On this special evening I gave something of my ancient Greek heritage to my American family. It was a proud night for me, mingling, as it did, my past, present and future with the leadership of our Church. Imagine, three bishops, the leaders of our faith, all from the tiny island of Imbroz! When the Patriarch gave the closing prayer marking the end of the evening, all present felt touched by the hand of God.

* * * * *

That fall the country was in the midst of a crisis. Saddam Hussein had attacked Kuwait, and American troops were deployed to the Gulf region. The military expense coupled with our weakened banking system was enough to plunge the country into a deep and protracted recession. The causes were numerous, and the effects were predictably painful. It was September 1990, but the crisis in the Gulf was literally a world away. In Ocean City there were no missiles, no troops, no war. Instead, it was fishing season, and, recession or not, I had a freezer to restock for winter.

The morning after I arrived, I was readying my fishing gear when Dr. Bill Greco knocked at my door.

"Chris, I'm ready!"

"Come on in, Bill," I called. Ever since Paul's illness and death, Bill and I had done a lot of fishing together. He knew exactly what to do and required very little supervision.

"They're calling for fair weather," Bill said by way of greeting. "It should be a good one."

"Good," I told him as we left the house and headed for the boat. "We'll go out to the ten-mile buoy for trout."

"I was thinking we might catch a few blues."

"We'll see. Did you bring the chum?"

Chum was a mixture of bait, usually fish chopped up into slivers which, when tossed out on the water, created a slick that attracted schools of fish.

"Right here," Bill said, lifting a bucket in his hand. "You have the lines?"

"Six of them, ready to go," I said.

"Well, we've got fruit, bread, cheese and beer...I think we're set."

"Then let's go!" I said.

When Bill and I fished, the pleasure was in the business of fishing. After travelling in the boat lanes about a mile and a half down the bay, I rounded the corner and faced the inlet where ocean meets bay. The inlet was surprisingly—almost eerily—calm, its normal chop and turbulence now but gently rolling small swells. As we passed through that sunlit morning, the only thing that disturbed the glassy calm of the water was the wake of our vessel.

Once safely through the inlet, I turned to Bill. "Trout or blues?" I asked.

"Blues," Bill voted.

"Trout," I suggested. "The sea doesn't have a tastier animal than fresh trout."

"That's true," Bill agreed. "Besides, we might run into some blues along the way."

Bill and I both loved the sport of fishing, and his tireless patience and attention to detail made us a perfect pair for these expeditions. Some of the biggest catches I've had over the years have been with Bill Greco.

The day remained perfectly clear and the morning sun shone brightly as it topped the horizon. A few stationary clouds were suspended overhead like giant balloons on a string. Four hundred yards to the east of my small runabout lay a commercial fishing vessel. Poles baited and ready, we trolled the calm waters looking for schools of fish.

"What a beautiful day God has given us, Bill!" I exclaimed.

"Yes, indeed He has," Bill rejoined.

At that moment we both saw a school of fish running between us and the commercial trawler.

"There they are!" Bill cried. "The commercial boat sees them, too. Should I toss out the chum?"

"No, wait a bit," I said, slowing the engine. "Let me throw out the lines first."

Quickly, I moved to the poles and began casting out the lines, three on each side of the boat. Bill followed behind me, tossing chum over the school of fish.

"Look, Chris," he said. "They're trout!"

Within seconds, the trout hit our lines with awesome intensity. Reels shrieked as the fish tore line from them, gobbling the bait and heading out to sea. I grabbed a pole with one hand and with the other I reached over and locked the reel of another. A minute later I pulled in the first trout of the day as Bill was struggling with trout number two. We were in fisherman's paradise. Our juices were flowing.

I slipped the hook from the mouth of my five-pound trout and held it aloft just as Bill finally landed his. "Look, Bill. On this beautiful day God has given us this beautiful sea creature. It's something, isn't it?"

As soon as I spoke I heard the shrill hum of another reel as a trout spun off yards of line.

"I'll get the pole, Chris," Bill called out. "You bait and cast the other two lines."

For a brief burst of time we were casting out one line as we were reeling in another. Over and over we performed this ballet of casting and reeling, casting and reeling, laughing with exhilaration and excitement. Eventually the torrid pace began to subside, but our catch remained steady until, by early afternoon, we had hauled aboard nearly ninety fish: some croakers, but mostly trout—and for Bill, even a blue.

"Chris," Bill said finally with happy exhaustion, "we've got to knock off. It's going to take us hours to clean this catch."

Tilting my head back, I wiped the perspiration from my brow as the warm, bright sun forced my eyes into a squint. All around us the peaceful sea glittered blue and golden with sunlight. We needed to get back to port and clean this catch. We had a big job ahead of us. For now, though, we would enjoy the peace and tranquility after the fervor and excitement of our bout with the sea.

I popped open two beers and we both sat and sipped in silence, contemplating the beauty of God's creation.

When we at last secured the vessel for travel, I suddenly realized I was starving. We had not eaten a bite all day. I broke out the fruit and cheese and tossed a hunk of bread to Bill. Winking in the sunlight as we headed westward toward land, we munched in silence on our simple meal as the gentle breeze playfully tossed spray across our bow and splashed our faces.

"Bill," I mused a little later, "what more could life give? A beautiful day and two old men having the time of their lives outwitting these beautiful sea creatures. Fresh air, calm water, a gentle breeze and the bounty of the sea. It is by God's grace we've been allowed to enjoy these things."

"We're lucky men, Captain," Bill smiled.

"Yes we are, very lucky," I agreed.

We made our way toward port and home on a perfect Indian summer day, cutting through a mesmerizing, luminous sea that had kindly yielded two old fishermen a most generous bounty.

23
A Grandson's Interview

...Do you think, O blue-eyed banditti,
Because you have scaled the wall,
Such an old mustache as I am
Is not a match for you all!
I have you fast in my fortress,
And will not let you depart,
But put you down into the dungeon
In the round-tower of my heart.
And there will I keep you forever,
Yes, forever and a day,
Till the walls shall crumble to ruin,
And moulder in dust away!

—Henry Wadsworth Longfellow
"The Children's Hour"

Operation Desert Storm wasn't the nation's only concern in 1991. The country also suffered through savings and loan closures and the near failure of the American banking system. This in turn triggered a recession the following year. In 1992, with the country still in the grip of an economic downturn, voters ushered in a new president—a young Democrat and ex-governor of Arkansas, William Jefferson Clinton. If it is true that leaders reflect the societies they oversee, then we should question our social and moral condition before flaunting the foibles of our elected leaders.

In the sixties and seventies a group of hippies had professed nihilism and anarchy. In the no-longer-surprising twists of fate and irony, by the nineties, many of these people had become religious, solid, working citizens. Nevertheless, the ethos of many was still tainted with the residue of the poisonous ideas they had so whole-heartedly embraced earlier. In the eighties and early nineties, society as a whole had lost its moral rudder. The state was replacing Christian morality with increasingly ridiculous ecumenical definitions of equality that parsed life into hyperbole and opinion. Indeed, morality itself, Christian or otherwise, seemed to be redefined as situational ethics. In the final analysis they were merely political expediencies. Although they sounded harmless, to me they had a very similar ring, akin to the "secular" reforms of the Young Turks in the years before the Christian Holocaust. It is my belief that simple truths remain simple truths despite the trappings of society, rich or poor, simple or sophisticated. We are all still men. Even if uttered by only a single voice, the truth remains the truth. Power, greed and politics—these are the motivators of time and history that often cause leaders to prey on the masses.

In my view, secularism was being transformed into fanaticism. Complacency fostered the loss of certain God-given rights and freedoms. This worrisome harbinger or precondition had established a firm grip in America and tragically tarnished her allure.

The recession and the Gulf War would end, but this silent moral shift from traditional Christian beliefs to political definitions of what is socially correct was undermining all that was great in America. Our individual freedoms were being stripped for the "good of the homogenous whole." So that no one may be offended by the beliefs of others, we were losing the right as individuals to hold those beliefs, or at least to speak them. The term "politically correct" was creeping into the American jargon, and "cultural diversity" became another phrase for strange and unprincipled behavior.

The working population remained apathetic and therefore was only half listening as it was led deeper and deeper into the soothing political rhetoric of economic distribution, equality and fairness. Who would, after all, argue with these principles? This was becoming the Age of Niceness. No one said anything that might be considered "insensitive." Indeed, no one, it seemed, was even saying "no" to his children any more. Besides, the government said you could be sued for that. Despite the more practical incentive of the threat of lawsuits, I believe the American people genuinely believed in being nice, and that was the driving force behind these shifts. No one was noticing, however, that the hidden result was an erosion of incentive and personal freedoms as the philosophy of "Niceness" was made into law. Instead of individuals taking responsibility for their own belief systems, the government was going to make sure we all had the same one...for the good of all, of course.

The loss of human rights under any pretext is unscrupulous and fosters corruption. The diminution of God-given freedoms and rights would most certainly be followed in lockstep by lost welfare and opportunity. Moreover, this wicked social impairment would not be easily reversed. The precursors for a future crisis were in place. Ironically, the holocaust that annihilated almost three-quarters of the Christian population of Asia Minor had begun under the guise of a politically correct doctrine professing equality for all minorities, a democratic constitution, and the lessening of religious influence over the state. As then, this new group of nihilists that has gained prominence over the political scene has intellectualized away the very chairs in which we sit. I was left wondering how my children and their children would face a future crisis, as we had become a nation of individuals lacking civility, cohesion, and moral courage.

Back in my own personal world, the recession left me with many vacancies in my rental stores and a serious reduction in my income. I was in need of a loan. My son Jon had borrowed a large sum of money to renovate the beer and wine carryout two years earlier, and although the carryout was busy, Jon seemed unable to get the kind of return on his investment I would have expected. After servicing his debt, he lived hand to mouth.

Anthony had sold his deli to a Korean family. It interested me to reflect that the Koreans were a new wave of immigrants, not unlike so many others over America's past, seeking opportunity and freedom. The Koreans managed to accomplish in twenty years in the restaurant business what it took the Greek people fifty years to do. They were hardworking and resourceful and I believed they would make a go of the deli. However, the recession brought on by the Gulf War, coupled with competition, caused the Koreans to go under two years later.

After he sold the deli, Anthony went to work for a mortgage lender and then moved back into investments as a broker. He was raising three children in a thousand-square-foot rambler on a quarter acre lot in Falls Church, about two-and-a-half miles away from his mother and me. Now that he was out of the restaurant business I saw a great deal more of him.

Meanwhile, Ianthe had moved back to Northern Virginia from Fredericksburg and acquired a teaching job in Fairfax County. Shortly afterward, I gave her the down payment on a condominium in Fair Oaks, a new development in Fairfax County, not far from our home. Already her return to Northern Virginia was paying dividends because there she was able to see Steve Yeatras more often. I continued to be the chief supporter of their relationship and had high hopes that she would be married by her thirty-sixth birthday. Steve's father had won a million dollars in the lottery in 1985 and so was doing quite well financially, so I asked his parents to match my contribution for a home after their marriage.

I didn't spend all my time worrying about my children and my finances, and I had interests other than stamps and fishing. A couple of years earlier my good friend John Delta had involved me in the Hellenic Society of Constantinopolitans, and eventually I become its treasurer. The society was composed of a handful of Orthodox Christians of Greek descent who had survived the holocaust in Turkey seventy years before, and others who were younger yet had immigrated from that part of the world.

It was an interesting group and I enjoyed the members very much. Their experiences as survivors of the Christian Holocaust were often compelling. After services at church on a Sunday near the holidays, Thomas Vasil, one of the members of the Society, told me his story. Tom was a retired engineer who was born in Smyrna and survived the slaughter of 1922. He was a slender man with a few white hairs combed back over a balding head, and he had thick glasses which magnified his eyes to appear as large as his nose and ears.

"I was born in 1912," he said, "so I am what, five years older than you? When I was a boy, my father was very successful in the ironworks business. We lived in Smyrna, and in 1922, the city grew dramatically as thousands of dislocated Christians were driven from their inland homes by the Turkish army and sought refuge in the seashore cities. By September of that year the population of the city had swelled, by some estimates doubling its normal population of around three hundred thousand souls. In the weeks before the Turkish military attacked, there were people everywhere seeking passage to any destination. Panic was in their eyes.

"When the slaughter started, we were at home. The soldiers broke in and looted our house. I watched in horror as they threatened to cut Papa's finger off to get his gold ring, but Mama pleaded with them and they finally got the ring without removing the finger. Others were not so lucky. By the time the soldiers were done, they had seized all our valuables except for a few gold coins that Mama had sewn into our clothes the day before.

"Then the fires came. Papa and Mama packed our belongings, and to escape the fires we joined the throngs in the streets. We wandered, dazed and distraught...until the killings began. You cannot imagine it, Christo. Young Christian girls were defiled in plain view of their fathers and brothers, who were bludgeoned and cut with long curved knives and left to bleed to death—and the rest of us...all we could do was watch. We were no match for the trained and well-armed Turkish army. It was unspeakable, the entire military might of Mustapha Kemal violently unleashed upon us...a horror I can never forget." His voice trailed off and he stopped speaking for a moment, almost absently, but then with a slight shake of his head he continued.

"After a day and a night in the streets we somehow managed to stay together and hidden from view by some miracle from God. To this day, I have no idea how we managed it. We finally escaped the crowds and hid in a foundry by the docks. All around us were billowing clouds of black smoke, the stench of fires and charred flesh and the screams of dying people. My two brothers, my parents and I made our way to the docks where a Greek merchant ship flying an American flag took us aboard. This is how we escaped. I might add, Christo, that the harbor was filled with ships from all over the world—Italy, France, Germany, Japan, Great Britain—but other than to evacuate their diplomats not a single one interceded nor offered refuge for the Christian masses trying to escape the slaughter. They served as silent witness to the Christian slaughter and annihilation of Smyrna, a city three thousand years old." He paused. "To this day, I do not understand why." Suddenly his tired sadness flashed into a harsh outburst. "The Turks I understand!" he said savagely. "They were brutal barbarians—zealots and fanatics bent on destruction in the name of their god! But the 'civilized nations'! To just stand aside and watch!" his voice shook with an involuntary sob, "and pretend they don't see." His bitter words trailed to a plea, a plea for understanding the incomprehensible. He stopped. I listened with sadness at his personal agony, one which so many had shared. At length, he sighed. "So many, many years ago, Christo. I was a boy of ten and still I have nightmares."

"God has blessed us and led us to a good life in America," I said gently. "We have found homes, raised families. God willing, our children and grandchildren will never know the horrors we endured in our youth."

"Chrysostomos," he said, "I cannot forget those days. So many innocent people were slaughtered and those who survived lost everything and were scattered to the winds."

Then it came to me as Thomas stood before me. "Thomas, do you remember making a brief stop on the island of Imbroz?"

"Yes," he nodded absently.

"One evening, a priest, a man, and a little boy, younger than you, came to visit."

He looked up with dawning recognition.

"You...you were the little boy!" he blurted out as the realization sprang across his face. The sheer coincidence left us speechless. The years and the sites we had seen flashed across our minds. Alive and in old age, our paths had crossed again in America. From that moment forward at the coffee socials following church, Thomas would find his way to my side.

"Not forgetting is one thing," I told him. "Obsessing with the past, keeping it alive instead of buried with the dead, can be unhealthy, even destructive."

"Perhaps," he agreed, "but I cannot forget that black part of my life. Our memories serve as guardians against future holocausts. There are so few of us left, so few who witnessed what happened, so we are obliged to remember. It is an obligation we owe the living and the dead. If we forget, our society will forget and we cannot allow that. Without a memory of what happened before, we are doomed to repeat it." Thomas looked at me sadly. "Yes, my friend, we must never forget.

"Chrysostomos, the majority of our Christian society does not associate martyrdom and holocaust with modern-day Christianity, but rather with the Jewish Holocaust. They must know it happened to Christians, too. Repression of this truth only increases the likelihood of another Christian holocaust someday. They think it can't happen to them!"

Thomas' story troubled me, and I found myself thinking of the past more often than I wished.

Respect for life as demonstrated in the Western Christian concept of social, political and economic freedom was taken for granted by the very people it most benefited. The comfort of our life was, in a way, the seed of its own undoing. We had become apathetic; we had forgotten our Christian roots and basic teachings and beliefs. Thomas serves us well as a sentinel who, through his horrific memories, challenges the securities of twentieth-century Christian men, stirring memories of antiquity, of martyrdom and Christian sacrifice. It is only through respect for and fear of God that we can find hope and motivation for a productive and peaceful world. It is a lesson we need to learn daily.

* * * * *

The Society of Constantinopolitans had about fifty members in the Washington area, with about eight or ten normally attending each meeting. Our average age exceeded that of the Nazi-holocaust victims by about two decades, and so explained our sparse attendance at meetings. We were a tiny organization of business people, teachers, doctors and the like, but we had a gigantic reverence for America, her freedoms and Christian traditions. Our respect made us particularly sensitive to her change, no matter how small.

For the first time in many years I felt bitterness toward the Turks over what they had done to my family. Reading the

Washington Post, I carefully clipped any article I saw on Turkey. I even began to quarrel with Katina for signing over Papa's small house and store to the Turks when she left the island in the 1960's. It wasn't the material loss that offended me most—the fields and other properties had gone to the Turks long before. Rather it was that Papa's house was a symbol of the lifelong toil of a Christian man who had stood on the shoulders of our ancestors, reaching back for generations that had similarly toiled on Imbroz. The loss seemed to disrespect Papa. Our small home represented Papa's unyielding protest to the conquest that surrounded it, and now, after all these years, all we had left was memory.

It struck me that the Jews had gotten some measure of justice in prosecuting their war criminals, and even reparation for loss of property, but very few people were informed enough to even acknowledge that a holocaust in Turkey had ever occurred. The world preferred to keep a blind and ignorant eye. Powerful interests had worked long and hard to conceal the truth, keeping it hidden from public opinion, and soon, no one would be left to remember.

* * * * *

The summer of 1991 brought equal doses of relief and joy into my life. Steve Yeatras had asked my Ianthe to marry him. At thirty-six, my little Cookie was finally getting married. I was ecstatic!

The Yeatras family was one of the many Greek families that frequented our store in Ocean City and with whom we exchanged pleasantries. The boy was a year older than Ianthe, but he was nice to her and I felt marriage and a family would be the sobering ingredient needed to help him fashion a good future.

"Chris, I want to invite Father John Travis, Ianthe's godparents and of course their children, too," Elenitsa told me one evening. "And Ianthe wants Father George Alexon to perform the service at St. Catherine's, and you wanted to invite Father George Papaiouniou. Oh, and our friends Christina Regis, Stan and Stacia Mastaracus, Terry and Gus Decalas, Mary and Gus Bochanos, Elenitsa and George Karambelos, and…"

The list went on and on. I rented the ballroom at the Radisson in Alexandria and planned all seven courses of the meal with the maitre d'. We had an open bar with hors d'oeuvres for two hours in the lounge. Over three hundred friends and relatives attended the wedding and the formal dinner reception. I was not an extravagant person, but when Greek fathers marry off their daughters, excess is the norm. The bill came to over $60,000, but the pleasure the day brought me was beyond measure. At long last, my beautiful little girl was married.

* * * * *

The 1991 commemorative stamps I received that winter included a set of stamps honoring the nine planets and our moon. Ten fascinating stamps commemorated events leading to World War II and five stamps commemorated fishing flies. The stamps were attractively mounted and captioned with a brief interesting narrative. I was fascinated with the history and beauty of stamps. It had been twenty years since I purchased my first set of commemoratives in America, and every year I waited for their arrival with the excitement of a child. To many, stamp collecting was not very exciting, but for me, it was colorful, historical, cultural, and it marked events as I passed through time, many of which I remember. With my lack of education, the stamps were another way of seeing the history I had never been taught. They also helped me relax after my busy days.

* * * * *

As Easter approached, I made a quick trip to Ocean City. I had ordered two legs of spring lamb, which I picked up along with other supplies for Easter dinner. I also went to see my old friend and creditor, Fred Parker, the president of Home Bank. I had an interest payment due on April 15th, but that wasn't what was on my mind. As soon as Fred and I had exchanged pleasantries, I got straight to the point.

"Fred, I need to borrow another ten thousand dollars."

"You want me to put it against the stores?"

"Yes. You know that our business is in the summer, Fred. I'll take care of it then."

"I know you will," he nodded. "I'll defer the interest on the present balance until then. I'll have the papers ready for you to sign by Friday. Will that work for you?"

"Thanks, Fred. That will be fine."

On the night of Good Friday, Elenitsa and I went to the late night service at St. Sophia Cathedral with Anthony and my grandson Brian. It was a lengthy service full of pageantry. Young girls threw flower petals on the symbolic tomb of Christ.

The next night, we attended the midnight service. As a procession of soft, glowing candlelight unfolded in the darkness in the first moments of Easter Sunday, the priest declared, "He has risen." The show of lights in the early morning hours of Easter was as inspiring as it had been in my childhood. Witnessing the age-old rituals always took me back in time to the tiny church of my childhood in Panayia on Imbroz and for a few brief moments I was flooded with pleasant memories, combined with the awe and inspiration of the Risen Christ.

* * * * *

The following autumn, Brian asked me if he could interview me for a school project. I was amused at the idea of being interviewed—even if it was by my nine-year-old grandson—and interested to know what his questions would be.

Brian arrived with a sheet of paper and a small tape recorder and, in a solemn voice, posed his first question:

"What country are you from?"

Easy so far! "Greece," I replied into the tape recorder.

"What was your school like?"

"Well, the school we had on our island was an elementary school. It went up through sixth grade, and I went up through fourth."

"How far away was the school?"

"The school, from our house, was more than a mile...we used to walk. We didn't have any transportation like here."

"Were the teachers very strict?"

"I'd say so. They were very strict if you did something wrong. You'd get spanked in school, which of course you don't have here."

"What was your childhood like?" Brian asked.

This question was more difficult, and I hesitated a minute. "...Ah, my childhood was not exactly what you all have here. You know, we had to work harder, had to do a lot of chores, help the family, because we were not as rich as in this country." I paused again, thinking for a moment of the many difficulties we had had under the Turks, yet it was nothing for public disclosure. How could I tell Brian about the purging of the Christians, the terrible deprivation and loss? How could I tell him that our language was banned, our records stolen and our property confiscated? The fact was, I couldn't tell him. There was no point in dredging all that up for a child who would not yet understand.

Sensing that I had more to say, Brian looked at me expectantly, but I shook my head. "That's it," I said.

"Okay..." He fumbled a bit with his paper. "What were your houses like?"

"They were not exactly what you have here. They were very small. We did not have the facilities we have in this country, of course, like running water. Most of the houses had no toilets. Toilets, they were outside, you know. In our little house we had only two rooms, and in one room we used to sleep four children, brothers and sisters, and my father and mother used to sleep in the other room."

"What traditional food did you eat?"

"Well, the foods we had there...we don't have the beef that's here. It was more olives, vegetables, cheese, fruit, and occasionally fish or lamb."

"Did you go fishing or hunting?"

"Yes, yes...we used to fish, of course, and hunt, too. Most of the food we grew ourselves."

"Where did you go to get your food?" Brian asked.

"We grew most of our food, but we had a market and if you needed anything you went there."

"What kind of games did you play?"

"We didn't have too many games like you have here, believe me," I told him. "All this...forget about electronics and everything else. We had...I personally had...one ball and that's all we had around the block. One ball, which we threw and kicked around."

"Okay...What sports did you play?"

I shook my head. "We didn't have sports. You're talking a few years back. We had soccer...and just chasing each other around the field."

Brian nodded his understanding, a mature nine-year old ready to press on with his interview. "What kind of money did you have?"

"It was Greek currency...drachmas, and later, the Turkish pound or lira."

"What kind of technology did you have?"

"Oh, technology." I paused. "We didn't have much technology," I smiled. "The biggest transportation we had was horses and, ah, stage coaches—you know, something like that—and street cars later in the city."

"What age were you when you left your country?"

"When I left it was during the war. I was almost twenty-eight years old when I left to come to America," I glossed over the years in Constantinople and the years prior to that on my uncle's island.

"What did you do after you left your island?"

"I came to the Embassy and I worked at the Embassy for three years. Then I got my papers and stayed here."

"Do you have any other interesting facts you can tell me?"

That was a good question, I thought, but I wasn't sure how to answer. "The interesting facts, really..." I paused, then began again. "There is no comparison with what we have here...and especially when I was a child many years ago. There is no comparison with this country. You can't know or even imagine how lucky we are here. Remember that."

"Where in Greece were you born?"

"On an island in the Aegean Sea. The name was Imbroz Island."

My grandson smiled and lowered his eyes to the tape recorder. "This is Brian Christ's interview," he intoned, "October 14, 1991."

378

* * * * *

"Chris, I'm getting dressed for the Constantinopolitan dinner. Are you ready?"

The Hellenic Society of Constantinopolitans held a New Year's dinner at St. George Greek Orthodox Church in Maryland early in January. I had invited my children and grandchildren to join us, hoping to give them a sense of our history. It was a special evening for celebrating, an evening for remembrance as well as for the future.

We came from Constantinople, Rankia, the Dardenelles, Imbroz and numerous other cities and towns in Byzantium, drawn together by our shared experiences and the hauntings of our past. Many members of the society had survived the two days of terror during the riots in 1955, and a handful dated back to the Christian Holocaust. As a group, we shared hardships and experiences that were almost unimaginable to our American families. I was often, for brief moments, flooded by memories, and every member I saw wore ghosts of the faces of those no longer there.

That night, interspersed among those haunting memories were the beautiful faces of my young granddaughters, Katelyn, now almost eight, and little Ashley, nearly four.

"Granddaddy, let's dance!" demanded Ashley as she grabbed me by the hand and headed toward the dance floor.

"Okay, Honey. How could I turn down such an offer?" In an instant, I felt another hand pull my free arm. Katelyn was not about to be left out! Fortunately, many Greek dances require dancers to join hands and rhythmically circle to the music, and this was one of them. Flanked by my delightful grandchildren, we danced up a storm.

"Chris, you never danced with me like that," Elenitsa teased as we returned panting with spent exuberance.

"Granddaddy did good," Ashley stated with authority.

I laughed. Yes, it was one of the dances of my life, spending precious time with two young jewels.

* * * * *

In the spring Ianthe gave birth to a healthy baby girl whom she named Krislyn, after me. I was thrilled about the baby and even though I had business in Ocean City to attend to, I postponed my trip until after the baby's birth. It was a joy and a relief to know that my little girl and her little girl were fine.

My joy was tempered one evening when Sultana called. We went through the usual greetings, asking about everyone's health, but when we got to Taki, Sultana's voice broke.

"I am worried, Chrysostomos. Taki is not well. There is something wrong inside...in his intestines. He should have surgery, but he won't go..."

I had no idea Taki was not well and the news was unpleasant. I spoke a few words to soothe my sister, then asked to speak with Taki. A few seconds later I heard his voice.

"Hello, Chrysostomos. Long time since I speak with you," he said in English, his familiar, heavy Greek accent ringing in my ears. As I had with Sultana, Taki and I went through the familiar ritual of inquiring after everyone's family. "How are you and Elenitsa, the children and grandchildren?" he asked.

"Everyone is fine, Taki. And your kids and grandkids?"

"Very fine, Chrysostomos, very fine."

"And you, Taki, how are you?"

"I'm all right, Chrysostomos," Taki told me, then paused. "To tell you the truth, a few months ago I passed some blood in my urine. The doctor did a test and thought he saw something, then they did the test again and the results were not conclusive."

"I see...and how do you feel?"

"I'm better, Chrysostomos...it's nothing, really."

In that moment I knew what Taki already knew...that his illness was something very serious.

"Can I do anything?"

"No, no, Chrysostomos, nothing, thank you. Nothing at all. "

"Take care of yourself, Taki," I said. "Please take care of yourself."

"Don't worry about me, Chrysostomos. I thank you for your concern, but please...don't worry...I am fine. God willing, I am fine."

"Goodbye, my friend," I told him.

"Goodbye, Chrysostomos, my good friend."

Taki and I were Greek Christians from Imbroz, which meant we believed very much in free will, but regarding our longevity we were fatalists. We believed that when it was our time, we would go…and yet we would be the last to admit our time had come. For a moment I felt my own mortality and I realized how little time there was to do so many things. Within a month, Taki had been hospitalized. A week later his condition became grave. Peter took his family up to New York to be with his father. Sultana was on the phone in need of support. Taki was in a lot of pain. He had abdominal cancer. Then he was gone.

I gathered my family, and we drove to New York for the funeral. It was quite a trip. The children thought highly of their uncle Jim. I remembered Taki in his sailor's uniform, cap in hand, asking permission to marry Sultana…our time as newlyweds in northern Virginia, drinking and singing, picnics to Great Falls with the kids.

Taki's passing was another link in the chain of my life now broken, and I spent the next few days contemplating our shared past. I was carrying forward, and he had moved on in a different direction.

* * * * *

When I returned to Ocean City in the late fall of '93, I had many thoughts on my mind and much to do. The recession was lifting but I still had not leased my vacant stores and Bob McGilligot, now my only tenant, was trying to sell his restaurant. I had managed to pay interest on the money I had borrowed from the bank and I was treading water on both sides of the balance sheet. Yet I was too busy that summer to worry. I spent time with Jon at the carryout, met with my attorney, visited with friends and business acquaintances and cooked with Elenitsa. People came to see me and I went to see them, taking pleasure in all the little things of life, and the summer moved along like a warm sea breeze.

"Mr. Christ!" a voice came through the screen door facing the bay one afternoon. It was Johnny Carroll, the boy who had been paralyzed in a motorcycle accident a few years before. He stood in front of my door just as he had as a child, only this time he was in full leg braces. The simple walk from his house next door to mine had been an ordeal.

"Hi, Johnny!" I called out cheerfully. "Come on in."

He struggled to open the door, but I was reluctant to help him. He would manage by himself. From childhood Johnny had visited me at my Ocean City townhouse, following me around, watching what I was doing, listening to what I was saying—although I can't recall that he ever followed my suggestions or learned a single thing from me. That didn't stop my proselytizing. I had always treated him matter-of-factly, and I would do so now. Johnny had sustained crippling injuries and life was proving a challenge for him, but I would treat him just as I always had.

A few days after Johnny's visit, I drove down to the southern edge of town. Four blocks beyond First Street on the right-hand side was Tony's fruit stand, a landmark that I had frequented for decades.

"Hello," I said, climbing out of the car.

"Hi," an unfamiliar voice replied. "What do you need?" Tony's absence overshadowed the fresh fruit arrangements and hung heavily in the air. Even the familiar flies presented an awkward testament to his absence and a reminder of the shortness of time and the fragility of life.

I had heard Tony had passed away that winter. For a moment I thought I should have known to pay respects, but how would I have known? Our paths only crossed during the brief summer season, yet we were good friends for brief moments over years. Our camaraderie was consummated among the plums and melons. I knew him as "Tony the Fruit Man," and he knew me as "Ocean City Chris." Years of memories compressed to fleeting moments of time.

The bounty of honeydews and cantaloupes stood starkly against the decades of summers past. For that instant, nothing was the same. The smell of fresh fruit in season was bittersweet. I lifted one ripe fruit and then another, making my selection, breathing the scent of old times, the vapor of memories past.

In a blink of an eye, it seemed that the summer of 1993 passed. Elenitsa and I went home to Virginia where I caught up on things that needed doing. Later in the fall I returned briefly to Ocean City to take care of some business at the bank and, of course, to fish. The day after my bank visit, I awoke to clear blue October skies and warm breezes—a perfect fishing day. I packed my gear and, dressed in sneakers, a windbreaker and my fishing cap, I headed out to sea alone to soak up the solitude of sun and sea once again. I couldn't overlook the allure of a warm, calm Indian summer day. I cut through crystal reflections on water set against a clear blue sky.

Within thirty minutes I rounded the point and faced the inlet. With my twin engine outboard I knifed easily through the chop and broke out into the ocean, heading for the ten-mile buoy and some trout. At the buoy I cut the engine, dropped two lines with double hooks and waited for a bite. While the sun warmed me and the sea gently rocked me in my little boat, I contemplated life. All problems were left at the shore. A long time ago I was a poor island boy whose family had lost everything, and now, half a world and a lifetime away, I was a man with plenty, only short on time. I had children, grandchildren.

As I fished, I touched the relic coin my father had given me the better part of a century before, and which I still kept pinned close to my heart. My fingers played over the ancient surface of the coin, this relic from my past, this generational hand-me-down from Papa, and I prayed. I felt in my heart that this relic of the True Cross had been my inspiration and guidance, my source of inner strength.

"Thank You, Lord, for my life and all its gifts. Thank You for all You have given me. Any time You wish, I am ready. I am an old man. I do not fear death. My only fears have been in life. Lord, please bless my family and their families as You have blessed me," I whispered. I wondered how many more fishing trips I would have...

I was startled out of my thoughts with a bite on my line, and I reeled in a beautiful five-pound trout. I recast my line but on this particular day, for an old man alone on the sea, it was the only fish I caught.

24

The Hauntings of
My Youth

She loves the bare, the withered tree;
She walks the sodden pasture lane....
The desolate, deserted trees,
The faded earth, the heavy sky,
The beauties she so truly sees,
She thinks I have no eye for these,
And vexes me for reason why.

—Robert Frost
"My November Guest"

My car meandered down a vacant Coastal Highway. Another summer season had come and gone. It had been thirty-eight years since I first crossed the Chesapeake to set foot on my sunny seaside home, a world so far removed from my beloved Imbroz, yet I had come to love it as much. It was the shining paradise of my second life. I had learned a new language and made many friends, raised a family and built a business...and much of what I loved, much of what I had achieved, was reflected in my narrow, sandy sunlit island.

I slowed the car, stretching out those few fleeting minutes as long as I could, inhaling the air tangy with salt. As I watched the gulls spin and soar over the blue waters of the sea, a drizzle began to fall. I know nothing is perfect and that each day serves up a new challenge, but that is part of the song of life, the high notes and the low. I took momentary survey of my work-worn body, then with an uncharacteristic sigh, surveyed sand and sea. As I turned westward toward Virginia, toward Fairfax, images of sea and sand were slowly swept away by the rhythmic pulsing wipers.

* * * * *

I never really gave much importance to political parties because I failed to see how they impact my life. No matter who was elected, I knew I would be doing the same things the next day. In America, no matter who was elected, I would be happy.

"Are you coming for Thanksgiving?" I asked my son Jon during a routine phone call to Ocean City one afternoon.

"Yes, Dad. I'll be there Wednesday, for sure."

"Did the beauty salon give you a check?"

"No, they didn't, Dad."

"How about the photo shop?"

"No, nothing there, either."

"Well, if you get anything from them, deposit it and let me know."

"Okay, Dad. See you Wednesday."

While for years my oldest son ran in a hundred different directions, Jon stayed with me. He was responsible and helpful and watched our small stores when I was not there. Yet, to my great regret, he was forty-three and still had not married. On the other hand, it was his life and I knew I could do little about it. Funny, as I look on it now, how different my attitude toward my unwed daughter was compared to my son.

That evening, I attended a disturbing meeting of the Hellenic Society of Constantinopolitans. Dr. Basil Delta brought the meeting to order and asked me to make my report as treasurer.

"We have about $1,450 in our treasury," I said, glancing at my notes, "and we plan to hold our New Year's dinner dance this year at the Marriott Inn. The proceeds after expenses will be donated to the Basil Orphanage."

I kept my report brief and to the point. Dr. Delta, as secretary, asked if there were any other business and then adjourned the meeting, thus ushering in a social hour. Of the members that gathered that evening, I was the eldest.

The group buzzed for several moments exchanging gossip and news. Then the discussion turned, as it typically did, to the Old World and the Turks. I listened somewhat absently as my thoughts drifted to Jon my unwed son, but I returned to the present when the discussion turned toward me.

"During the two days of terror in September of 1955, we lost everything in Constantinople," Vasili Assakopoulos, who was in his sixties, told us. "Many Christians were killed. Women were raped, graves desecrated and businesses destroyed. The Turkish authorities said the mobs were out of control—but it was common knowledge that they incited and even organized the mobs."

Gregory Papayoli, who was also in his sixties, nodded in vigorous agreement. "Yes, my family lost everything as well. Persecution against the Christian minority was unrelenting."

Vasil Uzunoglu, a professor and research engineer in his late sixties looked at me. "Chrysostomos, weren't you a child during the holocaust?"

"Yes, but it was long ago and I was very young, Vasil."

"Do you remember much of it?"

The truth was, when I chose to, I remembered too much of it. "Mama and Papa, our island of Imbroz, Byzantium, they are all gone, to the Turks and the passage of time, a generation of Christian culture was extinguished," I said, shaking my head. "Yes, those old, old years of my youth, I remember them, Vasil, as if they were yesterday." Then I added, "But before the Turks came, the years were not all bad." I said no more.

"I have studied the holocaust for many years," Vasil continued, "and although much of the truth is not publicized, I have discovered many things. It was Sedat Semari, a Turkish Jew, who, along with his relatives, published the two dominant newspapers in Constantinople in the fifties," Vasil told us. In addition to being a scientist, Vasil fashioned himself as a bit of a historian on the subject of the Christian holocaust and Turkish life. I looked at him expectantly.

"The newspaper was well funded by Jewish money," he continued, "and the paper was widely read by the Mohammedan population. In 1955, the newspapers published lies that stirred the mob concerning an alleged desecration of Atatürk's grave that had never happened. The publication was called the *Huriet News*. With the government's tacit support, two days of rioting, burning, rape and slaughter erupted. Christians were the targets, and not just

Greek Christians—Armenians, Serbs and even a few Italians were attacked by the mobs. The small Christian population of businessmen and shop owners, all survivors of the holocaust, was diminished even further. The paper is widely read today."

Vasil's interesting history lesson was attracting listeners beyond our little group, but he directed most of his lecture to me. "You see, Chrysostomos, the Jewish people have been persecuted for centuries. In 1492, during the first Spanish Inquisition, it was not only the Arabs who were evicted from Spain. The first Inquisitor General, Tomás de Torquemada, also expelled 170,000 Jews. A large number of these Jews settled in Salonika, Greece, where they lived uneventfully for over four hundred years as subjects of the Ottoman Empire on Greek Christian soil. They pretended to become Mohammedans, preserving their Judaism and seldom intermarrying. Then, in the late 19th century, members of the freemasons and the *dönme*, a secret Jewish religious sect, sponsored and populated a group of radical military officers known as the "Young Turks." They became members of the Committee of Union and Progress, or C. U. P., which courted the Christian minority against the Ottomans. They stood against the religious zealots of the time in appearance only." Vasil seemed to have quite a command of history, and I listened with interest.

"In 1908, they put forth a supposed democratic constitution and proclaimed that all Christian minorities throughout the Ottoman Empire would have equal rights. After the Balkan Wars of 1912 when Thrace was taken by Greece, many "Mohammedans" of Jewish ancestry left Salonika and migrated to Turkey, many finally settling in the Arabic section of Constantinople. Within this group were certain Young Turks, who became the new leadership of Turkey that initiated the Christian Holocaust from 1915 to 1923. They formed the units of the Army Nihilisto which were later assimilated into the existing Committee of Union and Progress, which then dominated the government headed by Kamil Pasha, the Sultan's vizier.

"In 1913, led by a group of expelled Salonikan Jews, the Committee staged an effective military coup of the Turkish government and put the triumvirate of Enver Pasha, Jamal Pasha, and Talaat Pasha in control." Fascinated, I nodded, urging him to continue, the full import of his words not even having struck me.

"Parading as secular reformers, this band orchestrated the first holocaust of our bloody century," he continued. Of course, I knew very much about the Young Turks, but memories of them had not stirred my mind for many years. "The central committee of the Young Turk party, the C. U. P., the original Jewish group, was the core group that carried out the genocide which exterminated roughly a million and a half out of two million Armenians, one million out of two million Greeks, and countless numbers of Christians throughout the Balkans and Asia Minor. The Young Turks gave assurances to the rest of the world that they were separating government from religion and civilizing Turkey, but, as we Christians can all attest, nothing could have been further from the truth. They were engaging in a heinous form of ethnic cleansing, and the rest of the world was too busy or too preoccupied to care."

By now Vasil had the complete attention of the group. "Over the years, it has been claimed that the Turkish government was not responsible for these slaughters. Hogwash!"—the grunts of common knowledge resounded among the group. "The authors of the Christian holocaust controlled the Committee for Union and Progress, which controlled the Young Turks who, in turn, controlled the military of Turkey long before Atatürk was proclaimed president. Among the notable men who controlled the Committee were Mehmed Talaat Pasha, Ismail Enver Pasha, and Ahmed Jamal Pasha. The Committee formed the "butcher battalions," viciously uprooting and murdering over seventy percent of a law-abiding Christian population that numbered as high as five million at the turn of the century.

"Talaat Pasha, Enver Pasha and Jamal Pasha, who orchestrated the Armenian Christian slaughter, were of Jewish ancestry. Along with Atatürk, a Jew with Greek blood, they were members of the Jewish *dönme*. So was Dr. Selanikli Najim, their chief ideologist and purveyor of their mental poison." All around, people were shaking their heads in dumbfounded disbelief. This was news to us all! Still, he continued with the shocking revelations. "Enver was from Salonika. Mustapha Kemal, who ruled Turkey from 1920 to

1938, was from Salonika. With them was Emmanuel Carasso, a Turkish Jew from Salonika, who was the Grand Master of the freemasonic lodge known as "Macedonia Risorto," the strong benefactor of the Committee of Union and Progress.

"In 1916, Talaat and Jamal let it be known that all Jewish shop owners in Constantinople should mark their shops with red so they wouldn't be mistaken for Christian businesses. The fact that many elitist groups within the Committee for Union and Progress were Jewish has been suppressed, deliberately or not, but the extraordinary irony can be lost on no one. Let us not forget, either, that Jews comprised the great majority of Bolsheviks in Russia. In fact, the Young Turks were the first government in the world to recognize Lenin's gang of cutthroats after the Russian Revolution. There is a lot of evidence that indicates close ties between the Young Turks, Bolsheviks, and other revolutionary movements before they even seized power. A common link between all these groups is an extremely high number of Jews in their ranks, as well as nihilistic and relativistic philosophies guiding their actions in seeking to violently overthrow the existing order. The Jews were, indeed, the controlling element that orchestrated the slaughters and benefited greatly from the theft of Christian cultural and material wealth—in plain view of the ghosts of their rightful owners—not only in Asia Minor, but wherever these parasites gained power."

"Yes," I agreed finally. "Although that may be true, the Jews have been widely persecuted themselves." Not sure whether it was a question or a statement, I let my words hang.

"It's ironic, Chris, that the Christian holocaust was carried out by people of Jewish descent, and twenty years later Hitler used the Christian Holocaust—initiated by Jews—as a blueprint for his own holocaust against the Jews and others in Europe," Vasil responded. From behind his spectacles, Vasil's eyes searched mine.

"Vasil, there have been many holocausts that followed this— China, Russia and Germany to name a few. Why can't we learn to live in peace with each other?"

Neither he nor I had an answer. "Vasil, my friend, nothing under the sun is perfect," was all I could think of to say. "It is something to aspire to, something to strive for, to pray for, but we are only human, after all. All of us—Jews and Christians and

Mohammedans alike—have our human frailties that keep us from attaining the perfection our minds seek." He nodded his acknowledgement. "Sometimes people, and peoples, go awry. Only God knows why. Sometimes even basic kindness is beyond the human race, but we must always keep trying. Our effort confirms our civility."

When the meeting ended, Vasili took me aside. "Chris, here's a book on the uprooting I'd like you to read," he said, pressing the volume into my hands. "These materials go a long way toward revealing those truly responsible for this hideous genocide," he added, handing me several other books and magazine and newspaper clippings.

"Let the ghosts of the past rest in peace." I thanked Vasil realizing that what he said was true

Later, when I was alone, I examined the books and articles with interest. The material graphically showed the dramatic uprooting we were subjected to. Generations of my family's labor were stolen, and a whole way of life was lost. These nihilists erased our Byzantine civilization, stole its wealth, and called themselves the Young Turks. God, in his infinite wisdom, had made mankind a very twisted puzzle. Though the materials Vasil gave me I was reluctant to accept, as I read them they made perfect sense. They filled in many gaps and answered gnawing questions that had silently plagued me for many years.

* * * * *

The family life I was deprived of in my youth was something I never got enough of now with my own children, no matter what their ages. Perhaps that is why I cherished so deeply every opportunity I had to spend with my children, why I wished to give them everything.

By nine-thirty Elenitsa was up and found me reading the paper for a brief minute.

"I'll need to put the spinach pie in the oven," she told me.

"We've got time," I said. "Everything is organized. I'll put the turkey in the oven in about half an hour."

By eleven o'clock, Jon was up and showered and preparing the salad. I showed him the turkey baking in the lower oven. It was Thanksgiving Day. We planned to eat at two o'clock, and by one everything was as it should be. I went upstairs to freshen up and to put on a tie and jacket. On holidays like Christmas, Easter and Thanksgiving, I always dressed up to show respect for my family and the occasion. This was the way I was brought up. It was my tradition. As I dressed, I felt tired already from my preparations. Even putting on my tie seemed more effort than it warranted.

As the kids arrived, I was revived by the warmth and conviviality of my noisy family. Shortly after one o'clock Ianthe, Steve and Krislyn arrived. I greeted them warmly. "Hi, Cookie," I said with a warm hug.

"Hi, Daddy."

Soon Anthony and Lee Ann arrived with their children. I greeted them warmly, with kisses for Lee Ann and the children, who threw their arms around me and gave me hugs. My precious, precious grandchildren. They were worthy of a feast prepared by their Greek Granddad and Yiayia. Each moment with them was a godsend.

For a while they chatted, sipped their drinks and munched on shrimp appetizers while I shuffled back and forth preparing to serve the various foods. Then I ushered my family into the dining room and seated everyone around the table. This year Katelyn, now seven, offered to say grace, and when she had finished I cleared my throat and offered some words of my own:

"Thank you God for allowing us to celebrate another year together and for looking over us. Thank you for the beautiful food you have provided. Please protect us and grant us good health for another year if it is your will. Amen."

"Amen," my family chorused.

Then I felt inspired. "I will offer a toast," I said, lifting my wineglass. "To all the children, to your health, happiness and successful lives. You have every opportunity in life. Remember, if you put your mind to it, nothing is impossible."

The older children raised their wineglasses to mine in acknowledgement, the younger ones their milk and Sprite, toasting each other, and me, and the festive occasion of being together.

Later that evening after everyone had gone, Elenitsa and I sat quietly reading and watching TV. "That went well, Chris, didn't it?" she remarked.

"Yes, very well," I said. "Everything was fine."

"Ianthe's baby, Krislyn...and Brian, Katelyn and Ashley...those kids are really something," she mused.

"You can say that again," I smiled. "They really are."

* * * * *

I had been thinking quite a lot about Anthony's growing family. A neighbor pointed out a house to me that was in a different development but just one block away. It was a split level, about twenty-four hundred square feet. I thought it would be perfect for Lee Ann and the kids, and I had mentioned it to Anthony before Christmas. His visit that Thanksgiving reminded me to ask him about it.

"I drove by the house the other day," he said casually. "It seems pretty nice."

"Pursue it, Anthony," I urged him. "The old lady who lived there died, so maybe her heirs will sell for a reasonable price."

"Okay, Dad," he said. "I'll check it out." Suddenly, he smiled. "Thanks."

* * * * *

That New Year's Eve, Elenitsa and I stayed up to watch the ball drop in Times Square.

"I'm tired," Elenitsa yawned.

"Only ten more minutes," I told her, handing her a glass of champagne.

"Shouldn't we wait until midnight?"

"Well, it's almost midnight. In fact, it's already midnight in other parts of the world."

"Well, that's a thought," Elenitsa smiled and took my hand in hers.

"Elenitsa, remember when we were first starting out? Remember the boarding house?"

"And how we used to leave the milk on the window sill to keep it cold?"

"Ah, yes," I chuckled. "The good old days. We were so happy to get an apartment with a kitchen. Do you remember the Tyler Garden Apartments?"

"Oh yes, with the paper thin walls you could hear your neighbors through."

"And the rambler, our little rambler," I said. "Our first home."

Elenitsa nodded. "I miss that house, except..."

"Except what?"

"Except you were never there. I felt like a single parent, raising the children alone," she said, beginning a replay of old complaints, but lacking the conviction of a current battle.

"My gosh, still talking about that... We've had a good life, Elenitsa," I told her. "God has been good to us. We have our children and grandchildren, and we have our health. My life has by some measures been more difficult than most, but I feel nothing but proud and blessed."

"Oh, Chris..."

In Times Square, the crowd counted off the last ten seconds of the old year as the ball descended. At the stroke of midnight, I raised my glass to Elenitsa.

"Happy 1994, Elenitsa."

After 46 years, she was still my Elenitsa, once my burning passion, and now my life's companion and confidante. I took her small, careworn face in my hands and looked deeply into her familiar eyes as I kissed her with the warm emotions of past and present.

"Happy New Year, Chris," she said.

In the days that followed, I experienced a little weakness in my arms and legs, and sometimes my heart would race when I went up the stairs. I told myself these were cold symptoms, but secretly feared it was more.

The Hellenic Society New Year's dinner dance was approaching, and I began to round up my family for the event. I called Ianthe and told her I had tickets if she could make it.

"I wish we could, Daddy, but Steve has to work late and—" Abruptly she switched topics. "Daddy, what's wrong with you?"

"Wrong?"

"You sound...breathless."

"Oh, I have a cold."

"Take care of yourself. Please, Daddy."

"I will, Cookie. Don't worry."

After I talked with her, I called Anthony, who promised to come.

"I'm glad Anthony is coming with us, Elenitsa. I want to introduce him to more of the members."

She nodded. "Yes, it's more fun when the children come."

I spent the rest of the evening in my flannel pajamas, drinking hot tea and reading my encyclopedias in an effort to shake that stubborn cold. My cold hung on, and later that week the first of three ice storms hit the Washington area. The weather was a mess with freezing winds and a four-inch snow topped by frozen sleet and rain. Despite my cold, I went out and broke a path through the ice down the steps to the cul-de-sac, then readied the car. That evening Elenitsa and I met Anthony, Lee Ann and the kids at the nearby Westpark Marriott for the New Year's dance.

I took Anthony around and introduced him to Vasili Uzanoglu, John Delta, his brother Dr. Vasili Delta, and a number of other Society members. We didn't discuss the Holocaust much that evening, but we did have fun. The turnout was pretty good—over seventy people attended the event, including about ten kids. It didn't merit a live band, but we had taped music and before I knew it I was holding hands with my two beautiful granddaughters and once again dancing in a circle to the music of a Greek mandolin...one, two, kick...one, two, kick. This time it was Katelyn who was leading.

The music excited the kids, and Ashley, laughing merrily, began to tease her big sister. Katelyn stood with her hands on her hips and fixed her sister with a stare.

"Shut up, Ashley!" she commanded, but Ashley was laughing and kicking and having such a good time that soon I began to laugh as well. Finally, Katelyn joined in the merriment and all three of us were happily dancing again. Here I was, an old man dancing with his two lovely granddaughters. What more fun could I imagine?

* * * * *

The next week my cold worsened and Elenitsa had me in to see Dr. Anderson, a heart specialist who had seen me over recent years, but the only thing he determined was that I had bradycardia, or a slow heart beat. Dr. Anderson suggested a pacemaker, but I replied that black coffee with a tad of skim milk had been sufficient to get my heart going each and every morning.

"Well, Chris, you sound a little congested, but otherwise you seem okay. I want you to walk on the treadmill for a while."

The treadmill, which was similar to the one at the health club I had recently joined, was wired to give the doctor all sorts of information about my cardiovascular system. The results of the tests showed nothing wrong, but the doctor prescribed an antibiotic, just in case. I also picked up some cold medicine.

My weakness continued intermittently, however, and I soon came to believe that something was indeed very wrong. I did not speak of it to Elenitsa or anyone, preferring instead to continue my daily activities, though at a slower pace. No matter what physical blows life dealt you, a positive attitude only served to brighten your prospects, which in turn improved the condition. There was nothing to be gained by turning morose.

One evening, my old friend Lincoln Vance called. For years he had been caring for his wife, Kitty, and was now mourning her recent death. Elenitsa answered the phone and talked to him first, so by the time she gave the phone to me Lincoln knew I was not exactly well.

"How are you feeling?" he asked right away. "Elenitsa sounded worried."

"Well, I have the flu," I told him.

"It's not anything more serious, is it?"

"Oh, no...just a bad cold. Listen, Lincoln," I said briskly, changing the subject, "as soon as the weather improves, we must go out for coffee and talk."

"You bet, Chris. It will be my pleasure." Lincoln paused, then added, "I have a lot of respect for you, Chris, and I always enjoy your company. Take care of yourself and I'll see you soon."

Not long after my conversation with Lincoln, a second ice storm swept the area, and for the first two weeks in February a weather pattern of extremely cold temperatures kept everything frozen. My flu seemed to parallel the weather—the colder it got, the worse I felt. Just climbing the stairs of my house left me weak and out of breath. I began to wonder if I would ever see the bloom of my azaleas again.

The freezing rain weighed down the power lines, toppled trees and left a glaze of ice on the hill surrounding my home, making it impossible to come and go until the weather broke. At least we still had electricity. Many families were without power.

After a week of being "frozen in," Anthony came to see if we needed anything, driving carefully over the ice-covered streets into our cul-de-sac. As soon as he saw me, a frown creased his forehead.

"How are you feeling, Dad?" he asked concerned.

I shrugged. "I'm okay. I still have that cold."

"He hasn't felt good for over two weeks," Elenitsa interjected.

Anthony looked at me in concern. "You need to go to the doctor," he said.

"I've been to the doctor," I told him. "I'll be fine. Look, I want to take you and Lee Ann and Ianthe and Steve and all the kids out for your mother's birthday. She's going to be 72, you know."

"Dad, no...you don't have the money to do that right now."

My son was right, although I didn't like to admit it. "Well then, would you prefer to come over here for dinner?"

"Yes, we'd like that, but I don't want you to wear yourself out."

"I'm not about to do that. I'll prepare something easy...it won't be the usual, nothing special, so don't worry."

I could see Anthony was not convinced. "Where's your snow shovel, Dad? I want to clear your walk and driveway."

"I'll get to it later..."

"No, Dad. You don't need to do that. Is it out in the garage?"

I told him where to find the shovel and then I stood at the window and watched as he scraped my driveway free of ice. When he left that afternoon, I reminded him about his mother's birthday, and told him to arrive at two o'clock on Sunday. Then I called Jon in Ocean City.

"I want you to come up next Sunday for your mother's birthday."

"I don't think I can make it."

"Yes, you can," I said firmly. "It's your mother's birthday."

Actually, this was an unusual request. Normally, I did not make such a big deal over our birthdays—Elenitsa's and mine—especially when it came to Jon who had a long way to come. Besides, Jon valued his privacy. Although he worked hard for six months of the year, the remaining six he stayed in Ocean City, leaving the island only for holidays and an occasional Civil War reenactment.

"But Dad..."

I heard the resistance in his voice. If Jon had a wife, it might not only civilize his lifestyle, but perhaps make it easier to get him off the island once in a while.

"Is there any special reason why I need to come?" he asked finally.

"Yes," I told him sharply "because I *want* you to come."

The truth was, I did not completely understand why this was so important to me. We had been together for Christmas and our usual protocol called for a gathering at Easter. This was only late February and Easter was not that many weeks away, but for some reason I felt an urgency to bring everyone together for Elenitsa's birthday, and if that meant arguing with Jon, so be it.

"Okay, Dad," he sighed. "I'll be there."

Relieved that all the children and grandchildren would come, I retired to my office to put some bills in order. That evening as I went through my bills, I realized that for the first time in twenty-two years, I had not sent in my monthly check or my order form for my 1994 commemorative stamps. Well, that was okay, I decided. The repetitive ice storms and my recent weakness had distracted me. Besides, money was a little tight. I would just take a pass on those stamps this year.

The frigid weather and my weakened condition had brought on a temperamental introspection that was uncharacteristic. The foreboding insistence with which I had made Elenitsa's birthday a family gathering in spite of the inclement weather gave the event an air of unintended urgency, the urgency of a tired old man short on time.

25
Twilight

"O Captain! my Captain!
Our fearful trip is done;
The ship has weather'd every rack,
The prize we sought is won;
The port is near, the bells I hear..."

—Walt Whitman
"O Captain! My Captain"

That Sunday, the ice had melted and cold, foggy drizzle shrouded the streets. The inclement drear made me wonder whether I would see the bud and bloom of my flowery little friends one last time. The weather had improved enough to allow everyone to arrive on time for their mother's birthday celebration. Elenitsa made the same lemon pound cake she always made for my birthday, and I prepared a simple meal with what was on hand— baked chicken, broccoli, pita bread and kasari cheese. I was a bit embarrassed by the ordinary meal. The simplicity was out of character for me, and I found myself apologizing for the sparse spread.

"Ianthe, I'm sorry I don't have much."

"Oh, Daddy, don't be silly," she said. "This is fine! We came to see you and mom anyway."

When we sat down at the table, I took a long lingering look at all the faces around me. The prayer I offered was simple.

"Thank you God for bringing us together. Thank you for this food. Please grant us health throughout the year and watch over us. Amen."

"Amen," my family chorused.

I sat my beautiful granddaughters on either side of me. Brian sat next to his sister Katelyn, and Krislyn sat in her high chair beside her mother but near enough so I could see her. Much of dinner I spent in humorous discourse with my grandchildren. I showed Ashley how to hold her fingers to make the sign of the cross, and then teased her until she squealed with laughter.

"I'm going to squeeze the juice out of you!" I joked, hugging her tightly in a big bear hug.

"No, Granddad," she protested between giggles. "No, no, no!"

Eventually we cleared the table and I brought the cake, complete with a single lit candle, to the dining room.

"Happy birthday to you..." I sang, and soon the rest of the family joined me, singing and honoring Elenitsa on her seventy-second birthday.

That evening when Ianthe bundled up Krislyn and prepared to leave, I held her close for an unusually long time.

"Good night, Daddy," she said a little quizzically, kissing my cheek.

"Good night, Cookie. You and Steve take good care of Krislyn."

"We will, Daddy," she smiled, and a minute later they were gone.

By now Anthony and Lee Ann were getting ready to go. I watched as Anthony snugged a cap over Brian's head, then I touched his arm and took him aside.

"Anthony, what have you done about the house?" referring to the one around the corner.

"I spoke with the people who own the house," Anthony told me, "and this week I'm going to see it."

"You need a bigger house to raise your children," I told him.

"I'm looking into it, Dad," Anthony smiled. "I promise."

Before I could reply, the children came up to hug me goodbye. Lee Ann kissed Elenitsa and then embraced me. I loved her as if she were my own daughter, and returned her hug with one of my own. Then I turned to embrace my son. Even though he towered over me, I sometimes felt like he was still my little boy. "Take care of your family," I said, reluctant to let him go.

"I will, Dad." Anthony pulled away from me a bit. "How are you feeling?" he asked, his voice low. "You should get checked, Dad."

I knew he noticed that I still wasn't quite myself. "I'm okay, Anthony," I tried to reassure him. "I have a cold, that's all. Don't worry about me."

Jon came up. "You're leaving in the morning?" I asked him.

"Yes, Dad," he said, eyeing me with a familiar concern.

Later that night Elenitsa and I spent a quiet hour watching TV and reading.

"You know, Chris," she said, putting aside her book and standing up. "I had a lovely time. It was so good to have all the children here today, wasn't it?"

"Yes it was," I smiled, poking the smoldering ash that remained in the fireplace.

"I'm going to go to bed," she said, kissing my cheek.

"I'll be up shortly," I told her, patting her hand.

I watched the news on TV and then followed Elenitsa upstairs. Halfway up the steps, I paused and looked down into the hall. This was my house and I loved it. At that moment, I knew that my time was short. Soon, God would call me home, but I felt no regret. I had led the life that Mama and Papa had wished for me, and I suddenly felt their presence very near.

* * * * *

My flu-like symptoms were growing in intensity. Elenitsa plied me with honey-lemon tea and various remedies, but nothing really worked. I tried to remain quiet, watching TV and reading, and I spent a couple of icy evenings thumbing through an interesting book I had ordered on Thrace. It covered the troubled eleven-year period from 1912 to 1923, beginning with the Balkan Wars and spanning World War One. Under the Treaty of Lausanne, during the exchange of populations, part of Thrace, which was a Greek province, was set aside for Mohammedans and, in return, part of Constantinople was set aside for Christians. At the time of the agreement, early in 1923, the population of Mohammedans in Thrace was approximately 150,000, with roughly the same number of Christians in Constantinople. Over the past seventy years, however, while the Mohammedan population in Thrace has grown, the number of Christians in Constantinople has dwindled to fewer than seven thousand, a testament to the ongoing difficulties Christians faced in Turkey. My mind wandered to Vasil Uzanoglu, to the genocidal tyranny of the Young Turks and their shrouded background.

I turned to my *Britannicas* and found an article on Atatürk. I read about his origins in Greece and his reputation as the "father of modern Turkey." There was little mention of his deadly actions against the Greeks and Christians.

In this century, the century of holocausts, it is correct to say that the Christian population and Byzantine culture in Asia Minor has been largely exterminated or uprooted. It is a bit ironic that a great country like America, whose population is largely Christian—a country that champions justice and undertakes to help so many downtrodden—is unable or unwilling to outline in a history book the details of this slaughter, or to help even the handful of Christians who remain at the holy site of the Patriarchate in Constantinople, a Christian shrine dating back to the fifth century. As the light of the Byzantine period is slowly extinguished, the Christian world seems uninformed or couched in indifference to its significance. Soon my thoughts strayed from my reading. Even it could not hold my energy or attention too long.

I shut my *Britannica*.

Late one evening after Elenitsa had gone to bed, I looked at the pages of photographs throughout my book on Thrace, arrested by pictures of lovely red and yellow flowers. The climate in Thrace, I decided, must be more European than Mediterranean. I closed my eyes for a moment, visualizing my azaleas in bloom and hoping that I would see them one more time.

Perhaps I fell into a doze, for suddenly I could see Papa and hear his voice. "America is a great country," he was saying. "Surely the civilized world will know the wrongs done here. In time, Chrysostomos, they will know."

"No, Papa, " I responded. "It has been over seventy years and I am sorry, Papa, but they don't know. I am an old man now, and they still don't know. I am sorry, Papa. I'm so sorry."

"Chris!" Elenitsa called down the stairs, startling me into wakefulness. "Are you coming to bed?

Startled and confused, I called back "Soon," and stopped before I added "Mama."

A little while later as I undressed for bed, I kissed the relic coin Papa had given me so long ago and whispered a familiar prayer: "Thank You, God, for giving me health and strength. Thank You for my family, for my wife and children, grandchildren—all the flowers of my life. Almighty God, if You are ready to take me, I will come to You without fear, for all my fears are in life, not death. I remain Your servant. Amen."

In the darkness, Elenitsa stirred. "Chris, did you say something?"

"No dear, nothing," I reassured her. "Go back to sleep."

* * * * *

In March, the temperature rose sufficiently to once again reduce the ice to a messy slush. That evening I called Jon.

"Have you talked to MacGilligot?"

"Not yet."

"See if you can get him to give us a check."

"Okay, Dad. I'll do that tomorrow. How are you feeling'"

"Not bad," I told him, hedging a little. "How about you?"

"I'm fine. I have a Civil War reenactment coming up in a couple of weeks."

"Jon," I said suddenly. "You know how we prepare the turkey at Thanksgiving, the lamb and rice pilaf at Christmas and Easter? I mean, you know how we do it, don't you?"

"Sure, Dad. Why do you ask?"

"I want you to continue the tradition every year with your brother and sister...you understand?"

"Of course, but—"

"Just remember," I said firmly, cutting him off. "I want you to stay together as a family."

"Yes, Dad. Of course, I promise."

"And be sure to take care of yourself."

"I will, Dad," Jon said, sounding puzzled. "Is anything wrong?"

"No, no, I'm just giving out some fatherly advice. I want you to try to straighten yourself up."

Everyone knew this was code for getting married. Jon knew I wanted him to marry and have a family—I had made no secret of that.

"Don't worry about me, Dad," he said, and I could hear the smile in his voice. "I'll be fine."

Later that evening I called Ianthe.

"I'm coming over to plant azaleas tomorrow," I told her. "They're from my garden."

"That will be fine, Daddy. I'm glad you're coming."

"You'll like the azaleas," I told her. "You'll see how beautiful they are when they bloom."

Digging up two azaleas the next morning was a tougher job than I remembered it to be. I was both tired and relieved when the planting was complete. Although my body was becoming quite frail, my spirits lifted as I worked in the sunshine and saw the early signs of spring all around me. Soon my beautiful friends would bloom.

When I finished planting, I went inside to say goodbye to my daughter.

"Thank you, Daddy," she smiled, "I can't wait to see them bloom."

"Take care of yourself," I said as I embraced her. "Take care of little Krislyn, too."

"I will Daddy," she said, hugging me back. "I'll see you soon."

"Perhaps not," I replied as I prepared to leave. "Perhaps…I may not see you for a while."

For an instant Ianthe appeared startled by my words. Then she shook her head and smiled, brushing her hand in the air dismissing such talk.

* * * * *

The following morning, I went about my routine, but had a heavy feeling in my chest, and I decided not to go to church. My mind was alert but my poor body was worn out. Over sixty-five years of long days and heavy toil had taken their toll.

"Is it my time?" I whispered in a prayer.

The weighty feeling in my chest had plagued me off and on in the past, but this time it had been seven weeks and I simply could not shake it. I went slowly downstairs to my den and sat at my desk. All the pictures of my life were arranged around that room: my children, grandchildren, sisters, brother, nieces, nephews, parents, aunts and uncles. My eyes rested on poor Uncle Russo and Aunt Cleo. How kind they were to me in my youth! How far away my boyhood seemed now. There was Mama with her warm smile and Papa with his handlebar mustache and gentle eyes. My, my, I missed them all so much.

For several long minutes I sat there surrounded by the pictures of my life. How quickly it all had passed! Days, weeks, months, years, decades...all gone to eternity, just so many specks in the infinite parade of time. I was filled with so many memories, fleeting moments held captive in my mind.

Suddenly I realized that after I died, Anthony, as my eldest son, would be responsible for my bills and obligations. I also realized that he had not inherited any of my organizational skills. Come to think of it, none of my children had. Unfortunately, in that department they took after their mother.

Anthony would need as much help as I could give him if he was to manage things after I was gone. So I got out my will and placed it squarely on the top of my desk. Beside it, I placed several other important papers that he would need to attend to, and I wrote specific instructions about each:

I have a fifteen-thousand-dollar note, interest due quarterly, from First Virginia Bank last fall. It is secured with my vehicle. If you need an extension, see Mrs. Seal. I have a second loan at Home Bank for twenty-five thousand dollars that I borrowed last April in addition to the loan on the stores. Jon can see Mr. Parker and he will extend the term if needed. My cemetery plot as well as Mother's are bought and paid for. Be careful of the other charges. The documents are right here. There are some coins that I have labeled for Ianthe, Jon and for you, Anthony—equally divided. I have collected them over the years.

I scribbled away for some time, clipping each set of instructions to the relevant documents. Then I straightened my desk and arranged everything neatly as was my habit. I had prided myself over the course of my life with not being a burden to anyone, and I certainly didn't intend to become one in death. All my worldly business was carefully stacked on the center of my desk where Anthony could not fail to see it.

* * * * *

Later that morning my nephew Peter—Taki's and Sultana's son—called to tell me he had found a book about Imbroz printed by Amnesty International. "It's fascinating!" he said. "It tells about all the atrocities that were committed there when you were young, Theo Christo."

Oddly, I was not as interested in this as I might have been a few weeks or months earlier, but I listened as he told me what he had read, and then I asked about his family. What had inflamed my passion just a short while ago seemed almost not to matter, as if it all had existed in a movie or a play.

That afternoon Lincoln Vance called and we made a date to go out for coffee the next day. "I'll pick you up at nine in the morning," I told him, pleased at the prospect of seeing him again.

As I watched the news that evening, I had the pleasant feeling of having accomplished a great deal. Truthfully, I was relieved to have gotten so many details out of the way in preparation for whatever tomorrow might bring, but there were still a few things left to do. There never seemed to be enough time to finish the work of life.

The next morning over coffee at McDonald's, Lincoln and I chatted about current events and caught up on each other's news. Since Lincoln didn't have children he was always interested in mine.

"I expect you're happy to get Ianthe married off," he said.

"You can't imagine, Lincoln."

"And Anthony, how is he?"

"He is well, Lincoln, but I am not sure he's accomplishing much in life."

"I've always thought very highly of that young man," Lincoln remarked. "Perhaps he's a late bloomer."

"Thank you, Lincoln—that must be it," I chuckled. "Now, if we could just get Jon married off—"

"You could die happy!" finished Lincoln with a laugh. It struck me, though, that I could most certainly, at any moment, die happy.

We chatted like this for an hour or so, and then I drove Lincoln home. As he got out of the car, he hesitated.

"Chris, you know, you're the only Greek I would ever do business with."

"Oh, come on, Lincoln," I laughed.

"It's true." He paused, looking at me seriously. Then, out of the blue, "Are you okay, Chris?"

"Oh, sure, Lincoln. I'm fine."

"I hope so, Chris," he offered in parting. "I sure hope so."

I lifted my hand in farewell, pulled away from the curb and headed home thinking I was getting a little tired of people asking me if I was okay!

Later that day Anthony called and wanted to show me the interior of the house I had found for him. I liked the house and said so. "You'll have lots of room here," I told him.

"Yes," he agreed, looking at the spacious rooms around us. "Twenty-four hundred square feet, compared to the thousand feet I have now."

"When will you close on it?"

"Well, I'm waiting to have my loan approved. I might close in a week or two."

I shook my head regretfully. "I wish I could help you, Anthony," I said.

"Dad, you've spent your whole life helping all of us. We'll be fine, honest."

"I'm very happy to have you and Lee Ann and the children only a block away. Very happy."

"Yes, it's a nice house."

"Anthony," I went on, "I want you to promise me something. I want you to promise me that you won't ever put your mother into a nursing home."

Anthony looked at me strangely. "Of course not, Dad," he said, his eyes on mine. "Are you okay?" he asked.

Was it that apparent? I felt my body failing. I might look a little tired, but I didn't think my physical appearance was alarming anyone. It must have been my need to prepare. I could not seem to contain my anxiety that my children would not be ready, and I think this was showing.

"Sure, I'm fine, thanks, just fine," I said, but I could tell that my son was concerned. As we drove back to my house I felt the same heaviness in my chest rendering me silent. This time I felt the heaviness in my arms, legs and torso as well, and I knew I couldn't blame it on the weather. I wasn't in pain, but I was very tired, and my breathing was increasingly short and shallow. My mind was alert and agile, but my body was winding down like an old clock.

That evening I called Katina in New York. Although Elenitsa kept in touch, Katina and I had not talked except briefly at Taki's funeral. My sister's voice brought forth feelings long gone to time and circumstance.

At first we inquired politely about each other's families, and then I came to the point.

"Katina, I am sorry for what happened, for getting mad at you about Mama's and Papa's house. It was wrong of me. You were alone and you had no choice."

For a moment Katina was silent. "It's been so many years, Chrysostomos," she said. "We are no longer there. What does it matter?"

"Katina, remember that time you and I roamed off to play and came home after sundown? Mama and Papa were so worried and angry."

My sister laughed. "Yes, and Papa spanked you."

"That was the only time he ever did. Poor Mama and Papa. I tried, but they wouldn't come to America."

"You know Papa, Chrysostomos. He was so stubborn. He would never leave our house, Turks or no Turks."

"That is true, Katina. And you...you gave up everything to care for them."

"Don't think of that. That was so many years ago. I have no regrets. My years with Mama and Papa are my fondest memories. Chrysostomos, they were so fond of you, so proud of you. Hardly a day would go by when it wasn't mentioned—'My son is a success in America!'"

We laughed.

"Besides," she went on, "thanks to you, Costa, and Sultana, I have so many lovely nieces and nephews!"

"Ah, Katina…"

"The years have gone, little brother. It doesn't matter now. Our island, Mama and Papa…even the Turks…None of it matters now."

I saw the sense of what she was saying. "I believe you are right," I said. "God bless you, Katina."

The next day, Anthony called. "Dad, our loan has been approved, and the owners don't mind if we move in some things before we go to closing. Lee Ann's boxing up stuff now and we plan to move in on Sunday afternoon."

Anthony's news pleased me. "Mother and I will help you, God willing," I said. "How about if we meet you at three on Sunday? Are you going to church?"

"I don't think so, Dad. Not this Sunday."

"Well, then, we'll see you at the house at three."

"Okay, Dad, thank you." He paused. "Are you feeling better?"

"Anthony…don't worry about me. Tend to your family."

"Dad…"

"I still have this cold," I admitted finally, "but I'm feeling better, thank you."

"Good, Dad. I'm pleased to hear that. I'll see you Sunday, then."

"Yes, Sunday, but…one thing…"

"Yes?"

"Remember what we talked about a few days ago? About your mother?"

"Yes…no nursing home."

"That's right. I just want to make sure you remember."

"I'll remember, Dad. Honest. What's this all about?"

"See you Sunday," I said.

The weather was finally warming and that afternoon I went out and surveyed my yard. Hands folded behind my back I walked the rows of azaleas, stopping occasionally to remove a fallen branch or twig from my plants. I busied myself like this for quite some time, as if preparing a stage for the colorful show my plants would make. They were just about to bloom and I longed to see them.

That evening I was restless and stayed up to watch the late news. Five minutes into the newscast there was a story from New York City. "A tragic accident occurred in Manhattan this evening. Two Greek Orthodox priests have been fatally stuck by a car driven by a drug addict. The deceased priests are Father Demetrios Frangos, secretariat of the Archdiocese, and Father Germanos Stavropoulos, Chancellor of the Archdiocese. Father Frangos was eighty years old and Father Germanos was in his fifties. The Hispanic driver of the car is reported to have been speeding and driving recklessly. This is a tragic accident and a big loss for the Greek Orthodox Church."

This was astounding news. I made my way upstairs and nudged Elenitsa awake. "Father Frangos and Father Germanos are dead," I told her, and gave her the details of the accident. "Imagine, two Christian priests who survived the Holocaust being taken this way," I lamented.

"Oh, Chris," she said, patting my hand. "How very, very sad."

"It is," I agreed. Then, thinking of Jimmy Coucouzes, I added, "And how hard for the old Archbishop!"

* * * * *

The next morning, Saturday, I was at the health club at precisely eight o'clock. After changing and stretching my legs, I got on the treadmill and began walking. I usually walked thirty to forty minutes, but after my winter layoff from exercise these last weeks I was uncertain how it would go. After twenty minutes, sweat was beading on my forehead and running down my neck. I was out of breath and my legs were tired. I would try to go another two minutes before quitting.

I gazed down at my feet as they methodically plodded along the treadmill and I almost dozed off. Suddenly, in my mind's eye, I saw an image of Mama.

"Chrysostomos, I have made you shoes...put them on, put them on..."

"Yes, Mama..." I started to whisper, then suddenly I snapped awake. Such an odd daydream, I thought, stepping off the treadmill. I changed back into street clothes and on the way home I stopped at the grocery store for some lentils. By the time I got home I was feeling weak and tired. I took out the lentils and began to prepare dinner.

That evening was marked by unusual peacefulness and quiet. As was our habit, after supper Elenitsa and I sat in the family room, read and watched the news.

"You know, Elenitsa, the kids are doing well," I said.

Elenitsa looked up from her book. "They are, aren't they? And you know, I love our grandchildren," she said happily. "If only Jon would marry..."

"Honey, Jon is grown, he will have to decide himself when to marry. There is little we can do." Then we began reminiscing, recalling old times when the children were small... It seemed like yesterday, and in our minds it was. Somehow the years had slipped by and now here we were, remembering fondly the things that once were.

"Elenitsa, it wasn't too bad, was it?" I asked. "Our lives...and everything."

"Of course it was good, honey. The children, their families."

"I mean us, Elenitsa, us."

She stared at me. "Of course it was. Oh, so many years and memories!" She smiled. "I'm tired, dear. I'm going up to bed."

"Let me give you a kiss," I said, "and I'll be up shortly."

I opened a volume of the *Encyclopedia Britannica* in my lap. There was never enough time to finish things, I reflected. Another half-hour...I'll read for another half-hour before I go up to bed.

* * * * *

The next morning as I dressed for church, I glanced out the window and there were the first signs of pinks, reds, whites and pastels. My azaleas had begun to bloom! I went outside to survey them in my church suit.

"Look, Elenitsa, my azaleas, they've bloomed! I called as I came back inside. "Look!"

"Yes, Chris, you can look at them some more later. Christina is waiting for us," she called back. Christina had been widowed twenty years before, and we made it a habit to take her to church.

We sat in the center row, directly in front of the altar, next to my physician, Tom Mandes, and his wife. For the first time in my life, I had to sit during the service.

Mrs. Mandes leaned toward me. "Chris, are you all right?"

"Fine, fine, thank you," I responded in what was now becoming a familiar refrain. "I am fine," I assured her and looked straight ahead to discourage further discussion.

After services we went downstairs for a few brief minutes of 'coffee and friendship.' The congregation was abuzz with news of the tragic deaths of the priests. It was not often that the Greek Orthodox Church made the evening news, and these were men many of us had met and known personally. Then I collected Elenitsa and Christina and took them to the Key Bridge Marriott for brunch. It was a beautiful spring day, and after such a harsh winter it was all the more welcome and appreciated.

A little later as I was changing my clothes I glanced out the bedroom window. There they were...my friends the azaleas, blossoming in a beautiful array of color. During that cold, frigid winter I had often wondered if I would see my beautiful friends again. I descended the stairs, hardly aware of my weakened state, and called out to Elenitsa.

"I'll be in the yard with my azaleas if you need me."

"When do we have to leave to help Anthony and Lee Ann?"

"Not until two forty-five," I told her, glancing at the kitchen clock. It was barely one o'clock. I had an hour on this beautiful spring day to be alone with my plants.

I went out the kitchen door and walked across the lawn to my favorite red azaleas that stood nearly seven feet high, sparkling with the new spring's dew drops on their little red buds.

"You didn't forget me," I said to them. Like a wide-eyed kid, I gazed at the glorious blossoms, a beautiful pageantry of stimulating colors.

"Honey, you see the azaleas?"

"Yes dear," she replied through the cracked kitchen door.

This quiet spring event never ceased to amaze me. It was the simplest things in life that revealed to me the glory of God's creation. God is in the little things. With a firm, formal gait, I moved down the long pastel row of reds, pinks, oranges and purples, one color spilling into another. Most of the buds, though not yet fully open, had begun to blossom, and the colors were brilliant and captivating. Hands clasped behind my back, I strolled the full perimeter of my yard, proudly surveying my rainbow of blossoms like a general inspecting his troops. The time passed unnoticed. Pleasantly tired by my rambles, I was back at the kitchen door.

"Elenitsa," I said, stepping into the kitchen, "I'm going to the other room to rest a bit before we go. Wake me a little after 2:30."

"Okay, Chris."

I opened the window and blinds, allowing warm shafts of sunlight to spill into the room. Then I turned and settled myself comfortably in a corner of the sofa next to the window. Hands folded behind my neck, as was my habit, I basked in the restful sunshine. Old habits do indeed die reluctantly. I dozed off with the warmth of the sun on my face, the blossoms of the azaleas dancing inside my eyelids, and the satisfaction of a life well lived.

Epilogue

My Dearest Son, ...my advice to you is (1) your expenses should not exceed your income; (2) self-interest shouldn't separate you from family; (3) if your country calls, go to her aid; (4) no matter how high you rise in life, never lose your humility.

—Papa Ioanni, April 11, 1945

He was a colored man, muscular and sinewy who, although sixty years of age, pedaled his twelve-speed bike with the ease of a man half his age. At dawn on the Bay Bridge, which stretches four-and-a-half miles across the Chesapeake Bay directly east of Washington, D. C., his muscular silhouette looked misplaced and at the same time artistic. He was biking from Berlin, Maryland, to St. Sophia Cathedral in Washington, a one-hundred-and-sixty-mile trip, to attend the funeral of his long-time friend Mr. Christ.

Bernard rarely attended funerals, but this was different. Mr. Christ had given him his first job, and Bernard had worked for him for nearly forty years, off and on. More than an employer, Mr. Christ was like the father Bernard had never had.

Bernard had peddled non-stop all night just to reach the bridge by sun-up, and the cathedral was still forty-three miles away. Bernard didn't think about the distance. Instead, he thought about the battery in the headlight of his bike, and was relieved it had survived the night.

In the morning's first light, on the suspension bridge two hundred feet above the Bay, the Maryland state trooper driving alongside did not know what to make of Bernard. At first he thought he should ticket him for riding a bike across the bridge. Then he wondered if Bernard was a vagrant, or if perhaps he should be taken to the state hospital in Cambridge. Using his spotlight he examined the bike as well as its rider, from the tassels hanging from the handlebars, to the horn and headlight, to the foxtail on the back. When the light flickered on Bernard's face, he offered the trooper an unthreatening, friendly smile.

Driving parallel to the bike at about twenty miles an hour, the officer picked up his microphone and switched on the speaker. "There are no bicycles allowed on the bridge," he announced sternly. Then curiosity got the better of the officer. "What are you doing?" he asked in a milder tone.

"Mr. Christ died, sir," Bernard replied as he pedaled, "and I'm going to his funeral in Washington the only way I know how. And you got to excuse me, sir, 'cause if I don't get going I'm gonna to be late."

The trooper, who had no idea who Mr. Christ was, considered the spectacle pedaling so intently across the bridge in the grey light of first dawn, and finally shook his head and turned off his spotlight. "Bike carefully," he finally admonished Bernard, then sped on past.

"Yes, sir," Bernard called after him, never wavering from his focus on Washington, still several hours away. He didn't want to be late for Mr. Christ's funeral.

* * * * *

"Theologos, get up...we'll miss the train. You don't want to be late, do you?"

The old man opened his eyes. The receded hairline outlined a worn and wrinkled face, engraved by decades. He threw back the covers and slid out of bed.

"Of course I'm going," Theologos told Anna, his wife. As he slowly pulled up his trousers he thought of his good friend. "We must pay our respects to Chrysostomos," he said quietly. Reaching into the closet for a fresh, white shirt, Theologos went on, half to himself, "He was my dear friend...he brought me to the Embassy...he introduced us to each other." He sat in silence for a moment, losing himself in memory. Snapping back to the present, Theologos glanced at the clock on the bedside table and calculated the time he needed to shower, dress and drive to the station. The train for Washington left Altoona at 6:30 a. m. and would arrive at Union Station at nine that morning.

415

"Honey, are you sure you should go?" Anna asked her husband worriedly as he finished dressing. "You haven't been feeling well, and you know you're not a young man any more."

Theologos sighed heavily at his wife's concern. "I'm an old man but Chris is from my island," his voice heavy but deliberate. "Like me, he struggled hard to come to America. I haven't seen him for many years, Anna, but Chris and I were very close and he was a special man." Anna knew it was true. She knew the depth of feeling her husband had for Chrysostomos. Theologos looked at his wife. "God has taken one of His finest from us. Anna, bring our coats."

Anna touched her husband's hand. "I know," she said gently.

Theologos gave his wife a quick, affectionate smile. "Now hurry, Anna," he said briskly, "or we'll miss the train."

* * * * *

The man sat in his chair by his bed with the lights out. He had dressed himself and was reaching for his shoes. He had lost his vision years earlier as a young man. Despite his blindness, he was a well-regarded shopping center developer who had renovated many shopping centers. Vincent Allan was Jewish, not a Greek, but he had met Chris while a patron at the Apollo Restaurant in 1950 and had remained a good friend.

He heard the bedroom door open and knew his wife, Sue, had entered the room.

"Chris was the hardest working man I ever knew," he mused aloud.

"I know, honey." She paused. "Do you need any help?"

"Not at all," he replied.

* * * * *

"Dad, get up," Johnny said, poking his head in his parents' bedroom door.

Johnny's father blinked and rubbed his eyes.

"Come on Dad, Mom," Johnny urged. "I don't want to be late."

Johnny turned on his crutches to leave. He had strapped on his leg braces and dressed himself carefully. His parents had owned the summer townhouse next to the Christ family for thirty years, and Johnny, who was only twenty-one, had known Mr. Christ ever since he could remember. Even after his motorcycle accident, Mr. Christ had always given him encouragement, and Johnny would never forget that. Apart from his family, Mr. Christ was the most important person in Johnny's life.

"Mom, Dad, come on or we'll be late!"

* * * * *

Early that morning, after dressing in a widow's attire, Mrs. Christ sat alone at the kitchenette table she had shared for so many years with "Bread Crumb." She fingered the mail gram that had been sent by courier from Archbishop Iakovos which contained a special prayer he had written upon this occasion. Rather than reread the card, she reflected on the call.

It was mid-afternoon when he called with great regret. Having taken sick, he was unable to attend. Archbishop Iakovos' voice was effusive and emotional, uncharacteristic of an archbishop. "Chrysostomos was different than most, he was a special man. We mourn our loss together, but the beloved memories will be cherished and will endure," he had said. The Archbishop, Jimmy Coucouzes, had once known her Chris as Bread Crumb. A moment passed between them.

The day before he called, his secretary had telephoned. "Mrs. Christ, this is Paulette, the Archbishop's assistant," a voice had said on the line. "The Archbishop wanted to attend, but he has not been well and is not able. When he heard your husband had died, he was conducting a prayer service and he collapsed…"

The words lingered as she looked tearfully across the small kitchen table at Bread Crumb's empty chair.

* * * * *

It was seven in the morning and Peter Hatzi was up and showering. Usually on a Saturday his wife Kathy had to rouse him, but this Saturday was different. He had lost his father four months earlier, now his favorite uncle had died at age 76 and Peter, stricken by grief and unable to sleep, was up early. Uncle Chris was always positive and supportive, and ever since childhood Peter had had a special bond with him.

Downstairs, Peter's mother and aunt, who were Uncle Chris' sisters Sultana and Katina, were readying themselves for the drive to the cathedral and their beloved brother's funeral. Possibly more than anyone else, they had been witnesses to—and at times beneficiaries of—Chris' strength and productive influence. He had been the patriarch of the family. They especially knew how he had, at a very young age and in a time of terrible need, provided and cared for his family. They knew how hard he had worked to come to America, and how he had sacrificed to bring them over as well. He had been the strength of their family for more than six decades, and the knowledge that he was there for them had given their lives security and warmth. He had provided the wherewithal, but more than that, he had shown a continuity in his humble working life that aided their transitions to America. Older than Costa and Sultana, but younger than Katina, he was the undisputed leader of their small family since Mama and Papa had died. His sudden and unexpected death had left his sisters with a terrible void in their lives.

Bread Crumb was not only special to his sisters and his nephew, Peter, but also to Peter's wife. Kathy, like Bread Crumb, was also from Imbroz. Like Bread Crumb, she was an accomplished cook, yet she always marveled at Uncle Chris' talents in the kitchen.

"I can't believe we've lost Uncle Chris," she told her husband sadly. "Poor Uncle Chris. I will miss him."

Peter swallowed hard. He finished dressing and ushered his wife downstairs where they joined Sultana and Katina. "Come on Mama, Thea. We have to get going," he said. "We're supposed to meet Anthony and Ianthe at Thea Helen's and go on to the cathedral together. We'll stop by Thea Afrodite's on the way. She and the kids will follow us."

At Thea Helen's house, intense grief filled the morning air. Sultana and Katina got out of Peter's car and embraced Elenitsa.

Elenitsa and Sultana were in tears, and Katina, older and more reserved, consoled them while Peter embraced his red-eyed cousins. Anthony, Chris' eldest son, sobbed like a baby at his father's death, just as Bread Crumb had sobbed long ago when his Papa had died. His best friend had left him. Jon stood next to his brother and wept quietly. Minutes later Ianthe, her eyes red and swollen with tears, arrived with her husband. With Bread Crumb's death, she had lost her greatest ally and her strongest source of material, emotional and spiritual support. Her face was pale with grief.

As the family climbed into their cars, each felt their personal loss in their separate ways. As they resumed their journey to the cathedral, a light drizzle began to fall. Bread Crumb was gone, and his loss was felt by everyone he had touched. Even a misty sky began to softly weep.

* * * * *

Struggling with his cane, Lincoln Vance righted himself and walked the five steps from his car to the door of Harry Jagoda, his business partner.

"Come on, Harry," he rasped, knocking at the door. "Let's get going before we're late."

"Hold on, Lincoln," Harry replied impatiently in a voice as raspy as his, "I'm coming, I'm coming."

Like Bread Crumb, Harry and Lincoln were both depression-era children. Even though they were born in different cultures—Harry was Jewish, Lincoln a Greek—they had faced similar challenges and difficulties in America. Their friendship with Bread Crumb was rooted in shared experience, Old World work ethic and mutual respect.

"You know, we've met a lot of people over the years," Lincoln said as Harry greeted him at the door, "but Chris was the best, most honest man I have ever known."

"That he was," Harry nodded as he and Lincoln made their way to the car. He had known Chris Christ for forty-five years and his affection for his Greek Christian friend was as great as Lincoln's.

Like Chris, Harry and Lincoln were hardworking, self-made men who had overcome adversity in youth to achieve success.

* * * * *

Two blocks from the Washington National Cathedral on Massachusetts Avenue is Saint Sophia Cathedral. Named after the historic Saint Sophia in Constantinople, its cornerstone was dedicated by President Eisenhower. Although not as large as the original, it is every bit as opulent as the original was years ago, with colorful mosaics and icons carved from marble and cast in gold. Although Bread Crumb had been married at Saints Constantine and Helen Cathedral, and was a founding member of Saint Catherine Church in Northern Virginia, it was Saint Sophia that he attended in his early years and where he had initially taken his children to Sunday School, and where he and Elenitsa had returned to attend services in their later years.

Father John, who had been the priest at Saint Sophia for thirty-five years, put on his vestments and came to the cathedral early that day. He and his wife had eaten with Chris on many an occasion. He trusted Chris, his confidant. He had sought out his judgment often. For several long minutes he stood at the altar and gazed motionless at the soaring, mosaic-encrusted dome overhead.

All over the Washington area, Greek Christians were preparing to attend the funeral of Bread Crumb from a tiny island in the Aegean called Imbroz. Gus Pappas, the dentist whose wife died at a young age of cancer, Mr. and Mrs. Markesas, who were in their eighties, John Simms and his wife, who twenty years earlier had purchased Anthony's Carryout. All were in states of grief and reflection, as were Arthur Clubb and Mike Herr, the managers of Anthony's Beer and Wine, the Tsentoloz family, Leo and Tasso Vondes, Gus Moshous, Bill and Mary Simons, Dr. and Mrs. Carroll and their son Johnny...the list went on and on.

* * * * *

Bread Crumb's widow, Elenitsa, and their children arrived at the cathedral, leading their small family procession from the suburbs. Father John instinctively moved toward the doors to greet the family he knew so well.

"Father, we have lost Chris," Elenitsa said simply as her eyes filled with tears.

"Yes, I know…" was all he could manage to say, and for a long moment he embraced her, consoling Elenitsa as well as himself. Then he stepped back and allowed her to lead her family down the aisle toward their seats. The two front pews on the right of the center aisle, traditionally reserved for the family, were soon filled with Chris' sisters, Sultana and Katina, his nieces and nephews, as well as his children, grandchildren and widow.

When the hearse arrived, Chris' eldest son, Anthony, composed now in his grief, turned to his brother and one of his cousins. "Jon, Peter," he said. "Come, let's help with Dad."

The three made their way back up the aisle to the doors of the cathedral and down the steps to the street. There they helped lift the casket up the stairs to the entrance of the church, where it was placed on rollers and moved down the center aisle to the altar, accompanied by Jon and Anthony. At the altar the casket was turned and opened for viewing.

Anthony wanted to see his father's face one last time. All his life, through failure and success, his father had given him his total, unconditional support. Bread Crumb's warm expression, his affectionate manner, had always comforted Anthony and placed him at ease, but when the casket was opened the lifeless face of his father was unrecognizable. The intelligent, passionate warmth that had served as a guiding light to his family and friends was gone. So, too, were the rosy cheeks and infectious smile. What Anthony saw was a longer, more somber face. Chrysostomos Chrysostomidis was gone, leaving behind in death the lifeless face of a stranger.

When filled to capacity, Saint Sophia held nearly a thousand worshippers. Today, the cathedral overflowed with Bread Crumb's friends and family who had come to pay their last respects. Father John, who had buried generals and congressmen, doctors and lawyers, could not remember a time in his thirty-five years at Saint Sophia that the church was any fuller for a funeral—but it had filled for Bread Crumb, waiter, cook and restaurateur, a common man who, through perseverance and discipline, led an uncommon life.

As the cathedral filled with mourners, an elderly black man on a bike stopped a mile or so up Wisconsin Avenue to ask directions of a stranger.

"Excuse me, sir…Where is Massachusetts Avenue? I'm looking for Saint Sophia."

It was Bernard, still wearing his goggles. Like the police officer on the Bay Bridge at dawn, the stranger's eyes took in the bike with its mirrors, horn, and the foxtail on the back. Finally his gaze returned to Bernard's face.

"Go straight down Wisconsin Avenue for nine or ten blocks," he said, choosing to overlook the eccentric sight Bernard and his bike presented, "then make a left on Massachusetts Avenue. You'll see Saint Sophia a block and a half further on the left."

"Thank you, sir," Bernard said with a somber smile, and pedaled away. Now he would be on time for Mr. Christ.

People were still filling the church when Father John finally began the service. One of the last to enter the cathedral, Bernard removed his hat and goggles, lit a candle, and stood in the back of the church. There he quietly mourned Mr. Christ, his employer, mentor and faithful friend.

After the formal part of the service, Father John, who had performed so many funerals, had to clear his throat. Finally he began to eulogize his parishioner.

"Chris Christ was more than a reverent man who had more than his share of adversity. He was honorable in all his dealings with his fellow man. He was humble before God and those who were less able, and he was honest through and through. He led a Christian life that many aspire to and few attain. He will be missed dearly by everyone who knew him…" Bread Crumb's family barely heard the words of the service. They could not focus beyond their grief.

In thirty-five minutes the service drew to a close. "Everlasting be your memory," the congregation sang melodiously. "Everlasting be your memory." Then Father John addressed the mourners once again.

"Holy Father," he prayed, "please save a special place for Your loyal servant, Chris Christ, who came to us from so far away, who worked his whole life unselfishly for his family and his Church, both here and in Turkey. Chris spent his life showing respect for all men. He was truly a rare man, an inspiration for many, never speaking an unkind word. Violently uprooted from his family at the age of ten, he not only endured, he triumphed. He endured poverty and deprivation, working rather than complaining, until he rose above his circumstances. Chris Christ was in every respect the best that mankind represents, and we pray for his soul..."

Then he added, with a touch of humor Bread Crumb would have enjoyed, "I realize many of you do not normally attend services at this cathedral, which is too bad. I wish I could get such a turn-out for my Sunday sermons."

A moment later the family rose, followed by the congregation, for final viewing of Bread Crumb. Elenitsa was the first to approach the coffin.

"I love you, Chris," she whispered.

Beside her, Anthony bent to kiss his father's forehead and then made the sign of the cross and bid farewell. Red-eyed, Ianthe and Jon followed him, and with them came the rest of the family, all sobbing as others followed.

As his mother and siblings were greeted by friends, Anthony watched the mourners slowly making their way past his father's casket. He saw Mr. Vance, leaning heavily on his cane, pause to look at Bread Crumb's face. After him came Mr. Jagoda, who tripped on the steps to the altar and had to be steadied by Gus Pappas. Then Johnny Carroll struggled up the altar steps on his crutches, followed by his parents. When they passed the casket they were replaced by Vince Allan, guided by his wife Sue, his sightless eyes gazing past the casket with head bowed in respect for his old friend. Behind him, hat in hand, was Bernard, patiently waiting his turn.

"Oh, Mr. Christ...what has happened...Oh, Mr. Christ!"

Eyes turned in empathy at the sight of the colorful man lamenting his lost friend. The sight of Bernard touching Bread Crumb's lifeless body was heartfelt by all. A familiar gentle smile lit Bernard's face. "I made it, Mr. Christ, and I'm on time. God bless you, Mr. Christ. God bless you and don't worry—I'll help your sons take care of business."

The drear and drizzle of that day supported a mournful, somber wintry mood, yet streaking boldly through the chilled colored panes of rain-speckled glass, scouting shafts of sunlight promised spring's return.

Postscript

On March 30, 1999, Bernard Coleman, at age 64, was found on Mary Francis's roof, dead of a heart attack. He was repairing roof shingles for his landlord. The mild-mannered man, who had cared for and spoken to pigeons as a youth and had been Bread Crumb's off-and-on employee for thirty-six years, was gone. Jon Christ planned the funeral for Bernard, and his sisters, Viola, Linda and Florence, were present and thankful.

In April 2000, Katina Pananis died in a nursing home in Brooklyn, New York. Nick, her husband of over thirty years, was by her side.

Sultana Hatzi, Bread Crumb's only living sibling, lives in Brooklyn, New York, close to her daughters, Theope and Urania, and their families.

His Eminence, Archbishop Iakovos, retired in Rye, New York, where in August of 2002 he celebrated his 91st birthday. In conversation recently he said how much he missed Bread Crumb.

Elenitsa still lives in the home on a half-acre she and Bread Crumb shared. His clothes are still in their closet and the pictures in his office have remained largely as they were.

Bread Crumb's American Dream and his legacy live on in his children, his grandchildren and his numerous nieces and nephews. Through the institutions they have attended, and the degrees they have attained, they remain a testament to his perseverance and will, and most importantly to our collective hopes and aspirations as Americans.

My name is Afrodite Christ, the wife of Chris' late brother Costa. I was born on Imbroz December 31, 1931. Although the Christian Holocaust ended eight years before my birth, persecution of Christians went on for decades. While the Turks tolerated our churches, they confiscated all church-related real estate that was given by the community. They would go to the property and announce the respective Christian saint's name, then cynically take the property when the saint did not respond. Many Mohammedans from the Black Sea were resettled on Christian property. In 1942, the Turks imprisoned the mayors from all seven towns on Imbroz along with certain dignitaries. They were imprisoned in Anatolia for five years and no reason.

In 1952, a Greek school was reopened on our island. It quickly gained a good reputation, with graduates advancing to second-year college students. The Greek schoolteachers were paid by the communities, and the classes were held after Turkish school.

In 1962, the Greek school was closed. In 1964, Christian properties became Mohammedan. I came to America in 1965 as Costa's wife. America has been good to us. Three of my four children graduated from Harvard and the fourth from the University of Virginia. Were it not for Chris, our families would probably not have come to America. *August 2001*

My name is Tom Vasil, the little boy Thomas in the book. I am a survivor of Smyrna. I was an electrical engineer before I retired. Chris and Elenitsa have been dear friends of my past wife and me, and we saw them almost every Sunday in church. *September 2001*

My name is Anthony Vondes and I was born in Albania in 1912. The Turks overran our village when I was a young boy. I left home as a teen and worked in hotel restaurants in Athens before coming to America. I met Chris at his store in Ocean City and we became instant friends. Although we only knew each other for fifteen years, I felt a closeness to him I have felt for few people—two men with nearly parallel lives. *October 1996*

My name is Christina Regas. My past husband and I have been close friends with Chris and Elenitsa. I am a Greek American; the Turks overran my mother's town of Rankia. We moved to Athens when I was very young. Chris was the finest of Christian men and it was a pleasure to have known him. After my husband died, Chris and Elenitsa would always take me to church. *Septmber 2001*

My name is Vince Allan. From Arkansas, I came to Washington to attend George Washington University in 1944. In and out of Johns Hopkins eye clinic for many years, I eventually went totally blind in 1961. I opened up a Chrysler dealership across the street from the Apollo restaurant and it immediately became a second office as many a potful of coffee was consumed. Chris and I became lifelong friends. I was one of the first to walk through the doors of the Apollo. He also bought his first car from me. We were similar in age and temperament and we even married about the same time. We attended the weddings of each other's children, and we lived near each other since 1953. He had boundless energy and an optimistic attitude. When you made friends with him, you had a friend for a lifetime. He was a man I greatly admired for his virtue and honesty. He was warm and genuine. *September 2001*

My name is Lincoln Vance. After graduating from Georgetown University in 1939, I maintained ties to the Greek community my whole life. In nearly 30 years of doing business with Chris, I never had a contract with him. His word was his bond and that was what most attracted me to the man. My instincts told me I could trust him, and many who knew him felt the same. His philosophy of life was the way he lived. He was the hardest working man I ever met and he never expected a handout. He was up every day at 5:30 and was always in the restaurant early. He was a religious man, and he brought up a wonderful family. *September 2001*